Carol Ann Tomlinson
Cindy A. Strickland

Differentiation in Practice

A RESOURCE GUIDE FOR DIFFERENTIATING CURRICULUM

Grades 9–12

ASCD
Association for Supervision and Curriculum Development
Alexandria, Virginia USA

Association for Supervision and Curriculum Development
1703 N. Beauregard St. • Alexandria, VA 22311-1714 USA
Telephone: 800-933-2723 or 703-578-9600 • Fax: 703-575-5400
Web site: http://www.ascd.org • E-mail: member@ascd.org

Gene R. Carter, *Executive Director;* Nancy Modrak, *Director of Publishing;* Julie Houtz, *Director of Book Editing & Production;* Katie Martin, *Project Manager;* Georgia Park, *Senior Graphic Designer;* Valerie Younkin, *Desktop Publishing Specialist;* Eric Coyle, *Production Specialist.*

All Web links in this book are correct as of the publication date below but may have become inactive or otherwise modified since that time. If you notice a deactivated or changed link, please e-mail books@ascd.org with the words "Link Update" in the subject line. In your message, please specify the Web link, the book title, and the page number on which the link appears.

Paperback ISBN: 1-4166-0050-7 • ASCD product #104140
s8/05
e-books ($31.95): retail PDF ISBN: 1-4166-0317-4 • netLibrary ISBN: 1-4166-0315-8 • ebrary ISBN: 1-4166-0316-6

Quantity discounts for the paperback book: 10–49 copies, 10%; 50+ copies, 15%; for 500 or more copies, call 800-933-2723, ext. 5634, or 703-575-5634.

Library of Congress Cataloging-in-Publication Data

Tomlinson, Carol A.
    Differentiation in practice : a resource guide for differentiating curriculum, grades 9-12 / Carol Ann Tomlinson, Cindy A. Strickland.
        p.   cm.
    Includes bibliographical references and index.
        ISBN 1-4166-0050-7 (alk. paper)
  1. Education, Secondary—Curricula—United States. 2. Curriculum planning—United States. 3. Individualized instruction—United States. I. Strickland, Cindy A., 1959- II. Title.

    LB1628.5.T66 2005
    373.19—dc22

                                                                                    2005011776

12 11 10 09 08 07 06 05   12 11 10 9 8 7 6 5 4 3 2 1

*For the high school students
who remind us, relentlessly and creatively,
that they are individuals seeking to find
themselves and discover purpose in learning*

✳

*For the high school teachers who remain
convinced that they must connect with students in
order to teach them well and to ensure that each
learner sees academic success as worthy of investment*

✳

*And for the high school principals who have the
courage to ask, "Why do we do this in this way?"
and seek solutions that make the best sense
for the young people in their care.*

Differentiation in Practice

A Resource Guide for Differentiating Curriculum, Grades 9–12

Acknowledgments

This book, like all books, represents the efforts and insights of many people. There are many hands, minds, and classrooms reflected in its pages.

We are particularly indebted to the current and former high school teachers whose work constitutes the heart of the book: Cheryl Dobbertin, Lyn Fairchild, Tracy Hamm, Suzi Juarez, Miki Reddy, Cheryl Franklin-Rohr, Cynthia Kelley, Kay Brimijoin, Kim Pettig, Kate Reed, Molly Wieland, and Andrea Trank. They are courageous teachers and representatives of other courageous colleagues. They have risked putting their work on paper and entrusting it to colleagues they may never meet. They have been willing to question their teaching practices and to tolerate the ambiguity of recrafting their work for the purpose of illuminating differentiation principles and strategies. And they enter their classrooms day after day in pursuit of the essential dream of making human connections with so many young lives under such difficult conditions for the purpose of commending learning as dignifying.

Other high school teachers who have recently affirmed the reality of high school classrooms that extend the minds, hearts, and souls of adolescents by attending to them as individuals are Katie Carson, George Murphy, Lori Mack, Chad Prather, and the administrators and faculty of Colchester High School in Colchester, Vermont. We have learned from you as your students do, and we have been invigorated by you as your students are.

At ASCD, we are indebted to Katie Martin, whose care and insight with this series of three books of differentiated units has extended their quality and reach; to Scott Willis, whose steadiness smoothes the writing journey; and to Leslie Kiernan, whose extended partnership with differentiation and eye for quality provide persistent motivation to probe and polish.

We continue to grow in the partnership of colleagues at the University of Virginia. Those whose influence found a way into this volume include Carolyn Callahan, Tonya Moon, Catherine Brighton, and Holly Hertberg, whose insights and efforts are constant sources for ideas and ideals; Susan Mintz, whose understanding of adolescents and emerging teachers of adolescents sets a high standard; and Joanne McNergney, who encourages our exploration of curriculum and instruction for adolescents.

Not surprisingly, the students at Curry School of Education, with whom we work daily, are an immense source of energy. They are believers and skeptics in just the right balance, and they never fail to keep us honest.

We are nurtured by the partnership of colleagues from the ASCD cadre of presenters on differentiated instruction: Karen Austin, Vera Blake, Deb Burns, Marcia Imbeau, Sara Lampe, Carol O'Connor, Sandra Page, Judy Rex, and Nanci Smith. Their good sense, good hearts, and dedication to the goal of quality classrooms point the way for us.

Finally, the people who are at the core of our lives have provided us compass, anchor, winds for the journey, and port along the way. For Cindy, they include her husband, Rob Strickland, and their two children, Amanda and Michael, who are high school students. For Carol, they include longtime colleague, neighbor, and friend, Doris Standridge, and four-legged buddies Dooley and Duff.

Of course, what we have assembled here with the help of those we have noted and others who have contributed in ways small and large amounts to little more than an exercise without educators who will use the work. We hope this book serves you—and your students—well.

Introduction

This book is part of a series of ASCD publications on differentiating instruction. Each is designed to play a particular role in helping educators think about and develop classrooms that attend to learner needs as they guide learners through a curricular sequence.

How to Differentiate Instruction in Mixed-Ability Classrooms (Tomlinson, 2001) explains the basic framework of differentiation. Such a framework allows teachers to plan in consistent and coherent ways. *The Differentiated Classroom: Responding to the Needs of All Learners* (Tomlinson, 1999b) elaborates on the framework and describes classroom scenarios in which differentiation is taking place. *Fulfilling the Promise of the Differentiated Classroom: Strategies and Tools for Responsive Teaching* (Tomlinson, 2003) explores the connection between affect and cognition in teaching and learning. It also provides examples of and tools for developing differentiated classrooms in which teachers link affect and cognition. A fourth book, *Leadership for Differentiating Schools and Classrooms* (Tomlinson & Allan, 2000), discusses how to use what we know about change in schools with goals of differentiation and seeks to provide guidance for educational leaders who want to be a part of promoting and supporting responsive instruction.

In addition to these books, an ASCD Professional Inquiry Kit called *Differentiating Instruction for Mixed-Ability Classrooms* (Tomlinson, 1996) guides educators, in an inductive manner, to explore and apply key principles of differentiation. Five video programs, all produced by Leslie Kiernan and ASCD, give progressively expansive images of how differentiation actually looks in the classroom. *Differentiating Instruction* (1997) shows brief applications of differentiating content, process, and products according to student readiness, interest, and learning profile in primary, elementary, middle, and high school classrooms. It also illustrates a number of instructional strategies used for purposes of differentiating or modifying instruction. A three-video set, *At Work in the Differentiated Classroom* (2001), shows excerpts from a monthlong unit in a middle school classroom as a means of exploring essential principles of differentiation, examines management in differentiated settings from primary grades through high school, and probes the role of the teacher in a differentiated classroom. *A Visit to a Differentiated Classroom* (2001) takes viewers through a single day in a multi-age, differentiated elementary classroom. *Instructional Strategies for the Differentiated Classroom, Part 1* (2003) and *Instructional Strategies for the Differentiated Classroom, Part 2* (2004) illustrate how teachers at varying grade levels and in a variety of subjects use seven instructional strategies to ensure academic success for a wide range of students. Each of these materials attempts to help educators think about the nature of classrooms that are defensibly differentiated and move toward development of such classrooms. Each of the publications plays a different role in the process of reflection, definition, and translation.

This book uses yet another lens to examine differentiation and support its implementation in classrooms. It presents educators with a series of actual curricular units developed by teachers who work hard to differentiate instruction in high school classrooms. The book thus moves from defining and describing differentiation to providing the actual curriculum used to differentiate instruction. It is the third book in the *Differentiation in Practice* series, joining earlier volumes exploring differentiation in grades K–5 (Tomlinson & Eidson, 2003a) and grades 5–9 (Tomlinson & Eidson, 2003b).

What the Book Is (and Isn't) Intended to Be

As we prepared to write this book and its companions, we had numerous conversations between ourselves, with editors, and with many colleagues in education. Each conversation helped us chart our eventual course. Our primary goal was to provide models of differentiated units of study. We wanted to move beyond episodic descriptions of differentiation to show how it might flow through an entire unit. We also wanted to present units at a range of grades and in a variety of subjects, and elected to do so in grade configurations that are reflective of most schools. In this book, we have included differentiated units in mathematics, science, history, language arts/English, world languages, and art in order to demonstrate how differentiation might look in high school classrooms focused on different disciplines.

And while we have developed the book with a high school focus, our intent is that it be useful to a broader range of teachers than the grade levels and subjects it specifically represents. This is a book designed to teach anyone who wants to learn how to differentiate curriculum how to do so—or how to do so more effectively. To that end, we intend that each of the units be more representative than restrictive. That is, an 11th grade history teacher should be able to look at a 9th grade science unit, see how it works, and use similar principles and formats to develop a differentiated history unit for high school juniors. A technology teacher should be able to study several of the units included in the book and synthesize principles and procedures she finds to guide development of a differentiated unit for 7th graders. In sum, we intend this book to be a vehicle for professional development.

What this book is *not* intended to be is off-the-shelf curriculum for any classroom. It is not possible to create the "correct" unit, for example, on teaching Shakespeare within a historical context. A teacher in one classroom will conceive that process differently than will teachers in other classrooms or teachers in a different part of the country, in a different type of community, or responsible for a different set of academic standards. In the end, then, we are presenting educators with a learning tool, not a teaching tool. If teachers and other educators can read this book and say, "There's something I can learn here," then we will have succeeded.

How the Book Is Designed

Because we want the book to be a learning tool for a maximum number of teachers, we have made key decisions about its presentation. First, we decided to begin the book with Part I's primer on differentiation—an essential piece for readers new to the topic and a helpful refresher for those already familiar with it. We also opted to include an extended glossary (page 349), which explains terms and strategies that might not be familiar to all readers. Collecting this information in the back of the book, we thought, was preferable to interrupting the units themselves with "sidebar" explanations.

Part II, the body of the book, is devoted to instructional units. We think it will be helpful to share some of our thinking about the layout and contents of the units, each of which is presented in four parts.

• **Unit Introduction.** The first component of every unit is the introduction, which includes a prose overview of the unit; a list of standards addressed in the unit; the key concepts and generalizations that help with teacher and student focus; a delineation of what students should know, understand, and be able to do as a result of the unit; and a list of the key instructional strategies used in the unit. Some of the units also make links across units and disciplines and promote connections with students' lives and experiences. Note that because of our desire to make the book a

learning tool and not a set of lesson plans, we have listed the subject area for each unit, but not a specific grade level. Similarly, our references to the specific standards around which teachers constructed the units do not include grade-level designations.

• **Unit Overview Chart.** The second component is an overview chart, designed with three goals in mind: 1) to provide orientation in the form of a "big picture" snapshot of the unit's steps or events; 2) to provide an estimate of the amount of time each step or event requires; and 3) to clarify which portions of the unit apply to the class as a whole and which are differentiated. Note that time designations vary from unit to unit; some are designed for 90-minute blocks and some for 45- or 50-minute periods, reflecting the original work of the teachers.

• **Unit Description.** The third component is the unit description itself. It appears in the left-hand column of each unit page and gives a step-by-step explanation of what takes place in the classroom during the unit. A starburst symbol (✳) in the margins highlights differentiated components. All referenced supporting materials (samples such as worksheets, product assignments, rubrics, and homework handouts) appear at the end of the unit.

• **Teacher Commentary.** The fourth component is an explanation, in the voice of the teacher (or teachers) who created the unit, of what she was thinking as she planned and presented instruction. For our purposes, this is a particularly valuable element. To listen to the teachers who developed and taught these units is to move well beyond what happens in the classroom and to begin to analyze why teachers make decisions as they do. At one point in the writing and editing process, we thought we should reduce the teacher commentary sections to the fewest possible words; we quickly discovered that when we did so, we lost the magic the book has to offer. We hope you enjoy listening to the teachers as much as we have.

We tried to balance two needs in our editing of the units. First, we wanted to maintain the integrity of each teacher's unit without providing so much nitty-gritty detail as to risk distracting from the larger purpose of the work: the illustration of differentiation practices and principles. Second, we wanted to be sure to have both consistency (of terminology, format, essential philosophy, etc.) and variety (in instructional strategies, use of groups, assessment methods, etc.). The teachers who created the units have approved the changes we made or have helped us see how to make necessary modifications more appropriately.

Also, please note that we have opted to make the units somewhat more generic than specific. As teachers, we sometimes have the habit of looking for exact matches for our classroom needs and jettisoning whatever doesn't match. As authors, we can't eliminate the habit, but we wanted to make it a little harder to exercise. For example, although we have taken great care to list state standards reflected in each unit, we have intentionally not listed the name of the state from which the standards came. (It's amazing how similar standards on the same topic are across states.) We hope to make the point that good differentiation is attentive to standards and other curricular requirements, but we want to help readers avoid the inclination to say, "Oh, these aren't *my* standards, so this would not work in my classroom."

Finally, we decided to include solid units rather than "showcase" ones. What's here is more roast beef than Beef Wellington. We wanted to include units that demonstrate coherence, focused instruction, thoughtful engagement of students, and flexibility; we *did not* want to include units that dazzle the imagination. After all, although it may be fascinating to watch someone tap dance on the ceiling, few of us are inclined to try it ourselves. Hopefully, the units in this book are familiar enough to be approachable, but venture far enough into the unfamiliar to provide challenge for future growth. In this regard, our aim for readers is similar to what we recommend for students: pushing them a little beyond their comfort zones. If all readers feel totally at ease with the units, we've lowered the bar. If we send all readers running, we've set the bar too high. (In the latter instance, some judicious rereading over a period of professional growth just might be worthwhile.)

It may well be that the greatest pleasure of teaching comes from learning. It is our hope that this book—and the *Differentiation in Practice* series as a whole—will serve as one catalyst for helping teachers become the very best professionals they can be.

PART I

A Brief Primer
on Differentiation

Today's high schools serve a more academically diverse student population than at any other time in history, and this diversity will only increase in the decades to come. The Educational Research Service (Marx, 2000) has identified 10 trends likely to shape the educational future in the United States; four of these frame much of the teaching and learning challenges in contemporary high schools:

1. *The United States is moving from a nation constituted by a majority population and a number of minority populations to a nation of minorities.* Multiple cultures, races, and language groups will be the norm in our classrooms, and the range of competency or "readiness" levels within every subject will expand. Yet many teachers are still operating as if diverse backgrounds and readiness levels had no relation to learner success.

2. *In order to teach culturally and academically diverse populations effectively, schools will have to move from standardized instruction to personalized instruction.* Our best knowledge of effective teaching and learning suggests clearly that teacher responsiveness to race, gender, culture, readiness,

experience, interest, and learning preferences results in increased student motivation and achievement. Yet we are prone to feel as if we are somehow being unfair—unegalitarian—when we plan differently for different students.

3. *The vast majority of students in a diverse population will need to master the sorts of high-quality curriculum once reserved for advanced learners.* An increasingly complex society in which nearly every career and profession requires problem solving and flexible thinking means that students must learn to be critical thinkers, problem solvers, and producers of knowledge (rather than just consumers of knowledge). Yet high school enrollment practices—our manner of determining which students will take which courses—ensure that only a small percentage of students will be expected to acquire these skills, competencies, and characteristics.

4. *To help more students master high-quality curriculum, schools will need to move away from defense of the status quo and seek new ways of thinking about "doing school."* Our personal experience and the research we see in educational journals underscores the need to revise instructional

practices to promote greater personal investment in learning and higher achievement for a broad range of adolescents. Yet too many teachers cling to the comfortable patterns of the past. Despite abundant and mounting evidence to the contrary, our high school classes still evince the belief that teaching is telling, that the teacher is the teller, that learning is repeating, that curriculum is coverage, that students are unmotivated and dependent, that assessment happens at the end of large blocks of teaching, that grades serve the purpose of "separating the sheep from the goats," and that "classroom management" is just a synonym for control. At the very least, high school teachers fear that if we don't "teach like the colleges do"—primarily through lecture and independently completed assignments—our students will be ill-prepared to succeed at the college level.

Calls for Reflection

For some time now, educators who have invested their professional lives in improving schools—particularly those who have focused on improving high schools—have called on colleagues to break free of past paradigms of teaching and invent new ones that reflect the realities of the students we serve and the professional knowledge at our disposal.

• Theodore Sizer (1992) reminds us that while it may be inconvenient that students differ, it is an irrefutable fact of life in the classroom. He goes on to issue a challenge: If we want productivity, high standards, and fairness for the students we serve in high schools, we have to attend to their diversity, not ignore it.

• Psychologist Robert Glaser (in Darling-Hammond, Ancess, & Ort, 2002) argues that high

schools must shift from modes that reflect only minimal variations in conditions for learning to modes that allow a range of opportunities for success—modes of teaching that adjust to each student's talents, interests, backgrounds, and readiness levels.

• Researcher Adam Gamoran (2003) demonstrates that when teachers try to respond to student differences through tracking, the students in low-track classes are inevitably shortchanged—taught in ways that provide them with less opportunity and ask less of them. Perry, Steele, and Hilliard (2003) remind us of the price of tracking paid by minority students from low socioeconomic backgrounds. High school teacher Joan Cone (1992) has spent her career demonstrating that it is possible to present and support high-level learning opportunities to a wide range of students without lowering expectations.

• Researcher Seymour Sarason (1990) notes that students themselves are calling for new ways of teaching. It is evident to them that one-size-fits-all delivery systems are failing them.

• The National Board for Professional Teaching Standards (2004) reminds us that high-level professionals recognize individual differences in students and adapt instruction accordingly. Failure to do so results in ineffective instruction and evaluation for students who lack prerequisite skills as well as for students who are ready to move beyond prescribed outcomes.

• The National Association of Secondary School Principals' *Breaking Ranks II: Strategies for Leading High School Reform* (2004) encourages emphasis on essential learning (instead of coverage), teachers connecting with students as a means to increased student achievement, classroom adaptations for students' learning differences, and flexible use of classroom time to encourage application of instructional strategies that are consistent with how students learn best.

The high school teachers whose work constitutes the majority of this book lend their voices to the chorus as well. They have accepted the challenge of change and are working to craft classrooms in which responsive instruction attempts to ensure that more students than ever learn at high levels of quality and achieve high levels of success. We are particularly excited about sharing their voices with a wider audience.

The journey to responsive instruction is neither short nor formulaic. Indeed, it calls to mind Nietzsche's idea of a "long obedience in the same direction." Our success as high school teachers in this modern age rests upon our willingness to look closely at where we've been, where we are, and where we need to go in the light of the full range of students we teach and our own escalating skill in addressing academic diversity. Perhaps a good first step in that direction is to examine the realities of a few students and teachers in high schools—and then to begin to examine a framework for thinking about teaching that responds to human beings as well as to the demands of a curriculum.

The Students

Lavon is very bright. He generally takes basic-level classes, and his work there is adequate. No one at school seems to know how smart he is. *He* knows it, but he doesn't know what to do with it—at least not in productive ways. There's hardly enough money at home to pay the rent, let alone pay for college. Besides, none of his friends talk about college. In fact, Lavon really doesn't know anyone who has been to college except for his teachers, and his life isn't like theirs.

Carlos is quiet in his classes. He began high school in this country just two months ago. Carlos misses his friends back home. He doesn't understand the teacher. He can't read the books. He fails the tests. He can't tell his parents how unhappy he feels. In school, it's like no one knows he's there.

Danielle has a learning disability. She likes the heated discussions that are sometimes part of her history class because she has strong opinions about history and she expresses them well. She can tell that people listen when she talks. She can't manage the books, however, and she's awful at taking notes. Danielle works on homework, but deep down, believes that it's pointless. Even when she finishes it, it's usually wrong—or muddled in her head. Danielle doesn't expect to do well in school. It's been that way for a long time.

Heather translates the words she reads into pictures in her mind. Poetry and history and science and math all become images. The images are interpretive and help her sort out ideas and meanings. Words don't work that way for her. They are heavy and awkward—not at all like the mental gallery she can call up at any moment. But in her classes, it's only the words that count.

Michelle is one of a small population of black students in a primarily white school. Sometimes she's the only black student in her advanced classes, and sometimes she's one of just two or three. Her parents value education and encourage her to learn. Nonetheless, Michelle's school feels like a pair of shoes that's the wrong shape and size. To go there is to leave the world in which she belongs and to enter one where she's at best a stranger and at worst an unwelcome stranger. Language, habits, the ways of working, textbook content, the push and pull of peers, the lack of eye contact from some of her teachers, and a hundred other elements send Michelle coded messages that she doesn't really belong. Anyhow, what is she supposed to *do* with what she learns in school? No one from the world where she does belong seems to use this stuff.

Jacob has a hard time with reading. He tried to get better at it for years, but it seems like he and his teachers gave up on that at about the same time. Now, teachers tell him what to read, but no one works with him on how to read. Jacob tries to get by without reading, but it's getting harder and harder to bluff his way through. He wonders if anyone knows how bad his reading really is.

Andrea is a graduate student living in the body of a 16-year-old high school junior. Her reasoning and writing are stunning. She wants to pursue her interest in genetics, but there's so much schoolwork to do. It's not challenging for her, but it's incredibly time consuming. Andrea knows she has to get excellent grades in order to get into the kind of college she dreams of attending—so she does the work and hopes there'll be a time when school is actually interesting.

Damon gave up on school so long ago he can't remember when that was. He hates the long days of sitting and listening. He hates what the teachers talk about. He hates most of the kids in his classes—and they return the favor. He comes to school pretty regularly—he gets grief at home if he skips—but he has no intention of investing himself in his classes. It's too painful to try over and over and fail over and over. School is pointless anyway.

Phaedra is incredibly creative, with a mind that continually manipulates ideas and asks questions. She wonders why things are they way they are. She ponders alternatives to nearly everything. She can do the work in school okay. Mostly she completes what's required to get respectable grades, but she's hungry for a place where she can move beyond "right" answers.

Jenna feels trapped. She's a straight-*A* student. Her parents and teachers praise her, but she feels like a hamster on a wheel. On the one hand, she's terrified of losing her class rank. On the other hand, she feels like a fraud for getting high grades in classes that don't actually challenge her to do much more than follow directions and memorize textbook facts. Jenna can't let people down, but she knows she's somehow letting herself down.

For *all* of these students, there are also incessant "distractions" that fill their time and draw their minds away from classroom demands. There are after-school jobs, boyfriends and girlfriends, school offices, team sports, drama club, and music groups. Things like video games, Web logs, skateboarding, and hanging out with friends nearly always seem more alive, compelling, and relevant than what goes on in the classroom. Add to all of that the inevitable emotional turbulence and physical changes that in many ways *are* adolescence, and it's easy to understand that being an adolescent student is something of an oxymoron. It also clarifies the need for teachers of adolescents to account for both the complexity of their students' lives and the variety of their individual learning needs. To do less is to lose ground as a teacher before teaching even begins.

The Teachers

Mr. McArthur has loved science for as long he can remember. Ten years into his teaching career, he's reconciled to the fact that many of his students don't share that enthusiasm. Still, he hasn't given up. Mr. McArthur works hard to make his lectures interesting and continues to develop them further each year. He sets high expectations for his students, even though he knows it's difficult for them to live up to those expectations. Increasingly, he has students who can't or won't read homework assignments and who don't know how to take notes effectively.

Ms. Ellison's general math class has 21 students, representing 4 different languages. She speaks only English, and she's uncertain about how to communicate with six students who speak little English. Some of Ms. Ellison's second language learners are proficient readers in their native languages. Some aren't. In addition, even though her students have a wide variety of gaps in their math knowledge, she's expected to cover the entire math text with them *and* make sure that they have the basic skills they need to pass the mandated exit exam.

Ms. D'Archangelis teaches history. She particularly enjoys her honors and AP classes, where students are bright and generally focused on success. Nonetheless, she feels driven by a curriculum that is too extensive to "do right" within the time she shares with these students. When she plans class activities, she often feels like she's sacrificing a degree of complexity that her students would really enjoy. Ms. D'Archangelis worries both about the students who struggle with the convergent thinking her class requires and about those students who are *too* comfortable with convergent thinking. She is also aware that at any given time, some of her students need greater challenge than she is providing while others are just barely keeping up.

Mr. Ortiz's Spanish classes includes students who speak Spanish as a first language but don't know its grammar; students who know English grammar well and those who don't; students who are great memorizers of patterns but shy about risking oral production; students with a great ear for language and no patience for homework; and students who somehow seem to be learning to

speak, read, and write the language faster than he's teaching it. As more and more of his students are required to take foreign language, the range of competencies and needs is growing accordingly.

Nearly all of these teachers feel escalating pressure to prepare their students for a high-stakes test—a test that reveals no concern for students who struggle with school or for students eager to learn at a more challenging pace or in greater depth. Even as classrooms are becoming more heterogeneous, the message from the test-makers seems to be one of mandated homogenization.

The dilemma is clear: How does a high school teacher who teaches nearly 150 students honor the uniqueness of individuals in classes that are likely to be overpopulated, undersupplied, perpetually short of time, and under the gun for test performance? Besides, high school students are nearing adulthood, leading some teachers to worry that doing too much to accommodate students' unique needs will leave them ill-prepared for life beyond high school, where they'll be expected to achieve without special supports.

There is no add-water-and-stir solution, of course. Complex challenges like this never have simple solutions. But those of us involved with writing this book hold tight to two beliefs. First, we believe that every teacher is a learner, and as such, every teacher can become better and better at the effective instruction of academically diverse student populations. Second, because all indications are that classrooms will continue to diversify, we believe there is no choice but to learn to teach well the students who trust us—voluntarily or involuntarily—to prepare them for the future. Based on these two beliefs, we find that the best response to the complex challenges today's schools present is differentiated instruction.

What Is Differentiated Instruction?

As we use the term in this book, "differentiated instruction" refers to a systematic approach to planning curriculum and instruction for academically diverse learners. It is a way of thinking about the classroom with the dual goals of honoring each student's learning needs and maximizing each student's learning capacity.

This approach to effective instruction of heterogeneous student populations—and in truth, all student populations are heterogeneous—suggests that teachers concentrate on two classroom factors: the nature of the student and the essential meaning of the curriculum. If, as teachers, we increase our understanding of who we teach and *what* we teach, we are much more likely to be able to be flexible in *how* we teach. After decades of educational research and classroom experience, we simply have no evidence that we teach as effectively as we might—as effectively as our students need us to teach—unless we teach in ways that vigorously seek to address the variety of student needs that are a reality in our classes.

There are five classroom elements that teachers can differentiate—or modify—to increase the likelihood that each student will learn as much as possible, as efficiently as possible:

- **Content**—What we teach and how we give students access to the information and ideas that matter.
- **Process**—How students come to understand and "own" the knowledge, understanding, and skills essential to a topic.
- **Products**—How a student demonstrates what he or she has come to know, understand, and be able to do as a result of a segment of study.

- **Affect**—How students link thought and feeling in the classroom.
- **Learning environment**—The way the classroom feels and functions.

In addition, there are three student characteristics to which teachers can respond as they craft curriculum and instruction:

- **Readiness**—The current knowledge, understanding, and skill level a student has related to a particular sequence of learning.
- **Interest**—What a student enjoys learning about, thinking about, and doing.
- **Learning profile**—A student's preferred mode of learning.

Let's take a few moments to focus on these characteristics.

Readiness is not a synonym for ability; rather, it reflects what a student knows, understands, and can do today in light of what the teacher is planning to teach today. It is very difficult to maximize the capacity of some learners if we are unaware of their learning gaps or if we are impervious to the fact that other students have already mastered the material we are planning to teach for the next week. The goal of readiness differentiation is first to make the work a little too difficult for students at a given point in their growth—and then to provide the support they need to succeed at the new level of challenge. Differentiation in response to student readiness does not suggest we abandon the curriculum, but rather that we adapt our teaching in ways that make the curriculum appropriately challenging for a range of learners.

Interest is a great motivator. A wise teacher links required content to student interests in order to hook the learner. The goal of interest differentiation is to help students connect with new information, understanding, and skills by revealing connections with things they already find appealing, intriguing, relevant, and worthwhile.

Individual *learning profile* is influenced by learning style, intelligence preference (see Gardner, 1993, 1995; Sternberg, 1988, 1997), gender, and culture. There is neither economy nor efficiency in teaching in ways that are awkward for learners when we can teach in ways that make learning more natural. The goal of learning profile differentiation is to help students learn in the ways they learn best—and to extend ways in which they can learn effectively.

It is not the purpose of this book to teach the key elements of differentiation; that has been done in other places. Nonetheless, a quick review of what it means to differentiate the five classroom elements in response to the three student characteristics should facilitate a common understanding among our readers.

Differentiating Content

Content is what students should know, understand, and be able to do as a result of a segment of study. It's the "stuff" we want students to learn, and therefore, it's the "stuff" we teach. Content is typically derived from a combination of sources. Certainly, national, state, and local standards provide guidance about what we should teach. That said, a set of standards is unlikely to provide complete and coherent content. Some standards documents emphasize knowledge and skill and largely omit the concepts and principles that lead students to genuine understanding of subject matter. Some standards documents are so general in nature that they omit the specific knowledge necessary to illustrate the principles identified.

Content is further defined by local curriculum guides and by textbooks. However, one of the most critical factors in determining content is the teacher's knowledge of both the subject and the students. The teacher is the source of synthesis for standards, texts, and guides. It's the teacher who must ask questions such as, "What matters most here?" "What is this subject really about?" "What will be of enduring value to my students?" "What must I share with them to help them truly understand the magic of this subject in their lives?"

When the teacher answers these questions, he or she is ready to specify what students should know, understand, and be able to do in a particular subject as a result of instruction presented over a day, a lesson, a unit, and a year. The teacher's overarching goal is to hold the essential knowledge, understanding, and skills steady for most learners. In other words, if the intention this week is to help students learn to solve quadratic equations, this will be the goal for all learners. Some may need to work (at the process stage) with more complex formats and more independence; others may need to work with greater scaffolding from the teacher and peers. In general, however, the knowledge, understanding, and skills related to solving quadratic equations belong to everyone.

There are exceptions to this guideline, of course. If a student already knows how to solve quadratic equations and more complex ones as well, it makes no sense to continue teaching him to solve quadratic equations. Likewise, if a student has serious gaps in number sense and basic operations, the solutions to quadratic equations are likely to be out of her reach until she can build the necessary foundation of knowledge, understanding, and skill.

Once the essential knowledge, understanding, and skills of a unit or topic are clear, the teacher also begins thinking about the second facet of content: how to ensure student access to that essential knowledge, understanding, and skill set.

Students access content in many ways. Teacher talk is one—and one of the most common in lots of high school classrooms. There are also textbooks, supplementary materials, technology, demonstrations, field trips, audiotape recordings, and so on. A wise teacher asks, "What are *all* the ways I might help my students gain access to new knowledge, understanding, and skills as we move through this topic or unit?"

Because students vary in readiness, interest, and learning profile, it is important to vary or differentiate content in response to those student traits. Figure 1 illustrates just a few ways in which teachers can differentiate content in response to student readiness, interest, and learning profile.

Differentiating Process

The line between process and content is a blurred one, but for purposes of discussion, we'll think of process as beginning when the teacher asks students to stop listening or reading and to begin making personal sense out of information, ideas, and skills they've accessed. Under this definition, process begins where students stop becoming consumers and start making meaning in earnest.

Process is often used as a synonym for "activities." Not all activities are created equal, however. A worthwhile activity is one that asks students to use specific information and skills to come to understand an important idea or principle. Furthermore, a worthwhile activity is unambiguously focused on essential learning goals. It calls on students to work directly with a subset of the key knowledge, understanding, and skills specified as content goals. It requires students to think about

ideas, grapple with problems, and use information. It moves beyond "giving back information" to seeing how things work and why they work as they do. Finally, a worthwhile activity is one that snags students' interest so that they persist at it, even when the task is difficult.

Figure 2 illustrates just a few ways in which teachers can differentiate process in response to student readiness, interest, and learning profile.

Differentiating Products

A product is a means by which students demonstrate what they have come to know, understand, and be able to do. In this book, we use the term *product* to refer to a major or culminating demonstration of student learning—that is, one that comes at the end of a long period of learning, such as a unit or a marking period, rather than a demonstration of learning at the end of a class period or a two-day lesson, for example.

As with activities, effective product assignments are likely to have certain hallmarks. Product assignments, too, should focus on the essential knowledge, understanding, and skills specified as content goals. They should call on students to use what they have learned—preferably working as much as possible as a professional would work. Product assignments should have clear, challenging, and specified criteria for success, based both on grade-level expectations and individual student needs. They should endeavor to capture student interest. Finally, high-quality product assignments are written and guided in ways that support student success with the process of working on the product.

Products can take many forms. In fact, their flexibility is what makes them so potentially powerful in classrooms sensitive to learner variance.

FIGURE 1

STRATEGIES FOR DIFFERENTIATING CONTENT

Student Characteristic	Strategy
Readiness	<ul><li>Provide supplementary materials at varied reading levels.</li><li>Use small-group instruction to reteach students having difficulty.</li><li>Use small-group instruction for advanced students.</li><li>Demonstrate ideas or skills in addition to talking about them.</li><li>Provide audiotaped materials.</li><li>Use videotapes to supplement and support explanations and lectures.</li><li>Use texts with key portions highlighted.</li><li>Use reading partners to support understanding of text or supplementary materials.</li><li>Provide organizers to guide note-taking.</li><li>Provide key vocabulary lists for reference during note-taking.</li></ul>
Interest	<ul><li>Provide materials to encourage further exploration of topics of interest.</li><li>Use student questions and topics to guide lectures and materials selection.</li><li>Use examples and illustrations based on student interests.</li></ul>
Learning Profile	<ul><li>Present material in visual, auditory, and kinesthetic modes.</li><li>Use applications, examples, and illustrations from a wide range of intelligences.</li><li>Use applications, examples, and illustrations from both genders and a range of cultures and communities.</li><li>Teach with whole-to-part and part-to-whole approaches.</li><li>Use wait time to allow for student reflection.</li></ul>

.... **FIGURE 2** ....

STRATEGIES FOR DIFFERENTIATING PROCESS

Student Characteristic	Strategy
Readiness	• Use tiered activities (activities at different levels of difficulty, but focused on the same key learning goals). • Make task directions more detailed and specific for some learners and more open for others. • Provide resource materials at varied levels of readability and sophistication. • Provide small-group discussions at varied levels of complexity and focused on a variety of skills. • Use both like-readiness and mixed-readiness work groups. • Use a variety of criteria for success, based on whole-class requirements as well as individual student readiness needs. • Provide materials in the primary language of second language learners. • Provide readiness-based homework assignments. • Vary the pacing of student work.
Interest	• Use interest-based work groups and discussion groups. • Use both like-interest and mixed-interest work groups. • Allow students to specialize in aspects of a topic that they find interesting and to share their findings with others. • Design tasks that require multiple interests for successful completion. • Encourage students to design or participate in the design of some tasks.
Learning Profile	• Allow multiple options for how students express learning. • Encourage students to work together or independently. • Balance competitive, collegial, and independent work arrangements. • Develop activities that seek multiple perspectives on topics and issues.

If, as a student, I can show the teacher that I have come to know, understand, and do the non-negotiables of the unit, *how* I do so may be open. Stellar product assignments are examples of teaching for success versus "gotcha" teaching. For example, a student with a learning disability that makes writing laborious (if not impossible) may do a better job of showing what he has learned in science by creating a high-quality museum exhibit, complete with tape-recorded narration, than he would by writing an essay.

Tests are certainly one form of product. In today's high schools, all students need guidance in how to take tests effectively. Nonetheless, when tests are the only form of student product, many students find that their ability to show what they know is restricted. With tests, it's important to remember that the goal should not be regurgitation of information, but demonstration of the capacity to use knowledge and skills appropriately. It's also important to remember that tests should *enable* a student's ability to show how much he or she has learned, not impede it. Thus, some students may need to tape-record answers to tests. Some may need to hear test questions read aloud. Some may need additional time to write their answers. When the goal is to see what a student has learned, those adaptations are "fair" for students with learning difficulties just as using Braille is "fair" for students who cannot see.

Figure 3 illustrates just a few ways in which teachers can differentiate products in response to student readiness, interest, and learning profile.

Differentiating Affect

Students, simply because they are human beings, come to school with common affective needs. They need to feel safe and secure, both physically and emotionally. They need to feel that they belong to the group and are important to it. They need to feel a sense of kinship with the group—a sense that they share common ground with their peers. They need to feel affirmed and receive assurance that they are valuable just as they are. They need to feel challenged and to know that they can succeed at a high level of expectation (which helps them develop a sense of self-efficacy). Humans have these needs in common. Nonetheless, our particular circumstances cause us to experience these needs in different ways.

For example, a student who struggles to learn has a need to belong and to contribute to the class—to feel important to the "wholeness" of the group. That need may go unmet if she finds herself always on the outskirts of class discussions and cast as a failure in most endeavors. If the teacher sees this student as a "fringe" member of the class, it is likely that other students will see her that way as well. To help this learner achieve a sense of belonging, the teacher must understand the student's need to be a legitimate contributor and must orchestrate class proceedings with the legitimate participation of this student in mind.

A highly able student also needs to feel a sense of belonging and importance to the group. This learner may already be a part of the social fabric of the group and may be recognized as an achiever. However, if he feels uneasy asking questions or making alternative proposals important to him because the teacher is impatient with or threatened by them, even this highly able student can feel uncertain about his status in the group. He may elect to act out a role that maintains the status quo, feeling that he is not free to be himself in the classroom. In a case like this, the teacher may not have to plan activities in ways that integrate this learner, but in order to address his need to belong, the

---

FIGURE 3

STRATEGIES FOR DIFFERENTIATING PRODUCTS

Student Characteristic	Strategy
Readiness	• Provide access to bookmarked Internet sites at different levels of complexity. • Lead optional, in-class, small-group discussions on various facets of product development (e.g., asking good research questions, using the Internet to find information, conducting interviews, citing references, editing, etc.). • Use similar-readiness critique groups during product development (especially for advanced learners). • Use mixed-readiness critique groups or teacher-led critique groups during product development (particularly for students who need extra support and guidance). • Develop rubrics or other benchmarks for success based on both grade-level expectations and individual student learning needs.
Interest	• Encourage students to demonstrate key knowledge, understanding, and skills in related topics of special interest. • Help students find mentors to guide product development or choice of products. • Allow students to use a range of media or formats to express their knowledge, understanding, and skill. • Provide opportunities for students to develop independent inquiries with appropriate teacher or mentor guidance.
Learning Profile	• Encourage students to work independently or with partner(s) on product development. • Teach students how to use a wide range of product formats. • Provide visual, auditory, and kinesthetic product options. • Provide analytic, creative, and practical product options. • Ensure connections between product assignments and a range of student cultures/communities.

teacher must make the class a place where legitimate questions and alternative approaches are sought, valued, and celebrated.

A student whose first language is not English cannot feel integral to the group when he can never read the text, understand directions, or make a real contribution to the work of groups to which he is assigned. The teacher in this instance must see the link between communication and belonging and develop multiple ways for the learner to have a voice in and make a contribution to the class.

A student from a minority culture feels anything but central to the operation of the group when all of her cultural peers are consistently placed in low-achieving groups and are assigned work that looks dull. Belonging is not a reality when the teacher is more likely to call on, chat more affably with, and make eye contact with students from cultures other than your own. Your importance diminishes when the teacher shows she expects less of you by settling for incomplete work, overlooking missed assignments, or failing to coach you on how to enhance the quality of a product.

These are just a few examples to make the point that every learner in a class needs the teacher to help him or her grow in affective competence, just as every learner needs the teacher to help him or her grow in cognitive competence. (In fact, the two are inextricably linked.) It is essential to remember that although our affective mileposts are similar, our journeys toward them may take many different routes. In a differentiated classroom, the teacher is continually attuned to student feelings, just as she is to student knowledge, understanding, and skills. She repeatedly asks herself, "What can I do to ensure that students of all readiness levels feel safe, integrated, affirmed,

valued, challenged, and supported here?" "What can I do to ensure that students know their interests and strengths are important to me as a person, important to their peers, and important to our success as a class?" "How can I increase the likelihood that each student comes to a better understanding of his or her particular learning patterns, finds opportunities to work in ways that are comfortable and effective, and respects the learning needs of others?"

A wise teacher takes a number of measures to support the affective climate of the classroom. These might include

- Modeling respect.
- Teaching about and for respect.
- Helping students develop an escalating awareness of and appreciation for the commonalities and differences among their classmates.
- Helping students see themselves and their peers in the important ideas and issues they study.
- Helping students examine multiple perspectives on important issues.
- Helping students learn to listen to one another so that they hear not only the words, but also the intentions behind the words and the implications beyond them.
- Helping students to develop empathy for each member of the class.
- Ensuring consistently equitable participation of every student.
- Providing structures that promote and support student success.
- Seeking and responding to legitimate opportunities to affirm each student.
- Establishing shared and individual benchmarks for success at the appropriate levels.
- Coaching students to work for their personal best.

• Celebrating growth.

• Helping students to be more reflective and effective in peer relationships.

• Helping students to be more reflective and effective in decision making.

• Helping students to become effective problem solvers, both personally and interpersonally.

In the case of affect, the teacher differentiates both proactively (in ways that are planned) and reactively (on the spot). She does both based on her understanding of the shared affective needs of all humans, the reality that we experience those needs in both similar and dissimilar ways, and her continued reflection on how each student's readiness levels, interests, learning style, intelligence preference, culture, gender, economic status, home experiences, and general development shape his or her affective needs.

Affect is, in large measure, the weather in the classroom. Its lights and shadows, sun and storms profoundly influence everything that a learner experiences within that classroom. The teacher's role is often that of "weather-maker." At the very least, it is the teacher's job to help students learn more effectively given the classroom weather.

Differentiating Learning Environment

It's helpful to think about learning environment in terms of both visible and invisible classroom structures that enable the teacher and the students to work in ways that benefit both individuals and the class as a whole. A *flexible* learning environment is a hallmark of a differentiated classroom. The teacher's guiding question for a differentiated learning environment is, "What can I do to allow students of varying readiness levels, interests, and modes of learning to grow most fully in this place?"

One way of thinking about a differentiated learning environment is to examine how space, time, and materials can be used flexibly. It's also critical to understand the rules and procedures that must govern a flexible learning environment. Although it is the teacher's responsibility to engineer a flexible classroom, a wise teacher involves students in decisions about how to make the environment work. This is smart not only because it gives students a sense of ownership of their classroom, but also because students are often able to see what needs to be done more quickly and creatively than the teacher, who may be bogged down with other responsibilities and pressures.

Decisions About Space

The goal of flexible space is to enable the teacher and the students to work in a variety of configurations and to do so smoothly and efficiently. To that end, teacher and students might ask questions such as

• What are the various ways we can rearrange the furniture to allow for individual, small-group, and whole-group work?

• How can we arrange space for conversation and movement as well as space for quiet concentration?

• What is the appropriate way to deal with student materials when students move from one place to another in the room?

• Who may move around the classroom? For what purposes? When? In what manner?

• What signal will we receive when it's time to move from one place or task to another?

• What will happen if someone's movement in the classroom is disruptive to others?

Decisions About Materials

Goals related to flexible materials in a differentiated classroom include making sure students have both what they need to pursue their own learning goals in preferred ways and what they need to work toward class goals individually, in small groups, and as a class. To make decisions related to classroom materials, teachers and students might ask questions such as

• What materials and supplies should always be available in the classroom?

• Which materials and supplies should students have ready access to and which should be accessible only to the teacher?

• How will students know which materials and supplies are appropriate for their tasks at a given time?

• What constitutes appropriate care for materials and supplies?

• What will happen if someone uses materials or supplies in ways that are inappropriate or disruptive to others?

Decisions About Time

Time is perhaps the most valuable classroom commodity. It enables or inhibits learning at every turn—and there is never enough of it. Because time is always nipping at our heels, it's easy to assume that the most efficient way to use it is to carve it into chunks distributed to everyone in an equal manner. When there is academic diversity in a classroom, however, that is seldom the judicious choice. Some students will need additional instruction from the teacher in order to move ahead. Some will finish work more rapidly than others, even when the work is appropriately challenging. Some will need more time on a few tasks. Some

will need more time on most tasks. It often makes sense for the teacher to teach a small group while other students are working alone or in small groups. Everyone knows what to do, how to do it, and everything works (at least most of the time—but that's true of classroom functioning in general). To enable flexible use of time, teacher and students might ask questions such as

• When will it be best to work as a whole class?

• When will it be helpful to work in smaller groups or independently?

• How will we know where to be in the classroom and at what times?

• How will we manage ourselves when we work without direct teacher supervision?

• What rules and procedures will govern our work at various places in the room and for various tasks?

• How will we get help when we need it and the teacher is busy?

• How will we let the teacher know we need help?

• What do we do if we finish a task before others do (even though the task was challenging and we worked at a high level of quality)?

• What do we do if we need additional time for a task (even though we have worked steadily on the task)?

• What do we do with our work when we finish it? Where and how do we turn it in?

• When is it appropriate to move around the room and when is it not appropriate to do so?

• How will we know which tasks to work on and which part of the room to work in at a given time?

• How can I tell if I'm succeeding in my work at a high level of quality?

• How do I keep track of my goals, work, and accomplishments?

There are, of course, many other questions related to flexible learning environments beyond those about space, materials, and time that we've listed. The reality is that students of any age can work both flexibly and successfully as long as they know what's expected and are held to high standards of performance. Ironically, we're most likely to see smoothly operating, flexible classrooms in kindergarten. Beyond that point, we teachers often convince ourselves that *our* students aren't capable of independent and flexible work. If that were really the case, it would be one of the few demonstrations of learners becoming *less* able to accomplish complex tasks as they get older! Besides, if we expect young people to become competent, self-guided adults, evidence that they are not moving in that direction should only serve as an impetus to ensure that they do.

Essential Principles of Differentiation

There are a number of key principles that typify a defensibly differentiated classroom, and they have been described in detail in other places. Still, at the outset of this book, it's important to review a few of them. These principles should be at the forefront of teacher planning and should serve as measures of the effectiveness of differentiation for teachers and administrative leaders alike.

Principle 1: Good Curriculum Comes First

There is no such thing as effective differentiation devoid of high-quality curriculum. Multiple versions of ambiguity will net only ambiguity.

Multiple avenues to boredom will only lead more students to an undesirable place. Multiple routes to trivia and irrelevance will never enhance learning in the long run. The teacher's first job is always to ensure that curriculum is coherent, important, inviting, and thoughtful. Then and only then does it make sense to differentiate that curriculum.

Principle 2: All Tasks Should Be Respectful of Each Learner

Let's be frank: Dull drills *do* have an occasional place in the classroom. They are the adult equivalent of balancing a checkbook or filling out tax forms. The vast majority of the time, however, student work should be appealing, inviting, thought provoking, and invigorating. And it should be all these things for *all* students. Every student deserves work that is focused on the essential knowledge, understanding, and skills targeted for the lesson. Every student should be required to think at a high level and should receive support when doing so. Every student should find his or her work interesting and powerful. Differentiation won't work (and shouldn't work) when some students are assigned tasks that look "privileged" while others are assigned tasks that merit avoidance.

Principle 3: When in Doubt, Teach Up!

The best tasks are those that students find a little too difficult to complete comfortably. Good instruction stretches learners. Differentiation should never be used as a way to mollycoddle or "protect" learners. If a student wants to tackle something you think may be too demanding, it might be wise to let him give it a try (with the understanding that once begun, the task must be finished). The student's efforts may have something important to show you. At worst, next time, you and he will both know a little more about what represents an appropriate challenge. Certainly when the teacher assigns tasks, it's critical to ensure that the tasks are tiered to provide meaningful challenge. Likewise, rubrics or other indicators of student success should push the individual student beyond his or her comfort zone. Be sure there's a support system in place to facilitate the student's success at a level he or she doubted was attainable.

Principle 4: Use Flexible Grouping

Before beginning a unit, a teacher needs to think about when it will be important for the class to work as a whole, when students will need to work and demonstrate competence alone, and when it makes most sense for students to work with small groups of peers. There must be time for the teacher to instruct small groups and time for conversations between the teacher and individual students.

Think about the ebb and flow of students in a classroom. Plan times for similar-readiness groups to work together—and times when mixed-readiness groups can work on tasks, with each individual making a meaningful contribution to the work of the group. Plan times for groups of students with similar interests to work together—but also plan times when students with varied interests can meld those into a common task. Likewise, plan for both similar and mixed learning profile groups. The former allows students comfort when working; the latter is one means of extending student awareness of working modes. Use randomly assigned groups too. Finally, be sure to provide both teacher-choice and student-choice groups.

There is little doubt that each of these configurations will benefit many students in the class in a variety of ways. Most certainly, using only one or two types of groups causes students to see themselves and one another in more limited ways. It also keeps the teacher from "auditioning" students in varied contexts and limits potentially rich exchanges in the classroom.

Principle 5: Become an Assessment Junkie

Everything a student says and does is a potential source of assessment data. Teachers are surrounded by assessment options. Trouble is, we often think of assessment narrowly—as something we do *after* learning ends so that we will have numbers to put in the grade book. It is far better to think of assessment as an ongoing process, conducted in flexible but distinct stages. First, there is pre-assessment, which is essential to a differentiated classroom. Whether a formal quiz, a journal entry, an exit card, or any of a dozen other means of determining student knowledge, understanding, and skill set related to an upcoming unit or lesson, it's critical for the teacher in a differentiated classroom to have a sense of student starting points. Throughout the unit, take notes in class discussions, as you check homework, and as you walk around the room to monitor student work and coach for quality. Again, use quizzes, journal prompts, exit cards, concept maps—whatever you like to use—to figure out students' level of knowledge, understanding, and skill at key points in a unit. Then differentiate instruction based on what you find out. When it's time for final assessments, plan to use more than one assessment format—for example, a product *and* a test. Think about ways you can modify even the final assessments to maximize the likelihood that each student will open the widest possible window on his or her learning.

Principle 6: Grade for Growth

A portion of a teacher's grading may necessarily reflect a student's standing related to grade-level benchmarks. A portion of grades, however, should reflect a student's *growth*. A very bright learner who gets consistent *A*s and never has to stretch or strive will become a damaged learner. A struggling student who persists and progresses will likely give up the fight if grade-level benchmarks remain out of reach and growth in that direction "doesn't seem to count." The most we can ask of any person—and the least we ought to ask—is that they be accountable for being and becoming their best. It is the job of the teacher to guide and support the learner in this endeavor.

*   *   *

We hope this primer on differentiation provides you with tools for reflecting on the units of differentiated instruction in Part II of this book—and on practices within your own classroom! Additional clarification on terms and strategies is available in the Glossary, beginning on page 349. To learn more about any of the topics discussed here, please consult the Resources on Differentiation and Related Topics, beginning on page 359.

Differentiated Units of Study

Readers read as they wish, of course, and there's great merit in that. We take away from a source what we are ready to take away, and we gather what we can in accordance with how we learn best. We would not deny our readers this freedom even if we could. Nonetheless, we offer a few suggestions and questions to guide your learning from the units that follow:

• See if you can find colleagues to read, analyze, and discuss the units with you.

• Read all of the units—or at least several of them—not just ones that address the grade levels or subjects you teach. Look for similarities and differences. Record what you see. What seem to be the non-negotiables in these units?

• Think about how the unit developers have included mandated standards and yet moved beyond them. What's the difference between "covering the standards" and the ways these teachers are incorporating standards?

• After you read and study a unit, go back to its list of standards and the teacher's listing of what students should know, understand, and be

able to do as a result of the unit. Check off those standards and goals you feel the unit addresses effectively. Develop ways to intensify the focus on any goals or standards you feel have not been addressed adequately.

• Look for the links between the learning goals (the standards plus what students should know, understand, and be able to do) and the individual lessons within these units. In what ways have the teachers used the learning goals to design the specific steps in the unit?

• What benefits for students are likely to occur when a teacher organizes a unit by concepts rather than teaching a list of goals without one or more organizing concepts?

• Think about some students you teach. Try to include students with a range of learning needs, not forgetting students who could be described as "typical." Jot down ways in which these specific students might benefit from the differentiated units versus nondifferentiated versions of the same units.

• For which students in your classes would you need to make additional adaptations in order to facilitate optimal learning? How might you make these adaptations if you were to revise one of the units? Would it be easier to make the additional modifications in these differentiated units or in nondifferentiated ones?

• How effective do you feel the various units are at

— Beginning with sound curriculum prior to differentiating?

— Making assessment a pervasive and useful element in instructional planning?

— Providing respectful tasks for all learners?

— "Teaching up"?

— Using flexible grouping?

• How did the teachers who developed these units seem to have decided when to use whole-class instruction and activities and when to differentiate instruction and activities?

• Where in each unit might you incorporate additional ways to differentiate content for particular students in your classes? What about additional ways to differentiate process? Products? Which instructional strategies that you currently find effective would you want to integrate into these units?

• Where in each unit might you incorporate additional ways to address student readiness? Interest? Learning profile?

• In what ways do these units call for flexible use of space, materials, time, and teacher contact?

• In what ways do these teachers seem to circumvent the constraints of short class periods?

• In what ways do these teachers exploit the benefits and avoid the pitfalls inherent in block scheduling?

• What classroom guidelines would you want to establish to ensure effective and efficient work in one or more of these units? How would you begin the process of developing a flexible but orderly learning environment? How might you enable your students to be your partners in establishing a flexible and differentiated classroom?

• Think about connections between student affect and differentiation as it's reflected in these units. In what ways is the general classroom tone likely to influence student affect? Why? In what ways is the differentiation likely to influence student affect? In what ways might differentiation enable teachers to develop connections with their students?

• What is the role of the teacher in these differentiated classrooms compared with classrooms in which whole-class instruction predominates? What opportunities do teachers have with flexible teaching that may not be so readily available in more traditional classrooms?

• Which elements of these units do you particularly like? Which do you question? Talk with colleagues about what you see as positive in the units and what is less positive for you. In each instance, be sure to explore why you feel as you do.

• Try adding your voice to a unit you have created by explaining why you have crafted the unit as you have—or why you might now think about modifying the unit in some way.

• How do you suppose the teachers who developed these units think about grading in a differentiated high school classroom?

• Apply in your classroom something you learn from the units in this book. It's wise to move at a pace and in a sequence that seems manageable to you—but it's important to grow as a teacher in ways that benefit your students.

*　　*　　*

Our great hope, of course, is that you will be "stretched" by the time you spend with these nine units. As educators, we invest our professional lives in the belief that learning is both dignifying and humanizing. We hope this will be your experience in the pages to come.

1

American Stories

An English Unit on Reading and Writing Historical Fiction

Unit Developer: Cheryl Becker Dobbertin

Introduction

This five- to six-week unit engages students in the study of historical fiction and culminates with them developing and sharing a piece of historical fiction that is based on one of their own family's stories or artifacts.

The unit opens with students using the concept attainment method (see Glossary, page 350) to develop a working definition of historical fiction. Students then work in heterogeneous literature circles in a reader's workshop environment to discuss, react to, and analyze a novel of their choice: *Roots* by Alex Haley, *Daughter of Fortune* by Isabelle Allende, *Cane River* by Lalita Tademy, *The Joy Luck Club* by Amy Tan, or *The Storyteller's Daughter* by Jean Thesman. Each of these novels, listed in order from most challenging to least challenging, uses a distinct cultural perspective to tell the story of a family's evolution. In cooperative groups comprising representatives from each of the literature circles, students identify and analyze the criteria for historical fiction and develop a rubric that they use to evaluate their own work.

By reading and watching interviews of well-known authors in the genre, students develop an understanding of the discipline of writing historical fiction and the process authors use to develop their craft. They also learn or review the process of examining primary sources for the kind of detail that supports a story's development.

Finally, students work throughout the unit to research their family's history, using all resources available to them: oral histories, letters and diaries, photo albums, Internet-based genealogical search tools, and the like. Those who cannot or do not wish to focus on their own family's stories work with material provided by the teacher. Supported by differentiated modeling and coaching from the teacher in

21

a workshop environment, they develop a vignette (character sketch), short story, or chapter of a longer work that demonstrates their understanding of the qualities of excellent historical fiction. Students who choose to rework or expand their writing further have the option to do so as an ongoing independent study.

Teacher Reflection on Designing the Unit

This unit is a reflection of my desire to help all students become critical readers, effective writers, careful listeners, responsive speakers, and most importantly, *engaged thinkers*. These competencies are at the heart of the standards movement, and I believe that students who become confident in their own ability to make sense of big ideas and communicate this understanding effectively will be successful throughout their schooling and beyond. Since discovering differentiation and the classroom energy created when students exercise *choice*, I have seen many of my students reconnect with learning. This unit represents the best that I know about moving students toward real engagement and, ultimately, toward deep and lasting understanding.

I started my planning with a careful examination of national and local standards. When it comes to designing lessons, I have found these standards to be liberating, because they emphasize the process of reading, writing, listening, and speaking over any particular canon. With my eyes firmly focused on the standards, my first planning question is no longer, "Which book should I teach next?" but, "How can I engage my students in thoughtful work?" The standards prompt me to step back and consider my real goals: to help my students to develop lifelong critical literacy skills. The books, then, are just the tools I use to get the students thinking.

It is essential that my students learn how to determine the key characteristics of a particular genre and that they know how to approach reading within that genre. It is essential that they know how to participate in respectful conversation about their reading. It is essential that they know how to consider the needs of their audiences and be able to carefully craft a piece of writing over time. Finally, it is essential that they realize that real authorship is hard, circuitous work. When I design with these essential understandings as the goal, the opportunity to differentiate becomes crystal clear.

The challenge of offering a respectful, high-quality curriculum in the heterogeneous secondary English classroom lies more in the design of the task than in the difficulty of the text. A struggling reader or developing writer can be just as highly engaged in developing the aforementioned essential understandings provided that he is matched with a book he *wants* to read and receives appropriate coaching and support throughout the reading and writing processes. This may include helping students build the background knowledge they need in order to make sense of challenging text or arranging for some students to read with others or to have access to an audio recording of their text. In short, all students can learn when the teacher plans a flexible starting point and then structures opportunities for them to make connections, synthesize ideas, analyze, and evaluate.

English and Reading Standards Addressed

SD1   Students read a wide range of print and nonprint texts (fiction and nonfiction, classic and contemporary) to build an understanding of the texts, of themselves, and of the cultures of the United States and the world; to acquire new information; to respond to the needs and demands of society and the workplace; and for personal fulfillment.

SD2   Students read a wide range of literature from many periods in many genres to build an understanding of the many dimensions (e.g., philosophical, ethical, aesthetic) of human experience.

SD3   Students apply a wide range of strategies to comprehend, interpret, evaluate, and appreciate texts.

SD4   Students adjust their use of spoken, written, and visual language (e.g., conventions, style, vocabulary) to communicate effectively with a variety of audiences and for different purposes.

SD5   Students employ a wide range of strategies as they write and use different writing process elements to communicate effectively with different audiences for a variety of purposes.

SD6   Students apply knowledge of language structure, language conventions, media techniques, figurative language, and genre to create, critique, and discuss print and nonprint texts.

SD7   Students conduct research on issues and interests. They gather, evaluate, and synthesize data from a variety of sources and communicate discoveries in ways that suit their purpose and audience.

SD8   Students use a variety of technological and information resources (e.g., libraries, databases, computer networks, and video) to gather and synthesize information and to create and communicate knowledge.

SD9   Students develop an understanding of and a respect for diversity in language use, patterns, and dialects across cultures, ethnic groups, geographic regions, and social roles.

SD10   Students participate as knowledgeable, reflective, creative, and critical members of a variety of literacy communities.

SD11   Students use spoken, written, and visual language to accomplish their own purposes (e.g., for learning, enjoyment, persuasion, and the exchange of information).

Unit Concepts and Generalizations

Culture, Values, Traditions, Heritage, Change

GEN1   The culture of the United States is rooted in the experiences, beliefs, and traditions of its immigrant families. People living within the culture are shaped by those experiences, beliefs, and traditions.

GEN2   A family's heritage, values, and traditions are captured in its stories.

GEN3   Families experience generational change but maintain unifying connections.

GEN4   Authors of historical fiction develop their stories based on research into the culture, values, and traditions of a particular event, time period, or person.

Unit Objectives

As a result of this unit, the students will *know*

- The characteristics of the genre of historical fiction.
- The processes and procedures for working in a reader's and writer's workshop.
- The similarities and differences between a short story, vignette, and chapter in a novel.
- The resources available to research family history.
- The steps in the process of developing a rubric.
- The process that authors use to develop a piece of historical fiction.
- The stages or phases of the writing process.

As a result of this unit, the students will *understand that*

- A family's stories preserve its heritage, traditions, and values.
- Authors of historical fiction blend both fact and fiction to engage their readers.
- Effective readers make connections among the text, themselves, other texts, and the world.
- Effective authors often reach beyond personal experience to acquire material for their work.
- In order to write well, one must read.

As a result of this unit, the students will *be able to*

- Analyze literature for the techniques used by the authors of a specific genre.
- Develop deeper awareness of their text-to-self, text-to-text, and text-to-world connections to literature.
- Reflect effectively on their own thinking and participate in discussions of literature.
- Apply genealogical research methods.

- Use primary and secondary sources to gather information.
- Use the writing process to create a piece of historical fiction.

Instructional Strategies Used

- Coaching
- Concept attainment
- Cooperative learning
- Demonstration/modeling
- Independent research
- Literature circles
- Pre-assessment
- Tiered activities

Sample Supporting Materials Provided

Unit Overview

LESSON	WHOLE-CLASS COMPONENTS	DIFFERENTIATED COMPONENTS
PRE-ASSESSMENT	Unit pre-assessment *20 minutes*	
LESSON 1 **What Is Historical Fiction?** *1–2 blocks*	Reflective journal writing *5–10 minutes*	Concept attainment activity differentiated by readiness *90–120 minutes*
	Definition sharing, discussion, and consensus *30–40 minutes*	

LESSON	WHOLE-CLASS COMPONENTS	DIFFERENTIATED COMPONENTS
LESSON 2 **Choosing a Novel and Introducing Literature Circles** *1 block*	Reflective journal writing *5–10 minutes* Overview of literature circle roles and expectations *60 minutes* Background knowledge self-assessment *20 minutes*	
LESSON 3 **Getting Started with Literature Circles** *1 block*	Introduction and discussion of the Critical Work Skills Rubric *20–30 minutes*	Literature circle meetings differentiated by interest *30–40 minutes* Reading in novels differentiated by interest *30–40 minutes*
LESSON 4 **Reading Workshops** *4–5 blocks*	 Artifact collection and reflective journal writing *ongoing*	Reading and literature circle meetings differentiated by interest *ongoing* Individual or small-group coaching sessions based on readiness needs *ongoing, time varies* Reader response options and sharing differentiated by learning profile and interest *ongoing, time varies* Anchor activity: Author research differentiated by interest *time varies*
LESSON 5 **(optional)** **Working for Quality** *1 block*	Rubric development practice *40 minutes*	Anchor activities: Reader response options and sharing, reading in novels, and author research *ongoing, time varies*

LESSON	WHOLE-CLASS COMPONENTS	DIFFERENTIATED COMPONENTS
LESSON 6 **Developing Graduated Assessment Rubrics** *1 block*	Whole-class activity: Graduated rubric development, part 1 *40 minutes*	
		Small-group activity differentiated by readiness: Graduated rubric development, part 2 *20–40 minutes*
		Anchor activities: Reader response options and sharing, reading in novels, and author research *ongoing, time varies*
LESSON 7 **Exploring the Process of Writing Historical Fiction** *1–2 blocks*		Concept attainment activity differentiated by readiness *50–80 minutes*
	Reflective journal writing *5–10 minutes*	
LESSON 8 **Narrowing an Idea** *1 block*		Artifact analysis or story brainstorming differentiated by interest *40–50 minutes*
	Reflective journal writing *5–10 minutes*	
LESSON 9 **Writing Historical Fiction** *5–6 blocks*	Whole-class review of the Critical Work Skills Rubric *10 minutes*	
	Mini-lesson on the writing process *10–20 minutes*	
		Independent research and journaling differentiated by interest, readiness, and learning profile *time varies*
	Mini-lesson on literary formats for the culminating product assignment *10–20 minutes*	

LESSON	WHOLE-CLASS COMPONENTS	DIFFERENTIATED COMPONENTS
		Independent writing differentiated by interest and readiness *ongoing*
		Individual or small-group coaching sessions based on readiness needs *ongoing, time varies*
		Anchor activity: Revision *time varies*
		Independent study extension opportunity *ongoing*
LESSON 10 **Reflecting on the Unit and Sharing Finished Products** *2 blocks*	Reflective partner work *50–60 minutes* Reflective journal writing *20–30 minutes* "Publication" of the differentiated products *80–90 minutes*	

Unit Description and Teacher Commentary

PRE-ASSESSMENT	*(20 minutes)*

LESSON SEQUENCE AND DESCRIPTION	TEACHER COMMENTARY
Unit pre-assessment. About one week before the scheduled beginning of this unit, ask students to complete an exit card or journal entry in response to the following three-part prompt: • *What are three things a writer of historical fiction must know, understand, and be able to do in order to develop a quality product?* • *What are two things you know about the way American traditions or values have been influenced by the traditions and values brought here by immigrants from other countries?*	The pre-assessment portion of any differentiated unit is always an interesting time. I often discover that I have misconceptions about my students' existing knowledge, understandings, and skills. An exit card is a simple strategy to help me get inside students' heads. Students write responses to these prompts on an index card (I use a different-color card for each of my sections) and drop it in a shoebox on the way out the door.

LESSON SEQUENCE AND DESCRIPTION	TEACHER COMMENTARY
• *What is one family story you have heard about your grandparents or great-grandparents? How have your grandparents or great-grandparents influenced what you and your parents believe or value? (It's okay if you haven't got a family story to write about, just answer the second question if you can. Please let me know if your family's history is a difficult topic for you.)*	✹ Students' responses to the first two prompts serve as the basis for the first lesson in this unit. Responses to the third question help me determine who will need historical documents or artifacts supplied to them in order to fully participate in the unit.
Note: Students use reflective journals throughout this unit. These can just be 20 pages of notebook paper stapled together, or they can be bound composition books. On the left-hand pages of the reflective journal, students record procedural information, research notes, drafts, and so on. On the right-hand page, they record personal reactions and reflections, sometimes in response to teacher-supplied prompts.	✹ The students' reflective journals provide invaluable information about what and how they are learning; I revise the lessons continuously, based on what I read in student journals. These journals aren't graded, but their thoughtful completion is one of the unit's indicators of success. I read the journals regularly, taking home only as many as I can read and return the next day, so that students will have them in class. When students are preparing for literature circles or reading, I use the unstructured time as an opportunity to conference with them about their journals.
✹ Students who "don't know what to write" in their reflective journals benefit from the **Reflective Journal Sentence Starters** (see Sample 1.1, page 48). Distribute these in a handout or post them in the classroom.	

LESSON 1	**What Is Historical Fiction?**	*(1–2 blocks)*
	Concepts: Culture, Values, Traditions, Heritage, Change GEN2, GEN4; SD6	

LESSON SEQUENCE AND DESCRIPTION	TEACHER COMMENTARY
Reflective journal writing. Have students record and respond to the following guiding question on the first left-hand page of their reflective journals:

What aspects of historical fiction make it a unique genre?

Sample responses might include "a wealth of historical detail, although not all of it is accurate"; "characters that fit the time and place in which they are set"; and "a story line that's intertwined with historical perspectives or events." | This particular prompt targets two important unit generalizations (see page 24). |

✹ = Differentiated Component

LESSON SEQUENCE AND DESCRIPTION	TEACHER COMMENTARY
Concept attainment activity differentiated by readiness. Divide the students into homogeneous groups of three students each, based on the exit card pre-assessment of background knowledge:	Concept attainment is an instructional strategy that enables students to construct the meaning of new concepts rather than just memorize definitions.
• *Groups of students who already know a great deal about the historical fiction genre.* • *Groups of students who know a few things about the genre.* • *Groups of students who have no idea about the genre and no prior exposure to it.*	When creating these three-person subgroups, I also make sure that group members are relatively homogeneous in terms of reading, writing, and thinking skills.
Give each group a folder of excerpts from the five pieces of historical fiction at the core of this unit (*Roots, Cane River, The Joy Luck Club, Daughter of Fortune,* and *The Storyteller's Daughter*) and four excerpts from other genres (perhaps Shakespearean drama, science fiction, modern young adult literature, and epic poetry). Label the five pieces of historical fiction as "Examples of Historical Fiction" and the four other pieces as "Nonexamples of Historical Fiction."	I determine which excerpts should go into each folder based on the readiness of the students in each group. Less proficient readers and writers receive more accessible excerpts of historical fiction and "nonexample" excerpts that are very obviously from different genres. More sophisticated readers and writers receive more challenging levels of text and other, less obvious nonexamples.
Based on the readiness levels of the groups, provide students with tiered scaffolds (in this case, graphic organizers) to help them complete a comparison matrix: *Very Concrete Thinkers* Give these students a copy of the **Historical Fiction Comparison Matrix** (see Sample 1.2, page 49), which includes specific comparison criteria in the column headings. *Developing Abstract Thinkers* Give these students a slightly different version of the comparison matrix with only some of the criteria filled in. (For example, fill in the column headings "Setting," "Point of view," and "Language," but leave the rest open for students to decide.) *Abstract Thinkers* These students should not require scaffolding on this task and therefore don't needed any criteria filled in. They will probably still benefit from having a blank chart.	"Scaffolding"—providing thinking support for students who need it—is an instructional technique that enables all students to participate in respectful, appropriate tasks. Scaffolds take on a variety of forms, including supplemental materials, highlighted text, and graphic organizers. Be aware, though, that some students do not need scaffolds and that providing scaffolds can sometimes limit students' thinking.

LESSON SEQUENCE AND DESCRIPTION	TEACHER COMMENTARY
Direct all small groups to do the following: 1. Compare and contrast the various aspects of the examples and nonexamples in their group folder. 2. Record in their reflective journals the aspects/criteria of examples and nonexamples that they used to complete their comparisons. 3. Use their comparisons to develop a small-group working definition of historical fiction.	
Definition sharing, discussion, and consensus. Reconvene as a whole class and have the groups share their small-group working definitions. Discuss the various definitions and then combine and refine them as necessary to create a whole-class working definition of the historical fiction genre. Ask students to record the definition in their reflective journals, writing it beneath the guiding question that they recorded at the beginning of the period and the criteria they recorded in their group.	The guiding question, criteria, and definition all go on a left-hand journal page.

LESSON 2   **Choosing a Novel and Introducing Literature Circles**   *(1 block)*
Concepts: Culture, Values, Traditions, Heritage, Change
GEN2, GEN4; SD1–3, SD6, SD9–11

LESSON SEQUENCE AND DESCRIPTION	TEACHER COMMENTARY
Reflective journal writing. Redistribute the excerpts from the novels and ask students to reread them and then to record and respond to the following prompts in their reflective journals: • *What connections do these stories have to the ideas of culture, values, traditions, heritage, and change?* • *In what ways are a family's heritage, values, and traditions evident in its stories?* • *Which of these stories intrigues you the most? Why? Which of these stories is not appealing to you? Why?*	Although I want students to enjoy the storylines in these excerpts, I also want them to keep the unit concepts in mind. The first two of these guiding questions bring the concepts to the forefront. I find that allowing students to choose a book to read is highly motivating. I have been consistently pleased to see many of my reluctant readers get excited about a book they have chosen.

LESSON SEQUENCE AND DESCRIPTION	TEACHER COMMENTARY
Collect all the reflective journals at the end of this lesson and set up heterogeneous literature circle groups based, if possible, on students' first-choice book.	
Overview of literature circle roles and expectations. Explain to students that for the next several weeks, they will be reading the novel that they found most intriguing based on its excerpt. Throughout the "reader's workshop" portion of the unit, they will be working in literature circles with others who are reading the same novel.	When I allow a student to work on a novel that is well above his or her reading level, I support that student by providing a reading partner or an audiotaped version of the novel.
Review and model the format and expectations of literature circles. Distribute the **Literature Circle Role Sheets** (see Sample 1.3, pages 50–54) and go over the roles students take on when they meet in literature circles. Make sure students understand that they will rotate these roles for literature circle meetings, meaning everyone will have the opportunity to work in areas of expertise and of challenge.	The literature circle is an instructional technique that helps teachers meet a variety of student needs. It gives struggling students peer support in comprehending text, and the open-ended discussion format encourages deep thought and exploration from advanced students. However, all members of each literature circle must understand that success lies in their willingness to prepare and participate. Be very explicit abut expectations for performance and behavior. Samples 1.3, 1.4, and 1.5 support students new to the technique and those who function best in structured environments.
Ask students to sum up the expectations for each of the roles on the left-hand page of their reflective journals.	
Next, review how the literature circle meetings will be assessed and distribute the **Literature Circle Assessment Rubric** (see Sample 1.4, page 55) and the **Continuum of Literature Circle Skills** (see Sample 1.5, page 56). Ask students to react to this method of evaluation on a right-hand page of their reflective journals.	
If possible, model a literature circle meeting for the students and ask them to use the rubric to assess the group's performance.	I ask colleagues to help out with this, and we use the role sheets to plan a conversation around one of the excerpts.
Background knowledge self-assessment. Tell students that reading is a process through which the reader combines what's on the page with his or her own background knowledge. The influence of background knowledge helps to explain why different readers often have different interpretations of the same text. Ask students to respond to the following prompt on a right-hand page of their journals:	Because background knowledge influences reading comprehension, I'm careful to reconsider students' readiness to read particular books in light of the background knowledge they have. I'm especially interested in what my English language learners have to say here.
What background knowledge are you bringing to this study of historical fiction? It may be things you have read or experiences you have had. How will the things you have learned or experienced influence your work?	

| LESSON 3 | Getting Started with Literature Circles | (1 block) |

Getting Started with Literature Circles *(1 block)*

Concepts: Culture, Values, Traditions, Heritage, Change
GEN2, GEN4; SD10–11

LESSON SEQUENCE AND DESCRIPTION	TEACHER COMMENTARY
Introduction and discussion of the Critical Work Skills Rubric. Begin by explaining to students that throughout this portion of the unit, they will work independently and at their own pace to read their chosen novels, record their thoughts and reactions in their reflective journals, and meet in their literature circle groups.	The purpose of this session is to set the standards and expectations for the "reading workshop" format of the next several class sessions. Being clear about processes and procedures is an essential component of successful differentiation, even at the secondary level.
Use the **Critical Work Skills Rubric** (see Sample 1.6, page 57) to show students how their time management during reading workshops will be assessed. Ask students to paste the Critical Work Skills Rubric on the left-hand side of their reflective journals. On the right-hand side, they should respond to this prompt: *Why are the critical work skills indeed "critical" in a classroom where students are working with different materials and at different paces?*	An excellent alternative to a predesigned or teacher-designed rubric is to work collaboratively with students to determine appropriate behaviors for a classroom where everyone is working on different things at different times and the teacher is not always available to answer questions and monitor behavior.
Literature circle meetings differentiated by interest. Give students time to meet for the first time with their literature circles and ask them to create a preliminary schedule for reading and meeting. They should create a group chart in which they will record which group members will take on which literature circle role for each segment of the reading, and they should copy the group chart into their reflective journals. These schedules should be updated regularly. Remind students that they should use the left-hand pages of journals to record procedural information, research notes, drafts, and so on. On the right-hand pages, they should record personal reactions and reflections.	Students feel empowered when they are allowed determine—in collaboration with their literature circle groups—how many pages they will read each day and when—within limits—they want to conduct their literature circle meetings. The charts showing the schedule students have committed to lets me know on which days I must be free to observe and assess literature circle meetings.
Reading in novels differentiated by interest. Students whose literature circle groups finish early should start reading their novels.	

| LESSON 4 | Reading Workshops | (4–5 blocks) |

Reading Workshops

Concepts: Culture, Values, Traditions, Heritage, Change
GEN1–2, GEN4; SD1–3, SD6, SD9, SD10–11

LESSON SEQUENCE AND DESCRIPTION	TEACHER COMMENTARY
Reading and literature circle meetings differentiated by interest. Students work both individually and collaboratively in groups to comprehend, analyze, and react to their novels while also considering the work and responsibilities of a writer of historical fiction.	Because students are reading different novels and are meeting on different schedules, flexibility is the key word during this portion of the unit.
The day-to-day flow should look something like this:	Some students find the freedom of this kind of classroom environment empowering; others find it over-whelming. Some are appropriately challenged by the opportunity to work and think independently. Others need scaffolding. I maintain a file folder containing 10 copies of various materials (graphic organizers, back-ground information, sample journal responses, etc.) to distribute to students if they need additional support.
• Students arrive in class and immediately begin reading, preparing for a literature circle, working on one of their reader response choices (see page 35), or meeting in a literature circle.	
• The teacher monitors students' performance by sitting in on literature circles and checking in to see that they have entered the dates of their literature circle meetings and their reading assignments in their reflective journals and to support and challenge students based on how they're performing.	
Students must know what role they will fulfill in each of their literature circle meetings (as roles will be rotated each time) and must prepare for each role appropriately.	The way students prepare for litera-ture circle meetings may be differenti-ated. Some students benefit from having and completing the Literature Circle Role Sheets (see Sample 1.3) prior to their literature circle meet-ings. Students who don't need as much scaffolding may only need to place sticky notes in their texts to mark the key ideas and passages they want to discuss.
The literature circle roles of Conversation Captain and Con-cept Connector (see Sample 1.3) are particularly important in helping students to explore this unit's concepts of culture, val-ues, traditions, heritage, and change, as well as some of the key principles and generalizations.	Based on what I know about students' readiness in regard to the material they are reading and the role itself, I may set aside time to ensure that each group's Conversation Captain and Concept Connector are prepared.

LESSON SEQUENCE AND DESCRIPTION	TEACHER COMMENTARY
Ask students to tape-record or videotape their literature circle meetings. Tell them that they will be able to review the meetings when they are creating products, and that they can include the tapes in their portfolios.	These tapes also serve as a permanent artifact that I can look to as a source for feedback and evaluation.
Individual or small-group coaching sessions based on readiness needs. Hold small-group mini-lessons or individual conferences with students who need additional support or challenge. *Struggling Readers* Possible lesson or conference topics include think-alouds (see Glossary, page 357), making connections, determining vocabulary meanings in context, and drawing inferences. *Advanced Readers* Possible lesson or conference topics include the subtleties of irony, extended metaphor, and other sophisticated literary devices, and the evaluation of a piece from a literary perspective. Students should record notes from these mini-lessons on the left-hand pages of their reflective journals and react or respond on the right-hand pages. Remind them to comment on connections they are making between their reading and writing and the unit concepts and generalizations.	One of the most beneficial aspects of the reading workshop is that it gives a teacher time to address student skill needs directly.
Reader response options and sharing differentiated by learning profile and interest. Throughout this phase of the unit, students must complete three **Differentiated Reader Response Options** (see Sample 1.7, p. 58), tasks coordinated to Sternberg's triarchic intelligences: creative intelligence, analytical intelligence, and practical intelligence (see Glossary, "intelligence preference," page 353). Each category of tasks includes some options that reflect the unit concepts and generalizations. Require students to complete at least two tasks that incorporate the unit concepts and generalizations and then allow them choose whatever else appeals to them. Distribute copies of the **Reader Response Options Rubric** (see Sample 1.8, page 59) to help guide students' development of high-quality work. Expand the assignment, if desired, by allowing students to select options that they've designed themselves.	These tasks are an opportunity for students to show me what they are thinking in ways that honor their learning profiles. As a creative thinker myself, it has always been easier for me to plan creative tasks rather than analytical or practical ones. By stretching my own thinking, I have come to see how students can become excited to show me what they're thinking about their novels based on learning profile. For example, students commonly ask to write and perform a song or create a piece of artwork.

LESSON SEQUENCE AND DESCRIPTION	TEACHER COMMENTARY
Once students get started on these tasks, ask them to meet in small, same-novel groups to share their ideas. At the end of the unit, ask students to choose their best work and submit it for evaluation. Use the Reader Response Options Rubric as the basis for evaluation.	This is a time when students' understandings of the unit concepts and generalizations will come sharply into focus. I sometimes ask them to write in their reflective journals about how their classmates' understandings of the concepts are the same as or different from their own understandings.
Anchor activity: Author research differentiated by interest. Have students who have completed their reading and discussions conduct research on the authors who wrote their novels.	Anchor activities (see Glossary, page 349) are a great strategy in a differentiated classroom, as students often complete tasks at different times. It's important that anchors not be "busy work." The activities must connect to what students need to know, understand, and be able to do.
Ask students to focus their research on how the novels were written, what steps the authors used, and any research methods the author employed. A school librarian can be a helpful partner during this anchor activity.	Students often think that good writing "just happens." Researching the work of real authors helps them see the depth of background work necessary before the writing even begins.
Artifact collection and reflective journal writing. Throughout this lesson, students should be working at home to collect family artifacts: household items, old photos, letters, diaries, birth certificates, marriage licenses, family trees or histories, family stories, and so on. These items will be instrumental during the upcoming brainstorming and research phases of the unit. If possible, model this "collecting" activity for students by bringing in personal family artifacts to share. Prepare a classroom collection of artifacts to be used by students who do not have access to these items from their own family's history. Resources to explore include the collections section of the Library of Congress's Web site (memory.loc.gov), the local historical society, or the school librarian.	When I first created this unit, I participated in this activity myself, working to uncover information about my family's history and sharing artifacts of my own. I have written short pieces of historical fiction based on my own family's history and have kept a reflective journal of my own. I believe that students benefit from seeing teachers do these kinds of activities and this kind of thinking. I know that some students may not be comfortable gathering their own items or may be unable to do so.

LESSON SEQUENCE AND DESCRIPTION	TEACHER COMMENTARY
Students should use their journals to record the things they are finding, how they found them, and their reactions. Share with students that they will be writing a vignette, short story, or chapter of historical fiction based on an artifact or story from their own family or on photos and letters from the artifact box.	

LESSON 5	Working for Quality SD10–11	(1 block)

LESSON SEQUENCE AND DESCRIPTION	TEACHER COMMENTARY
Note: This is an optional lesson to include if students do not have prior experience creating a rubric. An excellent resource for clarification on the procedures for writing a rubric is available from the Intranet of the Chicago Public Schools: intranet.sps.k12.il.us/Assessment/Ideas_and_Rubrics/Create Rubric_/create_rubric.html.	Because creating a good rubric is vigorous work, students need to evaluate something fairly concrete before moving on to the more abstract task of creating a rubric for historical fiction.
Rubric development practice. Begin by distributing copies of a blank rubric and some kind of treat. One popular approach is to use several kinds or brands of chocolate chip cookies.	The "Write a Rubric for Chocolate Chip Cookies" exercise is widely used in professional development circles. An overview of this idea is available at www.teachervision.com.
Break the class into self-selected groups of three. Using the overhead, review the key parts of a rubric: the criteria for evaluation (down the left-hand column), the score or statement of quality (across the top), and the descriptors (in the rest of the boxes). Students should record this information on a left-hand page in their journals.	Remember that students are using the left-hand pages of their journals to record procedural information, research notes, drafts, and so on. The right-hand pages are for personal reaction and reflections.
Ask: What criteria would you use to evaluate a chocolate chip cookie?	
To get the juices flowing, distribute several different brands of chocolate chip cookies, asking students to take just one bite of each cookie because there is going to be lots of cookie tasting but no more cookies!	
Ask students to share their ideas for evaluative criteria: cookie texture, cookie size, the quality of the chocolate, the number of chips per cookie, and so on. Write suggested criteria on the board. Then have everyone agree on which criteria they want to use and ask them to fill in the criteria columns of their blank rubrics.	

LESSON SEQUENCE AND DESCRIPTION	TEACHER COMMENTARY
Next, ask the small groups to discuss which kind of chocolate chip cookie they like the best. Group members should collaborate to write descriptors about what makes that cookie excellent—describe the texture, size, quality of chocolate, number of chips, and so on. (Tasting helps here.) Have them continue on to rubric descriptors for a chocolate chip cookie that's good but not great and then for one that's not so good. Share the rubrics and discuss the descriptors.	
Distribute one new cookie to all students (use a brand they haven't yet tasted). Ask them to evaluate it using the rubric and then share their evaluations. If they have very different opinions about the quality of the cookie, discuss why. Is it the differences in the descriptors? Is it that some important criteria were omitted from the rubric? Let them know that in the "real world," rubrics are usually revised several times.	
Anchor activities: Reader response options and sharing, reading in novels, and author research. If there is still time in the class session, give students the opportunity to finish any work (reading or discussion, reader response options) that they still have to complete.	

LESSON 6   **Developing Graduated Assessment Rubrics**   *(1 block)*
Concepts: Culture, Values, Traditions, Heritage, Change
GEN4; SD4, SD10–11

LESSON SEQUENCE AND DESCRIPTION	TEACHER COMMENTARY
Whole-class activity: Graduated rubric development, part 1. Explain to students that in this lesson, they will create rubrics for historical fiction. Collectively, they will develop the descriptors for excellence at three levels: • Practitioner-level (professional) historical fiction • Apprentice-level historical fiction • Novice-level historical fiction.	Creating these rubrics is an exercise in community-building. Students need to understand that it is possible for someone to do an excellent job at the practitioner level, an excellent job at the apprentice level, and an excellent job at the novice level. At this point in the unit, based on students' previous work and their self-assessments, I decide what level of work I expect from each student. If certain students have surprised me with unexpected effort or achievement, I encourage and support them as much as possible so that they can continue to work at a higher level.

LESSON SEQUENCE AND DESCRIPTION	TEACHER COMMENTARY
Ask students to reflect on the idea of graduated rubrics and, on the right-hand pages of their journals, comment on what they find appropriate or inappropriate about them. In addition, ask them to identify which level they think they should be asked to work (practitioner, apprentice, or novice) and why.	Teachers who don't differentiate regularly may encounter resistance to the idea of setting different performance standards for different students. (This can be a touchy issue for adolescents, who are usually highly attuned to "fairness.") I stress that I'm interested in helping each student grow as a writer; I'm *not* interested in comparing anyone to anyone else. All students, regardless of the level at which they are working, can create excellent work and be successful in this portion of the unit.
Distribute a blank rubric with "excellent professional-level," "excellent apprentice-level," and "excellent novice-level" as the quality descriptor column headings. The final criteria heading should be "Mechanics."	
As a large group, work to fill in the mechanics descriptors for each level. These should be similar, because excellent work at all levels is revised, proofread, and edited, and therefore does not contain errors that will interfere with the reader's comprehension.	Completing and discussing the mechanics portion of the rubric as a group is my way of stressing that writing is much more than mechanics, and that mechanical errors are not what sets professional work apart from novice work.
Small-group activity differentiated by readiness: Graduated rubric development, part 2. Put students in like-readiness groups and ask them to brainstorm (recall) the criteria for historical fiction. List the criteria on the board, then chunk and refine it.	Asking students to help create a rubric develops their critical thinking and evaluative skills. Plus, when students participate in rubric development, assessment becomes something that is done *with* them rather than something that is done *to* them. In the differentiated classroom, assessment tools like rubrics help students focus on growth and working for quality rather than on "getting it done."
Ask students to work in their groups to write descriptors for these criteria as they would be found in excellent practitioner-level work, using the novels they studied as exemplars. They should then record their ideas for excellent apprentice-level and excellent novice-level historical fiction.	
Collect the students' work and then combine and refine it to create the evaluation rubrics you will use to rate their finished products.	I opted for like-readiness groups here so that students would feel comfortable working at a common level of critical and evaluative thinking. An alternative would be to group the students working above grade level together (so that they can push each others' thinking) and place the rest of the class in mixed-readiness group (to provide peer scaffolding for students who find this type of thinking exercise difficult).

LESSON SEQUENCE AND DESCRIPTION	TEACHER COMMENTARY
Anchor activities: Reader response options and sharing, reading in novels, and author research. When groups finish, they should work on wrapping up anything left over from the reading workshop portion of the unit or continue to research their novel's author (see Lesson 4).	

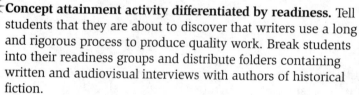

LESSON 7   **Exploring the Process of Writing Historical Fiction**   *(1–2 blocks)*
Concepts: Culture, Values, Traditions, Heritage, Change
GEN4; SD4–7, SD10–11

LESSON SEQUENCE AND DESCRIPTION	TEACHER COMMENTARY
Note: Prior to this lesson, create new homogeneous groups based on reading level—a change from the heterogeneous, interest-based composition of the literature circle groups.	
Concept attainment activity differentiated by readiness. Tell students that they are about to discover that writers use a long and rigorous process to produce quality work. Break students into their readiness groups and distribute folders containing written and audiovisual interviews with authors of historical fiction.	At the beginning of this lesson, I point out that we are now shifting our focus from being consumers and critics of historical fiction to becoming producers of historical fiction. The purpose of this activity is to familiarize students with the processes and procedures professionals use to create historical fiction.
The interviews should be "leveled"—that is, matched to the groups' reading-skill level. Here is an example set of materials for each readiness level:	There are many resources on the Internet that can help teachers create collections of leveled articles. I try to provide options for audio and video streaming at all levels, as many learners prefer these formats.

Advanced Readers
- "Historical Fiction or Fictionalized History?" by Joanne Brown (online at scholar.lib.vt.edu/ejournals/ALAN/fall98/brown.html).
- "Historical Fiction Author Roundtable" (online at www.authorsontheweb.com/features/0210-historical-fiction/historical-fiction.asp).
- "Isabel Allende" by Linda Richards (online at www.januarymagazine.com/profiles/allende.html).
- "Isabel Allende: A Life of Extremes" (audio online at www.bbc.co.uk/worldservice/arts/highlights/allende.shtml).

LESSON SEQUENCE AND DESCRIPTION	TEACHER COMMENTARY
Grade-Level Readers • "Tracing Her Roots: Lalita Tademy Quit the Corporate Life to Write a Novel About her Family History" by Heather Knight (online at www.sfgate.com; article published 6/1/01). • "Interview with the Author: Lalita Tademy" (online at www.oprah.com/obc/pastbooks/lalita_tedemy/o_bc2001 0914_profile.jhtml). • "Writing Backward" by Anne Scott Macleod (online at www.hbook.com/exhibit/article_macleod.html). • "Amy Tan: Best-Selling Novelist" (audio and video online at www.achievement.org/autodoc/page/ tan0int-1). *Struggling Readers* • "Writing Historical Short Fiction" by Bev Walton-Porter (online at home.san.rr.com/grady/writing/histfiction. html). • "Interview with Ann Rinaldi" by D. Ilana Dessau and Jenna Galley (online at scils.rutgers.edu/~kvander/ rinaldi1.html). • "Interview with Karen Cushman" by Stephanie Loer (online at www.eduplace.com/rdg/author/Cushman/ question.html). • "Cynthia Rylant" (video available from American School Publishers).	When matching students to articles and streaming audio and video via the Internet, I consider several factors. First is the complexity of the content itself. (For example, Isabel Allende tends to use sophisticated vocabulary even in interviews.) I also consider the complexity of the Web site. If it contains lots of links, has very busy graphics, or appears crowded, it can be easy for students to get confused or follow a link to a place that they don't need to go.
Ask students to read the material in their folders and access the audiovisual material and then, using chart paper, create a list of procedures used by writers of historical fiction. Urge them to add important thoughts or recommendations of interviewed authors.	Some of the students get this information from the reading phase anchor activity. Others encounter these ideas in the folder readings.
Students should post their group charts around the room and then use highlighter pens or sticky dots to indicate the procedures and recommendations that they can replicate while they are working on their own piece of historical fiction.	
Have one member of each group report out to the whole class about how their group has decided to proceed with their writing assignment.	I choose the group reporter randomly: the person wearing the most blue that day, for example.
Reflective journal writing. Have students write on the left-hand pages of their reflective journals about which procedures for writing historical fiction make sense to them, how they will use their family artifacts and stories to get started, and which tools and resources they have access to outside of school.	I go around the room and read students' responses in order to prepare for the next lesson.

LESSON SEQUENCE AND DESCRIPTION	TEACHER COMMENTARY
Remind students that they will need their artifacts and family stories (or materials from the artifact box) for the next lesson.	

LESSON 8   **Narrowing an Idea**   *(1 block)*
Concepts: Culture, Values, Traditions, Heritage, Change
GEN1–4; SD4–7, SD10

LESSON SEQUENCE AND DESCRIPTION	TEACHER COMMENTARY
Artifact analysis or story brainstorming differentiated by interest. Tell students that the time has come to select a detail from one of their family stories or one specific artifact on which to focus. This detail will be the basis for their culminating product: a short story, vignette, or chapter of historical fiction. Remind students that their writing should clearly reflect the culture, values, traditions, and heritage of their family.	The purpose of this lesson is to help students analyze their family artifacts (or the artifacts in the classroom collection) and gather details from their family stories, if applicable. As students begin the process of writing their own piece of historical fiction, all four of the unit generalizations take center stage. Students will reflect on these ideas in their journals as they work through the next couple of lessons.
If writing your own piece of historical fiction (or bringing in a local author to do so), do a think-aloud in which you share your family artifacts with the class, "thinking aloud" about the information and ideas you have so far. The think-aloud should include discussing the story idea you plan to pursue and the kinds of information you will need to research.	A "think-aloud" (see Glossary, page 357) is a comprehension-building strategy in which a competent reader verbalizes the connections, inferences, reactions, and questions that go through his or her mind while reading.
Get students started by asking them to set up a T-chart graphic organizer on a right-hand page in their reflective journals. In the space above the bar on the left-hand side, they write "Important Details in My Family Stories/Artifacts," and below it, they brainstorm a list of details that might provide the basis for an excellent piece of historical fiction.	
Above the right-hand bar, they write "How/Where I Could Find Out More," and below it, they brainstorm sources for more information: family members, online sources, print sources, and so on.	The school librarian is an excellent resource here. I've had our librarian come to class and meet with students to discuss their projects and research.
When their T-charts are complete, students should highlight the details they want to focus on. Review all highlighted charts and note what each student will be working on.	

LESSON SEQUENCE AND DESCRIPTION	TEACHER COMMENTARY
Reflective journal writing. On the right-hand pages of their journals, students should respond to the following prompt: *A family's heritage, values, and traditions are captured in its stories. Tell what you have discovered about your family or through your research that has had an effect on your life or the way your family is today. What similarities and differences are there between the way your family has changed over time and the way the family you read about changed over time?*	This journal response is important as it prompts students to connect to the "big ideas" in the unit.

LESSON 9 **Writing Historical Fiction** *(5–6 blocks)*
Concepts: Culture, Values, Traditions, Heritage, Change
GEN1–4; SD4–7, SD10–11

LESSON SEQUENCE AND DESCRIPTION	TEACHER COMMENTARY
Whole-class review of the Critical Work Skills Rubric. As a large group, review the Critical Work Skills Rubric (see Sample 1.6). Let students know that they will again be moving into a workshop environment; this time, it will be a writer's workshop.	This lesson transitions students into the creative phase of the unit, where they'll focus on writing historical fiction.
Mini-lesson on the writing process. Review the phases of the writing process, letting students know that when writing historical fiction, the brainstorming phase also includes collecting historical details about the setting, clothing, technology, culture, traditions, and values of the time period in which they will set their writing. Remind them that they may very well have to return to research after writing a draft, or even after revising it.	Sometimes, in an effort to teach the writing process, we give students the impression that writing is a linear process (brainstorm, write, revise, edit, publish) rather than a recursive process (brainstorm, write, brainstorm, write, revise, brainstorm, write, edit, write, brainstorm, etc.). It is important that students understand how real authors "use" the writing process. A good online resource about the craft of writing is Creative Writing for Teens: www.kidswriting.about.com/library/weekly/?oonce = true&.
✷ **Independent research and journaling differentiated by interest, readiness, and learning profile.** Students who need to continue work on their T-charts should do so. Others can move on to research.	Again, the school librarian can be a good resource.

LESSON SEQUENCE AND DESCRIPTION	TEACHER COMMENTARY
If necessary, provide scaffolds to help students scrutinize their primary source documents. Remind students to record information in their journals in a format that makes personal sense to them. Ideas might include the following: • One page of bulleted notes per source, with the source information recorded at the top of the page. • One web (or similar graphic organizer) per source, with the source information recorded at the top of the page. • Two columns of notes, with one column for source information and the other for notes. If students need a journal prompt, ask: *What connections have you discovered between your great-grandparents' or grandparents' values and traditions and your own? Your family has certainly changed over time, but how has it remained the same?*	The U.S. National Archives Web site (www.archives. gov/digital_class-room/lessons/analysis_worksheets/ document.html) contains excellent guiding questions. When I write along with my students, I share excerpts from my own journal entries in response to questions like these and then ask students to react. Another idea is to ask students to share and discuss their entries in small groups. It is through these discussions that students come to really understand the unit's concepts and generalizations.
Mini-lesson on literary formats for the culminating product assignment. Students also need to begin thinking about which of three literary format options is the best fit for the idea they are pursuing: a *vignette,* a *short story,* or a *chapter from a novel.* Explain the factors they should consider: • *Vignettes* are literary snapshots; they may be short, but every single word is essential. Vignettes sometimes have a well-developed plot, but not always. This format may be best for students who have a few specific details that have grabbed their attention. • *Short stories* have a definitive plot with a beginning, middle, and end. • *Chapters* have a definite setting, character development, and probably dialogue. However, the plot will be interrupted. Tell students that even if they decide on a format now, they can always change their minds later in the writing process if the format doesn't seem to suit their ideas.	By the time students reach high school, chances are they have written many short stories and read many chapters; they are likely to have far less experience reading or writing vignettes, which makes them a more challenging option. Additionally, a vignette that meets the criteria for excellent practitioner-level historical fiction is a rare thing. (Ernest Hemingway did it.) For examples of vignettes, see *In Brief: Short Takes on the Personal,* a collection of vignettes edited by Judith Kitchen and Mary Paumier Jones.

LESSON SEQUENCE AND DESCRIPTION	TEACHER COMMENTARY
Independent writing differentiated by interest and readiness. During this phase of the unit, students work on writing their chosen piece of historical fiction, using the appropriate rubric as a guideline for excellent work. Continue to provide whole-class modeling by sharing the development of your own work and excerpts from your reflective journal. Tell students that they may submit their finished pieces when they feel that they have written to the best of their ability and level. Evaluate completed work immediately and insist on at least one "improvement cycle."	This part of the unit is flexible, with time added or subtracted based on students' progress and needs. I might ask one student to work toward a higher level of excellence within her level (practitioner, apprentice, or novice) and ask another to lift his work to a more advanced level.
Individual or small-group coaching sessions based on readiness needs. Throughout the writing workshop class sessions, schedule "writing conferences"—basically coaching sessions—with individuals and small, homogeneous groups of students. Review their progress and provide mini-lessons on basic skills and the writer's craft, based on emerging needs. Ask students to record what they learn from these lessons on the left-hand pages of their journals and to react or reflect on the right-hand pages.	
Anchor activity: Revision/Independent study extension opportunity. Give students who have completed quality work the option of revising or expanding their historical fiction as an anchor activity. This should include several opportunities for self- and peer review. Students might also opt to continue to develop or expand their historical fiction as an independent study.	

LESSON 10 **Reflecting on the Unit and Sharing Finished Products** *(2 blocks)*
Concepts: Culture, Values, Traditions, Heritage, Change
GEN1–4; SD3–8, SD10–11

LESSON SEQUENCE AND DESCRIPTION	TEACHER COMMENTARY
Reflective partner work. Tell students that the purpose of this last session is for them to really delve into how reading and writing historical fiction has revealed aspects of themselves.	

LESSON SEQUENCE AND DESCRIPTION	TEACHER COMMENTARY
Bring in a partner for this activity and have the partner go through your reflective journal, reading passages aloud and stopping to discuss with you any "interesting things" noticed. These might include entries that are particularly revealing of your personality, the challenges you faced, and your break-throughs or triumphs while reading and writing. Add your own comments and reactions. As you and your partner engage in this discussion, a designated student should create a list of the kinds of topics addressed and comments shared. Post the list on the board so that students may refer to it during the next activity. Now it's the students' turn. Ask them to form pairs with a partner of their choice and go through the process that they have just seen modeled: One student reads aloud from the other's reflective journal, and the partners stop and talk about noteworthy and revealing entries that the reader notices. Remind students that they should make notes of things their reflective partner points out, along with their own reactions. Then they should switch roles. Circulate during this activity to hear what students are saying. Provide additional prompts as needed.	A colleague assists me with this modeling. Flexible grouping and a learning environment in which all learners feel safe and valued are two important hallmarks of a differentiated classroom. Allowing students to choose their partners at this point in the unit provides yet another grouping possibility, but perhaps more importantly, it ensures that students work with partners they trust.
Reflective journal writing. Using the notes from their reflective partner conversations, students should respond to the following prompt: *How did studying the historical fiction genre help you understand yourself better or in a different way?*	When time gets tight, reflecting on learning is an element of instruction that tends to be dropped. That's a big mistake, as reflective components are where students really connect to the learning.
"Publication" of the differentiated products. Writing work is not truly complete until it is shared. There are lots of options: • Sharing in homogeneous groups (practitioners together, apprentices together, etc.) • Whole-class sharing • A combination of these structures with a "Coffeehouse Reading" in the evening, with families invited to attend.	This is a celebration! This unit has most likely challenged each student to grow toward more sophisticated practice.

Teacher Reflection on the Unit

Designing and teaching this unit was a significant step in my journey toward employing quality differentiation, because it helped me to understand what it means to design learning experiences based on concepts rather than on discrete facts and skills. You may have noticed that I addressed standards 10 and 11 (see page 23) in every lesson in this unit. I believe that using these two standards as a consistent foundation helped me push students to become members of a literary community and use literacy skills for authentic purposes. It is these standards, along with worthwhile concepts and generalizations, that enable students—particularly secondary students—to connect with school in a meaningful way.

What was the most satisfying about this was watching the effect that my personal growth in differentiating curriculum had on my students. I saw them stretching, reaching to understand "big ideas" that were just off the edge of their personal horizons. The flexibility of the workshop approach enabled me to ask each learner to consider his or her individual growth (rather than asking them all to complete a common task); it let me support some students while setting others free. I saw my students developing both the ability and the desire to share their personal reactions, connections, and interpretations, and I saw them gaining confidence in their own voices. That is learning for a lifetime—the true meaning of being literate. Risking together, my students and I were more of a learning community than we had ever been before.

Cheryl Becker Dobbertin, a former high school English teacher, is the manager of professional development at Monroe 2-Orleans Board of Cooperative Educational Services (BOCES) near Rochester, New York. She can be reached at beckerdobbertin@yahoo.com.

SAMPLE 1.1—Reflective Journal Sentence Starters

I think . . .

I wonder . . .

What puzzles me is . . .

I am unsure about . . .

What's interesting is . . .

What's hard about this is . . .

One place where I will grow is . . .

A strength for me is . . .

Something I need to work harder on is . . .

It was great when . . .

I was surprised that . . .

I learned . . .

I already knew about . . . but learned that . . .

Others say/do/think/want . . .

I am concerned that . . .

I am affirmed when . . .

I feel secure when . . .

It's okay that . . .

I think what will happen is . . .

This is different because . . .

I feel connected when . . .

It made me think of . . .

I could visualize . . .

I figured out . . .

SAMPLE 1.2—Historical Fiction Comparison Matrix

Text	Setting	Characters	Plot	Literary Devices	Point of View	Language	Connections to Unit Concepts (Culture, Values, Traditions, Heritage, Change)
Example 1							
Example 2							
Example 3							
Example 4							
Example 5							
Nonexample 1							
Nonexample 2							
Nonexample 3							
Nonexample 4							

SAMPLE 1.3—Literature Circle Role Sheets

Conversation Captain

Name _____   Meeting date _____
Book _____   Assignment (p. _____ to p. _____)
Others in your group _____

Like a great host or hostess at a party, your job is to keep the conversation flowing. You should prepare for your role by developing a list of questions that your literature circle group can use as a starting place for discussion. Remember that you want to help people talk about the big ideas in the reading and share their reactions. Usually the best discussion questions come from your own thoughts, feelings, and concerns as you read. Think about finding connections between the text and the unit concepts of culture, values, traditions, heritage, and change. You may also use some of the general discussion questions below to develop topics for your group.

Here are some model questions. Caution! Your group can only use these once:

• How does this section reflect our working definition of historical fiction?
• What was going through your mind as you read this? What things, perhaps related to your own family's history, did you connect with?
• What values, traditions, and beliefs are shown through this family's story?
• Possible discussion questions or topics for your meeting:

_____
_____
_____
_____

Self-Evaluation: Rate yourself on a scale of 1 to 5. (Five = outstanding, 3 = you got the job done but you didn't really have to work at it, 1 = you did the bare minimum just to make it look like you were working.) Circle the number that you think is appropriate.

How well did you prepare?   1   2   3   4   5

How well did you participate?   1   2   3   4   5

Justify the score you gave yourself:

Adapted from *Literature Circles: Voice and Choice in Book Clubs & Reading Groups* by Harvey Daniels, © 2002, used with permission of Stenhouse Publishers.

SAMPLE 1.3—Literature Circle Role Sheets—*(continued)*

Literary Critic

Name _____   Meeting date _____
Book _____   Assignment (p. _____ to p. _____)
Others in your group _____

Your job is to locate at least three places in this section where the author has deliberately used an "author's tool" in order to affect the reader. Tools include literary elements or techniques: characterization, vivid description, metaphors, setting, tone, mood, and so on. After finding at least three places where tools are used, fill in the chart below. When you meet with your group, you will read the selection that incorporates the author's tool aloud to your group, identify the literary element or technique being used, and lead a discussion about how well the author has done his or her job.

1. Location: Tool (Literary Element):
   Page: Paragraph:

2. Location: Tool (Literary Element):
   Page: Paragraph:

3. Location: Tool (Literary Element):
   Page: Paragraph:

Below, reflect on the power of each tool. Did the author make a good choice? Did he or she use the tool well? What kinds of reactions did people have to the tool?

Tool #1:

Tool #2:

Tool #3:

Self-Evaluation: Rate yourself on a scale of 1 to 5. (Five = outstanding, 3 = you got the job done but you didn't really have to work at it, 1 = you did the bare minimum just to make it look like you were working.)

Circle the number that you think is appropriate.

How well did you prepare?   1   2   3   4   5

How well did you participate?   1   2   3   4   5

Justify the score you gave yourself:

SAMPLE 1.3—Literature Circle Role Sheets—*(continued)*

Word Wonder

Name _____   Meeting date _____

Book _____   Assignment (p. _____ to p. _____)

Others in your group _____

Your job is to be on the lookout for words that are unusual, puzzling, used in a different way, or essential to understanding this section. Try to figure out the meaning of these words from the context clues around them. Then look up the words and check to be sure that the definition makes sense in what you're reading. Write your own definitions and make sure that you really understand the words before you meet in your literature circle group! Lead your group through a discussion of the words and their meanings. Here are some things you might talk about:

* I thought this word meant . . . but then I found out . . .
* I had some trouble with this one because . . .
* This word was really important because . . .

Word:
Page number:
Sentence it was found in:
Meaning in this context:

Word:
Page number:
Sentence it was found in:
Meaning in this context:

Word:
Page number:
Sentence it was found in:
Meaning in this context:

Self-Evaluation: Rate yourself on a scale of 1 to 5. (Five = outstanding, 3 = you got the job done but you didn't really have to work at it, 1 = you did the bare minimum just to make it look like you were working.)
Circle the number that you think is appropriate.

How well did you prepare?   1   2   3   4   5

How well did you participate?   1   2   3   4   5

Justify the score you gave yourself:

SAMPLE 1.3—Literature Circle Role Sheets—*(continued)*

Plot Mapper/Detail Organizer

Name _____ Meeting date _____

Book _____ Assignment (p. _____ to p. _____)

Others in your group _____

Your job is to draw some kind of thinking map or graphic organizer that could be used as "notes" for what happens in specific sections of the text. You can draw or create a diagram, a web, an outline, or any other kind of graphic organizer you want. Use a separate sheet of blank paper for your work and attach it to this form. BE NEAT. Every member of your group will receive a copy of the organizer you create.

When you meet in your literature circle group, show your organizer to the other group members without comment. Everyone in the group will examine it, try to connect it to their own ideas about the reading, and clarify or correct anything with which they disagree. After everyone has had a say, you get the last word: Change the organizer based on the group's input or leave it as is. Remember, though, that your work is the permanent record of this section of the book, so it should be accurate.

Before you begin, make some notes of important aspects of the story that you will include in your organizer:

_____

_____

_____

_____

_____

_____

_____

_____

_____

Self-Evaluation: Rate yourself on a scale of 1 to 5. (Five = outstanding, 3 = you got the job done but you didn't really have to work at it, 1 = you did the bare minimum just to make it look like you were working.)
Circle the number that you think is appropriate.

How well did you prepare?   1   2   3   4   5

How well did you participate?   1   2   3   4   5

Justify the score you gave yourself:

SAMPLE 1.3—Literature Circle Role Sheets—*(continued)*

Concept Connector

Name _____   Meeting date _____

Book _____   Assignment (p. _____ to p. _____)

Others in your group _____

Your job is to use your own thinking, the text, and the things said by the people in your group discussion to develop, share, or capture the "big ideas" or generalizations about historical fiction and the unit concepts of culture, values, traditions, heritage, and change that results from your meetings. What you're trying to record is the "a-ha's"—the things that people in your group realized or learned as they worked and talked with one another.

Statements of big ideas often start like this:
- So what's important is . . .
- This is like . . .
- I/we realized . . .
- Oh! I get it . . .
- This means that . . .
- What I've learned is . . .

Big ideas developed:

_____

_____

_____

_____

_____

_____

Self-Evaluation: Rate yourself on a scale of 1 to 5. (Five = outstanding, 3 = you got the job done but you didn't really have to work at it, 1 = you did the bare minimum just to make it look like you were working.)
Circle the number that you think is appropriate.

How well did you prepare?   1   2   3   4   5

How well did you participate?   1   2   3   4   5

Justify the score you gave yourself:

SAMPLE 1.4—Literature Circle Assessment Rubric

Names of people in group _____

Selection/text being discussed _____ p. _____ to p. _____

Criteria	Advanced	Intermediate	Novice
Content	*Members of the group consistently* • Share prepared work as well as insightful new ideas. • Build thoughtfully on each other's comments while staying on topic. • Support ideas with rich examples and detailed evidence from the text. • Demonstrate inferential comprehension of the text.	*Members of the group* • Share prepared work as well as new ideas. • Build on each other's comments while staying on topic. • Support ideas with examples and evidence from the text. • Demonstrate inferential comprehension of the text.	*Members of the group* • Share prepared work. • Build on each other's ideas. • Inconsistently support ideas with examples and evidence from the text. • Demonstrate literal comprehension of the text. • Stray off topic.
Behavior	*Members of the group consistently* • Contribute insightful comments to the discussion. • Speak respectfully to each other. • Listen in order to understand. • Ask appropriate clarifying questions.	*Members of the group* • Contribute to the discussion. • Speak respectfully to each other. • Listen carefully. • Ask appropriate questions.	*Members of the group* • Contribute to the discussion when prompted. • Listen more to see if other people "get them" than to focus on others' points of view. • Ask questions.

SAMPLE 1.5—Continuum of Literature Circle Skills

Beginning	Developing	Advanced
☐ Fulfills role.	☐ Fulfills role and engages others.	☐ Dynamically moves between and among roles without "stealing thunder" or monopolizing the conversation.
☐ Makes text-to-self connections.	☐ Makes self-to-text and text-to-text connections.	☐ Makes self-to-text, text-to-text, and text-to-concept connections.
☐ Offers clearly stated opinions and ideas.	☐ Builds on the ideas and opinions of others.	☐ Is able to either build on or respectfully refute the ideas and opinions of others using support from the text.
☐ Pays attention when others are speaking.	☐ Actively listens and uses nonverbal gestures to encourage others.	☐ Actively listens with the intention of learning from others rather than being heard.
☐ Asks questions.	☐ Asks questions in order to help the speaker make his or her point more clearly and honors wait time.	☐ Asks questions to elicit critical thinking from others in the group.
☐ Sets aside prejudices and misconceptions.	☐ Acknowledges and sets aside prejudices and misconceptions.	☐ Examines own prejudices and misconceptions as growth opportunities.
☐ Maintains respectful tone and language when disagreeing.	☐ Embraces different points of view.	☐ Invites other points of view and restates and summarizes what others are saying.
☐ Helps the literature circle be successful.	☐ Helps the literature circle be a safe place for expression.	☐ Helps the literature circle be an authentic conversation.

SAMPLE 1.6—Critical Work Skills Rubric

Criteria	Advanced	Intermediate	Novice
Preparation	You are consistently prepared with the necessary materials.	You are inconsistently prepared.	Your lack of preparation interferes with your ability to participate.
Engagement	You are highly engaged in your work (sometimes you seem to be "lost in it").	You are visibly engaged in your work.	You are inconsistently engaged in your work.
Acceptance	You express and show acceptance of the challenge your tasks present and support others in their own growth.	You express and show acceptance of the challenge your tasks present.	You express or show a lack of acceptance of working at your own level of challenge.
Motivation	You are completely self-directed and do not require reminders to stay on task.	You are self-directed and rarely require reminders to stay on task.	You require reminders to stay on task.
Resource Use	You use resources (peers, librarian, teacher, other supports) responsibly.	You use resources (peers, librarian, teacher, other supports), but may sometimes seek support from the teacher that you could have gotten elsewhere.	You use resources (peers, librarian, teacher, other supports), but often seek support from the teacher that you could have gotten elsewhere.
Journaling	Your reflective journal is up to date and shows exemplary evidence of critical thinking and growth.	Your reflective journal is up to date and shows thought.	You are falling behind in your reflective journal and/or you are not recording thoughtful reactions and reflections.

Note: This rubric is based on the work of my friend and colleague, Christopher J. Potter.

SAMPLE 1.7—Differentiated Reader Response Options

Tasks for Creative Thinkers

A. Write poems that accurately reflect the values of the major characters.

B. Draw pictures of scenes that reflect the concepts of culture, values, traditions, heritage, or change.

C. Use a shoebox to create a model of a stage setting (props included) for a key scene that reveals a character's values or illustrates the family's traditions.

D. Draw a 10-panel comic strip of a chapter that reflects the concepts of culture, values, traditions, heritage, or change.

E. Get together with a couple of others who are reading your novel, turn a concept-based scene into a play, and videotape it.

Tasks for Practical Thinkers

A. Develop a list of items you would need in order to survive in the time period your novel is set in and explain why each item is essential.

B. Trace the route a character's life journey takes on a world map, noting the major events that happen in each location.

C. Write the last will and testament of one of the characters, including which personal items he or she would leave behind, to whom they would go, and why.

D. Describe a time when one of your major characters faced a challenging dilemma in relation to culture, values, traditions, heritage, or change, and compare and contrast that character's actions to what you would have done in the same situation.

E. Describe the life lessons in relation to the concepts of culture, values, traditions, heritage, or change that you are thinking about based on the experiences of the characters you are reading about.

Tasks for Analytical Thinkers

A. Describe which of today's social norms in regard to the concepts of culture, values, traditions, heritage, or change one of your major characters would have trouble adjusting to and discuss why.

B. Using a Venn diagram, contrast and compare the culture(s), traditions, and/or heritage(s) in your novel to those in another text that you've read this year.

C. Write a letter to one of your characters giving him or her advice about his or her family dynamics, and then write the character's letter back to you.

D. Use the computer to create an advertisement for the novel that could be displayed in a bookstore. Be sure to indicate why a potential reader interested in the way families change over time should buy this book.

E. Write a *New York Times*–style book review incorporating the concepts of culture, heritage, or traditions.

SAMPLE 1.8—Reader Response Options Rubric

Criteria	Advanced	Intermediate	Novice
Comprehension	*Your submitted product* • Reveals an inferential and analysis-level comprehension of your chosen novel. • Includes details about characters' actions, turning points, symbols, or other literary elements that are essential to deep understanding. • Shows unique and insightful understanding of the author's purpose and theme.	*Your submitted product* • Reveals accurate yet mostly literal comprehension of your chosen novel. • Includes many specific details about key events in the novel. • Shows that you share the general or commonly accepted understanding of the author's purpose and theme.	*Your submitted product* • Reveals a mostly accurate, literal comprehension of your chosen novel. • Includes some specific details, but they aren't necessarily important. • Shows that you are somewhat confused or uncertain about the author's purpose and theme.
Connections	Your submitted product reveals insightful, unique, and/or personal connections to the unit concepts of *culture, values, traditions, heritage, and change.*	Your submitted product reveals that you have made some strong yet obvious connections to the unit concepts of *culture, values, traditions, heritage, and change.*	Your submitted product reveals that you attempted to make connections to the unit concepts of *culture, values, traditions, heritage, and change,* but your connections were muddled or weak.
Quality	Your submitted product shows evidence of craftsmanship, revision, and the creative yet appropriate use of technology and/or interesting materials.	Your submitted product shows evidence of revision and the use of appropriate tools and materials.	Your submitted product appears to be in draft stage and your choice of tools or materials was uninspired.

2

Which Comes First, the Individual or Society?

An English and Humanities Unit on Macbeth

Unit Developer: Lyn Fairchild

Introduction

This five- to six-week unit on *Macbeth* focuses on the concepts of Elizabethan culture, figurative language, and directorial vision. Its purpose is to help students develop an understanding of how individual desires and choices affect a larger society and how society at large shapes an individual.

For the majority of the unit, class activities alternate between *mini-lesson days,* when tiered group assignments focus on specific skills, and *performance days,* when the class works in differentiated groups to analyze cinematic interpretations of Shakespeare's text, to perform scenes from the play, and to connect those scenes to unit themes. Other instructional components include nightly reading homework with tiered assignments; the use of a double-entry journal to track motifs, figurative language, and themes; and periodic quizzes to document student reading comprehension and inform targeted small-group and one-on-one instruction. A Socratic seminar concludes the reading, and students complete tiered expository or analytical essays.

Throughout, the students work toward a final group project: the presentation of a scene from *Macbeth* in a manner that expresses a particular motif or a particular era's "vision" about individual needs versus societal needs. While students are developing and staging their scenes, the teacher works with small groups to provide instruction in areas not yet mastered or to encourage extended learning.

Teacher Reflection on Designing the Unit

This unit draws on my career-long search for "hooks" into Shakespeare—interest areas that will most engage adolescents. My students respond well to the theme of the individual and society, perhaps because adolescence can seem like a constant navigation between the poles of the self and others. I decided that taking a humanities approach that asks students to look at *Macbeth* within the context of period politics and culture could help explain much of the initial strangeness of the play's language and action. In addition, incorporating an historical focus would also enhance the final project by asking students to juggle an understanding of similar and different historical periods. Finally, I've found that allowing students an opportunity to think like playwrights and producers helps them to approach the Bard's words with a distinct mission: to find a historical vision that can merge with Shakespeare's message and make it come alive for an audience. Class lessons on figurative language, character analysis, and narrative elements thus take on a practical relevance to the goal of presenting a Shakespearean scene.

English and Humanities Standards Addressed

SD1   Present a thesis and support it.

SD2   Recognize common themes and use evidence from the texts to substantiate ideas.

SD3   Relate cultural and historical contexts to literature.

SD4   Apply knowledge of literary terms.

Unit Concepts and Generalizations

Elizabethan Culture, Figurative Language, Directorial Vision

GEN1   Shakespeare's *Macbeth* presents an Elizabethan worldview in which the average individual occupies a submissive space in the "chain of being" below God, angels, and king, and where the absolutist political system uses divine right as its justification for the social contract.

GEN2   Shakespeare uses figurative language to create images in the audience's "mind's eye" in a manner that's similar to the ways in which modern filmmakers use cinematography.

GEN3   Figurative language, such as the paradox, functions as a symbol or summation of the Shakespearean worldview: the self-contradictory nature of human existence.

GEN4   Today's artists, including writers and filmmakers, present a particular vision that comments on the individual's place within society.

GEN5   The history of Western society since the Renaissance has been a tug-of-war between the rights of the individual and the rights of society.

Unit Objectives

As a result of this unit, the students will *know*
- Specific literary terms, including paradox, metaphor, simile, iambic pentameter, trochaic pentameter, split-level line, scansion, motif, theme, tragic hero, tragic flaw, exposition, rising action, climax, falling action, and denouement.
- The plot of *Macbeth* and the play's historical context, including the Gunpowder Plot, Jesuits in England, equivocation, divine right, and the reign of James I.
- Rubric standards and guidelines for an identification and comparison/contrast essay.

As a result of this unit, the students will *understand that*
- Individual goals can conflict with societal goals.
- Individuals make choices in an attempt to meet one or more needs: love and belonging, freedom, fun, and power.
- Citizens of the 21st century tend to attribute an individual's progress within a society to a combination of his or her personal choices and coincidence/providence.
- Certain individuals can change the course of a society's history.
- An individual's power is often bounded by society.

As a result of this unit, the students will *be able to*
- Identify paradox, motif, and figurative language techniques in Shakespearean text and explain how these devices contribute to the imagery and overall theme of *Macbeth*.
- Analyze a character or a concept in writing by identifying key traits and providing examples, or analyze characters in writing by comparing and contrasting one character's traits with another's.
- Research the motifs that support a theme and apply those recurring images to a thematic vision of *Macbeth*, or research the "character traits" of a particular era and apply those traits to a directorial vision of *Macbeth*.
- Create a thesis (a directorial vision) for a scene from *Macbeth*, based on unit themes and questions.
- Execute a directorial vision though conscious choices about acting, blocking, costumes, scenery, music, and other features that demonstrate the play's themes.
- Work cooperatively in a small group.

Instructional Strategies Used

- Double-entry journals
- Flexible grouping

- Mini-lessons and coaching
- Pre-assessment and post-assessment
- RAFT assignments
- Socratic seminars
- Tiered assignments
- Whole-class discussion

Sample Supporting Materials Provided

Unit Overview

LESSON	WHOLE-CLASS COMPONENTS	DIFFERENTIATED COMPONENTS
PREPARATION *45 minutes*	Pre-assessment of reading and writing skills *30 minutes* Interest and experience inventory *15 minutes*	
LESSON 1 **My World, Will's World** *3 class periods*	Brainstorming session: The individual versus society *10 minutes* Mini-lecture: Control theory *5 minutes*	

LESSON	WHOLE-CLASS COMPONENTS	DIFFERENTIATED COMPONENTS
		Control theory activity in flexible groups *30 minutes*
	Mini-lecture: Overview of Elizabethan culture *2–10 minutes*	Content varies depending on students' general familiarity with the period.
		Differentiated group activities: Plotting the Plot *45–90 minutes*
	Small-group presentations and whole-group discussion *30–45 minutes*	
	Unit understandings overview *5–20 minutes*	
LESSON 2 **Reading Language, Character, and Scene** *10–15 class periods*	Final project preview *5 minutes*	
	Introduction of the Director's Notebook *5 minutes*	Optional mini-lesson on double-entry journaling *20 minutes*
		Guided reading, discussion, staging, and viewing of Act I, Scene 1, differentiated by learning profile *60 minutes*
		Nightly homework: Reading and analysis differentiated by readiness *ongoing, time varies*
	Reading check-in activities *10–20 minutes*	
		Mini-lessons and related activities differentiated by readiness needs and/or interest *time varies*
		Performance activities differentiated by interest *time varies*
	Socratic seminar *90 minutes*	

LESSON	WHOLE-CLASS COMPONENTS	DIFFERENTIATED COMPONENTS
		Writing workshops differentiated by readiness and interest *90 minutes*
LESSON 3 Envisioning a Scene *7 class periods*	Discussion of unit understandings *20–30 minutes*	
	Cinematic models of directorial vision *10–30 minutes*	
		Final project work differentiated by readiness and interest *ongoing, time varies*
		Mini-lessons and workshops based on readiness needs and interest *ongoing, time varies*
LESSON 4 Presenting the Vision *3–5 class periods*	Final group project presentations and discussions *90 minutes or longer*	
	Self-evaluation and group evaluation *10 minutes*	

Unit Description and Teacher Commentary

PREPARATION   *(45 minutes)*

LESSON SEQUENCE AND DESCRIPTION	TEACHER COMMENTARY
Pre-assessment of reading and writing skills. Distribute the *Macbeth* Pretest (see Sample 2.1, page 83) to measure students' ability to read and interpret a passage of Shakespeare, analyze a character, and identify key character traits.	Some students who have struggled with Shakespeare in the past immediately groan at the sight of this pretest. I reassure them that its purpose is to help me figure out the best way to teach them.
Tell the students that you will read this passage through twice so that they may hear the language. If the class harbors a majority of novice students, it may be beneficial to show a cinematic clip of this scene before students begin the pre-assessment.	Because Shakespeare is meant to be performed, it is crucial that there be an auditory component in students' first encounter with the text.

LESSON SEQUENCE AND DESCRIPTION	TEACHER COMMENTARY
Ask students to complete the tasks that they know how to complete and make educated guesses about what they don't know. Encourage them to just try their best. Based on the pretest results, divide the students into three readiness groups—novice, on target, and advanced.	I let students know that if they can show sincere effort, I'll count completion of the pretest as a full-credit assignment; there will be no points off for incorrect answers. This relaxes the students and helps them be honest about what they know and don't know.
Interest and experience inventory. Distribute the **Production Skills and Interest Inventory** (see Sample 2.2, page 84) to determine students' background in acting, directing, scene design, and so forth; their interest in historical periods and cinematic genres such as fantasy, history, action/adventure, and romance; and their prior knowledge of *Macbeth*.	Students' responses inform interest- and learning profile–based grouping throughout the unit and also help me balance the final project groups in terms of skill and genre preference. I include a section for cinematography/editing because my school has access to video and video editing equipment—meaning that it's possible for us to "film" the final presentations.

LESSON 1

My World, Will's World

Concepts: Elizabethan Culture

GEN1, GEN5; SD3

(3 class periods)

LESSON SEQUENCE AND DESCRIPTION	TEACHER COMMENTARY
Brainstorming session: The individual versus society. Explain to students that the question, "Which comes first, the individual or society?" will be a central discussion point throughout the unit. Ask the class to brainstorm current-events issues where this question is in play.	This question about the individual versus society is relevant to many political issues, including free speech, security, privacy, and reproductive choice. Students relate to it easily and have little difficulty identifying current or recent events where leaders and citizens have been negotiating such issues.
Keep track of the brainstorming with a two-column list, recording the individual-rights perspective on one side and the societal-rights perspective on the other.	I'm careful to make sure this activity centers on the identification of issues rather than argumentation of political sides.
Mini-lecture: Control theory. Spend 5 to 10 minutes covering the concepts of William Glasser's control theory.	

LESSON SEQUENCE AND DESCRIPTION	TEACHER COMMENTARY
Note: Control theory is also known as "choice theory." For a quick and helpful survey of this theory, written in student language, consult Perry Good's *In Pursuit of Happiness: Knowing What You Want, Getting What You Need.* Key points include the following:	Control theory is a powerful tool to help students understand that a person's needs—such as Macbeth's ambition, which Glasser would call "a need for power"—are not problematic in and of themselves. What can get us into trouble are the choices we make and behaviors we pursue to meet such needs. My intent here is to help students understand that the ambitious methods that brought Macbeth success in battle are no longer the right strategy when he wants to pursue the power of the throne.

• Control theory teaches us to pursue what we need (love and belonging, freedom, fun, or power) in positive ways by making us aware of the moment-to-moment choices that we make in search of happiness.

• Control theory addresses the conflicts between personal choices and societal needs, asking us to consider how we can meet our own needs without preventing someone else from meeting his or her needs.

• Control theory encourages us to think in terms of this question of conscience: "Am I choosing to be the best person I can be right now?" This theory is in direct contrast to the medieval idea of fate and external locus of control, which, during Shakespeare's time, was being challenged by Renaissance ideas of human empowerment and creativity.

LESSON SEQUENCE AND DESCRIPTION	TEACHER COMMENTARY
Control theory activity in flexible groups. Ask students to divide a sheet of paper into four quadrants, one for each need to be met: love, power, freedom, and fun. Then, ask students to list recent choices that they have made in an attempt to meet particular needs. This task should be completed individually.	I've adapted this activity from Perry Good's *In Pursuit of Happiness.* It differentiates the content of whole-class instruction by interest, allowing students to begin from a subject of great personal interest: themselves. Good's task also harnesses the visual mode and uses examples and illustrations from a range of student experiences.
Ask: How do you achieve love/belonging, power, freedom, or fun in your daily life? What specific behaviors do you pursue?	
Ask students to meet in small, self-selected groups to share the various ways that they meet their needs. Share examples of your own.	Because the subject is personal, students should have a say about who is in their group.
Next, ask the class to generate a group list of needs and fill in the "power" quadrant with examples of both positive and negative behaviors people may choose in order to meet their need for power. Introduce the synonym "ambition" for "power," and invite students to offer specific strategies—positive and negative—of the ways in which people pursue power in politics, in personal relationships, at work, in athletics, and in other arenas where choices are evident.	

LESSON SEQUENCE AND DESCRIPTION	TEACHER COMMENTARY
Tell students to think about the results of one particular behavior in the "power" quadrant and identify a behavior that sometimes gets them into trouble. Offer some example responses of your own, and encourage students who are comfortable sharing their own responses to do so, as well.	Teacher modeling makes student sharing feel somewhat safer.
Working independently, students write a journal response to the following questions: 1. Did this behavior result in success for me? Explain. 2. Were the consequences ever opposite of what I hoped for? How so? 3. Did I come in conflict with another person, group, or institution? If so, what happened? Where did the conflict(s) occur? 4. Were there any obstacles to my achieving success? Did these obstacles arise from others trying to get what they wanted, or from my behavior in and of itself?	✸ This interpersonal moment in instruction helps students see how the choices of a medieval Scottish king are relevant to their own lives. Depending on class chemistry and students' comfort level with journals, I sometimes assign this journal work as a homework activity, especially if students are reticent about sharing personal experiences.
Mini-lecture: Overview of Elizabethan culture. Move on to a second short lecture focused on "Will's World"—the troubled times of Shakespeare's England. Incorporate visual representations of life during the period. Key points: • People in the Elizabethan age had firm cultural, spiritual, and philosophical beliefs about the "chain of being." • The revelation of The Gunpowder Plot (Guy Fawkes and his coconspirators' plot to destroy Parliament, James I, and the royal family) led to great mistrust of the individual as someone potentially treasonous to king and country. • There are parallels between the troubled times Shakespeare was writing in and our own, post-9/11 world.	✸ Although I present this lecture for the entire class, I vary it somewhat for different sections depending on the general level of familiarity students have with the time period. I do not provide a great deal of detail during this lecture because some of the students will be doing so as part of the next activity.
✸ **Differentiated group activities: Plotting the Plot.** Divide the class into two groups, based on their familiarity with *Macbeth* as revealed in Part 2 of the Production Skills and Interest Inventory (see Sample 2.2). *Group 1 (Students Who Know the Play Well)* Ask students who have previous experience with or exposure to *Macbeth* to conduct further online research into the Gunpowder Plot, an event that occurred in England the year before *Macbeth* was (most likely) written and that was a major influence on many plays of the period.	This activity differentiates content in response to student readiness. A Web investigation helps students with prior knowledge of the play to deepen their understanding of its context while giving me a snapshot of their familiarity with the text.

LESSON SEQUENCE AND DESCRIPTION	TEACHER COMMENTARY
Then, using their research, they will either prepare a dramatic re-enactment of the Gunpowder Plot or create an oral presentation that explores the event's historical context.	Giving students the choice of presenting the results of their research dramatically or through a formal, lecture-style presentation differentiates the activity in response to student interest and learning profile.
Group 2 (Students Who Do Not Know the Play) Divide these students into smaller heterogeneous groups of three to five. Distribute the **Ten-Minute *Macbeth* Activity Guidelines** (see Sample 2.3, page 87). Group 2 students will work in their groups to create a scene of 10 minutes or less that predicts the plot of *Macbeth* and uses as many of the Top 10 lines as possible. Stress that students' scenes should create a logical plot structure using one or more of the unit understandings.	I refer to students' Production Skills and Interest Inventory responses to ensure that each of these small groups is balanced. Each group needs a strong facilitator/director, a student with acting experience, and students who have visual/spatial and linguistic strengths.
Provide each group with index cards to use as optional cue cards.	For students new to the play, exposure to small amounts of text synthesized in a creative, playful manner helps reduce "Shakesfear." I sometimes let students choose which unit understanding will be the basis for their skit; at other times, I assign understandings to guarantee that all are addressed.
Small-group presentations and whole-group discussion. Begin with the Group 2 presentations predicting the plot of the play. After all of Group 2 has presented, ask the class to compliment the various "acting troupes" for creative ways in which they met the activity challenge and to identify the unit understandings in each skit. Follow with the Group 1 presentation on the Gunpowder Plot.	
Unit understandings overview. Close the lesson by returning to the unit understandings about the individual and society. Ask: Do these statements seem to be true to you? Why? As an alternative, time permitting, address unit understandings through inductive reasoning. Ask students to answer the following questions, thinking about the choices they make to meet their own needs:	Addressing the intrapersonal skill of self-reflection invites students to construct personal examples before a formal introduction to the text of *Macbeth*.

LESSON SEQUENCE AND DESCRIPTION	TEACHER COMMENTARY
1. What generalizations can we make about individuals and their relationship to modern society, based on Glasser's control theory? 2. What generalizations can we make about Elizabethan individuals and their relationship to their society? Be sure to add any missing unit understandings to the student-generated list.	

LESSON 2   **Reading Language, Character, and Scene**   *(10–15 class periods)*

Concepts: Figurative Language, Directorial Vision
GEN1–4; SD2, SD4

LESSON SEQUENCE AND DESCRIPTION	TEACHER COMMENTARY
Note: After an initial class session that sets the scene for the work to come, this lesson extends over two or three weeks, during which students read *Macbeth* (individually and aloud, with teacher coaching), conduct research, receive targeted instruction based on readiness needs, and perform scenes from the play. Mini-lesson days alternate with performance days.	
Final project preview. Begin the initial session of this lesson with a brief preview of the upcoming final project. Explain to students that they will be working in groups to perform scenes from *Macbeth* in a manner that reflects distinct directorial visions. Share the skill goals they will be pursuing, and explain that when directors see a script, they look for thematic elements—or patterns that repeat—in order to plan blocking, scenery, costuming, and so on. Time permitting, share additional details about the process and the project's evaluation criteria.	This preview of the unit's culminating, real-world task can help focus students' attention on identifying thematic elements throughout the unit.
Introduction of the Director's Notebook/Optional mini-lesson on double-entry journaling. Explain that the reading strategy for this unit—to help prepare their "director's eye" for the final project—will be to keep a "Director's Notebook" (a double-entry journal).	Keeping this notebook reminds students of the role they will be playing in the final project as they search for compelling imagery that will translate well to stage action or video.

LESSON SEQUENCE AND DESCRIPTION	TEACHER COMMENTARY
Distribute the **Organizer for the Director's Notebook** (see Sample 2.4, page 88), and review the procedure for two-column note taking. (A mini-lesson on double-entry journaling might be necessary.) In the left-hand column, students will copy text (a motif that they are tracking or any other meaningful passage that they choose); in the right-hand column, they'll analyze that text and make notes for the final project. Review the analytical strategies suggested in the organizer (see Sample 2.4) and ensure that students understand what is expected of them.	Double-entry journals are a great tool for analysis, and their format automatically differentiates process based on student interest. They can differentiate process by readiness, too, if you assign specific topics based on pretest findings. To support novice readers, I typically assign a few specific motifs and allow them to explore the one or two that interest them most.
Guided reading, discussion, staging, and viewing of Act I, Scene 1, differentiated by learning profile. Select student volunteers to read the first scene of *Macbeth* aloud three times through. After each reading, lead a whole-group discussion that includes these challenges for students: • *First reading: Paraphrasing the language into modern English.* Ask students what "fair is foul and foul is fair" might mean, and introduce the terms *paradox* and *oxymoron*. • *Second reading: Tracking the number of beats per line.* Here, talk briefly about trochaic meter (a stressed syllable followed by an unstressed syllable) versus iambic meter (the opposite: an unstressed syllable followed by a stressed syllable). *Ask:* Why might the witches speak in trochees while the other characters speak in iambs? • *Third reading: Noting and sharing all the motifs that appear* (e.g., witchcraft, weather, battles, light, animals). Ask students about the overall pattern—or theme—established by the combination of such motifs.	Multiple readings are essential to build students' comfort level with the text. This activity differentiates content based on learning profile, incorporating auditory, bodily/kinesthetic, and visual approaches. I want to challenge students to conduct intensive, close reading of the text not only for better comprehension but also (and ultimately) for better understanding of Shakespeare's genius. Because this activity provides an additional informal pre-assessment of students' comprehension of Shakespearean language, scansion, and imagery, I often jot notes as I listen to students' reading and discussion contributions.
Lead speculation about the number of ways a director might present Act I, Scene 1. Create a list of two to five generalizations on the board that finish this phrase: "The vision a director might present of this scene is . . ."	Here, I sometimes share some trivia regarding Elizabethan beliefs about witches to help students speculate about how Shakespeare himself might have directed the witches' scene.
Ask: Do the witches appear playful and mischievous? Fearsome and devilish? Wise? Psychic? Some combination thereof? Prompt students to support their opinions with evidence from the text.	

LESSON SEQUENCE AND DESCRIPTION	TEACHER COMMENTARY
Announce a fourth reading and select new volunteer actors who are willing to be "director's puppets." Choose a student director, who will make suggestions about ways to stage the scene and then direct the actors so that one of the generalizations the class agreed on comes to life.	The clues about theme are there (the witches' scene is foreboding, dark, and malicious), but there is still opportunity for lots of creativity in how to render that feeling. This activity is also a dress rehearsal for the kind of work necessary in the final group project. Throughout, I look for clues about individual student strengths and weaknesses.
Show two or more cinematic versions of the witches' scene. Options include the filmed versions of *Macbeth* by Roman Polanski (1987), Trevor Nunn and Philip Casson (1991), Orson Welles (1948), and Sue Pritchard and Michael Bogdanov (1997). Ask students to take notes on the differences between the cinematic version and the actual text. Which version seems most true to the text and why? Prompt students to talk about how their ideas about the mood and theme of scene, which they developed by reading the text, have been transformed by directorial choice.	This is a good way to show students how much liberty directors can take with Shakespeare while still remaining true to the text. I also point out to students that because Shakespeare's work is now in the public domain, directors may delete text or move it around as they please.
Nightly homework: Reading and analysis differentiated by readiness. Students should read an average of 10 to 15 pages a night, with longer reading assignments going to advanced readers. Assign novice readers as few as 5 pages of highlighted text each night, focusing on key scenes only. Provide these students with follow-up guidance and extended reading time during class. First Homework Assignment The first tiered reading/analysis homework assignment of this lesson breaks out as follows: *Novice Readers* Students read a brief, teacher-approved summary of the entire tragedy and Act I, Scene 2. Then, they highlight what they think are the most important plot elements to share with their classmates during the next class session.	Giving novice readers shorter and scaffolded reading assignments reflects my belief that the amount of independent reading novices do is less important than their success with it. The summary I use is a factual report of the plot, not an analysis of character or theme. Familiarizing novice readers with the entire plot gives them a head start and also allows them to share their new expertise with classmates the following day. This can be a confidence builder.

LESSON SEQUENCE AND DESCRIPTION	TEACHER COMMENTARY
On-Target Readers Students read Charles and Mary Lamb's summary of *Macbeth* (from the book *Tales from Shakespeare,* originally published in 1878) and Act I, Scenes 2 and 3, then paraphrase the passage where Macbeth's character is introduced in detail: "For brave Macbeth . . . upon our battlements" (I.ii,18–25). They should arrive in class ready to discuss Macbeth's character. *Advanced Readers* Students will read Act I, Scenes 2, 3, and 4 and then • Highlight instances of motifs and figurative language in the scenes read. • Scan a speech of five lines or more for iambic and trochaic pentameter. • Come to class ready to analyze the scenes and choose a speech to present.	I base students' reading group assignments on the results of the pretest, but keep the group assignments flexible, as students can become more comfortable with Shakespearean language as the unit progresses and move from "novice" to "on-target" quite quickly.
✸ Subsequent Homework During the remainder of this multisession lesson, students reinforce their nightly reading by responding to homework questions assigned from the **Making Sense of Shakespeare Tiered Question Sets** (see Sample 2.5, page 89). This hand-out provides three categories of reading comprehension questions designed to help students navigate Shakespearean verse, build key skills, and prepare for further analysis in their Director's Notebook.	I sometimes discontinue these tiered and structured homework assignments after a week or two, deciding that students' work in their Director's Notebook will suffice as follow-up for their reading.
Novice Readers Assign students questions from the "Plot Analysis" section, which focus on analyzing the plot events and progression.	Before novice readers take on questions from this handout, many of them benefit from completing a number of alternative assignments focused on paraphrasing key passages—soliloquies in particular.
On-Target Readers Assign these students questions from the "Character Analysis" section, which involve selecting a character (based on interest) and exploring his or her needs, motives, actions, and behavior.	These character-focused questions get to the heart of many of the unit concepts, generalizations, and understandings.

LESSON SEQUENCE AND DESCRIPTION	TEACHER COMMENTARY
Advanced Readers Assign these students questions from both the "Character Analysis" and "Language Analysis" sections. The language-focused questions address vocabulary, inferring theme from figures of speech and other textual features, and scansion.	Typically, advanced readers have all had some prior exposure to the plot of *Macbeth* and need to develop skills with character or language analysis. I ask for their input about which skills they feel they need to work on. In a differentiated classroom, the teacher and student must work together to identify learning needs and appropriate goals.
Reading check-in activities. Open each class session throughout this lesson with a "reading check-in," in which students reflect on the prior night's homework assignment and provide a brief review of the events that took place in the play. Give occasional reading quizzes that ask students to recall basic plot elements or interpret sections of Shakespearean text. These can range from a few basic questions to an entire passage that needs paraphrasing and scanning.	I focus daily reading check-ins on the text assigned to novice and on-target readers so that I can see how these students are faring. A convenient way to create computer-graded reading quizzes is to subscribe to www.quia.com. This Web site allows you to develop quizzes that present questions one at a time in varying combinations—allowing students to remain at different points in the reading while ensuring academic honesty.
A final reading quiz at the close of the unit should resemble the pretest (see Sample 2.1) but use Macbeth's final speech ("Tomorrow, and tomorrow, and tomorrow . . .") as the text.	The similar format provides good pre-to-post evidence of student growth in reading comprehension skills.
✴**Mini-lessons and related activities differentiated by readiness needs and/or interest.** Offer mini-lessons every other day throughout this part of the unit. They should provide information that is new to most, if not all, students. They may relate to reading assignments, as in the examples that follow. All mini-lessons should be interactive, highly visual, and dynamic, and they should feature flexible grouping and tiered assignments. No mini-lesson should exceed 20 minutes in length. Possible topics include character analysis; motifs; scansion; types of writing (e.g., identification, comparison/contrast); paradoxes and other figurative language (e.g., similes, metaphors, personification, hyperbole); and directorial techniques (e.g., casting, blocking, costuming, soundtrack composition).	Responses on the *Macbeth* Pretest and the Production Skills and Interest Inventory (see Samples 2.1 and 2.2) tell me where students' individual needs are and which students can skip these mini-lessons and move ahead with independent reading or research projects. Figurative language occurs frequently in this play, and students who have an eye for these "special effects" of the language can better appreciate the vision of Shakespeare and harness these visuals in their final projects.

LESSON SEQUENCE AND DESCRIPTION	TEACHER COMMENTARY
Sample Mini-Lesson on Character Analysis Begin by explaining that character analysis is an important skill for Shakespearean literature. For example, Macbeth is a complex individual: both a hero and a villain, much admired and much maligned. He disrupts the Great Chain of Being, yet he earns the tragedy's title role. It's Macbeth, not virtuous King Duncan, who is the designated hero. Lady Macbeth is equally intriguing: a powerful, self-seeking female in a time when women held few positions of authority. Ask students if they can recall any other literary, cinematic, cartoon, or anime characters who are similarly complex.	This mini-lesson is differentiated based on student learning profile and interest.
Now, guide students through the creation of a simple rubric for analyzing a literary character. Begin by drawing (or having a student draw) a human figure on the board or on a large sheet of paper. Ask students to label the figure with aspects of a person that might be important to consider. Ideas might be personality, point of view and beliefs, family background, speech, physical appearance, gestures, movements, what others say about this person, the person's actions, and so on.	
Next, divide this mini-lesson group into three smaller readiness-based groups to help reinforce the group discussion activity.	
Distribute the **Character Analysis Group Activities** handout (see Sample 2.6, page 90), designed to help build skill in character analysis and continue the previous lesson's exploration of the Elizabethan age. As part of this activity, each group presents a product to the rest of the class.	Occasionally, I allow students to self-select these kinds of tiered assignments, intervening only if I have serious concerns about students challenging themselves too much or too little. It's important to help students take responsibility for choosing activities appropriate to their needs.
Novice Readers These students complete Task 1 on the handout. Note that one element of this task is to create a poster or a human plot diagram representing the Aristotelian plot structure (exposition, rising action, climax, falling action, and denouement) and then teach the material to the rest of the class. Before the novice readers begin work on this component, check-in with them and give a short introductory lesson on the Aristotelian plot structure, noting that it is the norm for Shakespearean plays and Renaissance works in general. Use a graphic representation of this "plot triangle," but do not provide any adornments, as the students will develop visual symbols or kinesthetic gestures to represent each element.	Not all mini-lessons and their tiered group assignments should lead to presentations. However, the novice students' presentation on Aristotelian plot structure is crucial. This early experience of success and mastery builds confidence for what can otherwise be a very arduous unit. It also reinforces their previous night's homework assignment on plot analysis.

LESSON SEQUENCE AND DESCRIPTION	TEACHER COMMENTARY
On-Target Readers These students complete Task 2, which involves producing a poster.	
Advanced Readers These students work on Task 3, which involves casting and performing their choice of dramatic scene.	Advanced students have only one product option and less differentiation because they are most ready to direct.
For homework, students can go on to complete one of the **RAFT Activity Options** (see Sample 2.7, page 92), based on interest. This activity can also be an in-class assignment where students choose their own groups based on their interest in a particular character.	Because character identification is a key skill in this unit, I want students to explore the complex motivations of the most important individuals in this drama. The RAFT options in Sample 2.7 are keyed to Acts I and II and are typical for what I might provide for succeeding acts.
The **Tiered Worksheet on Paradox** (see Sample 2.8, page 93) illustrates the kind of assignment students complete to reinforce mini-lessons. Task A is designed for novice or on-target students; Task B is designed for advanced students.	On this handout, note that there are no perfect answers as to which pairs of paradoxes are truly oxymorons. The point is to get students discussing the concept of opposition and ambiguity as revealed in *Macbeth* and in real life.
✳ **Performance activities differentiated by interest.** Begin performance days with acting warm-ups. "Pass the prop" is a creative activity, where students pass an item such as a wooden spoon or a feather and pantomime its multiple uses (a spoon is no longer a spoon but a microphone, a lollipop, a radio antenna, etc.). There are two types of performance days. Language-Focused Performance Days With teacher involvement and coaching, students read aloud in front of the entire class. Some students play director, leading multiple rehearsals of certain lines in order to master the meter, convey meaning and theme, and communicate particular visions.	Performance days lay additional foundation for the final group project (see page 80). I like to use drama activities in the classroom and have found that acting warm-ups, such as those recommended in books like Viola Spolin's *Theater Games for the Classroom: A Teacher's Handbook*, can make a big difference in students' comfort level.

LESSON SEQUENCE AND DESCRIPTION	TEACHER COMMENTARY
Visual Performance Days On these days, small groups of students storyboard/sketch brief scenes and then present the visuals to the class or rehearse and present those scenes.	I provide a prop box stocked with random materials (plastic swords, hats, pots and pot lids, robes, etc.) that can quickly suggest lances, cauldrons, and other items needed for a Renaissance production of *Macbeth*. Sometimes I preview Option B of the Final Group Project (see page 81) by asking students to consider what props might be used if the scene were set in the present day.
Tell students that their groups should investigate and discuss the following questions as they rehearse their scenes: 1. What's the basic summary of the plot? What are the most important lines for this scene? Choose a passage of 5 to 10 lines and be ready to justify your choice. 2. What are the key stresses, motifs, and figurative language in the scene, and how do these "special effects" help express the scene's theme? 3. How will you present this scene to express a directorial vision—or theme—that also stays true to the text?	These discussion questions provide scaffolding. Note that they're similar to the homework questions (see Sample 2.5). The Director's Notebooks that students have been maintaining are excellent resources here. I remind them to use vocal, kinesthetic, or visual emphases to stress in performance the figurative language that they found significant while reading.
Hold whole-class discussions after students' visual performances. Follow-up questions might include the following: • What is the character's motivation (goal) in this scene? • What need is this character trying to meet? Is it representative of the individual, or does it appear to be a societal goal? • Is this character's situation a result of personal choice or coincidence/providence? • What is Shakespeare's "hidden message"—or theme—in this scene? Can you boil it down to a clear, succinct statement? • How do motifs present in the scene? • How much influence does this individual seem to have at this moment in the play? How much does society limit his or her power here? • How have the actors used props to suggest theme?	I like to ask certain advanced students and students with strong interest and skill in acting, directing, and staging theater to lead these discussions. Discussion provides an opportunity to review unit understandings, especially regarding the character of Macbeth.

LESSON SEQUENCE AND DESCRIPTION	TEACHER COMMENTARY
Certain scenes explore issues relevant to adolescent interests, so ask these questions, requiring that students defend their answer with textual evidence: • Are the witches in control? • How does a good man go bad? • Is Macbeth a hero or a villain? • How are situations in this scene both "fair" and "foul" simultaneously? • If a situation can be both "foul" and "fair," how would Shakespeare advise us to handle morally ambiguous situations? These questions might be extended as journal entries that explore students' lives. For example: • Do you believe in fate/supernatural forces at work? • Have you ever known a good person to "go bad"? Have you ever been tempted to do something morally wrong, and how did you handle it? • What situations have you been in where things were both "fair" and "foul" simultaneously?	When students submit their journals for my feedback, I give them the option of folding over—in effect, not submitting—a certain number of entries—perhaps one of every three. This allows students some personal space where they can reflect without fear of "judgment."
Socratic seminar. Conclude the reading of the play with a two-day discussion in a Socratic seminar format. Begin by establishing the ground rules: 1. Evidence-supported analysis is essential. 2. Everyone is expected to participate in the spirit of dialogue rather than debate. Students should question and challenge others' opinions while demonstrating respect, curiosity, and cooperation by engaging others and listening to one another. Here are some recommended questions. <u>Day 1: Opening Questions</u> • Was Macbeth a victim of fate or of his own choices? • What factors contributed the most to Macbeth's rise and demise? How much control, if any, did the witches wield? • Which of Macbeth's choices showed him at his best? Which showed him at his worst? • Which individual in this play is set up as a worthy role model? How do you know?	Socratic seminars (see Glossary, page 356) are discussions initiated by the teacher but perpetuated by the students. These opening questions are designed to prompt students to make a claim about Shakespeare's "message," using the text as the main source of evidence. My aim is to help them see Shakespeare as a "living author" who still speaks to us today. His text is complex and ambiguous enough to handle multiple interpretations.

LESSON SEQUENCE AND DESCRIPTION	TEACHER COMMENTARY
• What is Shakespeare's message to the average individual in his society? • What is Shakespeare's message about his society? • If Macbeth is not heroic at the end, why is the play called *Macbeth*?	I sometimes encourage advanced students interested in pursing independent research to examine the interpretations of famous critics A. C. Bradley, Harold Bloom, and Stephen Greenblatt.
<u>Day 2: Universal Questions:</u> • How does a good man "go bad"? • What is the nature of evil? • Does the story of Macbeth as a tragic and heroic individual have any relevance for us as individuals? Does it have relevance for us as members of our society? • How is our state or country currently balancing individual needs and societal needs in ways that compare and contrast with *Macbeth*?	These questions ask students to use their personal experiences, philosophies, and opinions to substantiate their arguments as they argue a theme of a more universal application. Depending on the trajectory of class discussions on the unit understandings, I reframe these Socratic seminar questions and invite students to create their own opening questions and universal questions.
Writing workshops differentiated by readiness and interest. Supply a variety of writing prompts to reinforce the skills of identification (character analysis) and comparison/contrast. See the **Tiered Writing Prompts** (Sample 2.9, page 95). *Group A (Novice and On-Target Readers and Writers)* Distribute a list of prompts focused on the identification skill. These prompts ask student to focus on one central idea, define it, and gather details about it. Some prompts within the identification analysis section (items B, C, D, H, and I) allow for greater challenge and can provide borderline novice or on-target students with an extra push. *Group B (Advanced Readers and Writers)* Distribute a list of prompts focused on comparison/contrast skills. These prompts asks student to juggle a range of definitions and details. To further differentiate the writing workshops, allow students to propose their own writing prompts. Develop graphic organizers for the different types of prompts as needed, and encourage novice writers—or advanced writers with complex ideas to prove—to use them.	I use in-class writing workshops for multiple reasons: They let me coach students via conferences and quick over-the-shoulder surveys; students can provide peer edits; and I am able to verify that this work is the student's and not a parent's or a Web site's. To further foil plagiarism—a challenge when the Web provides so many free, downloadable essays on *Macbeth*—I use writing prompts that are closely tied to unit understandings and generalizations, avoiding more traditional prompts like, "How does Macbeth fit the definition of a tragic hero?" There is no perfect prompt to suit a student except for the one he or she gets excited about. However, I do sometimes steer individuals toward certain prompts, based on past performances on essays.

LESSON 3   **Envisioning a Scene**   *(7 class periods)*
                        Concept: Directorial Vision
                            GEN1–2, GEN4–5;
                                 SD1–3

LESSON SEQUENCE AND DESCRIPTION	TEACHER COMMENTARY
Discussion of unit understandings. Ask students to share their latest thoughts on the unit generalizations in light of Macbeth's story. Good prompts include the following: • In the play, how do individual goals conflict with societal goals? • If you—as citizens of early–21st century U.S. society— could offer any advice to Macbeth at any point of the tragedy, what would you say to him? Why? What cause of Macbeth's fall might your advice help him to avoid? • Why do you think Shakespeare chose to tell his society this particular individual's tale?	Here is a chance for students to construct deeper understandings based on the work they've done so far.
Cinematic models of directorial vision. Remind students that the final project for this unit involves an expression of directorial vision. To help students grasp the concept of directorial vision, show a scene from a movie such as *The Matrix* (the blue pill or red pill choice scene) or *Stigmata* (the opening scene) and analyze it with students. Ask: What is the vision of the individual and society that this film presents? Follow this by showing a more traditional scene from one of the cinematic *Macbeth*s (see page 72).	These cinematic visions can help students grasp the sharp contrast between the Elizabethan worldview and the modern worldview.
Final project work differentiated by readiness and interest/ Mini-lessons and workshops differentiated by readiness needs and interest. Ask students to divide themselves into work groups to present a scene from *Macbeth*. To help facilitate the grouping, remind students of the various roles required and ask each student to introduce his or her talents to the class in a 30-second speech ("I'm a good artist and I am willing to play a small role," and so on). If the class community is strong and students are not prone to cliques, then there's a good chance of success with self-selected groups.	It's sometimes preferable to conduct these projects in teacher-selected groups, which can ensure balance in production-skill readiness and allow students with like interests to work together.

LESSON SEQUENCE AND DESCRIPTION	TEACHER COMMENTARY
Review the **Final Group Project Directions** (see Sample 2.10, page 97) and **Final Group Project Evaluation Rubric** (see Sample 2.11, page 98). There are two options, both of which revisit questions posed during Lesson 2's performance days. Encourage students to use their Director's Notebook and class notes and to refer back to their focus questions as they plan the acting, blocking, and design of their performance.	
Option A Students translate a motif into a greater theme for a directorial vision.	
Option B Students set a scene in a particular historical context and research that time period's prevailing attitudes toward individual rights versus societal rights.	Option B provides extra challenge in that students not only need to understand their scene thoroughly, but must also match the plot and characters with a different time period. Advanced students do well with this option, but I often allow novice students to take it on if they're interested in doing so.
Consult and assist students during the research and production process, as necessary. As groups work together, offer pull-out workshop sessions on topics like the following: • Specific roles (e.g., meet with directors to focus on how to storyboard/block a scene or "motivate the troops"). • Research strategies (e.g., note taking, paraphrasing, summarizing, and recognizing legitimate online sources). • Using the Final Project Evaluation Rubric to guide work. Workshop sessions can be voluntary or required, depending on teacher observation and student need or interest.	Another purpose of the role-specific workshops is to support "wisdom sharing." For example, I might prompt student directors to generate a list of dos and don'ts and student designers to compare their sketches and compliment and critique one another.

LESSON 4   **Presenting the Vision**   *(3–5 class periods)*
Concept: Directorial Vision
GEN4; SD1–3

LESSON SEQUENCE AND DESCRIPTION	TEACHER COMMENTARY
Final group project presentations and discussions. After each presentation (conducted live or shown on video), lead a whole-class discussion of its vision, strengths, and areas for improvement. Ask the students in the audience to share their compliments, questions, and critiques, referring to the rubric. Each group of performers fields these questions and shares their comments on the audience feedback.	To keep the tone of the post-presentation discussions positive, I take a few minutes before the first presentation to review and model some of the ways in which students can compliment others' performances and critique them (e.g., provide constructive suggestions in a positive way).

LESSON SEQUENCE AND DESCRIPTION	TEACHER COMMENTARY
Ask the audience to speculate on the group's vision for the performance. After the audience members have shared their hypotheses, have the performers share their actual thesis statement.	This speculation on the thesis helps the performers gauge the clarity of their communication and reinforces unit concepts and generalizations.
Self-evaluation and group evaluation. Ask all students to complete the **Final Group Project Assessment** (see Sample 2.12, page 99). This form asks students to rate and comment on their own work and performance during the final group project, and to comment briefly on the performance of their entire group. If desired, add a section to the evaluation for students to critique the project as a whole: what they liked and disliked, what could be different or better. Another option is to offer the final reading quiz at this time: a post-test modeled after the pretest but using a different text passage.	The results of this evaluation help me plan the next unit's group activities and design mini-lessons and coaching to help my students improve their collaborative skills.

Teacher Reflection on the Unit

Shakespeare really can come alive for students who are empowered to take directorial charge of the text. This unit concentrates on a few key skills while providing a highly interactive project as a focus for that skill set. I believe that stressing acting and the practice of that craft honors the dynamic, creative spirit of Shakespeare's work and highlights his brilliant language, timeless narratives, and compelling characters. The interdisciplinary overtones of this unit also open the door for interaction with history teachers and historical resources.

Lyn Fairchild has taught in public and private secondary schools for more than a decade and is currently a curriculum consultant and teacher for Duke University's Talent Identification Program. She can be reached at lfairchild@nc.rr.com.

SAMPLE 2.1—*Macbeth* Pretest

Directions: Read this soliloquy from Shakespeare's *Macbeth,* then respond to the prompts below.

Context: Macbeth, a medieval Scottish noble, is contemplating murder of his king, King Duncan.

Is this a dagger which I see before me,
The handle toward my hand? Come, let me clutch thee.
I have thee not, and yet I see thee still.
Art thou not, <u>fatal</u> vision, sensible   *causing death; important, fated*
To feeling as to sight? or art thou but
A dagger of the mind, a false creation,
Proceeding from the <u>heat-oppressed</u> brain?   *disturbed*
I see thee yet, in form as <u>palpable</u>   *tangible*
As this which now I draw.
Thou <u>marshall'st</u> me the way that I was going;   *lead*
And such an instrument I was to use.
Mine eyes are made the fools o' the other senses,
Or else worth all the rest; I see thee still,
And on thy blade and <u>dudgeon</u> gouts of blood,   *handle*
Which was not so before. There's no such thing:
It is the bloody business which informs
Thus to mine eyes. Now o'er the one halfworld
Nature seems dead, and wicked dreams abuse
The curtain'd sleep; witchcraft celebrates
Pale <u>Hecate's</u> offerings, and wither'd murder,   *goddess of the moon, witchcraft*
<u>Alarum'd</u> by his <u>sentinel</u>, the wolf,   *called to action/guard or sentry*
Whose howl's his watch, thus with his <u>stealthy</u> pace   *quiet; cautious; secretive*
With <u>Tarquin's</u> ravishing strides, towards his design   *Roman tyrant who raped his friend's wife*
Moves like a ghost. Thou sure and firm-set earth,
Hear not my steps, which way they walk, for fear
Thy very stones <u>prate</u> of my whereabout,   *speak*
And take the present horror from the time,
Which now <u>suits</u> with it. Whiles I threat, he lives: *follows; matches; agrees with*
Words to the heat of deeds too cold breath gives.

1. Use complete sentences or one small paragraph to paraphrase the text.

2. What are the key themes illustrated here in terms of figurative language, motifs, and scansion/meter? What do you know about Macbeth's key character traits? (REMEMBER: Create a clear topic sentence that answers these questions and provide specific details to support your topic sentence.)

SAMPLE 2.2—Production Skills and Interest Inventory

Name _____

Directions: Please respond to all prompts in the numbered sections so that we can form balanced groups for the final project in this unit.

1. Acting Skill, Experience, and Interest
Rate your skill on a level of 1 to 4, 1 being "poor," 2 being "on-target," 3 being "strong," and 4 being "excellent." If you have no stage experience, circle N/A and skip to the final question in this section.

Showing emotions on stage	1	2	3	4	N/A
Using the space well (blocking, etc.)	1	2	3	4	N/A
Playing comic roles on stage	1	2	3	4	N/A
Partnering with other actors	1	2	3	4	N/A
Learning lines	1	2	3	4	N/A
Taking directions from a director	1	2	3	4	N/A

Name some plays or shows you have performed in and indicate the parts you played.
_____
_____
_____

Have you ever performed in skits or scenes for another class? If so, elaborate on any skills you feel you have.
_____
_____
_____

Have you ever written a play or skit? If so, elaborate.
_____
_____
_____

How comfortable are you with reading Shakespearean language? How comfortable are you with Shakespearean acting?
_____
_____
_____

Overall, I would give myself a rating of _____ as an actor.

SAMPLE 2.2—Production Skills and Interest Inventory—(continued)

If you have no stage experience, how interested are you in the acting skills listed above? Circle 1 for "not at all interested" and 4 for "please let me act as soon as possible!"

1   2   3   4

2. Design Skill, Experience, and Interest

Rate your skill on a level of 1 to 4, 1 being "poor," 2 being "on-target," 3 being "strong," and 4 being "excellent." If you have no design experience, circle N/A and skip to the final question in this section.

Sketching figures and costumes	1	2	3	4	N/A
Sewing and making costumes	1	2	3	4	N/A
Sketching sets, scenery, and props	1	2	3	4	N/A
Building sets, scenery, and props	1	2	3	4	N/A
Painting and decorating sets and scenery	1	2	3	4	N/A
Creating a theme to connect costumes, scenery, and props	1	2	3	4	N/A

Overall, I would give myself a rating of _____ as a designer.

If you have no design experience, how interested are you in trying out the design skills listed above? Circle 1 for "I'm not at all interested" and 4 for "Please let me design as soon as possible!"

1   2   3   4

3. Directing Skill, Experience, and Interest

Rate your skill on a level of 1 to 4, 1 being "poor," 2 being "on-target," 3 being "strong," and 4 being "excellent." If you have no directing experience, circle N/A and skip to the final question in this section.

Creating a theme to plan the blocking and acting for a scene	1	2	3	4	N/A
Understanding character motivations and communicating them to actors	1	2	3	4	N/A
Showing actors how to speak and move on stage	1	2	3	4	N/A
Motivating and encouraging actors	1	2	3	4	N/A

Overall, I would give myself a rating of _____ as a director.

If you have no directing experience, how interested are you in trying out the directing skills listed above? Circle 1 for "I'm not at all interested" and 4 for "Please let me direct as soon as possible!"

1   2   3   4

SAMPLE 2.2—Production Skills and Interest Inventory—*(continued)*

4. Cinematographer/Editing Skill, Experience, and Interest

Rate your skill on a level of 1 to 4, 1 being "poor," 2 being "on-target," 3 being "strong," and 4 being "excellent." If you have no cinematography/editing experience, circle N/A and skip to the final question in this section.

Designing shots	1	2	3	4	N/A
Setting up shots (using camera angles, lighting, colors of props, etc.)	1	2	3	4	N/A
Creating an appropriate soundtrack	1	2	3	4	N/A
Familiarity with Final Cut Pro/Premiere (editing program)	1	2	3	4	N/A
Knowledge of razor blade editing	1	2	3	4	N/A

Overall, I would give myself a rating of _____ as a cinematographer/editor.

If you have no cinematography/editing experience, how interested are you in trying out the cinematography/editing skills listed above? Circle 1 for "I'm not at all interested" and 4 for "Please let me film/edit as soon as possible!"

1   2   3   4

5. Preferred Film and Theater Genres

Put a check next to your favorite film and theater genres.

- ☐ Action/Adventure/Thriller
- ☐ Drama/Psychological
- ☐ Comedy
- ☐ Fantasy
- ☐ Cartoon/Anime
- ☐ Historical and Period Pieces
- ☐ Horror/Supernatural
- ☐ Documentary
- ☐ Other: _____

6. Prior Knowledge of This Play

Have you read, acted in, or seen the play *Macbeth* before? If so, use the space below to list the plot events that you remember and as much information as you can about characters, themes, and other relevant background.

SAMPLE 2.3—Ten-Minute *Macbeth* Activity Guidelines

What's This Play About???

1. With your group, read aloud the 10 quotations from *Macbeth* listed below. Discuss what each quotation might mean in modern English.

"Fair is foul and foul is fair."

"And oftentimes, to win us to our harm,
The instruments of darkness tell us truths."

"Stars, hide your fires:
Let not light see my black and deep desires."

"If it were done when 'tis done, then 'twere well
It were done quickly."

"False face must hide what the false heart doth know."

"Out, damned spot!"

"Double, double, toil and trouble;
Fire burn, and cauldron bubble."

"Tomorrow, and tomorrow, and tomorrow
Creeps in this petty pace from day to day."

"Is this a dagger I see before me,
The handle toward my hand?"

"Sleep no more! Macbeth does murder sleep!"

2. Create a scene of 10 minutes or less that incorporates as many of these lines as possible and predicts the plot of *Macbeth*. Your scene should create a logical plot structure using one or more of the unit understandings listed below. In other words, create a scene where the conflict is based on one of these "truths." You may use cue cards or memorize the lines.

Unit Understandings

A. Individual goals can conflict with societal goals.

B. Individuals make choices in an attempt to meet one or more needs: love and belonging, freedom, fun, and power.

C. Certain individuals can change the course of a society's history.

D. An individual's power is often bounded by society.

SAMPLE 2.4—Organizer for the Director's Notebook

"Double-Journaling" in Your Director's Notebook

Here is an overview of the double-journal format, along with some suggestions about different kinds of notes to take and ways to comment on them.

TEXT	ANALYSIS
Copy a passage from the play and note its speaker and the act, scene, and line number(s).	Complete at least two of the following suggestions for every entry: • Paraphrase the text for basic understanding. • Identify a reaction to the text that relates personal associations, memories, and emotions. • Ask questions. • Agree or disagree with a character's choices. • Compare or contrast the passage with another passage or another work of literature. • Make a prediction about what will happen next based on reading already accomplished. • Identify the theme of the passage. • Explain how the passage relates to one of our unit generalizations. • Explain and interpret figurative language and motif as a representation of theme.

Themes to Track
• Individual goals can conflict with societal goals.
• Individuals make choices in an attempt to meet one or more needs: love and belonging, freedom, fun, and power.
• Citizens of the 21st century tend to attribute an individual's progress within a society to a combination of his or her personal choices and coincidence/providence.
• Certain individuals can change the course of a society's history.
• An individual's power is often bounded by society.

Motifs to Track
A motif is a physical element (such as blood) or some other image or idea that, in itself, does not have any particular meaning or represent any higher truth; it just is. However, when an author uses this element repeatedly in various places within a literary work, a reader can begin to draw conclusions about a higher truth or meaning. Here are some motifs that appear in *Macbeth*:

witchcraft	heaven	weather/nature	the soul
blood	sleep	animals	light and dark
battles/violence	clothing/armor	spirits/ghosts	male and female lineage/genealogy

SAMPLE 2.5—Making Sense of Shakespeare Tiered Question Sets

Making Sense of Shakespeare

Directions: After completing your nightly reading assignment, respond to your assigned analysis questions. Use complete sentences, and be sure to include the pages of your reading assignment and which questions you are responding to (e.g., P1, for Plot Analysis, question 1; C5 for Character Analysis, question 5, and so on). When you have finished, choose one passage from your nightly reading to include in your double-entry journal. For a format refresher, refer to the Organizer for the Director's Notebook.

Plot Analysis
1. Make a short list of the main events of the plot. What happens to whom? When? Where? Which event seems to be the most important?
2. Pose questions about the main events/actions in the plot. Does anything intrigue or confuse you?
3. Relate the scene to other situations in the play. Does it further the action? Retard the action? Repeat a situation? Mirror a situation? Provide its opposite?
4. What background and historical material helps with understanding the plot? Feel free to consult both the text notes and non-study–guide Web sites. Try these:

> www.shakespeare.com/faq/faq38.php
> www.encyclopedia.com/html/G/Gunpowde.asp
> www.gunpowder-plot.org/news/1998_04/macbeth.htm
> www.bard.org/Education/Shakespeare/macbethfair.html

Character Analysis
1. Pick a character of interest to you and summarize the key actions that best illustrate his or her personality.
2. What is your chosen character's desire? Why is it important to this character?
3. What plans and behaviors does your character use to achieve his or her desire?
4. What are the obstacles to the character achieving his or her desire?
5. What are the results of the character's behaviors?
6. How does the character interact with others? How do others see him or her?

Language Analysis
1. Pick a scene to analyze. Are there any words or phrases that are not defined in the footnotes? What sense can you make of them from the context? Look up these words and phrases and record the definitions.
2. What themes and significance are you noting in this scene? To defend your claims, identify common figures of speech (simile, metaphor, personification, hyperbole) and other text features, such as alliteration, paradox, or irony. For each, note (a) the timing of the usage, (b) the speaker of the phrase, and (c) the connotations of the images created.
3. Find a passage of 5 to 10 lines that is particularly interesting to you and scan it. Is it in iambic pentameter or in another type of meter? What words are emphasized? Why are they important in this scene?

SAMPLE 2.6—Character Analysis Group Activities

Task 1: Tough Audience

The events depicted in Shakespeare's historical plays were well-known to his audience, and the king was often among the first to check out a new play. Think about this situation as if you were a playwright in Elizabethan times: Everybody already knows the story you're going to tell, and the king will be your first audience. What do you have to do to grab both the king's and the public's attention and get great box office returns?

Directions:

1. Appoint a facilitator for your group.

2. Discuss with your group the social pressure Shakespeare was under and what that pressure might require of his writing. List five ways that this pressure could challenge Shakespeare as a writer and his possible solutions to these challenges.

3. Following a brief check-in with the teacher, make a labeled poster or a human plot diagram of Aristotle's plot structure, using symbols or gestures to indicate the key incidents that occur at the five points of the plot. Decide who will present to the class, and be prepared to teach the class about Aristotle's plot structure and explain your symbols or gestures.

4. On a separate sheet of paper with all group members' names listed, answer the following questions
   - What do you learn about Macbeth's character during Act I, Scene 2, even though Macbeth never actually appears? How does Shakespeare want us to first think of him?
   - What do you learn about King Duncan's character during Act I, Scene 2? Does the portrayal of the king have any connection to King James being in the first audience?
   - How do you know your analyses of Macbeth and Duncan are accurate? What supporting details confirm your opinions? List at least two quotations for each of your answers.

Task 2: Fair Is Foul and Foul Is Fair: Macbeth Under the Microscope

From the very first scene, we learn that things are not always what they seem. We also get the sense that Macbeth is soon going to be in deep trouble. Scenes 2 and 3 of Act I provide a lot of information—things that a casual reader could easily gloss over—that might reveal Macbeth's future (not unlike a sixth sense or a witch's prophecy). Sometimes all it takes is a good eye to "read" someone's character. And after all, like in the movie *Minority Report,* we know Macbeth's about to commit some crimes. What in his profile tells us from the beginning that he might be capable of such acts? Or are there things that suggest he was instead set up or led astray?

Directions:

1. Work as a group to reach a common agreement about what others said about Macbeth in Act I, Scene 2. Begin with the text you paraphrased. Once you agree on a translation, check it against the teacher-provided translation.

SAMPLE 2.6—Character Analysis Group Activities—*(continued)*

---

2. Agree on what Duncan says about Macbeth.

3. Create a Private Investigator Poster, a Metaphor Poster, or a skit.
   - In the P.I. Poster, draw Macbeth's profile, police line-up style, and label him with "Checks Out" traits (his good points) and "Warning Signs" traits (his weaknesses).
   - In the Metaphor Poster, create a metaphor for Macbeth: *Macbeth is a _____ in these three ways . . . .* Give three text citations to back your argument. Then illustrate the metaphor.
   - In the skit, create a scene among detectives who have been trailing Macbeth and putting together the puzzle pieces, looking for early signs of murderous intent. You may also wish to include a defender of Macbeth, such as his lawyer.

4. Be ready to share the posters or skit with the rest of the class.

Task 3: Totally Macbeth
What scene really "makes the man"? In Act I, we met Macbeth a few times. Which scene is the most telling of his character? Is it one in which others are talking about him, or is it one that shows something he does? Consider the opinions of Macbeth expressed by the witches, the captain, Duncan, Banquo, and Macbeth himself.

Directions:
1. Discuss and reach consensus—meaning that everyone agrees to live with the decision, even if it isn't their favorite—about the most telling or significant scene in Act I. Cite specific textual examples that support your group's claim using
   - Diction (specific word choice).
   - Figurative language, such as simile, metaphor, hyperbole, paradox, and so on.
   - Motifs (may also be figures of speech that you see repeated in other scenes).
   - Scansion (How do iambs and trochees work to emphasize key words and phrases? Where does Shakespeare break the pattern, and how does that change the emphasis?).

2. Present the scene for the class, involving as many members of the group as possible. Here are some suggestions for presentation formats:
   - *Freeze Frame:* Provide actors and an onstage narrator who on occasion stops the action to emphasize or explicate key moments or to ask the audience for feedback ("What do you think Macbeth's motivation is here?").
   - *Twin Time:* Act the scene with key characters having a twin who translates the text into modern language.
   - *What Was He Thinking?*: Act the scene and have on-the-spot interviews of the characters to get the "inside scoop."

SAMPLE 2.7—RAFT Activity Options

RAFT Options for *Macbeth* (Acts I and II)

Directions: Complete one of the RAFT options below for homework. In your product, be sure to replicate the character's concerns (the issues, ideas, and motives important to the character) and voice (both in attitude and in tone). These products will be evaluated not only for creativity and completeness, but also for evidence that you understand character action and motivation in *Macbeth*. For bonus points, use Shakespearean language in your product.

Role	Audience	Format	Topic
Macbeth	The witches	Missed connections advertisement in a local paper	When Will I See You Again?
Witches	Hecate, chief witch	Report	Mischief Made of Late: How We're Messing with Macbeth
Lady Macbeth	Macbeth	Diary entry, left open on her bed for Macbeth to see	Nice Guys Finish Last
Banquo	Macbeth	Letter	Patience Is a Virtue
Duncan	His Scottish subjects	Newspaper editorial	The Past Is Past and Here's What's Next
Macbeth	Himself	Diary entry	It's Time to Be Two-Faced

SAMPLE 2.8—Tiered Worksheet on Paradox

You Say Yin, I Say Yang: The Nature of Paradox

A paradox is a contradiction in terms, a truth that contains contradictory elements. For example, in your relationship with a family member or friend, you may experience the emotions of both love and hatred—two sentiments that are in deep opposition. The truth is, however, that you and this person are forever connected in this relationship, for better or for worse.

Also known as "compressed conflicts," oxymorons are opposites that attract to achieve a certain chaotic balance, or a peaceable war. Ambiguity is the name of the game in Shakespeare's world when it comes to human nature: Our motivations and dilemmas all take on varying shades of gray.

Task A: Oxymoron or Not? That Is the Question . . .

1. Review the list below and mark "yes" for the phrases that represent both oxymorons and paradoxes. Then mark "no" for phrases that are not oxymorons because they are actually synonyms or imperfect opposites.

Jumbo shrimp	☐ YES	☐ NO
Loyal friends	☐ YES	☐ NO
Fated coincidence	☐ YES	☐ NO
Blatantly obvious	☐ YES	☐ NO
Practical magic	☐ YES	☐ NO
Military intelligence	☐ YES	☐ NO
Treasonous malice	☐ YES	☐ NO
Real counterfeit	☐ YES	☐ NO
Wakeful sleep	☐ YES	☐ NO
Drenching rain	☐ YES	☐ NO
Reformed criminal	☐ YES	☐ NO
Violent love	☐ YES	☐ NO
Thunderous applause	☐ YES	☐ NO
Corporeal spirit	☐ YES	☐ NO
Marital bliss	☐ YES	☐ NO
Clearly obscure	☐ YES	☐ NO
Bloody execution	☐ YES	☐ NO

2. Come up with three oxymorons of your own.

3. Find at least three paradoxes in scenes from *Macbeth*.

4. Pick one of these paradoxes from *Macbeth* and either draw a symbolic picture that represents the paradox OR write a poem that provides multiple examples and ways that the paradox can be true in everyday life.

SAMPLE 2.8—Tiered Worksheet on Paradox—(continued)

Task B: Pick a Peck of Pickled Paradoxes

1. Identify which in the list below originate from *Macbeth*. Explain how they are apt expressions for the scene where they occur.

   Jumbo shrimp
   Loyal friends
   Fated coincidence
   Blatantly obvious
   Practical magic
   Military intelligence
   Treasonous malice
   Real counterfeit
   Wakeful sleep
   Drenching rain
   Reformed criminal
   Violent love
   Thunderous applause
   Corporeal spirit
   Marital bliss
   Clearly obscure
   Bloody execution

2. Paradox exists in the mind of the beholder. Something that strikes you as an oxymoron may not seem like one to someone else. For example, a grocery store where I shop has a sign claiming, "Our Fish Is Always Fresh." To me, "always-fresh fish" is an oxymoron. How can something perishable be "always fresh"? To the grocery store, "always-fresh fish" is *not* an oxymoron. It just means that fish will be for sale for a set period of time—until it's no longer fresh. Review the list of oxymorons and identify those that might NOT be oxymorons to someone in specific circumstances.

3. Identify the one paradox in *Macbeth* that is most emblematic of the truth of the play, and then choose one of the following product expressions:
   A. Create a mobile, a sculpture, or some other 3–D representation in which the truth, or thesis, is the hanging device and the suspended elements are quotations from the play that support your claim.
   B. Write lyrics for a piece of music that reflects the tone of the play's truth and that particular paradox.
   C. Write a dialogue in which two characters from the play, two famous philosophers, or two famous modern people analyze the play's truth and emblematic paradox.

SAMPLE 2.9—Tiered Writing Prompts

Identification Analysis (Group A)

Choose one of the following prompts and respond in writing. Before you make your choice, review the double-entry journal work you have completed in your Director's Notebook. If you have a hard time choosing, consult the teacher for a recommendation. Be sure to refer to the rubric for writing guidelines.

A. *I'm Here to Save the Day!* What is a hero and what is a villain? Define the words "hero" and "villain" using a dictionary definition backed by examples of particular individuals within the play.

B. *But What About Me?* What does it mean to be an individual within Elizabethan society? Define the word "individual" using a dictionary definition and historical research into Shakespeare's times. Back up your findings using examples of certain characters within the play.

C. *Utopia.* What would Elizabethans consider to be an ideal society? Define the word "society" using a dictionary definition as well as historical research of Shakespeare's times, backed by examples of the society presented within the play.

D. *Who's in Charge?* What is fate? Define the word "fate" using examples from the play.

E. *Be a Man.* How does the play define manhood? Use the actions of specific characters (especially Macbeth, Macduff, and Lady Macbeth) to illustrate Shakespeare's idea of true manhood.

F. *Women on the Verge of* . . . How does the play define womanhood? Use the actions of Lady Macbeth and Lady Macduff to identify Shakespeare's idea of true womanhood.

G. *The Devil Made Me Do It.* How does the play define witchcraft? Is it a craft of bewitching others or something else? Define it, referencing actions of any relevant characters within the play.

H. *Power Corrupts and Absolute Power* . . . What constitutes power within this play? Define "power" in *Macbeth*, referencing its healthy uses and its abuses within the play. To introduce or conclude your essay, provide a modern example of healthy use of power and an abuse of power.

I. *My Turn.* What would you like to identify in this play? Make a proposal for a prompt.

Comparison/Contrast and Interpretive Analysis (Group B)

Choose one of the following prompts and respond in writing. Before you make your choice, review the double-entry journal work you have completed in your Director's Notebook. If you have a hard time choosing, consult the teacher for a recommendation. Be sure to refer to the rubric for writing guidelines.

A. *Something Wicked This Way Comes.* Unquestionably, Macbeth is tempted in this play. What is the nature of the temptation? What tempts him and how does it tempt him? How does Macbeth handle this temptation? Examine the source of the temptation and the response of this battle-hardened warrior to the words of a few witches. Why is Macbeth an interesting person for us to watch being tempted?

B. *Which Comes First?* If Macbeth's personal goal is ambition, what is his society's goal for him? What role is he supposed to play? How do his goals and the goals of his society compare and contrast? Does his society support ambition or try to quash it?

SAMPLE 2.9—Tiered Writing Prompts—(continued)

C. *Love, Power, Freedom, or Fun?* Macbeth's most obvious need is for power, but does he demonstrate a longing for any other important need? Do his various needs compete or complement one another? What are the results of his behavior? What is Shakespeare's message to the audience?

D. *Full of Sound and Fury, Signifying . . .* Within the larger historical context that the play documents, were Macbeth's efforts meaningful or meaningless? What, if anything, is a tragic hero supposed to teach us?

E. *King for a Day.* What do we learn from Duncan the King versus Macbeth the King? Compare and contrast their actions while in positions of royal authority. Also note references to Edward the Confessor. What concept of ideal royal authority is Shakespeare presenting here?

F. *Be a Man, Why Don'tcha.* What is the play's commentary on manhood? What do we learn from Macduff the warrior and man versus Macbeth the warrior and man? Do any other "real men" step up to the plate? Compare and contrast Macbeth and Macduff according to a standard of ideal male behavior established in the drama.

G. *I Am Woman; Hear Me Roar.* What is the play's commentary on womanhood? What do we learn from Lady Macbeth, the childless wife, versus Lady MacDuff, the wife and mother? Compare and contrast these two according to a standard of ideal female behavior established in the drama.

H. *She-Man.* Is Lady Macbeth's role womanly or manly or something else entirely? Compare and contrast her with Renaissance and/or modern definitions of femininity and masculinity. Use the text to support your definitions.

I. *Come, You Spirits . . .* Lady Macbeth is power-hungry. What is the source of Lady Macbeth's power? Is she supernaturally connected—perhaps with the power of a sorceress? Or is she simply a power-hungry thane's wife? Compare and contrast Lady Macbeth with the witches and other powerful people in the play in order to determine what makes her tick and gives her strength.

J. *A Marriage Made in . . .* What kind of a marriage do the Macbeths have? Characterize each of them in terms of how they treat one another. Do their personalities complement one another or ultimately conflict? What in the language of the Macbeths' scenes together tells you how the actors who play the roles should behave toward one another while in character?

K. *Power Play.* What does Shakespeare tell us about the quest for power? Compare and contrast individuals such as Macbeth, Lady Macbeth, Duncan, Banquo, Macduff, and others to find Shakespeare's message.

L. *Vaulting Ambition?* Citizens of the 21st century tend to believe that an individual's progress within a society is a combination of personal choices and coincidence/providence. What is your hypothesis as to why Macbeth rose and fell from power in his society? Weigh the factors of individual choice and coincidence/providence, and produce a theory of what special cause or combination of causes determines the life that Macbeth leads.

M. *Motif, Schmotif.* How do motifs intersect and complement to produce a particular thematic message? For example, how do nature and weather intersect with the animal world? How do blood and sleep run parallel?

N. *My Turn.* What would you like to compare and contrast or interpret in this play? Make a proposal for a prompt.

SAMPLE 2.10—Final Group Project Directions

Final Group Projects: The Making of *Macbeth*

Option A

1. With your group, share the entries from your Director's Notebook and reach consensus about the motif you find most compelling.
2. Develop a group thesis statement: *We believe that the motif of X communicates the theme of* _____ : *that* _____ . In the first blank, write an abstract noun (your general theme). In the second blank, write an appositive (a phrase that further explains and represents that general theme).
3. Chose one scene from *Macbeth* to present in front of the class. Consider teacher-recommended scene options before making your final decision. Note that this scene must illustrate your thesis statement—your director's vision.
4. Assign roles. You'll need a director, actors, set and costume designers, and film editors.
5. Prepare the scene for class performance. Decide how to stage the scene so that it will be highly symbolic of your chosen theme and convey its motif in all aspects: through acting, blocking, set design, costumes, and props.

Option B

1. With your group, select a historical setting (a time and a place), then choose one scene from *Macbeth* to present in front of the class in a manner appropriate to that setting. Consider the following teacher-recommended options or propose your own. (You must provide a distinct date and specify the system of government.) Teacher recommendations:
   - Nazi Germany, 1939 (a fascist regime).
   - New York City, 2001 (a democratic republic, post–9/11).
   - Paris, 1789 (an absolutist regime on the eve of the French Revolution).
   - St. Petersburg, or Petrograd, 1917 (an absolutist regime fast becoming an autocratic communist regime).
   - Rwanda, 1994 (a presidential republic with a multiparty system on the brink of anarchy during the government-orchestrated massacre of Tutsis and moderate Hutus).
   - Our Town, USA, 2050 (the future of our democratic republic).
2. As a group, research your chosen historical setting, using electronic and print sources to understand the rules and attitudes that governed both individuals and their society. Here are some questions to consider:
   - How were figures in authority and government viewed at the time?
   - Who tended to be the heroes?
   - How aligned were individual and societal wants?
   - What are the powerful and symbolic visual images from this time period that represent the relationships between the individual and society?
3. As a group, discuss how to present your scene from *Macbeth* in a manner reflective of your chosen historical setting. What would remain the same? What would differ? Write a group thesis statement for your vision of the scene: *In (chosen historical setting), the individual and his/her society had a relationship that (describe it, using nouns and adjectives).*
4. Assign roles. You'll need a director, actors, set and costume designers, and film editors.
5. Prepare the scene for class performance. Decide how to stage the scene so that it will be highly symbolic of your chosen theme and convey its motif in all aspects: through acting, blocking, set design, costumes, and props.

SAMPLE 2.11—Final Group Project Evaluation Rubric

Criteria	Sophisticated	Strong	Adequate
Acting	Lines are fluent and delivered with comprehension, feeling, clear character motivation, and authenticity; actors own the space so that we forget we're watching a play.	Lines are strong and delivered with feeling; character motivation is evident; use of space is appropriate.	Line delivery is interrupted with lapses of memory and lack of clarity on character motivation, but more than 80% is memorized; inconsistencies in use of space detract from the performance.
Directing	Blocking directly relates to the theme and character motivations and is inventive, takes risks, and shows the group and director's vision; a clear unity links all aspects of the scene to demonstrate the theme and/or the time period's beliefs about the individual and society.	Blocking is creative and in keeping with theme and character motivations; the scene clearly demonstrates the theme and/or the time period's beliefs about the individual and society.	Unfocused or tangential blocking distracts from presentation of theme and character motivation; the scene is rendered more as a moment of Shakespearean text than as a clear vision of the theme and/or the time period's beliefs about the individual and society.
Sets, Props, and Costume Design	The theme and/or the time period comes alive with appropriate and symbolic sets, props, and costumes; all design elements are attractive and carefully constructed to support a unified vision of the theme.	Sets, props, and costumes strongly suggest the theme and/or the time period; appropriate and symbolic props appear; design elements are well made.	Sets, props, and costumes represent the theme and/or the time period, but lack a unity of vision or clear symbolism; certain design elements are very basic or missing.
Group Participation	The group is a true team, with work distributed equitably and enthusiastically, as shown by class meetings and final performance.	The group shows strong evidence of collaboration, but there are occasional ruptures in team unity, at which time certain members dominate or recede to the background.	The performance comes off well despite glitches in team unity, such as member domination or passivity; word of group disunity and discouragement gets out.
Historical Accuracy (Option B only)	The historical setting comes alive authentically through aspects of acting, directing, and design; the relationship between the individual and society is accurate, realistic, and compelling.	The historical setting is accurately presented through aspects of acting, directing and design; the relationship between the individual and society is accurate and realistic.	Anachronisms prevent ultimate believability, but acting, directing, and design attempt to render a historical setting.

SAMPLE 2.12—Final Group Project Assessment

Self- and Group Assessment for the *Macbeth* Final Group Project

Name _____

Directions: Rate thyself on thy performance: 1 = "poor," 2 = "on target," 3 = "strong," and 4 = "excellent." Circle N/A if you did not have that role.

My research	1	2	3	4
My acting	1	2	3	4	N/A
My directing	1	2	3	4	N/A
My scene, costume, and/or prop design	1	2	3	4	N/A
My daily work ethic	1	2	3	4
My consideration of others in the group	1	2	3	4

Here are a few specific examples of my performance that elaborate on the ratings provided above:

I would like to compliment the following group members' performances because

I would like to constructively critique the following group members' performances because

3

Toward Disunion: 1854–1861

A U.S. History Unit on the Path to the Civil War

Unit Developer: Lyn Fairchild

Introduction

This four-week Advanced Placement (AP) history unit challenges students to adopt the role of historian as they identify the causes of the Civil War and explore historical events in comparison to modern events. Students also adopt the role of a created persona from the antebellum or Civil War era who responds to large-scale events through a particular perspective. In addition to reading, taking notes on, and discussing such issues, students practice the skill of marshalling evidence to prove a thesis for free-response questions on the AP History test. Individuals who struggle in this area receive targeted instruction and support, while strong writers have the option to proceed with independent studies.

The culmination of the unit is the Living Time Line Project, which brings the class together on a variety of levels. It challenges everyone to walk in the shoes of an historical figure and to present a persona in an exciting and meaningful way while thinking about the larger themes of sectional tensions, political democracy, and individual contributions to societal trends.

Teacher Reflection on Designing the Unit

This history unit is built on national standards and draws on my belief that students should role-play the task of historian instead of simply reading what others have written. It's also important for students to realize that history is alive: The past events they study are immediately relevant to the current events they experience.

Considering the pressure on AP teachers to keep a breathless instructional pace, four weeks may appear to be a luxurious concession of time to any particular unit in an AP U.S. History course, particularly when only 20 to 30 pages of textbook reading frame the unit's historical events. However, the path to disunion raises core issues and helps students understand how the business of the American Revolution was unfinished and how the Civil Rights movement and other pivotal reforms of the 20th century were consequential developments stemming from events of the Civil War.

In designing this unit, I wanted to include a strong writing component. By the time that an AP U.S. History class typically reaches the unit on the Civil War, the AP exam is beginning to loom large on the horizon. For the teacher, the time has come to identify who can and cannot defend an historical interpretation with evidence. Many students who appeared qualified in August now could be "hitting the wall" in a class that may be the first advanced challenge of their high school career. Students who, at this point, might earn a 2 on the exam need special attention. Thus, I designed a differentiated unit that allows struggling students the chance to develop the skills they are lacking and at the same time allows advanced students who are eloquent thinkers and writers the opportunity to accelerate through unit material so that their progress is unimpeded.

United States History Standards Addressed

SD1   Understand the extension, restriction, and reorganization of political democracy after 1800, and explain the combination of sectional, cultural, economic, and political factors that contributed to the formation of the Democratic, Whig, and "Know-Nothing" parties.

SD2   Analyze how the disruption of the second American party system frayed the durable bonds of union, leading to the Republican Party's ascent during the 1850s.

SD3   Explain how events after the Compromise of 1850 and the Dred Scott decision in 1857 contributed to increasing sectional polarization.

SD4   Analyze the importance of the free labor ideology in the North and its appeal in preventing the extension of slavery in the new territories.

SD5   Understand how the debates over slavery influenced politics and sectionalism.

SD6   Explain the causes of the Civil War and evaluate the importance of slavery as a principal cause of the conflict.

SD7   Chart the secession of the Southern states and explain the process and reasons for secession.

Unit Concepts and Generalizations

Sectional Tension, Cause and Effect, Individual Impact, Perspective

GEN1 Sectional tensions brewing in the pre–Civil War United States were heightened by the actions of significant individuals: Harriet Beecher Stowe's publication of *Uncle Tom's Cabin*, abolitionist John Brown's violent actions, and Dred Scott's legal battle.

GEN2 Historians present the causes of the Civil War from diverse perspectives: as the peak of many years of social reform, as a significant period in U.S. racial history, as the most violent episode in the conflict between regional subcultures, and as the collapse of a democratic political system.

Unit Objectives

As a result of this unit, the students will *know*

- The major themes and events in American history as the United States drifted toward Civil War.
- The basic causes of sectional conflict prior to the Civil War.
- A variety of historical schools of thought regarding the causes of the Civil War.
- The individual impact made by influential historical figures of the era, including Harriet Beecher Stowe, John Brown, and Dred Scott.
- Important facts about a selected historical figure's perspective on pre–Civil War tensions or the progress of the Civil War.
- Standards and guidelines for effective outlining.
- Rubric standards and guidelines for writing AP free-response essays, particularly those in response to document-based questions (DBQ). (Advanced Placement standards for free-response essay questions require that the writer present a clear, well-developed thesis that effectively analyzes the topic's complexity in depth while presenting substantial, relevant evidence. For document-based free-response questions, the writer must also identify key themes and significant supporting details to marshal as evidence for the essay.)

As a result of this unit, the students will *understand that*

- A history of slavery distinguishes American society from other societies.
- Pre–Civil War tensions were the outgrowth of differing geographical, economic, and technological factors within the North and South; these factors influenced the development of sectional cultures and, thus, oppositional perspectives and politics.
- The history of governance and authority in the United States has been tumultuous and complex.

- An individual event may be interpreted from a variety of historical perspectives.
- Modern historical events, issues, and political parties are outgrowths of past events.

As a result of this unit, the students will *be able to*

- Identify and analyze multiple events that contributed to the outbreak of the Civil War.
- Examine the connections between antecedent and modern circumstances.
- Evaluate the credibility of and identify bias in primary and secondary sources.
- Synthesize historical data while writing a reliable historical interpretation in accordance with Advanced Placement standards.
- Synthesize historical data in order to present a coherent identification of a historical figure's perspective on pre-Civil War and Civil War events.
- Communicate effectively in discussion and marshal salient data and reasoning in debate.

Instructional Strategies Used

- Coaching
- Flexible grouping
- Multiple-intelligence, open-ended projects
- Self-assessment
- Compacting
- Mini-lessons and coaching
- Pre-assessment and post-assessment
- Tiered assignments
- Whole-class discussion

Sample Supporting Materials Provided

Sample #	Title	Page
3.1	"Hello, I'm Harriet" Presentation Guidelines	123
3.2	Living Time Line Project Overview	124
3.3	Living Time Line Project Planning Guide	125
3.4	Living Time Line Project Evaluation Rubrics	128
3.5	Chapter Outlining: Guidelines and Standards Handout	130
3.6	Chapter Outlining: Question It! Handout	131
3.7	Tiered Jigsaw Document Analysis Assignment	132
3.8	Living Time Line Project Checklist	133
3.9	Causes of the Civil War Handout	134
3.10	Build Your Own DBQ Assignment	135
3.11	Living Time Line Project Self-Assessment	137

Unit Overview

LESSON	WHOLE-CLASS COMPONENTS	DIFFERENTIATED COMPONENTS
PREPARATION	Pre-assessment	
		Individual assignment of the Living Time Line preview presentation
LESSON 1 **Meet a History Maker** *1 class period*	Unit kickoff *10 minutes*	
	Living Time Line preview presentation: "Hello, I'm Harriet." *15 minutes*	
	Whole-class discussion and quick-write for informal pre-assessment *15 minutes*	
	Preview of the Living Time Line project *15 minutes*	
		Homework: Textbook reading and outlining assignment differentiated by readiness and learning profile
		Optional independent study *ongoing*
LESSON 2 **On the Road to War** *4 class periods*		Chapter outline review and text mapping differentiated by readiness *45 minutes*
		Homework: Textbook reading and outlining assignment differentiated by readiness and learning profile
		Document analysis and Jigsaw differentiated by readiness *90 minutes*
		Homework: Planning for the Living Time Line project differentiated by interest and learning profile
	Living Time Line project check-in *5 minutes*	

LESSON	WHOLE-CLASS COMPONENTS	DIFFERENTIATED COMPONENTS
		Peer review of current research differentiated by interested *10–15 minutes*
		In-class independent project research differentiated by interest *30 minutes*
		One-on-one coaching sessions based on readiness needs *2–5 minutes per student*
	Homework: Test preparation	
LESSON 3 **What Caused the War?** *3–5 class periods*	Optional in-class review *10 minutes*	
	Multiple-choice test *30–45 minutes*	
		Homework: Living Time Line project work differentiated by interest and learning profile
	Living Time Line project check-in *5–10 minutes*	Optional mini-lessons on research skills based on readiness needs
	Discussion seminar preparation in heterogeneous groups *40 minutes*	
	Homework: Seminar preparation	
	Discussion seminar *45–90 minutes*	
LESSON 4 **The Write Stuff** *4 class periods*	Living Time Line project check-in *10 minutes*	Optional mini-lesson on research skills based on readiness needs
		AP writing skills activities differentiated by readiness *125 minutes*
	Free-response essay writing *45 minutes*	

LESSON	WHOLE-CLASS COMPONENTS	DIFFERENTIATED COMPONENTS
LESSON 5 **Back in Time** *6–7 class periods*		Living Time Line project work and peer feedback sessions differentiated by interest and learning profile *90 minutes* One-on-one coaching sessions based on readiness needs *ongoing, times vary*
	Living Time Line dress rehearsals in self-selected pairs *45 minutes*	
	Living Time Line presentations and response questions *90 minutes*	
	Self-assessment and response-question discussion *15 minutes*	
	Sharing of DBQ insights *30 minutes*	
	Reflective journal writing *30 minutes*	

Unit Description and Teacher Commentary

PREPARATION

LESSON SEQUENCE AND DESCRIPTION	TEACHER COMMENTARY
Pre-assessment. Prior to this unit, pre-assess students' ability to outline textbook chapters and write free-response AP essays. A good option for a writing pre-assessment is the 2002 AP History exam, which addresses the antebellum reform movements. It is available at apcentral.collegeboard.com.	Taking notes from reading, outlining reading, and writing free-response AP-style essays are the major components of this unit. I use the assessment results to inform my differentiated readiness groups: novice, on target, and advanced.

LESSON SEQUENCE AND DESCRIPTION	TEACHER COMMENTARY
Individual assignment of the Living Time Line preview presentation. Provide a selected female student with the **"Hello, I'm Harriet" Presentation Guidelines** (see Sample 3.1, page 123) and explain that on the first day of the unit, she will provide classmates with a model of the culminating Living Time Line project. Consider allowing the student to prepare her presentation as an independent study project during the unit preceding this one.	I assign this role to an advanced student who is gifted in speech and acting. I vary the historical figure depending on the student's sex, abilities, and preferences. Other good subjects for this living time line model would be Dred Scott or Hinton S. Helper.

LESSON 1

Meet a History Maker

(1 class period)

Concepts: Individual Impact, Perspective
GEN1–2; SD1–7

LESSON SEQUENCE AND DESCRIPTION	TEACHER COMMENTARY
Unit kickoff. Introduce the concepts, generalizations, and content standards of this unit by asking one of the students to read them aloud from a posted list that will remain visible for the duration of the unit. Note to students that today, the class will be focusing on the unit concepts of individual impact and perspective.	To promote comprehension, I sometimes color-code the list of concepts, generalizations, and standards, or I ask students to illustrate them with visual symbols.
Living Time Line preview presentation: "Hello, I'm Harriet." Tell students that a special guest is visiting today—a guest who will help everyone better understand unit standards 1 and 5 (see page 101).	An alternative way to inaugurate this unit is to contact a local historical society, museum, retired teacher, or theater professional and arrange for an in-class presentation.
Before introducing "Harriet Beecher Stowe," encourage students to be thinking of questions related to the focus standards that they might pose to the guest. Then bring out Harriet, who will make her presentation.	The point of asking students to employ the language of content standards while they pose questions is to promote their facility with the unit's larger understandings.
Whole-class discussion and quick-write for informal pre-assessment. Tell students that they have met an individual who played a significant role in the debate over slavery, which is one of the important themes of the path to disunion and the Civil War. Do they already know of other important individuals who had an individual impact on events leading up to disunion or on the events of the Civil War?	This quick gauge of student content knowledge establishes the individual's essential role in "making history" and helps me find out if students see this era in terms of exciting and unique individual people and events. It also shows me if their knowledge is broad or ill-defined or both.

LESSON SEQUENCE AND DESCRIPTION	TEACHER COMMENTARY
Ask students to consider the second unit generalization (see GEN2, page 102). Of the many causes of the Civil War debated by historians, which one (or ones) seems most plausible? • *Social trends:* The Civil War was the natural result of many years of social reform. • *Slavery:* The Civil War was a significant period in America's racial history. • *Sectional tension:* The Civil War was the most violent episode in the conflict between regional subcultures. • *Political dissolution:* The Civil War was the collapse of a democratic political system.	We'll revisit this exercise on the final day of the unit, at which time students can apply the understanding they've developed to extend their original theory or revise it.
Ask students to write for five minutes on this topic, using any evidence from past unit studies that would support one of these theories.	This constructivist approach is an important preview and review.
To differentiate this assignment, ask students to sketch, web, or outline their response.	
Preview of the Living Time Line project. Explain the idea behind this project: taking on the role of a person who has witnessed an historic event and whose life was affected by that event.	This assignment differentiates process and product based on student interest and learning profile.
Distribute the **Living Time Line Project Overview** (see Sample 3.2, page 124) and the accompanying **Living Time Line Project Planning Guide** and **Living Time Line Project Evaluation Rubrics** (see Samples 3.3 and 3.4, pages 125–129).	The Planning Guide includes a list of suggestions for events (and the option of proposing another event), a template for character development, and a checklist for the various stages of the project. All these provide a degree of scaffolding and support.
In this project, students choose the presentation mode they find most appealing (a speech or dramatic reading or a multimedia presentation) and also choose how they will approach the project: • Invent a character and then do research. • Do research and then invent a character. • Think about the presentation format first and then decide what kind of character would be most compelling in that format.	The creative process here is differentiated by student learning profile as presented by Sternberg. The creative learner enjoys diving into imagination first, whereas the analytical and practical learners prefer to assess available information and frameworks before beginning work.

LESSON SEQUENCE AND DESCRIPTION	TEACHER COMMENTARY
Explain to students that the Sources sheet contained in the Planning Guide is the equivalent of a Works Cited page for a research paper.	APA or MLA format is a familiar structure for many students. I also add particular specifications for how I want this page to look.
Ask students to think about the project and bring questions to class in the next few days. Encourage them to explore the Web links listed in the Planning Guide or browse the media center's offerings of Civil War–related books. Also point out that some students might also be interested in conducting family and genealogical research to pursue the story of an ancestor who lived during this era.	This surfing and browsing activity helps students see the wealth of information available and gets them thinking about the people who lived through historical events. (I've found that seeing photographs of these people can help.) The idea is to get students to build a scaffold of possibilities so that when it comes time to develop their project, they have some options.
Homework: Textbook reading and outlining assignment differentiated by readiness and learning profile. Ask students to begin their textbook reading and start on an outline of the text.	The textbook reading I use for this unit is Chapter 20 in *The American Pageant* (12th ed.), edited by Thomas A. Bailey and others.
The number of pages assigned should reflect the students' median level of reading speed and reading comprehension. Novice readers may need a shorter reading assignment. To guide chapter outlining, give each student one of two handouts, based on readiness. *Novice Readers* The **Chapter Outlining: Guidelines and Standards Handout** (see Sample 3.5, page 130) provides these students with straightforward practice in the chapter-outlining standards.	Knowing how heavy my students' workloads are, I try to limit nightly reading assignments to about 45 minutes. Focusing on median levels helps me do this. For example, if a majority of the class can read 5 pages in 20 minutes and answer at least 85 percent of the follow-up comprehension questions correctly, a typical nightly reading assignment might be 7 to 10 pages, with the expectation that students will also create an outline. Outlines are an important study tool for the AP exam.
On-Target and Advanced Readers The **Chapter Outlining: Question It! Handout** (see Sample 3.6, page 131) focuses on predicting outcomes, identifying main ideas, and supporting and synthesizing summative arguments.	Most readers in an AP class need to hone their analytical and synthesis skills rather than their factual recall skills.

LESSON SEQUENCE AND DESCRIPTION	TEACHER COMMENTARY
Remind students that the outlines they create now will be what they'll use to study for the AP exam. For this reason, they should create the kind of outline that they will find most helpful: *traditional outlining*, which verbal/linguistic learners and mathematical/logical learners tend to prefer, or *webbing/mapping*, which visual/spatial learners tend to prefer.	Offering two different types of outlining is an ideal way to capitalize on learning preference.
Optional independent study. Offer advanced students the opportunity to read ahead into the next unit on the Civil War, taking multiple-choice, comprehension tests as they feel ready; to move on to other unit activities and projects; and to conduct independent research projects. (The Web provides myriad quality American history sites, including dohistory.org and www.archives.gov.)	Students authorized to pursue independent study have proven themselves to be voracious readers and have achieved consistently high scores on multiple-choice tests and practice AP writing tasks.
Encourage these students to expand the Living Time Line project to whatever degree they are capable of. For example, they might • Explore the Web and discover new Internet resources for their peers to consult during their own project research. • Come up with another presentation format beyond the options mentioned (speech/dramatic reading, dramatic scene, or multimedia presentation). • Adopt a persona who will comment on a historical incident from the Civil War (the focus of the next unit), thus providing their classmates with a preview of subject matter to come. Work with these students individually to tailor the project guidelines to their specific needs and abilities.	I ask students who are working independently to maintain a brief log of daily tasks completed and to sign in (on a sheet or on the board) to indicate where they will pursue their work if they must leave the classroom to do it.

LESSON 2

On the Road to War   *(4 class periods)*

Concepts: Sectional Tension, Cause and Effect,
Individual Impact, Perspective
GEN1–2; SD1–7

LESSON SEQUENCE AND DESCRIPTION	TEACHER COMMENTARY
Chapter outline review and text mapping differentiated by readiness. Divide students into three readiness-based groups (novice, on target, and advanced) and ask them to review their outlines with one another.	I use practice AP essays as my readiness assessment. Novice students score in the 1–4 range, on-target students score in the 5–7 range, and advanced students score in the 8–9 range.

LESSON SEQUENCE AND DESCRIPTION	TEACHER COMMENTARY
Novice Students Meet with the novice students to develop a scroll-style text map: a page-by-page horizontal time line of the actual textbook, photocopied and laid out on the floor or board so that students may see all headings and subheadings in a single view. Ask students to work as a group to highlight and mark the essential details that support the headings and subheadings.	Text mapping is a graphic organizer technique that helps students master a large quantity of reading material. For more on the scroll approach, see www.textmapping.org/scrolls.html. This time with the novice students also lets me get an informal assessment of their chapter outlines.
On-Target and Advanced Students Give students in these two groups the choice of completing a scroll text map or simply sharing information with one another and updating their outlines using a different-colored pen.	Providing choice here supports visual learners' success, and the flexible grouping arrangement also helps build a sense of community.
Reassemble as a large group, and pose content-standard–based questions to gauge students' reading comprehension. For example: *What is a sectional, cultural, economic, or political factor that contributed to the formation of the Democratic, Whig, and "Know-Nothing" parties?*	I typically take content standards and convert them into questions. Questions like these can also provoke discussion of the meaning of key vocabulary like "sectional" and "political."
Structure this exercise not as a lively discussion but as an oral examination that invites students to return to their notes to find the answers.	
Collect about 50 percent of the on-target students' outlines and a few from the other two readiness groups. Evaluate these outlines according to the rubric standards available on the Chapter Outlining: Guidelines and Standards Handout (see Sample 3.5).	Time does not permit an instructor to collect outlines from four or five sections of students within one week. I narrow my focus to those who can most benefit from feedback: the on-target students, who can fall behind or jump ahead in skill. I keep a close eye on those who are diligent note-takers but have troubling assimilating the information and those who struggle to make connections among larger topic ideas and themes. Of course, I give feedback on everyone's outlining work at least once during every unit.
If time permits, provide detailed written feedback and a grade, asking students who do not earn a *B* or better to revise their outlines until they reach a *B* (or grade-level standards).	
Return the outlines to students later in the week.	
Homework: Textbook reading and outlining assignment differentiated by readiness and learning profile. Have students read and outline the remainder of the chapter. Remind them to think about the Living Time Line project and bring questions to class.	

LESSON SEQUENCE AND DESCRIPTION	TEACHER COMMENTARY
✳ Document analysis and Jigsaw differentiated by readiness. Divide the class into three groups and distribute the **Tiered Jigsaw Document Analysis Assignment** (see Sample 3.7, page 132): • Group 1 (advanced students) work on Topic 1. • Group 2 (on-target students) work on Topic 2. • Group 3 (novice students) work on Topic 3. Students pursuing the independent study may start this activity ahead of time or skip it altogether. When the Groups 1, 2, and 3 have completed their document analyses, ask them to jigsaw into new groups to share their topic findings. Regroup randomly—by having students count off, for example—or form groups based on which students will work well together.	The online readings for this Jigsaw allow students to analyze primary source documents and hear the voices of those who lived the historical incidents. The topics vary in the quantity of documents, the number of categories of information for synthesis, and historical chronology. When disparities in student skill levels are minor, I run this activity as a regular, untiered Jigsaw, assigning Topic 1, Topic 2, and Topic 3 to an equal number of students. It usually takes students one class period to complete steps 1 through 5 (see Sample 3.7). The Jigsaw is held during the third class session of this four-session lesson.
✳ Homework: Planning for the Living Time Line project differentiated by interest and learning profile. Before the end of class, go over the Project Overview (see Sample 3.2), the Planning Guide (see Sample 3.3), and the Evaluation Rubrics (see Sample 3.4). Allow students to ask questions about project parameters. If desired, ask advanced students who have already begun the project to share or model a rough draft of their presentation. Explain to students that over the next two nights, they should use the Planning Guide to decide their *persona* (age, gender, class, race, education, etc.) and *event* (historical incident) so that you can approve these by the end of the week. Review the importance of the Source sheet and the research guidelines.	I encourage my students to follow their interests in their project. For example, I steer students who are into high-action, combat-style video games toward military topics and personas. I prompt my clothing and fashion–obsessed students to investigate the millinery trade, dressmaking, uniform design, or the ways in which clothing expresses class and social status, and encourage them to think about creating a persona from that research. With a good topic match, students really enjoy discovering new information and sharing their research findings with others.
Living Time Line project check-in. Begin the last session of this four-session lesson by asking students to share a few facts from their project research that will show how their persona had an individual impact and unique perspective on the historical events they are researching.	

LESSON SEQUENCE AND DESCRIPTION	TEACHER COMMENTARY
Peer review of current research differentiated by interest. Divide the class into mixed-readiness groups based on the time period they have chosen to focus on for the Living Time Line project. For example: "If the persona you are creating in your project is responding to an event that occurred from 1850 to 1852, meet here. If your persona is responding to an event that occurred from 1853 to 1855, meet there."	
Tell students that over the next 10 to 15 minutes, they should talk about what they've uncovered in their research. Encourage students to help one another using the **Living Time Line Project Checklist** (see Sample 3.8, page 133), which lays out all the project expectations, including performance criteria.	This exchange lets peers remind one another of what they should be doing before a grade suffers. It's also a way of "sharing the labor" with me so that I don't have to constantly remind students of these various aspects.
In-class independent project research differentiated by interest/One-on-one coaching sessions based on readiness needs. Supply students with additional resources (beyond those provided in the Planning Guide) and ask them to continue their Living Time Line project research during class time.	My media center provides overviews of historiography as well as encyclopedic surveys of the path to disunion and the Civil War.
While students work, schedule individual coaching sessions with students.	Brief conferences like these help me identify obstacles and steer students toward topics (in this case, a persona and an event) that they would find interesting. It's a particular priority for me to have a personal conversation with students whom I suspect have not attempted the Planning Guide because they are wary of research, are disinterested in school, have reading difficulties, have problems at home, or have limited home access to research materials and technology.
Novice Students Meet with these students to review Planning Guides and provide direct feedback and guidance.	
Advanced Students Working Independently Meet with these students to review compacting logs and folders of completed work and find out where they're succeeding with independent learning. Remember: Even students with great inspiration can lack organizational strategies.	
At the end of class, collect the Planning Guides of those students who did not participate in a one-on-one coaching session and provide written feedback within a day or two.	
Homework: Test preparation. Ask students to review their reading outlines in preparation for a multiple-choice test during the next class session.	

LESSON SEQUENCE AND DESCRIPTION	TEACHER COMMENTARY
Provide the following review questions and ask students to generate a response of least one paragraph for each: 1. How were these pre–Civil War tensions the outgrowth of geographical developments? Economic developments? Technological developments? Cultural developments? Political developments? 2. How did the debate over slavery influence politics and sectionalism? 3. What were the differences among the cultures that had developed in the Northern states, Southern states, and territories? 4. What evidence have you gleaned that political democracy in the United States has a tumultuous and complex history? Announce that if everyone in the class completes the review questions for homework, there will a 10-minute in-class review before the test.	These questions encourage students to revisit content standards and help to bring order to the long list of historical incidents they've already outlined. The short-response format—a paragraph or so rather than a full essay—supports fast assessment while still reinforcing writing skills. This sort of motivational tool encourages the class to think of itself as a team.

LESSON 3

What Caused the War?   (3–5 class periods)

Concepts: Sectional Tension, Cause and Effect,
Individual Impact, Perspective
GEN1–2; SD1–7

LESSON SEQUENCE AND DESCRIPTION	TEACHER COMMENTARY
Optional in-class review. Ask students to hand in their completed review questions as they enter the classroom. Do a quick check, and if all students have completed the homework review as directed, hold a 10-minute, whole-class review before the test.	Theoretically, any student who completes the review questions should be well prepared for the test, but a whole-class review provides many students with a kind of psychological advantage. It's that last-minute oral processing during which they tell themselves, "Yes, I really *do* know this material!"
Multiple-choice test. Provide students with a multiple-choice test based on the information catalogued through their chapter outlines. Test questions should correspond directly with the unit understandings and should be modeled on the AP format.	Both the intuitive skill of identifying broad themes and the sensing skill of providing specific details to defend that theme are skills required on the AP exam and also important problem-solving and writing skills.

LESSON SEQUENCE AND DESCRIPTION	TEACHER COMMENTARY
Here is an example: *The Compromise of 1850 and the Dred Scott decision were both triggers for* *a. the rise of free labor ideology* *b. increasing sectional polarization* *c. the creation of* Uncle Tom's Cabin *d. Lincoln's rejection of the proposed Crittenden Compromise* Similar examples are available at apcentral.collegeboard.com. *Note:* A convenient way to create computer-graded reading quizzes is to subscribe to www.quia.com, a Web site that lets teachers develop quizzes that present questions one at a time, in multiple formats, and in varying combinations. This means you can let students go through the reading at their own pace while still ensuring academic honesty. Another advantage of Quia is its individual and group statistics provision, which can show how many and which students missed a particular question. The statistics can help teachers "teach to the test" during individual conferencing and mini-lessons for the whole class or small groups. For example, when faced with four choices, a student may always be able to eliminate the two least likely responses, but may always get stuck on which of the last two to choose. You might note that some students tend to choose the more general response when a specific answer is the best option.	This question requires students to be familiar enough with two incidents (items *c* and *d*) to recognize that neither is the correct answer. To evaluate the items *a* and *b* as possible answers, students must understand key vocabulary ("free labor ideology" and "sectional polarization") and they must also reason that the free labor ideology was one of the causes of the Compromise rather than one of its effects (see SD3, page 101). Notice too that this question requires students to build on knowledge from a previous unit and link that information to their current unit understandings. Helping students see their habits in testing helps them improve their scores.
Homework: Living Time Line project work differentiated by interest and learning profile. Distribute the evaluated Planning Guides collected during Lesson 2 and explain the homework assignment: taking detailed notes on Source 1 (see Sample 3.3, page 125–127).	
Living Time Line project check-in/Optional mini-lessons on research skills based on readiness needs. Begin class by asking students what successes they have had with research for the Living Time Line project and if any particular issues have arisen during the research process so far. To keep the concepts alive in students' minds, ask them to report on their characters' individual perspectives and impacts. Then announce that for this evening's homework, they should continue their research, using Source 2.	

LESSON SEQUENCE AND DESCRIPTION	TEACHER COMMENTARY
Depending on student progress thus far, offer mini-lessons on topics related to the research process: note taking, avoiding plagiarism, summarizing, citation, and synthesizing research.	
Discussion seminar preparation in heterogeneous groups. Explain to students that this next activity is a precursor to a discussion seminar on the Civil War and whether or not it was an avoidable conflict. Their task is to add to the understanding they developed through the Jigsaw documents analysis activity so that they can make a case during the discussion.	A successful discussion seminar is one initiated by the teacher but perpetuated by the students. Preparation is essential.
Distribute and review the **Causes of the Civil War Handout** (see Sample 3.9, page 134). Based on the complexity of the historical perspective, assign students to readiness-based groups to complete the handout tasks. Work on this assignment should take two class periods. During the first day, students conduct research; during the second day, they finish their research and create a symbolic poster that communicates the key tenets of their assigned school of thought.	The kind of source documents called for here reference a number of historians and provide basic descriptions of their theories. The idea is not for students to complete involved research, but for them to get a taste of the historians' arguments and then apply their past reading and activities to find supporting evidence for these arguments.
Homework: Seminar preparation. Students prepare their notes for the seminar and review their chapter outlines, highlighting sections that answer the seminar question: *Was the Civil War an inevitable conflict?*	Here, students are assembling evidence to support their analyses. The specificity of this assignment helps ensure better participation in the discussion.
Discussion seminar. Form a circle and ask students to bring their posters and sit near the other members of their school-of-thought group. Each group will present in turn. Ask the seminar question: *Was the Civil War an inevitable conflict?* All students must participate in the discussion, including students working on independent studies. In the spirit of dialogue rather than debate, they should question and challenge others' opinions while demonstrating respect, curiosity, and cooperation by engaging others and listening to one another. Gradually let students take control over the discussion. Compliment students when they demonstrate active listening skills, provide substantive evidence, reason effectively, and ask analytical and evaluative questions. Take notes so that you can corroborate or debunk students' perceptions.	Because a class typically comprises students with quite a broad range of academic and social skills, I base my evaluation of student participation in whole-group discussion on the quality of each student's contribution rather than on the number of times he or she speaks. One option is to develop a class discussion rubric (a checklist of standards like "provided substantive evidence," "reasoned effectively," "asked analytical and evaluative questions," and "actively listened to others"). We discuss each standard, and I ask students to grade their discussion performances.

LESSON SEQUENCE AND DESCRIPTION	TEACHER COMMENTARY
Depending on the success of the discussion seminar, it may extend to a second day to ensure full student participation and understanding.	

LESSON 4   **The Write Stuff**   *(4 class periods)*
Concepts: Sectional Tension, Cause and Effect
GEN1–2; SD1–7

LESSON SEQUENCE AND DESCRIPTION	TEACHER COMMENTARY
Living Time Line project check-in/Optional mini-lesson on research skills based on readiness needs. Ask students if they have any questions at this point in their character research. Discuss what they have learned to support or refute the unit generalizations. What has their research helped them understand about sectional tension, cause and effect, individual impact, and perspective?	
Conduct a mini-lesson on note taking, summarizing, citation, and synthesizing research as needed.	
AP writing skills activities differentiated by readiness. Divide the class into two groups: advanced students (those who have regularly received scores of 8 or 9 on practice free-response essays) and on-target and novice students (the rest of the class). Explain to both groups that they will spend the next three days working on skills they will need for the written portion of the AP exam.	The document-based, free-response questions on the AP exam demand strong historical knowledge, astute document analysis, the ability to synthesize information gathered, and the ability to compare and contrast effectively in writing. Practicing these skills is essential.
Day 1 *Group 1 (Advanced Students)* These students work independently on the **Build Your Own DBQ Assignment** (see Sample 3.10, page 135), which challenges them to develop comparison/contrast essay prompts appropriate for the unit content. Online resources are provided in this handout, but encourage students to stretch beyond those lists.	This task is a definite stretch for even advanced students, as it requires them to be familiar with DBQ standards and essay prompts and to gather meaningful and challenging (but not too challenging) readings from two disparate time periods. In addition, they must develop a question that adequately embraces the scope of the comparison and contrast.
A mini-lesson on online research may be advisable here, covering topics like how to identify legitimate sources: Does the site provide clear authorship? Is it updated frequently? Is information attributed to recognizable institutions or credentialed individuals?	

LESSON SEQUENCE AND DESCRIPTION	TEACHER COMMENTARY
Check in with this group periodically to provide direction and answer questions as needed. Students should continue their DBQ prompt preparation for homework.	
Group 2 (On-Target and Novice Students) Meet with these students to review important writing skills for the AP free-response essay, including how to build a thesis, how to cite evidence, and how to construct a commentary.	Thanks to the recent discussion seminar, reading, and chapter outlining, these students have the historical knowledge they need to address the prompt. My role is to help them demonstrate that knowledge.
Distribute the following standards for AP free-response essays and ask students to examine online models of student essays for evidence of these standards:	Other information on AP essay scoring standards and online models are available at apcentral.collegeboard. com.
Students who received the top scores (8–9) • *Presented a clear, well-developed thesis.* • *Supported their thesis with substantial, relevant information.* • *Understood the complexity of the question.* • *Offered an effective analysis.*	
Next, provide the following essay prompt, drawn directly from the discussion seminar:	
Evaluate whether or not the Civil War was an inevitable conflict. You have 5 minutes to plan your answer and 30 minutes to write it.	
Allow students in Group 2 to self-select into pairs or triads to outline their answers or work alone, as they prefer. Then, after approximately 10 minutes of work, have everyone reconvene to share potential outlines.	Allowing choice in work partners is helpful for students who prefer active discussion. Other students do best working on their own.
For homework, Group 2 students will write a documents-based, free-response essay to the prompt provided. Ask them to spend no more than 30 minutes writing their response.	
<u>Day 2</u> *Group 1 (Advanced Students)* Students continue their DBQ prompt preparation.	
Group 2 (On-Target and Novice Students) Divide Group 2 into mixed-ability subgroups of three to four students. Subgroup members read one another's essays and evaluate the writing according to AP standards by underlining thesis statements and topic sentences and by numbering the amount of substantive evidence used for each idea argued. Ask each subgroup to nominate the best essay. Consider having a few read aloud.	Students are often nervous about or discouraged by the thought of the looming AP assessment. Collegial sharing in a peer review environment helps lessen some of the tension while promoting skill development.

LESSON SEQUENCE AND DESCRIPTION	TEACHER COMMENTARY
<u>Day 3</u> *Group 1 (Advanced Students)* Meet with Group 1 students to preview the DBQ prompts they are creating. Then, ask them to work together to review all the prompts that have been created, evaluating them based on the rubric in the Build Your Own DBQ Assignment (see Sample 3.10). After nominating and reaching consensus on the best and most accessible prompt, Group 1's final task is to revise that prompt until it is stage-ready for the whole class. *Group 2 (On-Target and Novice Students)* Group 2 students work on revising their AP essay responses based on the evaluations received during the previous day's peer review sessions. At the end of class, they will turn their essays in for assessment.	Students are the toughest critics. Here, they let one another know whether or not they view an essay prompt as too difficult to attempt. Although assigning a formal grade is an option, I usually just give practice credit (as students still have another essay to write for this unit) and use these essays as a formative assessment: a way to gauge the progression of these students' skills. These essays also show me who needs extra attention and practice on free-response DBQs and where I might need to revise "novice," "on-target," or "advanced" groupings.
Free-response essay writing. Introduce the student-created DBQ prompt that was determined the best and have all students write in response for 45 minutes.	

LESSON 5   **Back in Time**   *(6–7 class periods)*

Concepts: Sectional Tension, Cause and Effect, Individual Impact, Perspective

GEN1; SD1–7

LESSON SEQUENCE AND DESCRIPTION	TEACHER COMMENTARY
Living Time Line project work and peer feedback sessions differentiated by interest and learning profile/One-on-one coaching sessions based on readiness needs. Place students in their Time Line groups to share the work they've done thus far. At this stage, they should have completed most if not all of their research and should have written a few paragraphs of their speech/dramatic reading presentation or composed labeled sketches/rough Web pages for their multimedia presentation.	

LESSON SEQUENCE AND DESCRIPTION	TEACHER COMMENTARY
Encourage students to consult the Evaluation Rubric (see Sample 3.4) and the Project Checklist (See Sample 3.8) for suggestions they can give one another and as a basis for informal peer evaluation.	Revisiting these documents reminds students of all the performance aspects.
Ask students to challenge one another with the kind of questions they might receive from their audience, which may include other students, teachers, parents, and the larger community.	"How do we know excellence?" is the larger framework for these questions. Inviting students to share ideas on that topic as a closing activity for each lesson throughout this unit helps them reflect specifically on what makes student work "excellent."
While the groups work, meet with students individually to review their project process, their prompts and essays, and their multiple-choice test results. Provide skill-development assistance and reinforcement as needed.	These one-on-one coaching sessions can meet multiple skill needs uncovered during the unit. They're most crucial for generally on-target students who are struggling with various aspects of the research process or project development.
Living Time Line dress rehearsals in self-selected pairs. Ask students to choose a partner and perform their presentations for one another. Again, they should base their feedback, compliments, and critiques on the unit standards and the Project Checklist.	The museum aspect of the Living Time Line, with students being both the "objets d'art" and museum-goers, is a strong support for self-assessment. Watching others perform gives everyone a clearer idea of the differences among standards of "sophisticated," "strong," and "adequate."
Living Time Line presentations and response questions. Students present in chronological order. Direct the rest of the class to take notes on their peers' presentations. Their follow-up task is to use actual statements of fact and opinion offered by the characters they meet in the Living Time Line to answer the following questions: • How were the pre–Civil War tensions the outgrowth of geographical developments? Economic? Technological? Cultural? Political? • How did the debate over slavery influence politics and sectionalism? • What were the differences among the cultures that had developed in the Northern states, Southern states, and territories?	This activity feels informal, but actually reinforces the skill of evidence building, helping students gain confidence in their ability to construct an argument by pulling facts from memory. In addition, students who are not always successful with the reading and writing activities of an AP classroom may surprise everyone by shining in this type of artistic presentation.

LESSON SEQUENCE AND DESCRIPTION	TEACHER COMMENTARY
• What evidence can you cite to support the statement that the history of political democracy in the United States has been tumultuous and complex?	
Self-assessment and response-question discussion. When all presentations are complete, ask students to fill out the **Living Time Line Project Self-Assessment** (see Sample 3.11, page 137). Once these are all turned in, ask students to report on their answers to the response questions.	It's very validating for students to hear their research cited in their peers' responses to the review questions. Those whose presentations leave a strong impression hear themselves quoted, and their work becomes a model of an excellent product.
Sharing of DBQ insights. Distribute the (ungraded) DBQ essays written during Lesson 4, making sure every student receives someone else's essay. Ask everyone to take a highlighter and highlight a "golden line"—something that meets one or more of the following criteria: • It is a substantive piece of evidence defending an argument. • It is a particularly well-summarized topic sentence. • It is an insightful bit of commentary on a piece of evidence. • It is a particularly eloquent, well-worded line of writing. Ask every student to read aloud at least one line that compliments another student.	Again, compliments and cheerleading for one another promotes a "team approach" to the upcoming hurdle of the AP exam.
Reflective journal writing. Ask students to reflect on the Living Time Line presentations and their own reading and research and to reconsider the following unit generalization: *Historians present the causes of the Civil War from diverse perspectives: as the peak of many years of social reform; as a significant period in America's racial history; as the most violent episode in the conflict between regional subcultures; and as the collapse of a democratic political system.* Ask: Of the various causes of the Civil War that historians cite, which one—or ones—seems most plausible? Have students write on this topic for at least 15 minutes, citing evidence presented in both this unit and past units to support one historical school of thought. Afterward, encourage any students willing to read aloud a few lines from their journal entries to do so.	This closing activity highlights student strengths and informally reminds the whole class of unit understandings and content knowledge. It also incorporates the students' voices—their interpretations of the events we've been exploring. This helps to ground history in the modern era. It's so important to me that my students see that history lives on in current events.

Teacher Reflection on the Unit

History can come alive for students when they listen to individual voices from the past and imagine what a person from that era would say in response to the events of the day. The unit's focus on writing provides an excellent assessment of student understanding and incorporates the format of the AP exam to help students concisely and substantively analyze the United States' path toward disunion in comparison with modern events.

Lyn Fairchild has taught in public and private secondary schools for more than a decade and is currently a curriculum consultant and teacher for Duke University's Talent Identification Program. She can be reached at lfairchild@nc.rr.com.

SAMPLE 3.1—"Hello, I'm Harriet" Presentation Guidelines

"Hello, I'm Harriet . . ."

Objectives: During this unit, each student will have an opportunity to step into the moccasins of a particular character from antebellum or Civil War history. You will be providing your classmates with a taste of this experience by taking on the persona of Harriet Beecher Stowe, an influential figure on societal trends that contributed to the Civil War.

Directions:

1. Gather 7 to 10 key facts about Harriet Beecher Stowe's life—ones that you find most relevant to the historical period we are about to study and that you believe would intrigue your classmates.
2. Use the facts you select to develop a brief paragraph of paraphrased summary, speaking in the voice of Harriet Beecher Stowe and introducing yourself to an audience (your classmates). If you are not sure how to paraphrase, use the following Web site as a reference: www.indiana.edu/~wts/pamplets/plagiarism.shtml.
3. Prepare a dramatic reading of a section of Stowe's most famous work, *Uncle Tom's Cabin*. Note that some historians have postulated that if Stowe had been a man, she would have chosen the profession of minister.
4. Be prepared to answer impromptu questions from your classmates about your (Stowe's) life.

Online Reference Sites on Stowe:

Biographical information
www.online-literature.com/stowe/
digital.library.upenn.edu/women/stowe/StoweHB.html
www.fembio.org/women/harriet-beecher-stowe.shtml

Biographical and artifact information
www.harrietbeecherstowecenter.org/

Stowe's words
womenshistory.about.com/library/qu/blqustow.htm
xroads.virginia.edu/~ma97/riedy/calvin.html

Print Sources on Stowe:
The Limits of Sisterhood: The Beecher Sisters on Women's Rights and Women's Sphere
    by Jeanne Boydston, Mary Kelley, and Anne Margolis (1988)
Harriet Beecher Stowe: A Life by Joan Hedrick (1993)

SAMPLE 3.2—Living Time Line Project Overview

The Living Time Line Project: Living Disunion and Civil War

Directions: In this project, you will create a persona: a "common man/common woman" who lived in a particular region of the United States between 1850 and 1865. Based on research you will do, you will invent a fully developed, authentic character of a specific age, gender, class, race, education level, personality, employment status, life history, family, political affiliation, and religious belief (or lack thereof). Use the **Living Time Line Project Planning Guide** to help you organize your work and keep track of your progress.

Your objective is to make this individual come alive and answer two questions:
1. *"What was it like to view a historical incident, up close and personal?"*
   Choose an important event from the chapter(s) we have read and provide an eyewitness testimony adapted to your character's perspective and circumstances. Event possibilities are listed on the Planning Guide.
2. *"How has the nation's drift toward disunion affected my life?"* Or, if you are working independently during this unit: *"How has the Civil War affected my life?"*

Presentation Format: Choose one of the following formats for your project presentation.

<u>Format 1: Speech or Dramatic Reading</u>
- *Let Me Tell You How It Was* . . . This is a formal speech explaining your perspective on the historical incident as well as the growing disunion or the Civil War. You must give your speech in costume and with appropriate props.
- *Let Me Take You Back* . . . This is a dramatic reading of a monologue or another kind of theatrical performance illustrating the historical incident as well as its influence on your life. You may request to work with a peer on this option if more than one person is essential to the scene.

<u>Format 2: Multimedia Presentation</u>
- *My Scrapbook* . . . This is a multimedia presentation showing visuals (photos, cartoons, artistic renderings) and/or providing the soundtrack of the historical incident as well as daily life as it has been affected by the growing disunion or the Civil War. This presentation can take the form of
   a. A poster accompanied by other multimedia components, such as sound effects.
   b. An electronic slideshow presentation.
   c. A Web page.
   d. An alternative form proposed to and authorized by the teacher.
You must be present throughout the multimedia presentation, acting as a tour guide to answer questions about your character's viewpoint.

Regardless of your chosen project option, you must be prepared to answer audience questions about the time period you are representing and your character's role.

Project Resources: Use online resources (I will distribute a list of Web sites to get you started) and print resources (available in the school media center). Consider films such as *Amistad, Glory,* and *Gods and Generals* and the TV series *The Civil War.*

SAMPLE 3.3—Living Time Line Project Planning Guide

Step One: Brainstorming
There are several ways to begin the creation of your living history character.

☐ Choose the characteristics of the kind of person you wish to know more about and then do your research looking for evidence of how such a person would have experienced and perceived the road to disunion or civil war. For example, you might be surfing the Web links that post Civil War pictures and find a picture of someone who captures your interest or imagination.

or

☐ Choose the event and then think of an individual who would have mostly likely seen and heard this event in person.

or

☐ Choose the presentation format (a speech, a multimedia presentation, or a dramatic reading/scene) and identify both the event and the type of person who would be most interesting and effective for your presentation.

Step Two: Character Development
Begin by filling in the character information below:

☐ Age:
☐ Gender:
☐ Class:
☐ Race:
☐ Education:
☐ Employment:
☐ Other significant characteristics:
☐ Life history: (What are the most significant events, both public and private, in this character's life? Be sure to verify that each event is era-appropriate. For example, how likely would your character be to finish high school, as high school education was not compulsory?)

_____
_____
_____
_____
_____
_____
_____
_____
_____

SAMPLE 3.3—Living Time Line Project Planning Guide—*(continued)*

☐ Family:

_____

_____

_____

_____

☐ Political affiliation (optional):
☐ Religious beliefs (optional):
☐ Decide on an event that your character will witness. Where will he or she be as it is happening? Here are
some event suggestions:
  • Harriet Beecher Stowe publishes *Uncle Tom's Cabin* (1852)
  • The Republican Party forms (1854)
  • Buchanan defeats Frémont and Fillmore for the U.S. presidency (1856)
  • Brooks beats Sumner in the Senate chamber (1856)
  • Brown's Pattawatomie Creek Massacre (1856)
  • Brown raids Harper's Ferry (1859)
  • Civil War in Bloody Kansas (1856–1860)
  • The U.S. Supreme Court issues the Dred Scott decision (1857)
  • The Lincoln-Douglas debates (1858)
  • Seven seceding states form the Confederate States of America (1861)
  • Any landmark incident (battle, raid, etc.) of the Civil War (1861–1865)

Have another idea? Propose it to the teacher.

Event Chosen: _____

Step Three: Research
Find at least four sources (two print and two electronic) to complete your research. Use two primary source
documents and two secondary source documents.

☐ Source 1 _____ Primary or secondary?
                                                         Print or electronic?
☐ Source 2 _____ Primary or secondary?
                                                         Print or electronic?
☐ Source 3 _____ Primary or secondary?
                                                         Print or electronic?
☐ Source 4 _____ Primary or secondary?
                                                         Print or electronic?

SAMPLE 3.3—Living Time Line Project Planning Guide—*(continued)*

☐ Take paraphrased notes. (Refer back to the rules for paraphrasing.)

☐ Keep a good record of where you find your notes. Workable systems include using color-coded index cards (e.g., yellow cards for notes from one source, pink for notes from another) or putting notes from different sources in different sections of a notebook. For print sources, *always indicate the page numbers where you find your information.* For online sources, *always include the complete URL and the name of the Web site or online publication.*

☐ Prepare a Sources sheet to accompany your final presentation.

☐ DO NOT copy lines from famous speeches, no matter how good they may sound. *Remember, you are creating a character.* However, do pay close attention to the diction, style, and syntax of authentic speeches, diaries, and other primary source documents. You should imitate that sentence structure and style as you write your own material.

Step Four: Drafting

☐ For a speech, dramatic reading, or dramatic scene, write a first draft of a script that integrates your research in a creative way while taking on the voice(s) of the character(s).

☐ For a multimedia presentation, use a storyboard, a sketch, or webbing software to plot out the different images and text that will tell your character's story.

Step Five: Revision

☐ Using feedback from peer groups and teacher conferences, evaluate your project's adherence to the Living Time Line Project Evaluation Rubrics.

☐ Practice the oral components of your presentation. Speaking aloud can help you catch mistakes that silent reading does not. Revise accordingly.

SAMPLE 3.4—Living Time Line Project Evaluation Rubrics

Format 1: Speech/Dramatic Reading

Criteria	Sophisticated	Strong	Adequate
Poise, Volume, Authenticity, Blocking, Costumes, and Props	The speaker is completely in character, believable and authentic, and delivers the speech from memory and with excellent poise; costumes and props are striking and appropriate; movements are intentional and completely in character, advancing the scene seamlessly.	The speaker is in character and authentic, delivering the speech with some speech aids; poise is strong; costumes and props are appropriate; movements relate to overall purpose of the presentation.	The speaker demonstrates an effort to render the character but lacks authenticity and/or enthusiasm and/or relies too heavily on speech aids; costumes and props meet basic expectations; movements lack intention and focus.
Factual Accuracy and Substance	The content is not only factually accurate but substantive, creative, and memorable; the speaker goes above and beyond to answer questions completely, and with depth and style.	The content is factually accurate and substantive; the speaker answers questions fully.	The content is factually accurate while lacking depth or creativity; the speaker answers questions sufficiently.
Diction	Speech patterns and language are appropriate to the era and the character.	Attempt to imitate speech patterns and language of the times is clear.	Era- and character- appropriate speech patterns and language are missing.
Sources Sheet	The sources sheet follows appropriate format and lists four sources.	The sources sheet follows appropriate format and lists four sources.	The sources sheet follows appropriate format and lists four sources.

SAMPLE 3.4—Living Time Line Project Evaluation Rubrics—*(continued)*

Format 2: Multimedia Presentation

Criteria	Sophisticated	Strong	Adequate
Visuals, Sound, and Text	Visuals, sound, and text provide compelling and exciting answers to the question.	Visuals, sound, and text work well together to answer the question.	Visuals, sound, and text compete and distract but do provide a basic answer to the question.
Speaker's Role	The speaker guides the audience through the presentation effortlessly and with expert knowledge.	The speaker guides the audience well, demonstrating good background knowledge.	A lack of organization and/or supporting details impedes the presentation.
Factual Accuracy and Substance	The presentation is substantive and accurate, built on well-researched facts, and organized thematically.	The presentation follows a theme of organized ideas and facts.	The presentation follows a theme supported by main ideas and facts.
Sources Sheet	The Sources sheet follows appropriate format and lists more than four sources.	The Sources sheet follows appropriate format and lists four sources.	The Sources sheet follows appropriate format and lists four sources.

SAMPLE 3.5—Chapter Outlining: Guidelines and Standards Handout

Chapter Outlining: Guidelines and Standards

Directions: Please read the assigned text and create an outline. You may use the traditional method or the webbing/mapping method—it's your choice.

Traditional Method

- As you complete the reading assignment, create a roman numeral–style outline with a heading for each major section, followed by subheadings.
- Under each subheading, list (using bullets or numbers) the crucial facts you will need to understand the subheadings when you review for the AP exam in May.
- Paraphrase. *Avoid plagiarism.* If you are not sure how to paraphrase, use the following Web site as a reference: www.indiana.edu/~wts/pamphlets/plagiarism.shtml.
- At the end of your outline, provide a brief, bulleted chronology of the main events to answer this question: *Why is this chapter titled "The Road to Disunion"?*

Webbing or Mapping Method

Note: You may use Inspiration or other webbing software for this assignment.

- Scan through the reading and find all parallel headings and subheadings—those that are the same size, the same font, and so on—and create boxes, circles, or other categorizing shapes for headings and subheadings. Differentiate between headings and subheadings in terms of size.
- Using connecting lines (and other categorizing shapes, if you choose), attach crucial facts that define the sub-headings. These facts should be those you will need to understand the subheadings when you review for the AP exam in May.
- Paraphrase. *Avoid plagiarism.* If you are not sure how to paraphrase, use the following Web site as a reference: www.indiana.edu/~wts/pamphlets/plagiarism.shtml.
- At the end of your outline, provide a brief, bulleted chronology of the main events to answer this question: *Why is this chapter titled "The Road to Disunion"?*

Chapter Outline Scoring Rubric

1. Headings/shapes reflect main ideas and subsets of those ideas.
2. Essential historical facts follow main ideas and their subsets.
3. Chronology/timeline details most significant historical events.
4. Language is paraphrased.

SAMPLE 3.6—Chapter Outlining: Question It! Handout

Chapter Outlining: Question It!

Directions: Please read the assigned text and create an outline. You may use the traditional method or the webbing/mapping method—it's your choice.

Traditional Method
- Skim the title of the reading assignment, its introduction, and its conclusion.
- Develop an analytical or evaluative question—a "how" or "why" or "should" question—to ask about the reading. The question should address the broad themes rather than a particular event. As you read, if you discover that you have misjudged what the reading is about, choose another question.
- Outline an answer to your question by gathering the crucial facts and create a roman numeral–style outline with a heading for each major section, followed by subheadings.
- Under each subheading, list (using bullets or numbers) the crucial facts you will need to understand the subheadings when you review for the AP exam in May.
- Paraphrase. *Avoid plagiarism.* If you are not sure how to paraphrase, use the following Web site as a reference: www.indiana.edu/~wts/pamphlets/plagiarism.shtml.

Webbing or Mapping Method
Note: You can use Inspiration or other webbing software for this assignment.
- Skim the title of the reading assignment, its introduction, and its conclusion.
- Develop an analytical or evaluative question—a "how" or "why" or "should" question—to ask about the reading. The question should address the broad themes rather than a particular event. As you read, if you discover that you have misjudged what the reading is about, choose another question.
- Create a web or map to your answer by placing the question in the center of a page and connecting it relevant facts. Use lines and select categorizing shapes to denote main topics (headings) and subtopics (subheadings). Select facts that you will need to understand the headings and subheadings when you review for the AP exam in May.
- Paraphrase. *Avoid plagiarism.* If you are not sure how to paraphrase, use the following Web site as a reference: www.indiana.edu/~wts/pamphlets/plagiarism.shtml.

Chapter Outline Scoring Rubric
1. The question addresses the central theme(s) of the chapter.
2. Headings and subheadings reflect main ideas and subsets of the theme(s).
3. Essential historical facts follow main ideas and their subsets.
4. Language is paraphrased.

SAMPLE 3.7—Tiered Jigsaw Document Analysis Assignment

Pivotal Points on the Path to Disunion

Directions:
1. Appoint a group facilitator.
2. Read your group's assigned key question aloud.
3. Go to the online source and divide the documents to be read among group members. As you read, look for significant details that answer your key question. Take notes.
4. In a group discussion, share your findings. Take notes on what others tell you.
5. Ask one person to read aloud his/her summative notes of the group's answer to the key question(s).
6. At the teacher's direction, jigsaw into a new group. Representatives from Groups 1, 2, and 3 should report their findings, and everyone should take notes.

Topic 1: Union or Confederate? Mobilization Toward War
Key Questions: As a Virginian in 1861, would you have chosen a Union or Confederate position? To mobilize for war, what sacrifices would the Southern states have had to have make?

Online sources
www.wadsworth.com/history_d/special_features/ext/ap/chapter14/14.1.module.html
www.wadsworth.com/history_d/special_features/ext/ap/chapter14/14.2.module.html

Topic 2: From Bleeding Kansas to the Election of 1860: Nails in the Coffin?
Key Question: What made each of these events influential in driving the country toward Civil War?

Online source
www.wadsworth.com/history_d/special_features/ext/ap/chapter13/chapter13.html

Topic 3: John Brown's Raid on Harper's Ferry
Key Question: Why did Americans find this event so significant?

Online source
www.wadsworth.com/history_d/special_features/ext/ap/chapter13/13.3.module.html

SAMPLE 3.8—Living Time Line Project Checklist

Name _____

1. Research
Sources
- [ ] I have examined at least two electronic and two print sources.
- [ ] I have examined at least two primary sources and two secondary sources.

Notes
- [ ] My notes are paraphrased.
- [ ] My notes are organized and clearly indicate the source of the information and, where applicable, the exact page location.
- [ ] I am building my Sources sheet.

2. Presentation Content
Text
- [ ] My text communicates the details of what it was like for my character to witness a historical incident up close and personally.
- [ ] My text communicates the answer to this question (mark one):
      "How has . . . ○ the nation's drift toward disunion? ○ The Civil War . . . affected my life?
- [ ] I have written project text in (mark one) . . . ○ the character's voice ○ the characters' voices . . . as authentically as possible. I have tried to emulate the diction, style, and syntax of a person from this time period.

Visuals and Sounds (multimedia presentations only)
- [ ] I have gathered relevant visuals and sounds that support the text I am creating.
- [ ] I have a visual sketch or plan to organize the text, visuals, and sounds.

3. Presentation Performance
- [ ] I have practiced my presentation so that it is convincing, well organized, and polished.
- [ ] I have appropriate props, costumes, and supporting materials.
- [ ] I can answer practice questions posed by my peers.
- [ ] I have a neat and complete copy of my Sources sheet.
- [ ] I have reviewed the rubric to see if my project is missing anything.

SAMPLE 3.9—Causes of the Civil War Handout

Causes of the Civil War: Various Schools of Thought

Directions:

1. Appoint a group facilitator.

2. Read the brief summary provided about the school of thought or group of historians that you will be researching.

3. Divide the resources (online and print) among group members and begin individual reading and note-taking.

4. Once everyone has completed their research, reconvene as a group and discuss the questions below. Write your answers on a sheet of paper with all group members' names included.
   a. What are the most important beliefs—or tenets—of these historians' school of thought as to the causes of the Civil War?
   b. What are the strengths of this theory? What have we learned from our reading, discussion, and activities that might support this theory?
   c. What are the potential weaknesses of this theory? What have we learned from our reading, discussion, and activities that might cause us to question this theory?
   d. If we could classify this school of thought under a heading, which of the following unit concepts would be the best fit? (1) Sectional Tension; (2) Cause and Effect; (3) Individual Impact; or (4) Perspective. Or do we need to create a new phrase altogether?
   e. What symbol would best convey the main ideas of this group of historians, or school of thought, to our classmates?

5. Develop an image and create a small poster based on your answer to question *e*, copying the key tenets of the school's argument in bulleted or numbered form on the poster or integrating them as part of the overall symbol/metaphor.

6. Plan how your group will present its poster to the class so that all group members can explain the ideas.

Schools of Thought

Nationalist School: James Ford Rhodes
Progressive School: Charles and Mary Beard
"Repressible" Conflict School: James G. Randall and Avery Craven
Neonationalist School: Allan Nevins and David M. Potter
Free Labor Ideology School: Eric Foner and Eugene Genovese
Party Politics School
Ethnocultural School: Michael Holt

SAMPLE 3.10—Build Your Own DBQ Assignment

Ever wanted to be The College Board for a day and create those challenging and intimidating prompts that get millions of juniors and seniors shaking in their boots? This is your chance to play the role of a test creator who designs a thoughtful, free-response documents-based question asking students to see the similarities and differences between historical periods. If you create one that is particularly strong, yours may be the prompt for the entire class!

Directions:

1. Review the standards for free-response documents-based questions at apcentral.collegeboard.com.

2. Choose one of the following "Then and Now" topics (or propose a new topic, based on an antebellum or Civil War incident of interest to you):

THEN: 1852 . . . Harriet Beecher Stowe publishes *Uncle Tom's Cabin*.

NOW: Over the past 50 years, who has written the most influential fiction or nonfiction focused on African American issues? (Lorraine Hansberry? Toni Morrison? Ralph Ellison? Martin Luther King Jr.? Malcolm X? Ella Baker? Randall Robinson?) How is the effect of this person's work similar to or different from the effect of Stowe's *Uncle Tom's Cabin*?

THEN: 1854 . . . The Republican Party forms.

NOW: What is the platform of today's Republican Party? How is it similar to or different from its original formation?

THEN: 1856 . . . Buchanan defeats Frémont and Fillmore for the presidency.

NOW: What were the positions of our most recent presidential candidates? What were the significant events during our most recent presidential election? What similarities and differences do you find between these elections?

THEN: 1856 . . . Sumner is beaten by Brooks in the Senate chamber.

NOW: What are the contentious issues in the U.S. Congress today, and how do representatives and senators treat one another? What is the level of civility or lack thereof? What is the level of partisanship and division? What similarities and differences do you see between these historical periods?

THEN: 1856 . . . Brown leads the Pattawatomie Creek Massacre and 1859. . . Brown leads the raid at Harper's Ferry.

NOW: In the past 20 years, what civil insurrections, riots, and other forms of disobedience have reflected American society's tensions regarding race relations? What incidents and types of civil disobedience have reflected the relationship of the citizen to government policy? How are these incidents similar to or different from John Brown's Massacre?

SAMPLE 3.10—Build Your Own DBQ Assignment—(continued)

THEN: 1856–1860 . . . Civil war rages in Bleeding Kansas.

NOW: What states have been the battlegrounds for recent, momentous events or political dramas? How have incidents there shaped events on a national level? Consider the 2000 and 2004 presidential elections and the ballot and polling problems in Florida and Ohio. What similarities and differences do you see between the presidential elections of 1856 and 2000?

THEN: 1857 . . .The Supreme Court issues the Dred Scott decision.

NOW: Which Supreme Court decisions of the past 75 years have had a strong impact on racial relationships in the United States? Consider decisions such as *Brown v. Board of Education* (1954) or *University of California Regents v. Bakke* (1978). What similarities and differences do you see between these decisions?

THEN: 1858 . . . Lincoln and Douglas debate.

NOW: What landmark presidential debates have tackled crucial issues in American history? Consider such debates as those between Nixon and Kennedy or Carter and Reagan. What similarities and differences do you see between these debates?

THEN: 1861 . . . Seven states secede to form the Confederate States of America.

NOW: What struggle between states' rights and the federal government's authority was the most significant during the 20th century? Consider the conflicts between federal and Southern state authority over civil rights in the 1950s and 1960s. What similarities and differences do you see between these disputes?

3. Find four to five excerpts of relevant readings from online or print sources. If you can find more, wonderful! *Each time period* ("Then" and "Now") *should have at least two readings.* One of your readings may be a visual: a captioned cartoon, map, chart, photograph, and so on. Excerpts from written documents should be 250 to 500 words in length. For documents for the antebellum and Civil War periods, search the online source "From Revolution to Reconstruction" at odur.let.rug.nl/~usa/D/.

Caution: If you are pulling readings from an online source, be sure to VERIFY THE LEGITIMACY OF THE WEB SITE YOU ARE USING. Sites that end in ".edu" or ".gov" are often legitimate, but some .edu sites are created by students for a college or high school class—students who may not have taken a lot of time—so be careful.

4. Create a prompt question that sounds like one that the College Board would have written. Use all or part of the follow-up questions provided in the "Then and Now" topic list. Remember that students answering the question will need to draw on outside knowledge, both from history class and current events, so the wording of the prompt needs to be comprehensible and accessible and should follow the format available on the College Board Web site.

SAMPLE 3.11—Living Time Line Project Self-Assessment

Name _____

Directions: Rate your work on your project: 1 = "poor," 2 = "on target," 3 = "strong," 4 = "excellent."
Circle N/A if you did not have that aspect in your project.

My research	1	2	3	4
My writing	1	2	3	4
My acting	1	2	3	4	N/A
My Web page/poster/station's visual display	1	2	3	4	N/A
My costume, prop design, and sound effects	1	2	3	4	N/A
My nightly work ethic	1	2	3	4

Here are a few specific examples in my project that elaborate on the ratings provided above:

_____
_____
_____
_____
_____
_____
_____

I would like to compliment the following classmates' projects for the reasons stated below:

_____
_____
_____

I would like to constructively critique the following classmates' projects for the reasons stated below:

_____
_____
_____

The next time you assign this project, please keep this element or component:

_____
_____

The next time you assign this project, please make this change or use this new idea:

_____

4 It Has to Hang

A Visual Arts Unit on 3–D Ceramic Sculpture

Unit Developers: Tracy Hamm with Suzi Juarez, Miki Reddy, and Cheryl Franklin-Rohr

Introduction

This nine-week unit for an advanced-level 3–D studio art course explores the challenge of designing a three-dimensional ceramic or paper clay sculpture that can be hung. The finished piece may be functional or nonfunctional, and the project incorporates the following elements:

- Wheel-thrown and/or hand-built techniques.
- Raku or Sagger firing techniques or an experimental combination of Sagger and Raku firing.
- A surface treatment that may include Raku glazes, slip coating, and textural methods.

As in all studio art classes, students spend the majority of their time working on their artwork. Each student determines the personal theme to explore in his or her piece, the building method for it, and the surface and firing techniques to use. Instruction highlights the problem solving required to develop a personal theme, the necessary skill competencies in ceramic materials and techniques, and the elements of art and principles of design. Throughout students' studio time, the instructor focuses on individual support and guidance.

Textbooks are usually not part of the learning process in studio art courses. Instead, the resources are primarily visual: videos, slides, art reproduction posters, Web sites, and art books. Because there are so many resources that can influence the design process, in this unit, students use a sketchbook/journal to store and explore the visual ideas and techniques they encounter in their research. The sketchbook provides a means of recording, practicing, reflecting on, and keeping track of all the components of the unit and provides ongoing process differentiation based on learning style.

Teacher Reflection on Designing the Unit

I created this unit while working with the art coordinator of the district where I was completing my student teaching. The master ceramics teacher I was assigned to knew that ceramics is my own studio emphasis, and she encouraged me to develop a challenging unit.

I knew I wanted students to gain a better understanding of how contemporary ceramic arts is moving away from "functional craft work" toward a more fine-art focus. In the contemporary context, for example, a ceramic piece will morph into another form—one that is not always ceramic-like. The content and theme being communicated guides the design and building process.

I began the design of this unit with my state's five visual arts standards, each of which directs a component necessary to create a piece of artwork. The creation of art naturally lends itself to independent learning, and I knew I'd need to use several differentiated instructional strategies to meet the wide variety of needs I'd already observed in the students. To clarify needs further, I included a pre-assessment related to students' experiences with building and firing techniques and student learning style, aiming to use the results to help me select and apply appropriate instructional strategies, including scaffolding techniques and other accommodations. The sketchbook/journal would provide ongoing informal assessment—a way to monitor students' successes and struggles.

Because reflective thought on creative decisions can't be done in isolation, I wanted students to "Think–Pair–Share" to gain deeper understanding of the design process. Another key decision in this unit's design was the decision to include the Process/Complex Learning Log as a way to help students document their artistic process and organize the many parts of the unit. Finally, the requirement to create a written artist's statement and the incorporation of rubric-based self-assessment was my way of helping students connect what they learned with the artwork they produced.

Visual Arts Standards Addressed

SD1   *Communication.* Students recognize and use the visual arts as a form of communication.

SD2   *Perception.* Students know and apply elements of art, principles of design, and sensory and expressive features of visual arts.

SD3   *Application.* Students know and apply visual arts materials, tools, techniques, and processes.

SD4   *Heritage.* Students relate the visual arts to various historical and cultural traditions.

SD5   *Aesthetics.* Students analyze and evaluate the characteristics, merits, and meaning of works of art.

Unit Concepts and Generalizations

Ceramic Sculptural Form, Individual Design, Construction Techniques, Surface Treatment, Firing Methods, Hanging Methods, Reflection

GEN1   Artists develop unique design interpretations in their artwork.

GEN2   Artwork is influenced by historical, cultural, and personal contexts.

GEN3   Artists are problem solvers and find solutions through creative thinking that incorporates analysis and synthesis skills.

GEN4   Artists develop skills in media, tools, techniques, processes, and specialized equipment.

GEN5   Artists reflect on their artwork by using relevant information from their own experience and point of view.

Unit Objectives

As a result of this unit, the students will *know*
- How to apply their creativity to solve problems.
- How artists choose themes and methods to communicate their message.
- How to use a process/complex instruction log to plan and manage the creation of a piece of art.
- The art vocabulary and terms used throughout the unit.

As a result of this unit, the students will *understand that*
- There is a relationship between the idea/theme behind a work of art and the techniques and materials used to create it.
- The artist's statement is a bridge between artist and audience and a way to reflect on the artist's work.

As a result of this unit, the students will *be able to*
- Design a solution to a 3–D sculpture challenge and implement it.
- Use hand-built or wheel-thrown skills to create a piece of 3–D sculpture.
- Apply a surface treatment to a sculpture using glaze and firing techniques.
- Design a successful hanging method for a 3–D sculpture.
- Write an artist's statement about a finished piece of artwork.

Instructional Strategies Used

- Coaching
- Creative Problem-Solving Process Chart
- Independent research
- Learning centers/stations
- Pre-assessment
- SCAMPER
- Think–Pair–Share

- Complex Instruction
- Double-entry journaling
- Individualized instruction
- Metacognition
- Rubric-based assessment
- Self-assessment
- Tiered assignments

Sample Supporting Materials Provided

Sample #	Title	Page
4.1	Project Overview	155
4.2	Sketchbook/Journal Model Page	156
4.3	Process/Complex Learning Log Template	157
4.4	Pre-assessment	160
4.5	Process Chart for Creative Problem Solving	161
4.6	SCAMPER Creative Thinking Checklist	162
4.7	Sculpture Plan Example	163
4.8	Project Rubric	164
4.9	Guidelines for Writing an Artist's Statement	168
4.10	Tiered Graphic Organizer for Writing an Artist's Statement	170

Unit Overview

LESSON	WHOLE-CLASS COMPONENTS	DIFFERENTIATED COMPONENTS
LESSON 1 **Unit Introduction** *2 blocks*	Discussion introducing the unit and the unit concepts *20 minutes*	
	Discussion of the sketchbook/journal *15 minutes*	
	Introduction to the process/complex learning log *15 minutes*	
		Presentation and discussion of artists and cultural sculpture examples *30–45 minutes*

LESSON	WHOLE-CLASS COMPONENTS	DIFFERENTIATED COMPONENTS
		Pre-assessment of 3–D art skills and learning style *15 minutes*
	Think–Pair–Share discussion of the pre-assessment *15 minutes*	
	Sketchbook self-assessment and preliminary notes *15 minutes*	
LESSON 2 **Theme Research and Problem Solving for Construction and Hanging** *1 block*	Discussion of design concepts and resources *15 minutes*	
	Problem-solving skills activity #1 *20 minutes*	
	Problem-solving skills activity #2 *15 minutes*	
	Think–Pair–Share on design solutions *25 minutes*	
		Sculpture plan development and creation based on interest, readiness, and learning style *ongoing, time varies*
LESSON 3 **Skill Building in New Techniques and Materials** *3 blocks*	Safety overview *15 minutes*	
		Individual sculpture plan presentation and approval conferences *ongoing, time varies*
	Review of the process/complex learning log *10 minutes*	
	Learning center #1: Paper clay *10 minutes*	Individual studio time *ongoing*
		Mini-model creation *1 block*
	Learning center #2: Firing methods *25 minutes*	

LESSON	WHOLE-CLASS COMPONENTS	DIFFERENTIATED COMPONENTS
	Think–Pair–Share on appropriate methods and techniques *30 minutes*	
LESSON 4 **Studio Time** *14 blocks*	 Informal assessment with the instructor and peers *ongoing, time varies* Artist's statement exercises *time varies*	Rubric discussion and customization differentiated by readiness and interest *30 minutes initially, then ongoing* Individual studio work *ongoing* Individual learning log check-ups/assessment *ongoing, time varies* Problem-solving demonstrations in flexible groups *ongoing, time varies*
LESSON 5 **Reflection, Assessment, and Critique** *3 blocks*	Introduction to writing an artist's statement *30–45 minutes* Critique protocol review *10 minutes* Critique sessions *1 block*	 Artist's statement development and approval differentiated by writing readiness *45 minutes* Formal rubric assessment differentiated by readiness and interest *time varies*

Unit Description and Teacher Commentary

LESSON 1	Unit Introduction	(2 blocks)
	Concept: Individual Design	
	GEN1–2; SD1, SD4	

LESSON SEQUENCE AND DESCRIPTION	TEACHER COMMENTARY
Discussion introducing the unit and the unit concepts. Distribute the **Project Overview** (see Sample 4.1, page 155). Begin with a group discussion about ceramic sculpture. Points to investigate include the following: • Who has had experience creating ceramic sculpture? What challenges did you face? Were the challenges related to the media or the technique? • What challenges will hanging ceramic sculpture bring? Brainstorm some design ideas that might work: mobiles, figurative representations, masks, vases, light fixtures, small altars, containers, and so on. • How can an artist make a personal statement with a sculpture?	The purpose of this handout was to give students a "big picture" view of the project and help them understand the challenge being presented. This beginning discussion was intended to generate interest and motivate students to solve a presented design problem. I wanted students to think about the many ways that 3–D ceramic pieces could be designed to hang. The first step was to investigate a personal theme that might be the basis for the sculpture.
Discussion of the sketchbook/journal. Explain to students that throughout this unit, they will keep a sketchbook—a standard tool of a professional artist. In their sketchbooks, they will take notes and do quick sketches as a way to store ideas and images that they can revisit when designing and creating their sculpture. Distribute and discuss the **Sketchbook/Journal Model Page** (see Sample 4.2, page 156).	The use of the sketchbook— essentially a reflective journal with a two-column structure—is a way to help students solve problems and create, store, and record their learning. ✷Sketchbook entries are differentiated by process based on learning style.
Introduction to the process/complex learning log. Next, introduce another tool students will be using throughout the unit as a way to track their progress and their deadlines. Distribute the **Process/Complex Learning Log Template** (see Sample 4.3, pages 157–159) and explain the following: • Like a grade book, the learning log is a way of keeping a weekly check on each student's work. • Each student will paste a copy of the learning log in his or her sketchbook and use it to check off what needs to be done during each lesson. • Each week the instructor will go around to each student while they are working and will review his or her log to monitor progress.	✷Learning logs are an excellent way for students to keep track of complicated, individual projects that include multiple tasks. Learning logs show students exactly what they have done, what they may have missed, and what they need to do in future lessons. As a tool for differentiation, it supports flexible use of time, provides ongoing guidance for all students, and allows advanced students greater independence because they can work through the steps at their own accelerated pace.

LESSON SEQUENCE AND DESCRIPTION	TEACHER COMMENTARY
Presentation and discussion of artists and cultural sculpture examples. Give students access to a collection of slides, books, and videos that show 3–D sculptures that hang or that illustrate relevant techniques. Make sure a few physical examples are available as well. Ask students to look for information and design forms that relate to subject or theme, 3–D forms, materials and techniques, and designs for hanging. Possible resources include the following:	Providing a variety of resources allowed me to vary the ways in which students encountered research resources. I wanted to make sure there was opportunity for visual, auditory, and kinesthetic learning and that I would be able to build students' interest in the project.
<ul><li>Videos: *Raku Ceramics* by Jim Romberry, *Hand Build Clay Sculpture* by Christine La Page, and *Basic Throwing Skills* by Robert Piepenburg (technique); and *Potters of Oaxaca* (culture).</li><li>Slides: Images of the works of Henry Moore, Alexander Calder, George Segal, Paul Soldn, Hans Bellmar, Barbara Cichocka, and John Ahearn.</li><li>Books and art reproductions: *Sculpting Clay* by Leon Nigrosh, *Making Ceramic Sculpture* by Raul Acero, and *The Craft and Art of Clay* by Susan Peterson and Jan Peterson.</li><li>Web sites: witcombe.sbc.edu/ARTLinks.html, claystation.com, and studiopotter.org.</li></ul>	Exploring the ways that other artists and cultures have used ceramics in a sculptural manner helps expose students to design components that might influence their own work.
Pre-assessment of 3–D art skills and learning style. Distribute and explain the **Pre-assessment** (see Sample 4.4, page 160). Students will write short responses to questions about how they like to work and their familiarity with the materials and the techniques that will be used in this unit.	I decided to create a pre-assessment to determine both students' existing skills and their learning styles. The information from the pre-assessment helps me choose appropriate instructional strategies and indicates which students might need scaffolding techniques and other accommodations throughout the unit.
Think–Pair–Share discussion of the pre-assessment. After students have finished the pre-assessment, have them find a partner with whom they will share their responses and determine their knowledge and new learning.	The Think–Pair–Share format enhances the thinking and learning process of each individual student.
Sketchbook self-assessment and preliminary notes. Ask students to use an outline form in their sketchbook to list skills and knowledge they have and feel confident they can use in this assignment.	When I taught this unit, the pre-assessment results told me that the majority of my students had not had any experience with the firing methods used in this unit. However, I learned from this component that the majority did have some idea of how they would make a ceramic piece hang.

LESSON SEQUENCE AND DESCRIPTION	TEACHER COMMENTARY
Students should also list what kinds of new learning they will need to meet the challenges in this unit. Ask them to write a short statement summing up the notes they took on a theme or subject based on what they encountered exploring the slides, books, and videos. Stress that they should highlight ideas they might want to consider for their own sculpture.	

LESSON 2　　　**Theme Research and Problem Solving**　　　*(1 block)*
for Construction and Hanging
Concepts: Individual Design, Construction Techniques
GEN1–4; SD1–3

LESSON SEQUENCE AND DESCRIPTION	TEACHER COMMENTARY
Discussion of design concepts and resources. Lead a class discussion on the main concepts covered in the pre-assessment and various example artworks they were exposed to in the previous lesson. Topics to explore include the following: • How objects hang • What type of objects hang • Figural possibilities • Thrown possibilities • Abstract objects • Mobiles • Wall sculptures • Suspended sculptures • Ceiling sculptures	The videos, slides, books, and physical ceramic pieces shown in class gave students a common set of references. Throughout the unit, I noticed they referred to these artists and hanging pieces when they were discussing and explaining their own art-form ideas. Incorporating a discussion of the various aspects of a hanging sculptural form was a way to help students begin to visualize their own interpretation of the project, including what problems they might need to solve.
Display physical, ceramic examples of hanging pieces and the various hooks, chains, nails, rope, and wires that will be available for students to use as hanging apparatuses.	I used my own sculpted wall forms here, and so was able to have the students examine a physical example of a ceramic hanging form unique to my interpretation.
Point out the interrelation of the sculptures' forms and their hanging methods. Encourage students to take notes, sketch forms, and brainstorm ideas for their own sculptures in their sketchbooks.	The idea was to get students to think about this early so that they would create a form with its hanging method in mind.

LESSON SEQUENCE AND DESCRIPTION	TEACHER COMMENTARY
Problem-solving skills activity #1. Hand out copies of the **Process Chart for Creative Problem Solving** (see Sample 4.5, page 161), which outlines a series of steps in the problem-solving process and provides associated questions to move the process along. Using an overhead transparency of the chart, explain to students that they will use their copy of the chart as an ongoing guide to help them think about the design of their sculpture and solutions for hanging. Review the various components of the chart and ask students to offer possible solutions.	My goal here was to encourage students to apply their creativity to solving the design challenge.
Then, ask students to work independently to begin applying the chart to their own design challenge.	While students worked, I moved around the classroom, checking for understanding and reteaching as necessary.
Problem-solving skills activity #2. Distribute copies of the **SCAMPER Creative Thinking Checklist** (see Sample 4.6, page 162) and explain that the class will be exploring ways to alter a ceramic piece so that it is more complex and interesting. Display a thrown pot and go through each step of the SCAMPER process, soliciting ideas from students.	SCAMPER (see Glossary, page 356) is a tool to help develop creative thinking skills. Its use here enabled students to see the methods of altering 3–D designs and provided moments of excitement and great interest.
Think–Pair–Share on design solutions. Having thought over solutions to their design challenge as part of the two problem-solving skill activities, students self-select into pairs to discuss solutions they are considering.	
Sculpture plan development and creation based on interest, readiness, and learning style. Tell students that during the next lesson, which will consist of three days, they must decide on their sculpture idea and submit a formal sculpture plan for the instructor's approval. If desired, provide students with a **Sculpture Plan Example** (see Sample 4.7, page 163).	Requiring students to submit formal sculpture plans was both a way to ensure I'd have a forum for offering advice and suggestions and a way to help students clarify their understanding of the project.
Tell students they may sketch their idea with approximate measurements (as in the plan example), write about it, or create a small-scale model.	I offered a choice of plan formats to appeal to varied learning profiles.
Let students know that during the next lesson, they will explore the various materials and techniques available to them, which will help to inform their final design decisions.	

LESSON SEQUENCE AND DESCRIPTION	TEACHER COMMENTARY
This process replicates how artists work: 1. They develop a unique design that might be influenced by other images. 2. They use problem-solving skills to get there. 3. They evaluate and analyze the process as it is happening.	

LESSON 3   **Skill Building in New Techniques and Materials**   *(3 blocks)*
Concepts: Construction Techniques, Surface Treatment,
Firing Methods, Hanging Methods
GEN3–4; SD2–3, SD5

LESSON SEQUENCE AND DESCRIPTION	TEACHER COMMENTARY
Note: This lesson uses learning centers to build students' skills with the various materials, construction techniques, and firing methods they will use to create their artwork.	I used the pre-assessment responses to determine which students needed to work on which skills. Each student's learning log included spaces to check off learning center work with the type of clay, technique, and firing methods (see Sample 4.3).
Safety overview. Begin this lesson by discussing safety expectations for the ceramic studio. Administer a safety test that all students must pass before working with the specialized equipment and materials. Next, distribute the standard safety contract required by the district (translated for ESL students or with slightly modified language for students with behavioral issues). Explain to students that both they and their parent or guardian must sign the safety contract before they can begin their studio work. Keep these documents on file as proof of shared agreement on student safety responsibilities while in class.	Both safety tests and contracts are required in my school district, and all art teachers and students must practice and enforce the safety contract measures. Agreements like this are necessary to keep things running smoothly and safely in environments where students are working independently.
Individual sculpture plan presentation and approval conferences. During these one-on-one conferences, held throughout Lesson 3, students formally present their sculpture plan. Discuss ideas and plans, and review decisions related to materials and techniques.	As noted, having a "design approval" requirement was a way to ensure I met individually with all students to review their plans. But it was also a way to get students started on their sculptures right away. I didn't want them to sit in class for days just thinking about possible designs.

LESSON SEQUENCE AND DESCRIPTION	TEACHER COMMENTARY
Review of the process/complex learning log. Remind students that they should be using their learning log to stay on top of tasks and due dates and should make progress toward each of the goals in every lesson.	
Individual studio time/Learning center #1: Paper clay. Students who do not need to practice specific techniques begin work on their sculptures, using the learning log as a guide. The others participate in the first materials-and-process demonstration in this lesson. Remind students to use their sketchbooks to take notes during each learning center, being sure to record information about both the material and the process. For the paper clay demo: • Demonstrate the material's pliability, stability, and easy maneuvering. • Explain that it is well-suited for hanging pieces because it fires to a light weight. • Note that it stays pliable for longer amounts of time than other clays do. • Explain and display the process of hand building with paper clay and throwing it on a wheel. • Prompt students to think about whether they want to use paper clay as the media for their sculpture.	I used pre-assessment results to determine which students needed to learn and practice new skills and methods. During the demos, what was most successful was encouraging the students to take notes in various formats to address their various learning styles by sketching parts of the demo, taking traditional lecture notes, drawing annotated diagrams.
Mini-model creation. As part of skill development in ceramic clay or paper clay, students create a maquette—or small model—of their anticipated sculpture. Stress to students the advantage of executing a design plan on a small scale before starting on the final sculpture. During the planning and construction process, consult with students on the design parameters and skill level for the techniques they are using.	Model creation was required—a part of students' grades that they had to check off in the learning log. The material used (ceramic clay or paper clay or both) was the students' choice, based on interest. I encouraged them to take on new challenges in choices and materials. Here, I focused on encouraging students to take risks and challenge themselves. It was about pushing for excellence.
Learning center #2: Firing methods. Due to safety issues and the continued development of skills, all students participate in this demonstration, which gives a variety of firing choices.	Students with experience and high skill knowledge assisted with the demonstration.

LESSON SEQUENCE AND DESCRIPTION	TEACHER COMMENTARY
For the firing methods demo: • Lecture and demonstrate each firing choice the students have. • Explain how each firing method could complement their final sculpture differently and how to go about choosing the right one for their personal piece. • Display various examples of Sagger firing and Raku firing. • Cover the chemistry of each type of firing, the chemical reactions, kiln temperature, and so on. • Explain to students that they may also combine firing methods or opt for a cold finish: a color treatment technique such as stain, acrylic paint, ink, and so on.	This demonstration component allows student to learn about vital firing processes, which involve an understanding of chemical reactions in glazes and the relationship to low- versus high-fire temperatures in kilns. ✸I reminded students to take notes in their sketchbooks, using whatever note-taking format suited them best.
Think–Pair–Share on appropriate methods and techniques. Have students discuss their design choices, using their sculpture plans and mini-models. Divide students into pairs based on their choice of similar firing techniques and finishes.	

LESSON 4

Studio Time   *(14 blocks)*

Concepts: Ceramic Sculptural Form, Individual Design, Construction Techniques, Surface Treatment, Firing Methods, Hanging Methods
GEN3–5; SD2–3

LESSON SEQUENCE AND DESCRIPTION	TEACHER COMMENTARY
✸**Rubric discussion and customization differentiated by readiness and interest.** Begin this lesson by distributing the **Project Rubric** (see Sample 4.8, page 164). Review the criteria in the rubric pertaining to class participation and unit standards, and then tell students they will need to create additional individual criteria pertaining to their personal goals for their sculpture. Their assignment is to make a rough draft of their rubric using the template provided. After the instructor has reviewed and approved the draft, they will create a final version. Stress to students that they should use their rubric to guide their studio work and should be prepared to self-assess based on the criteria agreed to.	I designed the criteria-based rubric shown in Sample 4.8 to address the unit's main objectives and standards. Having students add their own personal criteria allowed them to have a major say in the way in which their artwork would be assessed. It empowered them to challenge their own learning and skills. Finally, it reflected the way in which artists really work.

LESSON SEQUENCE AND DESCRIPTION	TEACHER COMMENTARY
Individual studio work. Lesson 4 is largely devoted to students' studio work time. Every student will need to devote the duration of Lesson 4 to sculpting, shaping, refining, and firing their project in clay. Encourage students to start their final glaze firing as soon as they finish their individual sculptural forms. Students will reach this stage at varying speeds and paces, depending on the complexity and size of their sculpture.	It was in these class blocks that I implemented my essential art skills and knowledge and applied my knowledge of differentiation to address the needs of an entire class of individual learners. I had to be able to coach, critique, track progress, and make suggestions on a daily basis.
Individual learning log check-ups/assessment. As students work, monitor their progress by examining their learning logs at least once a week. Four and a half weeks into this unit, conduct a formative assessment by giving each student a letter-grade based on progress documented in his or her learning log, time spent on task, and conversations during one-on-one mini-conferences.	During this section of the project, the learning log serves a vital purpose: tracking every student's progress and aiding in creative problem solving.
Informal assessment with the instructor and peers. Studio work time is the most important aspect of an art class. It is during this time that creative and complex thinking processes come into play as students work to develop successful skills in the materials, techniques and processes. Encourage and prompt students to conduct periodic, informal, self-assessments and to hold informal Think–Pair–Shares to get peer assessments of their work in progress.	These informal assessments were highly effective solutions for creative problem solving. Establishing this type of conversation among the students, their artwork, and me made for an amazing studio atmosphere.
Problem-solving demonstrations in flexible groups. As part of studio time, it is important to illustrate some of the ways that artists solve problems they encounter while producing the artwork. Recurring problem-solving demos might include the following: • Using a student's piece that broke during firing to demonstrate epoxy glues or using a piece that broke during the wet-clay phase to demonstrate clay reattachment techniques. • Sharing a student's significant technique, breakthrough, glaze results, or solution. • Pointing out common problems observed during informal check-ins.	I conducted these sessions as a whole class or in small groups depending on the particular problem and solution and what else was going on during studio time. I saw all of these occurrences as excellent opportunities for learning and encouraged my students to do the same.

LESSON SEQUENCE AND DESCRIPTION	TEACHER COMMENTARY
Artist's statement exercises. On the last day of this lesson—at which time all students' sculptures will be complete—distribute the **Guidelines for Writing an Artist's Statement** (see Sample 4.9, page 168). This handout includes an example of an artist's statement and five preparatory exercises for students to complete in their sketchbooks.	This was my way of getting students started on developing the artist's statements for their sculptures. These exercises are not graded individually, but are part of the learning log requirements.

LESSON 5   **Reflection, Assessment, and Critique**   *(3 blocks)*

Concept: Reflection

GEN5; SD5

LESSON SEQUENCE AND DESCRIPTION	TEACHER COMMENTARY
Introduction to writing an artist's statement. As a whole class, review and discuss the artist's statement exercises from Lesson 4. Explain that an artist's statement is a medium for reflection, focus, and closing in on what has been created. It allows an artist to express a personal perspective on a piece's concept and function.	The format for an artist's statement should be open enough to address each student's individual writing abilities and personal expressions.
Artist's statement development and approval differentiated by writing readiness. Distribute the **Tiered Graphic Organizer for Writing an Artist's Statement** (see Sample 4.10, page 170). Explain to students that they'll be using their graphic organizer and the earlier artist's statement exercises to guide them through the process of writing an artist's statement for their sculptures.	Artist's statements can be difficult to write regardless of the artist's age or expertise. Incorporating tools like graphic organizers and writing exercises was vital for success.
Level 1 Graphic Organizer This organizer is highly structured, with very specific prompts to aid students who struggle with writing. *Level 2 Graphic Organizer* This version is less regimented and allows more freedom for students who are proficient writers. If a student is particularly skilled at writing, the artist's statement can be as involved and detailed as he or she chooses to make it.	As I looked over the writing exercises in the students' sketchbooks, I assessed their writing readiness and decided that a tiered organizer was the best way to assist students of varying skill levels.
Encourage English language learners to write the artist's statement in their native language and then ask a teacher, parent, or another student to help translate it into English.	This connected students to an authentic task in their language learning.

LESSON SEQUENCE AND DESCRIPTION	TEACHER COMMENTARY
Tell students that after they create a rough draft (pasted in their sketchbooks), they will submit it for assessment and approval. Next, they will Think–Pair–Share on their artist's statements, make any additional revisions, and complete a final version with correct grammar and punctuation.	Writing an artist's statement prompted students to reflect on their learning and make a bridge of understanding between their artwork and their audience. When grading these artist's statements, I focused on content and format over grammar and punctuation.
Formal rubric assessment differentiated by readiness and interest. Students use their individualized rubrics to examine their sculptures and then self-assess. Using the criteria and requirements they created on their rubrics, they write a final grade for themselves. Then each student turns in a copy of the filled-in rubric for instructor evaluation.	The rubric's purpose is to guide self-assessment by helping the students focus on how well they met their criteria.
Critique protocol review. Prior to students' formal presentation of their sculpture, explain the critique format: • Students will talk about their sculpture and its hanging qualities, using their artist's statement and appropriate art vocabulary and concepts. • The entire class will be expected to question, compliment, or offer comments on their fellow students' artwork, using appropriate art vocabulary and concepts.	Because a sculpture project is a visual form of communication, I knew a visual assessment and discussion was necessary. What's more, any studio art class students take in college and graduate school will use a critique format like this one.
Critique sessions. Students present their sculptures, share their artist's statements, and take questions from the instructor and their classmates. The formal summative assessment for this unit is a written sheet returned to the student. The final grade is based on every factor of the sculpture project, including the student's on-task/class participation, sketchbook assignments, design/sculpture plan, mini-model, learning log, individualized project rubric, artist's statement, and class critique.	From an instructor's point of view, the critique is an excellent way to compare student work, assess each student, and provide verbal accolades to every student who has completed such an involved assignment.

Teacher Reflection on the Unit

As a student teacher, I found that designing and presenting this unit was an extraordinary experience. On the basis of its success, I have since modeled all of my lesson plans around the differentiated practices I used here.

There were so many positives. First, the open-ended design meant students could expand upon the basic premise—create a hanging piece of ceramic sculpture—in any way they chose to. Each student communicated and interpreted the project in a unique manner, and they thrived on each other's variations in form and concept. However, using uniform preparation exercises, like the graphic organizers, really enhanced students' ability to communicate their concepts. Finally, all the pre-assessments were amazing tools for me. Pre-assessment is not especially common in art classes, but I discovered in this unit just how important it is. Knowing what skills and knowledge students were beginning with enabled me to plan how I could reach every student instead of noticing much too late that I had strugglers.

Looking back on this unit, I am flooded with the imagery of all the stunning sculptures that developed. This unit allowed for creativity, but also guided, assessed, and stretched this concept for my class and me.

Tracy Hamm completed her student teaching at Jefferson County Schools in Denver, Colorado. She can be reached at thamm@jeffco.k12.co.us.

Suzi Juarez is the art curriculum coordinator for Jefferson County Schools. She can be reached at sjuarez@jeffco.k12.co.u. Miki Reddy is a former teacher of the gifted and a veteran art teacher. She can be reached at kmmreddy@earthlink.net. Cheryl Franklin-Rohr is the gifted education secondary resource consultant for Jefferson County Schools. She can be reached at cfrohr@ jeffco.k12.co.us.

SAMPLE 4.1—Project Overview

"It Has to Hang"

Date Due _____

In this unit, you will design and create a ceramic sculptural piece that must hang instead of sit flat on a surface or the ground.

Your piece may be *thrown or hand built,* but must either *hang from the ceiling* or *attach to the wall.* It cannot be a piece made to stand on a flat surface. You will choose among *various firing methods* and *surface treatments* to finish your pieces, and then add the necessary materials to make your piece hang.

You will also record ideas from class, research ideas, create a sketch and a model, learn skills you'll need to complete the artwork, develop an instructional rubric, and reflect on your work through critiques and a written artist's statement.

What will you create? Here are some object ideas:

plant hanger	mobile	light switch
key holder	mask	plaster mold (face, body parts)
altar piece	light fixture	figural sculpture (bust, face, etc.)
gargoyle	door knocker	object sculpture (car, vase, etc.)

How will you get the piece to hang? Here are some hanging ideas:
• metal hooks that go into a hole in the back of the piece
• epoxied wire loops on the back of the piece that hang on a nail in the wall
• rope or wire that holds the piece from the ceiling
• mount the piece to a flat object (using epoxy, rope, wire, etc.) and hang like a painting

Instructional and Assessment Components
1. Your **sketchbook/journal** will be used for recording the design process, sketching ideas, note-taking, research references, reflections, critiques, your artist's statement, and assessments
2. You will keep a **process/complex learning log** to track the learning process and the completion dates of the steps leading to the final artwork. This will be a collaborative effort between student and instructor.
3. Your **grade** will be determined by the design process recorded in the sketchbook, keeping a process/complex learning log, critiques, artist's statement, and an instructional rubric.
4. You must pass a **safety test** on your responsibility to maintain a safe and clean art studio environment.

SAMPLE 4.2—Sketchbook/Journal Model Page

Two-Column Note-Taking for the Sketchbook/Journal (S/J)

- Include the title or date for lecture, demonstration, or video.
- List main ideas, topics, and key words on the left.
- List information on the right, using words, phrases, or abbreviations when appropriate.
- Indent subtopics under key words or topics.
- Write neatly.
- Include any sketches in the right-hand column to support the words.

This is an example of what the note-taking might look like:

		Name: *Michael S.* Date: *March 7, 2005* Class: *Per. 7*
	Title: *Video on Henri Matisse*	
General Info	1869–1954 French Important innovator of 20th century art	

Modernist	Emphasis on formal innovations
	    Used blocks of color to define form and content
	    Commitment to progress	

Sculpture	Figure work
	    Figures' twisting poses suggest movement
	    Keep it simple—refine forms to simple shapes.	

Essential ideas	Favorite technique: clay modeling "I have always tried to hide my efforts and wished my works to have the light joyousness of springtime, which never lets anyone suspect the labors it has cost me." "A sculpture must invite us to hold it like an object."	

SAMPLE 4.3—Process/Complex Learning Log Template

Problem/Project: Design and create a ceramic or paper clay sculptural piece that must hang.

Lessons	Goals	Progress	Next Steps	Completed
Lesson 1 Dates:	Track learning progress and deadlines for unit in process/complex learning log.			
Unit Introduction	Sketchbook/Journal (S/J) used for sketching, note taking, research, and storing samples.			
	Pre-assessment results attached in S/J.			
	Pair-share responses discussion recorded in S/J.			
Lesson 2 Dates:	Begin the process of using the SCAMPER Chart and Creative Problem Solving Chart to create unique ideas for design.			
Theme Research and Problem Solving for Construction and Hanging	Record in S/J ideas from whole class or pair-share brainstorming sessions.			
	Results of research on theme, subject, technique, and methods recorded and sketched in S/J.			
	Final approval for design from instructor.			

SAMPLE 4.3—Process/Complex Learning Log Template—*(continued)*

Problem/Project: Design and create a ceramic or paper clay sculptural piece that must hang.

Lessons	Goals	Progress	Next Steps	Completed
Lesson 3 Dates:	Complete safety test and contract.			
Skill-Building in New Techniques and Materials	Record and sketch in S/J information from each skill-building learning center on clay, building technique, and firing: Ceramic clay Paper clay Hand-built Wheel-thrown Raku Sagger			
	Ongoing consulting with instructor on process of design.			
	Approval from instructor for final construction method for design.			
Lesson 4 Dates:	Record in S/J the discussion and design of instructional rubric that will guide and be the final assessment for the artwork.			
Studio Time	Bisques firing complete.			

SAMPLE 4.3—Process/Complex Learning Log Template—*(continued)*

Problem/Project: Design and create a ceramic or paper clay sculptural piece that must hang.

Lessons	Goals	Progress	Next Steps	Completed
Lesson 4 (cont.)	Glaze firing or surface treatment complete.			
	Record in SJ any informal critique discussion with instructor or peers.			
	Record the five exercises for how to write an artist's statement in SJ.			
Lesson 5 Dates:	Complete the artist's statement graphic organizer.			
	Instructor approval for final artist's statement.			
Reflection, Assessment, and Critique	Formative assessment mini-conference with instructor.			
	Self-assess final artwork using the instructional rubric; return to teacher for assessment.			
	Participate in class critique of artwork and record in SJ.			
	Final display: Hang artwork with artist's statement.			

SAMPLE 4.4—Pre-assessment

Name _____ Period _____ Date _____

Directions: Answer the following questions based on what you know.

1. Do you prefer functional ceramics (like thrown or hand-built bowls and plates) or sculptural ceramics (like human figures, animals, abstract pieces)? Explain your preference.

2. If you had made a bowl (thrown or hand-built), how could you shape it or change it to hang it on the wall?

3. Do you like art assignments that give you straightforward guidelines to work under, or do you prefer an assignment that is more open to your own ideas? Why?

4. What do you know about Raku firing and Sagger/salt firing?

5. What do you know about artist's statements?

6. Describe a product you have made with paper clay.

SAMPLE 4.5—Process Chart for Creative Problem Solving

Problem/Project: Design and create a ceramic or paper clay sculptural piece that must hang.

1. Fact Find Use fluent thinking; many ideas trigger new ones.	What do I already know?	
	How do I find out more? Research, resources (online, books, interviews)	
	What do I need to learn or practice?	
2. Problem Find Use flexible thinking and different kinds of ideas.	How can I look at this problem in different ways? Narrow it down to the specific ideas?	
	Revise: How can I design this piece differently?	
	Illustrate: How could it be hung or attached?	
3. Idea Find Use original thinking—unusual or new ideas.	Look for all possible ideas—new combinations.	
	Practice or try first using small models.	
4. Solution Find Use elaborate thinking; make ideas clear and add the detail.	Explore new ideas—materials or methods. Are they appropriate and feasible?	
	Do I enjoy what I have designed? Does it excite me?	
5. Acceptance Find Evaluate; examine all sides, the pros and cons.	Will this really work? Is it the best idea for the design?	
	What problems do I anticipate in the process? How will they be solved?	

SAMPLE 4.6—SCAMPER Creative Thinking Checklist

S

SUBSTITUTE: What could be used instead of it?

C

COMBINE: What could be added?

A

ADAPT: How can it be adjusted to suit a condition?

M

MODIFY: How can the color, shape, or form be changed?

MAGNIFY: How can it be made larger, stronger, or thicker?

MINIMIZE: How can it be made smaller, lighter, or shorter?

P

PUT TO OTHER USES: What else can it be used for?

E

ELIMINATE: What can be removed or taken away from it?

EXAGGERATE: What about it can be enhanced?

R

REVERSE: How can it be turned around or placed opposite its position?

REARRANGE: How can the pattern, sequence, or layout be changed?

SAMPLE 4.7—Sculpture Plan Example

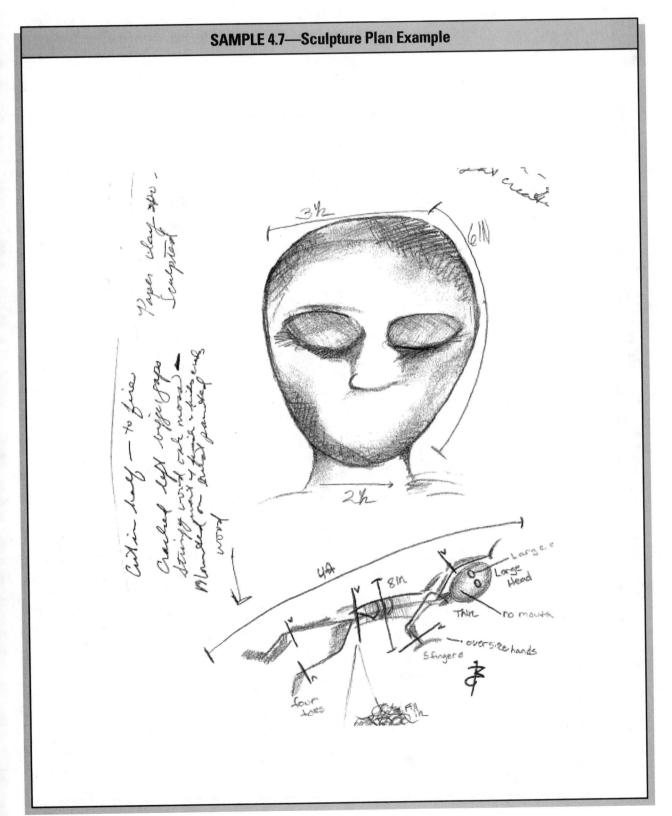

Drawing by Tyler Matson

SAMPLE 4.8—Project Rubric

I. Class participation

Criteria	3—Exceeds	2—Meets	1—Missed/Not Yet	*S	**T
Punctuality	In seat when bell rings.	In seat when bell rings.	Tardy or absent often.		
On-Task Behavior	Self-motivated; focused on work.	Focused, but needs occasional redirection.	Unfocused; easily distracted.		
Cooperation and Respect	Supportive of others; engages in peer teaching; shows mastery of material.	Supportive of others; uses materials appropriately.	Disruptive; rude to teacher and classmates.		
Learning Skills	Capable of working independently.	Follows directions well; requires occasional redirection.	Does not follow directions; requires regular redirection.		
Clean Up and Safety Compliance	Cleans table area and assists others; models and uses safe behavior.	Cleans own table area; is cooperative; demonstrates safe behavior.	Rarely helps clean up; sits and watches; demonstrates unsafe behavior.		
			Total		

*S = Student self-assessment, **T = Teacher assessment

SAMPLE 4.8 Project Rubric—*(continued)*

II. Artwork Evaluation

A. Unit Requirements

Criteria	3—Exceeds	2—Meets	1—Missed/Not Yet	*S	**T
Adherence to Deadlines	Completed by due date.	Completed by due date.	Late.		
Use of Process/ Complex Learning Log	Completed every task in the log.	Some tasks not completed.	Many tasks not completed.		
Use of Sketchbook	Sketchbook has highly developed evidence of design research, including notes and sketches, skill learning, diagrams, reflective writing and is well organized.	Sketchbook shows evidence of an attempt to include quality notes, sketches, and reflective writing, but could be better organized and developed.	Sketchbook has not been used for collecting evidence of learning, many concepts are not present, and there is little organization.		

B. Unit Standards

Communication and Heritage (SD1, SD4)

Criteria	3—Exceeds	2—Meets	1—Missed/Not Yet	*S	**T
Ability to Communicate the Theme and Concept	Theme and concept are evident and understandable.	Not a strong representation of original theme/concept as expressed in the original plan.	No evidence of theme or concept.		

SAMPLE 4.8—Project Rubric—*(continued)*

Perception (SD2)

Criteria	3—Exceeds	2—Meets	1—Missed/Not Yet	*S	**T
Evidence of Research and Planning	The theme/concept shows original and unique aspects.	Theme/concept shows some original ideas, but does not go beyond usual images.	Little evidence of an original theme.		
Design Development	Advanced design elements are evident.	Strong design elements are evident.	Design elements are lacking.		
Plan Execution	The final work resulted in completion of the original plan.	The final work shows some variation from the original design.	The final work does not reflect the original design.		

Application (SD3)

Criteria	3—Exceeds	2—Meets	1—Missed/Not Yet	*S	**T
Techniques and Skill for Ceramic Materials	Advanced work in all aspects of the construction.	Some portions of the construction, firing, and surface techniques were not successful.	Very little evidence of skills developed.		
Solution to Hanging the Work	Hanging solution is visually balanced and pleasing to the eye.	The work hangs, but the hanging solution does not complement the work.	Work was not able to hang.		
Level of Craft	Work shows excellent use of ceramic media and techniques.	Work shows good use of media and techniques, but lacks some finishing.	Work shows evidence of poor use of media and techniques, below the level of course expectations.		

SAMPLE 4.8—Project Rubric—*(continued)*

Aesthetics (SD5)

Criteria	3—Exceeds	2—Meets	1—Missed/Not Yet	*S	**T
Critique Participation (Informal and Formal)	Consistently offers highly developed comments in informal (verbal) and formal (written) critiques.	Shows average participation in informal critiques; higher-level art vocabulary was not evident in formal critiques.	Shows below-average participation in informal critiques; formal critiques showed a lack of art vocabulary or included trite responses.		
Written Artist's Statement	Artist's statement reflects the high level skills developed through the exercises and from the graphic organizer.	Developed a good artist's statement that shows evidence of some learning gained through the five exercises and graphic organizers.	Artist's statement was incomplete and offered little personal information.		

Personal Criteria

Criteria	3—Exceeds	2—Meets	1—Missed/Not Yet	*S	**T

Grade scale for Artwork Evaluation: A total of 42 points are possible (36 points as set, plus up to 6 points related to student's personal criteria).

A = 38–42   B = 34–37   C = 30–33   D = 26–29   F = 25 and below

---

SAMPLE 4.9—Guidelines for Writing an Artist's Statement

What is an artist's statement? It's about your work and your thoughts about your work. It's about words, which are different than wedging clay, painting with a brush, or drawing with charcoal; these are the world of senses, while words are the landmarks in our mind.

Why bother with a statement? It builds a compelling bridge between you and your audience and becomes a way to reflect on your work.

How are learning to paint, draw, or shape clay and learning to write an artist's statement the same? Both have to be learned and practiced, and both can be scrapped and started over.

Here is an example of an artist's statement.

Night Creature
by Tyler Matson

Inspired by characters and fantastic beings from popular culture, I chose to sculpt a ceramic Night Creature. Taking on an almost lizard/humanoid form, Night Creature definitely seems surreal.

Because I had never done a life form, I wanted to really push the figure and make it large-scale. The sculpture form was made to appear as if it were scaling a wall or ceiling, increasing its surreal effect. As a creature of the night, the piece was designed with large eyes and no mouth. It is a silent animal.

Night Creature was sculpted in one piece. Due to it being so large, I had to adapt my form in order to fire it. I had to cut it in half to fit it into the kiln. I cut it in such a way that the divisions would look like the natural way a creature would be crawling and climbing.

I chose to use an experimental slip coating that was fired in the Raku kiln. I envisioned a high-contrast, smoky black-and-white finish. The firing was successful and the surface treatment made the Night Creature look out of this world. However, the firing was high stress and cracked the piece in many places. I problem solved and decided a way to use the cracks as part of the piece: I mounted it on a rust-colored board and put "stringy" oak wood moss in the cracks. This firing problem and my solution not only hid the cracks, it enhanced the form immensely.

The Process

Step 1: The Warm Up
- Work in your sketchbook.
- Set a timer for 3 minutes or watch the clock.
- Then, without thinking about spelling, grammar, or punctuation, quickly write about the work you've done. Imagine that it's a note to a friend.
- Stop. Read what you wrote, but do not erase, edit, or do anything to change it. What is important is *that you wrote,* not *what you wrote.*

SAMPLE 4.9—Guidelines for Writing an Artist's Statement—*(continued)*

Step 2: Silence Your Inner Critic
- These exercises prompt you to reflect on your work and make a personal revelation about it. Remember, the goal of an artist's statement is to create a bridge between you and your viewing audience.

Complete the following exercises in your sketchbook. Take no more than 3 minutes for each exercise.

Exercise 1
Your art piece starts talking to you. Write down everything it says, no matter how absurd, and be free, truthful, or funny.

Exercise 2
Imagine that a friend you have not seen in a long time wants to know about your work. The words should spill out—so much to write, so little time.

Exercise 3
Imagine your piece of work comes alive and can move around and interact with the world. What does it do? Think about the adventure, the magic that could happen.

Exercise 4
Write personal comments on the technical aspects of your work. What were you thinking as you created the ceramic piece, painting, or drawing? Reflect on the way the media or tools worked, your mistakes, if and how you started over, or how you solved a problem or challenge you encountered.

Exercise 5
Do a "pair-share" with a classmate.
Talk together about what you've done to create your piece and why you have done it. As your partner is talking, take notes to record your conversations. Sometimes the perfect words come from talking, not from writing.

An artist's statement can easily take shape while executing the art piece. As you work, take notes on the learning process: the problems you encounter and the solutions you come up with; the choices you make and how and why you make them. Writing about your work will become easier and you will be able to communicate its uniqueness. GOOD LUCK.

SAMPLE 4.10—Tiered Graphic Organizer for Writing an Artist's Statement

Level 1 Graphic Organizer

Directions. Each box contains a question or statement to answer that will help you to write your artist's statement. Use the word prompts to guide your answers.

What influenced your design?

Artists:
Periods of art:
Cultures:
Functional/nonfunctional considerations:
Popular culture:
Other:

Describe your sculpture.

Elements of its design:
Principles of design followed:
Adjectives:
Subject:

What processes did you use to create your sculpture?

Materials:
Techniques:
Skills:
Tools/equipment:
What was hard?
What was easy?

What did you want your sculpture to communicate to viewers?

Is there a story?

Emotion:
Mood:
Commentary on Social Issues:

Do you feel your sculpture is successful?

Subject:
Design:
Materials:
What it communicates:

Develop a main idea sentence for your artist statement.

It should be the main goal or concept behind your sculpture. Use this space to start your artist's statement, and then elaborate using ideas from above.

SAMPLE 4.10—Tiered Graphic Organizer for Writing an Artist's Statement—(continued)

Level 2 Graphic Organizer

Directions: Each box contains a question or statement to answer. Use the answers to help write your artist's statement.

What influenced your design?

Think about artists, periods of art, cultures, functional/nonfunctional, popular culture, and so on.

Describe your sculpture.

Talk about the elements and principles of design and the subject. Use adjectives.

What processes did you use to create your sculpture?

Cite materials, techniques, skills, tools and equipment, and methods of overcoming difficulties.

What did you want your sculpture to communicate to viewers?

Consider emotion, mood, and aspects of social commentary.

Do you feel your sculpture is successful?

Support your opinion with ideas from above.

Develop a main idea sentence for your artist statement.

It should be the main goal or concept behind your sculpture. Use this space to start your artist statement, and then elaborate using ideas from above.

5

The Eyes of Experience

An English Unit on Perspective and Identity

Unit Developers: Cynthia Kelley and Kay Brimijoin

Introduction

This three- to four-week unit explores how identity is shaped by life experiences. As students study selected poetry, art, music, and film representing a variety of perspectives across the World War I and World War II eras, they develop an "eye" for the elements that contribute to personal and group identity. They wrestle with issues of self, patriotism, justice, honor, and conflict from an individual and societal point of view and go on to refine their own perspectives on these issues through critical, reflective writing. Ultimately, students examine the notion of how individuals and their unique experiences are memorialized and create a culminating product: a memorial to be housed in a Web-based "Virtual Memorial Museum."

The beginning of the unit spotlights the relationship between interpretation and perspective and how this shapes people's views of themselves and their culture. Through examining poetry of World War I, students consider the implications of being a soldier in both literal and symbolic terms. Students investigate ways to honor someone who has died for a cause and begin research on their culminating products by visiting a memorial museum. Next, students develop definitions of patriotism and contrast them with a variety of viewpoints from both World War I and II poets and the modern era. After considering an unusual account of the shooting at Columbine and a friendly fire incident from World War II, students construct explicit and implicit arguments about the justifiability of war. Excerpts from literature and music of the Nazi era help students discover how different perspectives can shape the assumptions that underlie arguments. They explore the relationship between propaganda and perspective and examine the unique experiences and contributions that women, African Americans, and Native Americans made to the World War II effort. These explorations lead students to reflect on their own self-concepts within their current cultural landscape. At the end of the unit, students take a field trip to a simulated World War II canteen, where they experience how culture responds to and is shaped by war. Finally, students present the products they have created for the Virtual Memorial Museum, and the Web site is posted for the school community to visit.

Throughout the unit, students reflect on their understandings of identity and perspective by responding to journal prompts aligned with unit concepts. This journaling is done electronically: Students send their entries to a course Web site, where responses can be shared and highlighted by the teacher in class. The journal prompts are designed to bring clarity to students' thinking about the key concepts of the unit and to tease out their own unique perspectives on these issues. This juxtaposition of individual views and understandings of identity within a group reiterates the purpose of the unit.

This unit is designed for an advanced high school English class with a range of student knowledge, understanding, and skills. It also works well as a collaborative effort between English and history teachers. There are many opportunities for individual conferencing, mini-lessons, and small-group work, all of which can provide scaffolding for students struggling with language, critical thinking, or writing. Assessment is ongoing, varied, and includes multiple self-assessments. Rubrics are provided to encourage students to set and meet personal learning goals.

Teacher Reflections on Designing the Unit

Our school division's curriculum, aligned with state standards, outlines many standards which may be addressed for this literary genre and era. With these standards in mind, we designed this unit to help students formulate and refine their conceptions of personal identity as they progress toward a different academic and social environment in college or in the workplace. Around this time, students begin to realize that they are approaching the end of their high school education, and as they mature, they encounter natural contradictions in archetypal concepts such as honor, patriotism, and the justifiability of war. Struggling to cope with these issues further refines their sense of self, within both the community and the culture at large. By prompting students to understand and identify with the experiences of young poets at war, we hoped to guide them through an examination of their own feelings about tough issues. Accordingly, we worked to tie in historical and cultural concepts relevant to the modern American social and political landscape.

We also wanted to provide students with structure for this self-examination and help them refine their skills in writing, argumentation, critical thinking, and analysis. Students self-examine at different levels and can respond to a variety of materials. Providing opportunities for differentiation reaches students at their present level of self-understanding and helps them move—academically and introspectively—at their own pace. The teacher's role is that of facilitator and coach, enabling students to receive individual help from both the teacher and from other students.

English and History Standards Addressed

The student will read and analyze the development of British literature and literature of other cultures.

SD1   Recognize major literary forms and their elements.

SD2   Recognize the characteristics of major chronological eras.

SD3   Relate literary works and authors to major themes and issues of their eras.

The student will read and analyze a variety of informational materials, including electronic resources.

SD4   Identify formats common to new publications and information resources.

SD5   Recognize and apply specialized informational vocabulary.

The student will read and critique a wide variety of poetry.

SD6   Explain how the choice of words in a poem creates tone and voice.

SD7   Explain how imagery and figures of speech (personification, simile, metaphor) appeal to the reader's senses and experience.

The student will develop expository and informational writings.

SD8   Generate, gather, and organize ideas for writing.

SD9   Consider audience and purpose when planning for writing.

SD10   Write analytically about literary, informational, and visual materials.

SD11   Elaborate ideas clearly and accurately.

SD12   Revise writing for depth of information and technique of presentation.

SD13   Apply grammatical conventions to edit writing for correct use of language, spelling, punctuation, and capitalization.

SD14   Proofread final copy and prepare document for publication or submission.

The student will make a 5- to 10-minute formal oral presentation.

SD15   Choose the purpose of the presentation: to defend a position, to entertain an audience, or to explain information.

SD16   Use a well-structured narrative or logical argument.

SD17   Use details, illustrations, statistics, comparisons, and analogies to support purposes.

SD18 Use visual aids or technology to support presentation.

SD19 Use grammatically correct language, including vocabulary appropriate to the topic, audience, and purpose.

The student will evaluate formal presentations.

SD20 Critique relationships among purpose, audience, and content of presentations.

SD21 Critique effectiveness of presentations.

The student will demonstrate skills for historical and geographical analysis.

SD22 Identify, analyze, and interpret primary and secondary source documents, records, and data, including artifacts, diaries, letters, photographs, journals, newspapers, historical accounts, and art to increase understanding of events and life in the United States.

SD23 Formulate historical questions and defend findings based on inquiry and interpretation.

SD24 Develop perspectives of time and place, as well as various time lines of events, periods, and personalities in American history.

SD25 Communicate findings orally and in analytical essays and/or comprehensive papers.

SD26 Develop skills in discussion, debate, and persuasive writing with respect to enduring issues and determine how divergent viewpoints have been addressed and reconciled.

SD27 Interpret the significance of excerpts from famous speeches and other documents.

The student will demonstrate knowledge of the effects of World War II on the homefront.

SD28 Describe the contributions of women and minorities to the war effort.

SD29 Explain the internment of Japanese Americans during the war.

SD30 Describe the role of media and communications in the war effort.

Unit Concepts and Generalizations

Identity, Connections, Conflict, Honor, Patriotism, Perspective, Voice

GEN1 People struggle to understand their individual identities in relation to a group identity through life experiences.

GEN2 Poets, artists, filmmakers, and musicians use art as a way of comprehending their own individual life experiences as well as the state of human existence.

Unit Objectives

As a result of this unit, the students will *know*

- Specific literary terms, including metaphor, simile, imagery, allusion, voice, tone, symbolism.
- Specific conceptual vocabulary, including patriotism, justice, honor, identity, conflict, and perspective.
- Key historical events from the World War I and World War II eras.
- Names and major works of the primary American and British war poets of the early 20th century.
- Names and major works of artists, musicians, and filmmakers whose work focused on war issues.
- Structure and elements of critical reflective writing.

As a result of this unit, the students will *understand that*

- People struggle to understand their individual identity in relation to their group identity.
- Society uses art to communicate understandings of individual life experiences.
- Moral implications are evident in war.
- Moral implications of war can be expressed through poetry, film, art, and music.
- Differing perspectives occur on key concepts such as patriotism, justice, honor, identity, and conflict.
- Perspective is shaped through critical reflective writing.

As a result of this unit, the students will *be able to*

- Analyze and critique war poetry and historical nonfiction.
- Develop writing skills and an awareness of different perspectives.
- Gain a sense of different perspectives, cultures, and viewpoints by examining literature and art.
- Explore the key concepts of patriotism, justice, honor, identity, and conflict.
- Synthesize information to construct new concepts.
- Use the works of writers and artists as a model for creating a culminating product.
- Collaborate more effectively.
- Self-assess more effectively.

Instructional Strategies Used

- Brainstorming
- Flexible grouping
- Jigsaw
- Field trips
- Independent projects
- RAFT assignments

- Reflective journals
- Self-assessment
- Think–Pair–Share
- Transparency talks
- Web-based lessons differentiated by learning modalities

- Rubric assessment
- Simulation
- Tiered assignments
- Varied product assignments
- Whole-class discussion

Sample Supporting Materials Provided

Unit Overview

LESSON	WHOLE-CLASS COMPONENTS	DIFFERENTIATED COMPONENTS
PRE-ASSESSMENT *30–50 minutes*	Pre-assessment *30–50 minutes* Homework: Preparatory reflective journal assignment	
LESSON 1 **Introduction: Looking Through the "I"s** *1 block*	Introduction of unit concepts *10 minutes* Poem by Yeats and class discussion *25 minutes* Introduction of the Virtual Memorial Project *15 minutes*	Readiness group assignments and interpretations discussion *25 minutes* Homework: E-journal assignment differentiated by readiness

LESSON	WHOLE-CLASS COMPONENTS	DIFFERENTIATED COMPONENTS
		Introduction of the real world video diary option *15 minutes*
LESSON 2 **It's Not Just a Job** *2 blocks*	Carousel brainstorming in random small groups *20–25 minutes*	
		Tiered poetry reading and "transparency talk" classification differentiated by readiness *35 minutes*
	Whole-class categorization activity and discussion *15 minutes*	
	Homework: Prewriting activity and e-journal assignment	
	Whole-class homework categorization and e-journal entry sharing *15 minutes*	
	Explanation and modeling of a soldier's job description *15 minutes*	
		Self-selected tiered writing prompts differentiated by readiness and interest *55 minutes*
	Homework: E-journal assignment	
LESSON 3 **Never Forget** *2 blocks*	Article reading and Think–Pair–Share activity *15 minutes*	
	Short film presentation and discussion *35 minutes*	
		Memorial Art Web lesson differentiated by learning profile *15 minutes*
	Whole-group discussion of the Web lesson *10 minutes*	

LESSON	WHOLE-CLASS COMPONENTS	DIFFERENTIATED COMPONENTS
		Assignment of the Virtual Memorial Project differentiated by interest and learning profile *15 minutes*
	Field trip to a memorial museum *2–3 hours*	
	Whole-class field trip follow-up and criteria formation for the Virtual Memorial Project evaluation rubric *20–25 minutes*	
		Homework: E-journal assignment differentiated by intelligence preference
LESSON 4 **I Pledge Allegiance** *1 block*	Flexible group discussion and class definition of patriotism *15 minutes*	
	Jigsaw poetry activity in small, mixed-readiness groups *30 minutes*	
	Whole-class follow-up discussion to revise the class definition *15 minutes*	
		Self-selected RAFT assignments differentiated by learning profile and interest *20 minutes*
	Homework: E-journal assignment *10 minutes*	
LESSON 5 **Because He Was My Foe . . .** *1 block*	Independent reading and note-taking *15–20 minutes*	
	Film clip presentations *10 minutes*	
		Small-group poetry reading and response activity differentiated by readiness *20 minutes*

LESSON	WHOLE-CLASS COMPONENTS	DIFFERENTIATED COMPONENTS
	Whole-class discussion in Socratic seminar format: "Is War Ever Justifiable?" *25 minutes*	
		Self-selected "position projects" differentiated by interest and learning profile *10 minutes*
		Homework: Reading assignment differentiated by learning profile
LESSON 6 **From All Sides . . .** *2 blocks*		Reading discussion/synectics based on intelligence preference *50–55 minutes*
		Graphic organizer creation in "segregated" groups based on intelligence preference *25 minutes*
		Anchor activities *time varies*
		Synectics transparency talks and process discussion *25 minutes*
	Sharing of position projects *30 minutes*	
	Whole-class discussion on perspective *25 minutes*	
		Homework: E-journal assignment differentiated by interest
LESSON 7 **A Fool Is Born Every Minute** *1 block*	Brainstorming activity and direct instruction on World War II propaganda *20 minutes*	
	Historical research in heterogeneous pairs *15–20 minutes*	
	Poetry Think–Pair–Share in heterogeneous pairs *15–20 minutes*	

LESSON	WHOLE-CLASS COMPONENTS	DIFFERENTIATED COMPONENTS
	RAFT presentations on patriotism in World War I poetry *25 minutes*	
	Homework: E-journal assignment	
	Film night (optional)	
LESSON 8 **I Am an American . . .** *2 blocks*	Introductory discussion and direct instruction on historical events *20 minutes*	
		Web-based historical research differentiated by interest *30 minutes*
	Group research presentations and discussion *25 minutes*	
		Writing assignment differentiated by interest and learning profile *10 minutes*
	Sharing and discussion of writing assignments *30–35 minutes*	
		Tiered target notes activity differentiated by readiness *30 minutes*
	Virtual Memorial Project rubric review and presentation scheduling *25 minutes*	
	Homework: E-journal assignment	
LESSON 9 **In Memory of . . .** *2 blocks*	Directions for presentation note-taking *10 minutes*	
		Virtual Memorial Project presentations and documentation *60 minutes*
	Homework: Presentation notes review and e-journal assignment	

LESSON	WHOLE-CLASS COMPONENTS	DIFFERENTIATED COMPONENTS
	Sharing of e-journal reflections *10 minutes*	
		Virtual Memorial Project presentations and documentation *45 minutes*
	Small-group categorizing activity for the Virtual Memorial Museum *15–20 minutes*	
	Whole-class transparency talk on memorial categorization *20 minutes*	
LESSON 10	Film excerpt viewing *50 minutes*	
		"Break-out" seminar sessions differentiated by interest and learning profile *50–60 minutes*
Wherever You Are . . .	Whole-class discussion on identity and the media *15 minutes*	
	Lunch and "canteen" simulation celebration *90–120 minutes*	
	Homework: E-journal assignment *15–20 minutes*	
(field trip)	Homework: Unit evaluation	

Unit Description and Teacher Commentary

PRE-ASSESSMENT	*(30–50 minutes)*
LESSON SEQUENCE AND DESCRIPTION	TEACHER COMMENTARY
Pre-assessment. Before beginning this unit, use an informal assessment, like a questionnaire, to pre-assess the students' prior knowledge of the historical era and related cultural genres, their technological skills, and their learning styles. Ask students to rank their interests and strengths in areas relating to the topic. It is also helpful to review students' performance on any secondary English and history standards assessments (particularly students' writing skills) to determine students' areas of strength and areas for improvement.	As expected, we found that the depth of prior knowledge varied from student to student. Because a portion of the unit deals with technology, it was necessary to determine student readiness for technology application so that we could provide appropriate scaffolding. The culminating project requires both technological skills and independent work, so we also needed to determine which students should receive coaching and direction to meet time lines and ensure high standards.
Homework: Preparatory reflective journal assignment. The day before the beginning of the unit, ask students to view Felix Vallotton's *Verdun* (1917) on a bookmarked Web site (or provide a color photocopy of the painting for those who do not have access to the Internet). Ask students to discuss the painting in a journal reflection. Their task is to interpret the action or "plot" of the painting, citing visual cues that support their assertions.	We wanted students to prepare for the first day of the unit by writing about their perspectives on the painting the night before.

LESSON 1	**Introduction: Looking Through the "I"s**	*(1 block)*
	Concepts: Identity, Perspective	
	GEN1; SD3; SD6–14; SD23; SD26	

LESSON SEQUENCE AND DESCRIPTION	TEACHER COMMENTARY
Guiding questions: How does your view of the world compare to others' views of the world? How can this shape personal identity? What causes us to see through others' "I"s and what happens when we do?	We like to begin lessons by providing students with guiding questions that support the principles we will explore that day.

LESSON SEQUENCE AND DESCRIPTION	TEACHER COMMENTARY
Readiness group assignments and interpretations discussion. Divide students into readiness groups and distribute copies of the **Tiered Discussion Questions** (see Sample 5.1, page 207) focused on Vallotton's *Verdun*. The different question sets serve as "lenses" in that they're designed to solicit a particular interpretation of the painting. Students present their group findings to the whole class. Discuss why and how they interpreted the painting from different perspectives and what that reveals about personal identity.	We placed students in differentiated groups here based on the outcomes of ongoing assessment of student writing and critical thinking conducted during the early part of the semester. The discussion questions are differentiated based on increasing complexity and abstractness. Our purpose here was to help students discover the disparity between differing views among groups and their personal views. We wanted them to inductively experience the connection between the concept of identity and the varied perspectives illuminated in art and other media.
Introduction of unit concepts. Explain the concept of the unit through an analogy of looking through bifocal lenses. The view that seems farther away and more encompassing— the identity of a larger group—is contrasted to the view that is nearer—the identity of the individual. Use prepared transparencies during this discussion: one showing a pair of bifocal eyeglasses, a plain black circle (to suggest a contact lens), and a set of various colored overlay "lenses" displaying symbols that represent major concepts and groups of the World War eras (a red swastika, a green Star of David, a blue U.S. Army star, a yellow peace symbol, and so on). Place each symbol transparency, in turn, on top of the "contact lens," and briefly note the views the symbol represents. Conclude by covering the contact lens with a transparency depicting a question mark. Tell students that throughout the unit, they will work on identifying their own views.	The goal of this discussion was to draw the distinction between the macro and micro view of perspective. This activity appeals to visual/spatial learners and offers another venue for students to explore the unit's fundamental concepts.
Poem by Yeats and class discussion. Students read and discuss W. B. Yeats's poem "The Second Coming," focusing on a "vision" of war and its effect on human experience.	We chose Yeats's poem because we decided its apocalyptic nature would make an impression on students and set the serious tone of the unit.

LESSON SEQUENCE AND DESCRIPTION	TEACHER COMMENTARY
After students read the poem, ask them the following questions: <ul><li>What would you expect to appear at a *second coming* and how does that differ from Yeats's view?</li><li>What is the symbolism of his vision?</li><li>What historical forces do you think prompt people, including poets, to predict vast upheavals, new civilizations, and even the end of the world?</li><li>What shapes the poet's views?</li></ul>	
Introduction of the Virtual Memorial Project. Explain the final project, which involves the creation of a Web site of a "Virtual Memorial Museum" displaying the students' culminating unit project.	Introducing the culminating project at this point was a way to inspire students and show them this unit would lead to an authentic product.
✸ **Homework: E-journal assignment differentiated by readiness.** Assign each student one of three reflection prompts based on readiness. *Prompt 1 (Below Grade-Level Learners)* What do you think the poets of today "see" in our world? *Prompt 2 (Grade-Level Learners)* How does looking through "different lenses" explain the events of September 11, 2001? *Prompt 3 (Advanced Learners)* What might be a modern symbol to represent the 21st century? Explain. *Note:* Arranging for students to use an "e-journal" to chronicle their reflections throughout this unit is a way to reinforce the technological component of the final project and increase student accountability. Under this arrangement, students log into a Web site to record their reflections and responses to prompts. They also have the option to read classmates' reflections. The teacher has the option of accessing e-journals during class discussions.	Students' groupings for the painting determined their prompt assignment. We decided journal prompts would be a regular, ongoing assignment. Programs such as Blackboard and CyberLearning Labs are useful for setting up and coordinating this type of activity.
✸ **Introduction of the real-world video diary option.** After explaining the e-journal process, instruct students that at arranged times throughout the unit, they may respond to any of the concepts from the lessons in a "real-world" video diary entry. This response is optional. These entries can be edited and streamed onto the Web site with student and parent permission.	Video diary entries are featured in a variety of current television shows popular with our students. We felt that giving them the opportunity to do such an entry would not only reinforce the concept of struggle with individual identity, but would also motivate students and heighten their interest in the unit.

LESSON SEQUENCE AND DESCRIPTION	TEACHER COMMENTARY
Note: The video diary entry requires both equipment and a separate location where students can be alone with the camera for 5 to 10 minutes each. Students might make appointments with the media specialist before or after school, or during lunch or any other free time during the school day.	

LESSON 2   It's Not Just a Job   *(2 blocks)*
Concepts: Identity, Conflict, Perspective
GEN1; SD3, SD6–14, SD22, SD25–26

LESSON SEQUENCE AND DESCRIPTION	TEACHER COMMENTARY
Guiding questions: What does it mean to be a soldier? Is it a job? What are the qualifications or tasks? Should a soldier's job be classified as an "occupation"?	In general, we like to use guiding questions as anticipatory sets, posting them in the class and using them as seeds for discussion. In this unit, some questions are more rhetorical and some are more literal, but all frame the thinking for the day's lesson.
Carousel brainstorming in random small groups. Assign students randomly to groups of approximately four or five. Post sheets of chart paper for each group at various points in the room, or use sections of whiteboards/chalkboards. Groups brainstorm answers to the question, "What jobs do soldiers perform?" elaborating as much as possible. On cue, groups classify the soldier's jobs they brainstormed, categorizing like tasks and assigning a name to each category. For examples, the categories might be equipment preparation, guard duty, and active battle. Next, also on cue, the small groups move from chart to chart, adding helpful feedback to the other groups' key category definitions. Finally, reconvene as a whole group and agree on the key categories of a soldier's jobs.	This lesson features flexible grouping, with random groups in the carousel brainstorming and readiness-based groups in the poetry study that follows. Flexible grouping is a way to ensure students are working with a variety of peers in one class period.
Tiered poetry reading and "transparency talk" classification differentiated by readiness. Divide students into readiness groups and assign specific poems that match reading and writing levels.	Students' readiness group assignments were based on reading level, prior writing products, ongoing informal assessment (observations, discussion, etc.), and ability to self-assess.

LESSON SEQUENCE AND DESCRIPTION	TEACHER COMMENTARY
Group 1 (Below Grade-Level Learners) "The Happy Warrior" by Herbert Read "Back" by Wilfred Gibson *Group 2 (Grade-Level Learners)* "An Irish Airman Foresees His Death" by W. B. Yeats "Wirers" by Siegfried Sassoon *Group 3 (Grade-Level Learners)* "Naming of Parts" by Henry Reed "I Have a Rendezvous with Death" by Alan Seeger *Group 4 (Advanced Learners)* "Gone, Gone Again" by Edward Thomas "The Soldier" by Rupert Brooke.	The higher the readiness level, the more complex the assigned poems, which move from concrete descriptions of a soldier's physical tasks ("The Happy Warrior") to a more abstract view of soldiers' reflections on these tasks ("Gone, Gone Again"). Choosing to blend the poetry from both World War eras helped to focus the lesson on the guiding questions rather than moving chronologically through history. Our aim was to emphasize theme, voice, and concept within a historical context.

The students' task is to define the jobs soldiers perform as expressed in the poetry and analyze the soldiers' understanding of themselves within that role. In each group, students read their assigned poems, identify the tasks of the soldiers evident in the poems, and categorize the various tasks, using the key categories identified during the previous activity.

Give each group blank transparencies and water-based markers, and explain that they will be giving a "transparency talk" (see Glossary, page 358) to share their insights with the rest of the class. During each group's presentation, every group member is responsible for explaining some of the information included on the transparency.

It is sometimes helpful to model a four- to six-minute transparency talk before students begin this type of activity. For more information on the transparency talk strategy, see the Glossary and Winebrenner (1992).

Whole-class categorization activity and discussion. After each group has presented, work as a class to define the major categories of soldiers' jobs that emerged from the poetry reading. How do these categories differ from the various categories suggested by the groups? Why do they differ?

Have students discuss how the poets saw themselves as soldiers. As individuals, how did they handle potential conflict stemming from their role as soldiers?

Homework: Prewriting activity and e-journal assignment. For homework, students make a list of tasks that they have to perform in their personal lives and categorize these tasks.

This list is a prewriting activity to prepare students for an assignment during the next class session.

LESSON SEQUENCE AND DESCRIPTION	TEACHER COMMENTARY
Students also respond to the following e-journal prompt, submitting their comments electronically: *How well do you handle your role as a student? Do you experience conflict with this role as the soldiers in the poems did with theirs?*	
Whole-class homework categorization and e-journal entry sharing. Begin the second day of this lesson by conducting a whole-class brainstorm of the jobs students identified for homework and the correlating categories of those jobs. Using a computer projector and Internet link, highlight samples from the e-journals.	The idea here was to expose students to multiple individual perspectives.
Explanation and modeling of a soldier's job description. Explain to students that, in the business world, tasks and categories like the ones they have generated become job descriptions. Share examples of descriptions for jobs that would be familiar to them. Then share a job description you have written for a soldier, based on the general categories the class developed on Day 1 and using the template(s) you wish students to use.	We put together a sample job description that followed standard technical-writing guidelines, but was still accessible to high school students who might not have seen much professional writing. General templates for writing a job description are readily available on the Internet; we provided them as scaffolds to support students who were struggling.
Self-selected tiered writing prompts differentiated by readiness and interest. Explain to the class that their next task is to write a job description of a student, based on the categories and descriptors they created for homework. Distribute the job description template(s) and tell students that they may choose to write the description from one of the following perspectives: • The perspective of a high school senior. • The perspective of a college admissions director. • The perspective of a parent of a high school senior. • The perspective of an employer of high school seniors. It can be helpful to model a response to get students off on the right foot. If possible, have students use a laptop or desktop computer to word process their work. Students should turn in their job descriptions for assessment.	Offering the option of writing job descriptions from a range of perspectives was a way to reinforce how perspective can alter a role. Although the self-selection allows for interest-based differentiation, there are varying degrees of complexity implicit in the writing options. For example, it's easier to write from the familiar perspective of a student than from the perspective of a college admissions director. We also noted the options each student chose, factoring it into our picture of his or her self-concept, interests, and readiness.

LESSON SEQUENCE AND DESCRIPTION	TEACHER COMMENTARY
Homework: E-journal assignment. Students respond to the following prompts: *How well do you handle your role as a student? Can you lose yourself in your role, as the soldiers lost themselves in theirs? Do the perspectives of others, such as employers or parents, influence you to act out your student role in different ways? At different times?*	

LESSON 3   **Never Forget**   *(2 blocks)*

Concepts: Honor, Perspective
GEN1–2; SD2–14, SD22–25

LESSON SEQUENCE AND DESCRIPTION	TEACHER COMMENTARY
Guiding questions: Why do we honor people who have died in war? Do we honor people who die on the job? Is there a difference? Why do people choose to give their lives for a cause?	In this lesson, students differentiate between honoring war dead and honoring people who die in the line of duty on the job today.
Article reading and Think–Pair–Share activity. Students read an excerpt from the *Harvard Magazine* article "What I Read at War" by Chris Hedges. Post the following questions on the board or on the classroom Web site: 1. How does this excerpt change or reinforce your understanding of what people fight for in a war? 2. What do you think you would do in a situation like the one the author describes? 3. Are there other situations in which you would agree with the author's statement that "heroism never feels like heroism"? Explain your answer. For the Think–Pair–Share, students think about the questions for two or three minutes after reading them, possibly writing down answers. Then they pair with someone seated near them and share their thoughts. After all pairs have discussed the questions, ask for sharing across the class.	The pairs here were self-selected or random. It is important to provide students the opportunity to work with a wide variety of peers and grouping configurations.
Short film presentation and discussion. Screen the film *Into the Breach*, and afterward, discuss why the men featured in the film felt the soldiers of D-Day deserve to be honored. Talk about some of the traditional ways of honoring people.	This 30-minute film is included on the DVD of *Saving Private Ryan*. It's a behind-the-scenes series of compelling interviews in which the cast, crew, and veterans discuss the intense emotional impact of making the film.

LESSON SEQUENCE AND DESCRIPTION	TEACHER COMMENTARY
Memorial art Web lesson differentiated by learning profile. This activity involves students in learning profile groups working online to access and analyze poetry texts, sound files, and images. Set up a page for this activity on the classroom Web site, making sure that all the links are correct and functional.	It would be possible to conduct this lesson "offline" by setting up the three groups in different parts of the classroom and providing them with multiple copies of the images and tape players and headphones for the audio components. However, using Web technology is a way to condense the media and reduce extraneous movement and noise.
Divide students into groups based on Gardner's multiple intelligences. Tell them that their task is to uncover meanings within a set of assigned works, which they will access on the Web.	Group assignments were based on learning profile data gathered earlier in the year. The three groups here (visual/spatial, musical, and verbal/linguistic) reflect a particular class's composition; with a different class, we might design tasks for different intelligences.
Group 1 (Visual/Spatial Learners) "In Flanders Fields" by John McCrae (poem) *Poppy Field in a Hollow near Giverny* (painting) by Claude Monet *Note:* An image of the painting is available online at www.artofmonet.com.	The idea here was for students' work in these groups to help them make decisions about how they would design their culminating product.
Group 2 (Musical Learners) "Let Them In" (song) by Anonymous, performed by David Wilcox *Note:* This song can be streamed via MP3 onto the Web site or recorded from Wilcox's *Home Again* CD.	
Group 3 (Verbal/Linguistic Learners) "Song IX (Funeral Blues)" by W. H. Auden, performed by John Hannah *Note:* This audio may be streamed via MP3 onto the Web site (drew.frubel.com/songix.html) or recorded from the DVD of the film *Four Weddings and a Funeral*.	
All groups use the following questions to guide their analysis:	
1. Who does the work honor? 2. What tone does the artist/poet set? What is the effect on the reader/audience? What elements suggest or support the tone? 3. How does the way in which the artist presents the memorialized person influence the observer's understanding? 4. Discuss the ways that our society has honored people who have died for a cause.	We based these questions on the lesson's guiding questions.

LESSON SEQUENCE AND DESCRIPTION	TEACHER COMMENTARY
Whole-group discussion of the Web lesson. Reassemble as a whole class to discuss the differentiated Web lesson.	The purpose of this discussion was to provide the framework for evaluating the culminating product.
Assignment of the Virtual Memorial Project differentiated by interest and learning profile. Remind students that the culminating product for this unit is a mini-memorial in a format of their choosing (a poem, song, piece of art, or another product as approved by the teacher) that will honor a person or a group who has died for a cause. Students' products will be posted online in a class-created "Virtual Memorial Museum." Distribute (or provide online access to) the **Virtual Memorial Project Guidelines** (see Sample 5.2, page 208).	Using a virtual museum format allows student work to be displayed in electronic exhibits for an unspecified length of time. Instead of restricting sharing to scheduled performances, other students and school staff have the chance to view the products at their leisure.
Field trip to a memorial museum. Arrange for the class to take a field trip to a memorial museum that honors the sacrifice of people who have died for a cause. On the way to the museum, explain to students that they should gather information about characteristics of memorial museums as they are touring.	If a field trip option hadn't been available to us, students would have viewed virtual museum memorial exhibits online. Good examples are the United States Holocaust Museum's site at www.ushmm.org and the National Shrine of the Immaculate Conception's site at www.nationalshrine.com.
Whole-class field trip follow-up and criteria formation for the Virtual Memorial Project evaluation rubric. On the trip back to school, discuss the characteristics students observed and generate a list of essential elements for the virtual museum they will create. Have a student volunteer record the list for the class, and use these criteria as the foundation for the **Virtual Memorial Project Rubric** (see Sample 5.3, page 209). Explain to students that this rubric will be used to evaluate their culminating products, and thus they should use the rubric to guide their work. When they present their products, they will also submit a filled-in rubric as a self-assessment.	
Homework: E-journal assignment differentiated by intelligence preference. Ask students to choose one of the following prompts and write a reflective response: *Option A (Analytical Intelligence)* Identify the key parts of a memorial museum and how they work together to create an appropriate environment.	These options reflect Sternberg's triarchic intelligences.

LESSON SEQUENCE AND DESCRIPTION	TEACHER COMMENTARY
Option B (Practical Intelligence) Reflect on why this memorial museum is important for the community. What does it contribute? *Option C (Creative Intelligence)* What would you do to improve this museum? Would you present anything differently, add new exhibits, take anything away?	

LESSON 4   **I Pledge Allegiance**   *(1 block)*
Concepts: Patriotism, Perspective, Voice
GEN2; SD1–3, SD 6–14

LESSON SEQUENCE AND DESCRIPTION	TEACHER COMMENTARY
Guiding questions: What is the definition of patriotism? Are there criteria for judging degrees of patriotism?	In this lesson, students wrestle with differing perceptions of patriotism. We wanted them to understand that what one person or group claims is patriotic isn't necessarily what every individual must subscribe to in order to be patriotic.
Flexible group discussion and class definition of patriotism. Divide students into heterogeneous small groups and ask them to develop a definition of patriotism. After a few minutes, have each small group share its responses with the rest of the class. Record the various definitions on the board or on chart paper and, as a group, reach consensus on a class definition of patriotism.	We used mixed-readiness groups here so that students could support one another and share knowledge.
Jigsaw poetry activity in small, mixed-readiness groups. Students remain in their groups to examine one of the following poems and then answer text-specific **Jigsaw Discussion Questions** (see Sample 5.4, page 210): • "The Soldier" by Rupert Brooke • "The Wirers" by Siegfried Sassoon • "Dulce et Decorum Est" by Wilfred Owen • "This Is No Case of Petty Right or Wrong" by Edward Thomas • "Base Details" by Siegfried Sassoon After students have analyzed a poem in their mixed-readiness home groups, recombine them into new heterogeneous specialty groups to discuss all the poems.	The scaffolding that lower-readiness students receive in mixed-readiness expert groups can give them confidence when they jigsaw into their specialty groups. This is one of the great benefits of flexible grouping. The text-specific discussion questions in Sample 5.4 are designed to focus students' attention on tone, imagery, and theme.

LESSON SEQUENCE AND DESCRIPTION	TEACHER COMMENTARY
Whole-class follow-up discussion to revise the class definition. Re-examine the criteria for defining patriotism. Ask students to add or delete criteria and synthesize a class definition of patriotism.	This definition appears again as a component of the RAFT activity.
Self-selected RAFT assignments differentiated by learning profile and interest. Distribute the **RAFT Activity Options and Rubric** (see Sample 5.5 page 211), telling students to choose one option to complete and share by Lesson 10. Explain to students that they should use both the rubric and the class definition of patriotism to guide the work they do.	These RAFT options are designed to appeal to both learning profile and interest. The rubric defines performance criteria.
Homework: E–journal assignment. Students respond to the following prompt: *Has your own personal definition of patriotism changed as a result of the readings? Explain how it has or has not changed.* *How does your understanding of patriotism relate to the definition of justice? Can war ever be justifiable?* Tell students that their responses to these questions will launch the next day's discussion.	This is another example of how we used e-journal entries to help students make part-to-whole connections and apply what they were learning to other concepts.

LESSON 5   **Because He Was My Foe**   *(1 block)*
Concepts: Identity, Conflict, Perspective, Voice
GEN1; SD3, SD8–14, SD22–26

LESSON SEQUENCE AND DESCRIPTION	TEACHER COMMENTARY
Guiding question: Is war ever justifiable?	"Justifiable" means capable of being proven fair or equitable. By crafting the question this way, we emphasized obtaining proof rather than voicing opinion.
Independent reading and note-taking. Have students read "The Monster That Is High School," an article written by high school student Daeha Ko and published in *Writing Arguments* by John D. Ramage, John C. Bean, and June Johnson. This article is about the Columbine High School shooting that took place on April 20, 1999. It presents the idea that the true victims of the shooting were the perpetrators.	Having students read this article was a way to help them connect the lesson's guiding question to their own lives, particularly their struggles within the high school context. We wanted them to wrestle thoroughly with this issue and seek out unstated assumptions.

LESSON SEQUENCE AND DESCRIPTION	TEACHER COMMENTARY
As they read, students should use sticky notes to target puzzling passages, commentary, or key questions they have.	"Sticky note discussions" are a great way to get all students involved in and contributing to a topic. They also help to define specific questions students have about vocabulary, concepts, or inferences.
Film clip presentations. Show short passages (approximately 10 minutes total) from the movie *Memphis Belle*. Be sure to show the "friendly fire" incident (where shooting down an enemy airplane inadvertently leads to the death of a rookie crew) and the commanding officer's views on the deaths of many of the men in his unit.	
Small-group poetry reading and response activity differentiated by readiness. Group students based on reading and analytical reasoning readiness. Each group reads an assigned poem and responds to this prompt: *How does the speaker of the poem justify his actions? How are the actions within the poem justifiable?* Here are the reading assignments: *Group 1 (Advanced Learners)* "On Seeing a Piece of Our Heavy Artillery Brought into Action" by Wilfred Owen *Group 2 (Grade-Level Learners)* "Vergissmeinnicht" by Keith Douglas *Group 3 (Grade-Level Learners)* "The Parable of the Old Man and Young" by Wilfred Owen *Group 4 (Grade-Level Learners)* "The Man He Killed" by Thomas Hardy *Group 5 (Below Grade-Level Learners)* "Does It Matter?" by Siegfried Sassoon	Each of these poems addresses the justifiability of war. Most of them are quite literal and filled with concrete imagery.
Whole-class discussion in Socratic seminar format: "Is War Ever Justifiable?" Ask students to generate questions and generalizations, based on their sticky notes from the Columbine article and their findings from the group poetry assignment. Compile their suggestions on a piece of chart paper. Use these generalizations and questions to provide a framework for a Socratic seminar.	The Socratic seminar provides a solid structure for discussing and analyzing this emotion-laden topic. Again, the dialogue format invites every student to participate, making the discussion a very democratic experience.

LESSON SEQUENCE AND DESCRIPTION	TEACHER COMMENTARY
	Helpful references on the Socratic seminar process include Ball & Brewer (2000), Moeller & Moeller (2002), and www.socraticseminars.com.
Self-selected "position projects" differentiated by interest and learning profile. Offer students the choice of two possible tasks. *Option 1 (Explicit Argument)* Write a position paper or a speech (minimum two pages) on the essential question, "Is war ever justifiable?" Draw on personal experience to support your position. *Option 2 (Implicit Argument)* Create a product (a visual representation in two or three dimensions such as a brochure, advertisement, poster, painting, photograph, sculpture, or any similar medium), that takes a position on the guiding question: "Is war ever justifiable?" Draw on your personal experiences to support your position. Tell students that they will share their papers, speeches, and art projects in class two days after this lesson.	We want to emphasize not only the concept of the justifiability of war, but also that arguments can take either explicit or implicit forms. At the same time, we felt the unit would be strengthened at this point by differentiating an assignment based on interest and learning profile. Both task options offer multiple and varying project options. We also designed this assignment to promote media literacy and prepare students for Lesson 7's focus on propaganda. This time line allows students the opportunity to complete these projects outside of school.
Homework: Reading assignment differentiated by learning profile. In preparation for the next lessons, divide students into two groups based on their intelligence preference, and give each group a different reading assignment, posted online or distributed in hard copy. *Group 1 (Logical/Mathematical, Musical, Verbal/Linguistic, and Intrapersonal Intelligence)* These students read excerpts from *On Race and Nation* by Adolf Hitler. *Group 2 (Visual/Spatial, Kinesthetic, Naturalist, and Interpersonal Intelligence)* These students read excerpts from *All But My Life,* Gerda Weissman Klein's memoir of her life during the Holocaust.	At this point in the unit, we move to events and poetry relating mainly to the World War II era.

| LESSON 6 | From All Sides | (2 blocks) |

Concepts: Identity, Conflict, Perspective
GEN1–2; SD2–3, SD8–14, SD22–27

LESSON SEQUENCE AND DESCRIPTION	TEACHER COMMENTARY
Guiding question: Why do different people have different perspectives on the same issue?	

Reading discussion/synectics based on intelligence preference. Students remain in the intelligence preference groups established at the end of Lesson 5. Group 1 consists of students identified as logical/mathematical, musical, verbal/linguistic, and intrapersonal. Group 2 consists of students identified as visual/spatial, kinesthetic, naturalist, and interpersonal.

When students enter the classroom, announce that everyone in Group 2 must take their belongings and follow you to a new classroom location. (Ideally, this will be smaller room, where the students might be slightly crowded.) Group 1 will stay in the classroom with a volunteer facilitator (e.g., a school specialist, student teacher, or administrator) who will guide their work.

Group 1
1. Students consider and discuss the following question: "Which people from world history could be considered people whom everyone "loves to hate"?
2. Students review the excerpts from *On Race and Nation* that they read for homework and discuss them as a group.
3. Students listen to selections of music composed by Richard Wagner and other German nationalist composers.

Group 2
1. Students review and discuss the excerpts from *All But My Life.*
2. Students watch *One Survivor Remembers*, a 30-minute film based on *All But My Life.*

Both groups will be asked to make a connection between their perspectives on the homework reading and the music (Group 1) or film (Group 2) they have just experienced.

Teacher Commentary:

For an overview of the synectics technique, please see the Glossary, page 356.

Leaving one group to work comfortably in the classroom emphasizes the stereotypes of "status" and separation from "other" learners. This complements the theories students will be struggling with in the lesson.

We used intelligence preferences as entry points to offer students easier access to the abstract content and complex tasks.

Our objective here was to help students develop a broader understanding of the issues and gain a new perspective on them.

LESSON SEQUENCE AND DESCRIPTION	TEACHER COMMENTARY
Group 1 The volunteer facilitator guides these students through a synectics thinking model, using a series of questions to help connect the reading and music with the analogy of a machine.	Our volunteer facilitator was, of course, familiar with the synectics technique. This part of the unit did require prior coordination.
Group 2 Use leading questions to help this group of students make connections between the reading and film with the analogy of something from the natural world that undergoes transformation.	These activities offer students a challenge, but it's within a comfort zone that has been created by all the reading, writing, and discussion in the unit leading up to this point.
Graphic organizer creation in "segregated" groups based on intelligence preference. After the discussions are concluded, both groups use transparencies and markers to create a graphic organizer explaining their synectics model.	We provided several models of graphic organizers and also gave students the option of coming up with their own organizer format.
Anchor activities. Once students complete their work in these groups, they may work on their RAFT options and/or their position projects on the justifiability of war.	
Synectics transparency talks and process discussion. Open the second day of the lesson with everyone back in the classroom. Both groups share their synectics model in a transparency-talk format, selecting a speaker to explain their model.	
Sharing of position projects. Students informally share the position papers, speeches, and artwork they created on the justifiability of war (see Lesson 5).	As noted, these projects were differentiated by interest and learning profile.
Whole-class discussion on perspective. Segue into a discussion related to the guiding question for Lesson 6: "Why do different people have different perspectives on the same issues?" Use these questions to guide the discussion: • How are perspectives shaped by events and circumstances? • Why is it beneficial to examine varied perspectives on a problem or issue? • How do you evaluate the strengths, weaknesses, and implications of differing viewpoints? Optional: Remind students that their activities during the previous class session took place in distinctly different settings (one spacious, one crowded). Ask them to discuss how their surroundings affected their ability to complete their tasks and how they felt while working.	The justifiability issue is predicated on perspective. Our goal for Lesson 6 was to push students to discover that perspective shapes the underlying assumptions of any argument.

LESSON SEQUENCE AND DESCRIPTION	TEACHER COMMENTARY
Homework: E-journal assignment differentiated by interest. Distribute a list of the discussion questions or post them on the Web site. Students select one and respond to it in their e-journals.	Giving students the opportunity to reflect on these questions a second time, in writing, allowed them to deepen responses shared in the class discussion and incorporate or counter perspectives shared by classmates. It also was a way of acknowledging that some students express themselves better in writing than they do through speech.

LESSON 7

A Fool Is Born Every Minute   *(1 block)*
Concepts: Conflict, Perspective, Voice
GEN1; SD2–14, SD22–27, SD29–30

LESSON SEQUENCE AND DESCRIPTION	TEACHER COMMENTARY
Guiding question: What role does propaganda play in war?	In this lesson, students investigate the relationship between propaganda, perspective, and patriotism.
Brainstorming activity and direct instruction on World War II propaganda. Read the following quotation aloud: "War, at its most basic, is about seduction and then tragic betrayal." Use the students' thoughts about this quotation as a springboard into a brainstorming activity about their prior knowledge of the use of propaganda in this country during World War II, specifically propaganda about the Japanese.	
Next, provide direct instruction on propaganda as a persuasive tool. A key point to address is that argumentation has elements of both truth-seeking and persuasion. In contrast, propaganda relies almost exclusively on persuasion.	We limited the direct instruction to 10 minutes.
Historical research in heterogeneous pairs. Have students, working in assigned pairs, view excerpts from the CD-ROM *Executive Order 9066: The Incarceration of Japanese Americans During World War II* (available through Grolier Educational publishers). Select excerpts that present factual information about the internment as well as some showing how Japanese Americans were incarcerated solely because of their ethnic identities, and how they subsequently lost their homes, businesses, and livelihoods.	We paired students here based on how they described their own political views on a continuum from very conservative to very liberal. (One of our colleagues, a government teacher, administers a political views self-assessment tool based on current issues.) The idea was to partner students with opposing political views and ask them to work together throughout this lesson.

LESSON SEQUENCE AND DESCRIPTION	TEACHER COMMENTARY
Students may also want to explore the Web site on Manzanar War Relocation Center at www.nps.gov/manz.	
Poetry Think–Pair–Share in heterogeneous pairs. After viewing sections from the CD-ROM, the paired students read and discuss poems written from a Japanese American child's point of view: • "In Response to Executive Order 9066: All Americans of Japanese Descent Must Report to Relocation Centers" by Dwight Okita • "Be Like the Cactus" by Kimii Nagata • "The World" by Jessica Hoshino • "My Plea" by Mary Matsuzawa • "Faith" by Yukio Ota	The natural differences in the paired students' perspectives enhanced this activity.
Have pairs synthesize their understandings by focusing on the following questions: 1. How do differing perspectives affect patriotism or expressions of patriotism? 2. How is patriotism fueled by propaganda? 3. Does propaganda always lack elements of truth seeking in order to have persuasive power? 4. Does propaganda change perceptions of "truth"? Give examples.	These questions provided a bridge between the focus on propaganda (Executive Order 9066) and the RAFT projects on patriotism that students took on in Lesson 4 and would present shortly.
After pairs share their thoughts, initiate a whole-class discussion centered on the students' responses.	The goal here was to target the key understandings about the effect and form of propaganda as an argument.
RAFT presentations on patriotism in World War I poetry. Students present their RAFT projects (see Lesson 4). Collect self-assessments.	As noted, RAFT options were self-selected, based on interest and readiness.
Homework: E-journal assignment. Students complete an e-journal entry discussing how their discovery of the connections between patriotism and propaganda relates to the aspect of patriotism they presented in their RAFT projects.	This assignment helped to make the connections explicit.
Film night (optional). Invite students to attend a "film night" screening of *Snow Falling on Cedars*, a film based on David Guterson's novel of the same title. Executive Order 9066 directly affects the main characters.	

LESSON 8

I Am an American . . .
(2 blocks)

Concepts: Identity, Honor, Patriotism, Perspective
GEN1; SD4–14, SD22–28

LESSON SEQUENCE AND DESCRIPTION	TEACHER COMMENTARY
Guiding questions: How did other groups, with their own unique perspectives, contribute to the war effort? Did their contributions change the majority's views?	This lesson examines the unique experiences and contributions to the World War II effort made by women, African Americans, and Native Americans.
Introductory discussion and direct instruction on historical events. Begin Day 1 of this lesson with an introductory "perspectives talk" on how women, African Americans, and Native Americans were involved in the war effort.	Again, we kept direct instruction very brief—15 minutes or less.
Web-based historical research differentiated by interest. Students choose the subject that they would like to learn about and research it, using the following bookmarked Web sites: • *Women:* Rosie the Riveter Memorial Museum at www.rosietheriveter.org. • *African Americans:* Tuskegee Airmen Memorial Museum at www.fortdesmoines.org/tuskegee.shtml. • *Native Americans:* Code Talkers Memorial Museum at www.codetalkermemorial.com. As students choose the group that will be their research subject, have them move into proximity with other students researching the same topic—either in pods, if using a mobile lab, or in the same area in a computer lab. All students use the following questions to guide their research: 1. What were this group's major contributions to the war effort? 2. How were their contributions viewed during the war and afterward? 3. What are some characteristics of this memorial Web site that are effective in expressing this group's perspectives during the war era?	This activity allowed students to be the primary constructors of their own knowledge and understanding. Each of these Web sites has its own historical section, including photographs. We wanted students to choose which group to investigate because this was fairly new territory for them, and we knew their engagement would be greater if they selected the group that piqued their interest. Guiding questions are really important in focusing students' independent research on the Internet. Here, because the content was relatively new to most, we made the questions generic; at this point, we wanted students to gather some basic knowledge.

LESSON SEQUENCE AND DESCRIPTION	TEACHER COMMENTARY
4. What conflicts and opposing points of view arose between the individuals in this group and the larger society? 5. Discuss ways in which these conflicts paved the way for later societal changes. As students conduct their research, they should share findings with others performing similar research.	
Group research presentations and discussion. After students have completed their research, initiate a general class discussion where the members of each research group offer their findings to the other groups.	This was a way for the entire class to learn the history of each of these groups.
✱**Writing assignment differentiated by interest and learning profile.** Students choose a method of written expression (monologue, poem, speech, letter, song, or journal entry) and write a piece that conveys the point of view of someone from the group they investigated: how that character sees his or her identity vis à vis society. For example, students might take on the role of a code talker, a woman working in a munitions factory, or a Tuskegee airman and express how that person's point of view might compare and contrast with the point of view of the larger society at the time.	This wasn't a major project—just a way to help students understand personal point of view versus societal point of view and the conflict that can arise between them. The idea links back to Lesson 1's concept of looking at identity through varying lenses.
Sharing and discussion of writing assignments. Begin by having students share their writing. Discuss any relevant discoveries about perspective.	
✱**Tiered target notes graphic activity differentiated by readiness.** Divide students into three readiness-based groups and distribute the **Target Notes Guidelines and Template** (see Sample 5.6, page 214). Each group has a different subject to focus on, and students work independently to fill in their organizers in response to a differentiated set of prompts. *Group A (Basic Readiness)* Students focus on their individual identity: how others see them in their personal lives. *Group B (Higher Readiness)* Students focus on their identity as a young adult: how others see members of their generation.	With this activity, we began to connect all of the concepts in the unit, reinforcing the understanding of perspective and tying it to the main concept, identity. The activity also allowed for the visual distinction between an individual view versus a societal view. Notice that the subjects become more and more complex with each tiered group, as students are asked to consider their identity within larger constructs. Readiness to tackle complex concepts was the main consideration in each student's group assignment, but we also considered maturity and self-concept.

LESSON SEQUENCE AND DESCRIPTION	TEACHER COMMENTARY
Group C (Highest Readiness) Students focus on their identity as part of the larger culture: how others see them as Americans. After students finish their graphic representations, they write a summary combining the perspectives they have outlined.	We knew that some students would benefit from focusing on themselves, while those who had a solid understanding of their identity needed the challenge of more complex issues. Close reading of e-journals and video diary entries also helped with appropriate placement.
Virtual Memorial Project rubric review and presentation scheduling. Remind students that they will be presenting their culminating products—their memorials—during the next class session. Briefly review elements of the Virtual Memorial Product Rubric (see Sample 5.3) and assign the order of presentations.	The presentation order was random.
Homework: E-journal assignment. Students respond to the following prompt: *Based on the summary of how you perceive others' views of you, explain how these views are accurate, inaccurate, or a mixture of both. What factors do you feel account for any inaccuracies in others' perceptions of you? What connections have you made between your own life and our discussions and investigations this week?*	This assignment was another way to link back to the metaphor of looking at identity through lenses. Anyone who was uncomfortable with classmates or others reading this entry was permitted to use a privacy viewing mode when posting it or to submit the entry via regular e-mail or hard copy.

LESSON 9

In Memory of . . .

(2 blocks)

Concepts: Identity, Honor, Perspective
GEN2; SD8–21, SD22–25

LESSON SEQUENCE AND DESCRIPTION	TEACHER COMMENTARY
Guiding questions: What purpose does a memorial serve for those who mourn lost people? What elements within a memorial connect to people in a meaningful way?	
Directions for presentation note taking. Explain to students that they will need to take notes during each of the product presentations. Distribute copies of the **Spreadsheet Note-Taking Template** (see Sample 5.7, page 216).	

LESSON SEQUENCE AND DESCRIPTION	TEACHER COMMENTARY
The template is divided into columns with blocks for note-taking: • *Column 1:* Students record the presenter's name. • *Column 2:* Students record the memorial's title. • *Column 3:* Students record the subject of the memorial and several qualities about the honoree(s) that are evident in the project. • *Column 4:* Students record elements of the product that they felt were effective in relaying those important qualities about the honoree(s).	We wanted to encourage active listening and help audience members respond to the presentations in a structured way. The template helped students generate appropriate feedback, and the notes also provided a record that students used to organize the Virtual Memorial Museum.
Virtual Memorial Project presentations and documentation. Students present their culminating products individually while the class takes notes. Encourage students to ask questions and allow time at the end of each presentation for them to record notes. Collect self-assessments. If there is time left at the end of the lesson, have students take a "gallery walk" so that they have a closer look at the memorials and speak to other students individually about them. Enlist volunteer student photographers (perhaps yearbook staff) to take digital photos for the Web site.	
Homework: Presentation notes review and e-journal assignment. Students review their presentation notes and respond to this journal prompt: *Thinking back on the products presented today, what are some of the elements that you connected to the most? Were you surprised by any of the choices of memorial subjects? What were some of the similarities and differences among the products?*	
Sharing of e-journal reflections. Begin by having students share reflections about the products that have been presented. Ask them to discuss similarities and differences among the first set of memorials.	At this point, students began to see similarities in the projects and were able start grouping them in a variety of ways.
Virtual Memorial Project presentations and documentation. Each of the remaining students presents his or her product while the class takes notes. Encourage questions and allow time at the end of each presentation for students to record notes. Collect self-assessments.	
Small-group categorizing activity for the Virtual Memorial Museum. At the end of the presentations, divide students into heterogeneous groups and provide them with transparencies.	Students used their spreadsheet presentation notes (see Sample 5.6) to guide work on this activity.

LESSON SEQUENCE AND DESCRIPTION	TEACHER COMMENTARY
Direct the groups to create a web- or map-style graphic organizer that classifies the memorials into an order for their display in the Virtual Museum. Each group must identify their unifying concept and present reasons why they organized the museum in a particular way.	
If necessary, model the process using a general web organizer.	
Whole-class transparency talk on memorial categorization. Have all the groups share their organizers and explain their classification schemes and rationales. When all ideas have been shared, solicit student volunteers to serve as a "building committee." These students agree to review the ideas and develop a scheme for the museum.	

LESSON 10

Wherever You Are . . .   *(2–3 blocks)*

Concepts: Identity, Perspective

GEN2; SD8–12, SD22–24, SD28–30

LESSON SEQUENCE AND DESCRIPTION	TEACHER COMMENTARY
Guiding questions: How does popular culture respond to war? What role does the media play in shaping our identities?	In this lesson, students "experience" how culture responds to and is shaped by war. The various ways in which the media shapes identity is an underlying theme throughout the unit.
Note: Ideally, this lesson is conducted as a "mini-conference" or academy-style field trip, where students travel off site to attend seminars on the elements of popular culture in the World War II era. An alternative is to bring experts in for a "in school" field trip held in the auditorium or gymnasium. Either way, the lesson should end with a celebration.	Involving outside experts is a great way to enrich students' educational experiences. The resources available at nearby Sweet Briar College were perfect for this lesson. The students took a field trip to Sweet Briar's Florence Elston Inn and Conference Center, and faculty members served as seminar presenters.
Film excerpt viewing. Begin the field experience by showing excerpts of the film *Accentuating the Positive: America Goes to War: The Home Front* (available from pbs.org). The excerpts should focus on popular culture's response to the war, including the USO, music, and Hollywood.	We chose clips that best mirrored the mini-lessons that would follow.

LESSON SEQUENCE AND DESCRIPTION	TEACHER COMMENTARY
"Break-out" seminar sessions differentiated by interest and learning profile. After the film, students choose to attend a seminar on one of the following topics: • Advertising's Response to War: Persuasion and Propaganda • The World of War Art: The Artist's Eye • Accentuate the Positive: Music and the War • Forties Fashion and the Feminine Ideal • Political Strategy: Washington's Response to War.	These specific topic categories reflect the experts we had available to present. We were careful to seek out topics that would appeal to different intelligence preferences.
Whole-class discussion on identity and the media. After the sessions, reconvene to share experiences and to respond to the following questions: 1. How did the media help to shape the popular attitude in World War II? 2. In what ways do the media affect our choices today? 3. How do the media affect our individual identity? How do they affect our group identity?	
Lunch and "canteen" simulation celebration. Move to a larger room where a "canteen" has been created—decorated to look like the canteens of the World War II era. After lunch, invite a dance instructor to lead a session on popular dances of the era. Play period music while students practice and enjoy dancing. Appoint or request a photographer to take pictures for the Web site.	Parent volunteers assisted with the lunch and helped with decorations. Simulations like this, although a little daunting to plan and pull off, really resonate with students and bring concepts together. Students' educational experiences are greatly enriched by learning with and from community members.
Homework: E-journal assignment. Ask students to respond to a final prompt: *How important is it for us to "step outside" our ongoing struggles with identity? When you tire of the struggle, what do you do to "step outside"?*	We used excerpts of these journal prompts as captions for the pictures on the Virtual Memorial Museum Web site.
Homework: Unit evaluation. Distribute a unit evaluation for students to complete at home. It should ask students to articulate their likes and dislikes as well as the essential understandings they've acquired through the entire experience of the unit.	

Teacher Reflection on the Unit

We like that the unit design pushed students beyond content knowledge and asked them to uncover meaning, apply what they were learning in new ways, and make judgments in order to gain wisdom—all valuable processes for adult life. The unit also consistently recognized and honored individual differences and asked students to reflect on the kinds of choices we make in defining, understanding, and appreciating diverse perspectives. Finally, it offered plenty of opportunity for creativity—a helpful way to offset the vagaries of "senioritis." Since the unit was first designed and taught, Cynthia's increasing sophistication with technology has inspired her to integrate additional Web-based activities. She is hopeful that more online elements will help to further intrigue and motivate imaginations ready for college and adult life.

Each time she teaches the unit, Cynthia must coach a few students who are unsure about its nontraditional approaches. In general, though, we've found that most students really enjoy displaying their understandings through unique and different products. Participating in many of the activities connected to the unit has been meaningful and fun for us as well. We have enjoyed watching students move through connection, empathy, reflection, and then application. In the process, they have gained not only knowledge about the literature of war, but essential self-knowledge for the future.

Cynthia Kelley teaches at Amherst County High School in Amherst, Virginia. She can be reached at ckelley@amherst.k12.va.us.

Kay Brimijoin, PhD, is a former Amherst County Public Schools teacher and administrator and is currently an assistant professor in the education department at Sweet Briar College, Sweet Briar, Virginia. She can be reached at brimijoin@sbc.ed.

SAMPLE 5.1—Tiered Discussion Questions

Directions: In your discussion group, answer the appropriate questions below, being sure to identify elements of the painting that support your answers.

Group 1
1. How does the subject seem to be viewing the battle? Do you feel he is a soldier or a civilian?
2. What might the colors of the incoming missiles suggest? Do you think they have any symbolic meaning?
3. What type of format did the artist choose for this subject? What elements suggest this?
4. What statement about war could Vallotton be making in this painting?

Group 2
1. From what perspective is the subject viewing the forest fire? Do you think the subject is part of the rescue effort or a victim of the fire?
2. What might the colors of the light beams suggest? Do you think they have any symbolic meaning?
3. Why would an abstract format be logical for this subject?
4. What statement about environmentalism could Vallotton be making in this painting?

Group 3
1. From what perspective is the subject viewing Ground Zero? What does this perspective tell you about the subject?
2. What might the colors in the painting symbolize? Are their any other symbols in the painting?
3. What is the artist's message about 9/11?
4. How does use of an abstract format relay the artist's message effectively? How would a realistic format change the message?

SAMPLE 5.2—Virtual Memorial Project Guidelines

In Memory of . . .

As we have discussed, one way that people put the lives and contributions of others into perspective is to honor them by constructing a memorial. Memorials not only showcase the life and work of the honoree, but also say something about the way in which the honoree has affected the individuals who create the memorial. From our research, we know that although memorials are often symbolic and can take a variety of forms, they have some basic elements in common: Memorials present a <u>message</u> honoring a specific <u>subject</u> for a particular <u>audience</u> in an expressive, creative, and individual way.

Directions: Your assignment is to create a memorial for an honoree (or honorees) of your own choosing. Follow the guidelines below.

1. Choose a person or group (the <u>subject</u>) whom you feel is deserving of a memorial. It can be a public figure or someone who has had a direct, personal effect on your life.
2. Research and identify which aspects of the subject's life might be important to share with others.
3. Identify aspects of the subject that have affected you personally to share with others.
4. Choose a method to present your <u>message</u> about the subject that is creative and individual to you.
5. Create the memorial and then present it to the class (the <u>audience</u>) for inclusion in our Virtual Memorial Museum.

Your product (the memorial) can incorporate art, music, drama, writing, domestic arts, technical arts, or any combination from these broad categories. You may incorporate varying levels of symbolism in the product's design as long as your message about the subject is clear. Use the assessment rubric to guide your creation.

You are welcome to discuss any ideas on subject, message, or method with the teacher before you begin.

SAMPLE 5.3—Virtual Memorial Project Rubric

Name _____

Memorial Project Title _____

Quality of Thought

The product clearly demonstrates an understanding of the elements of a memorial for the subject chosen, including subject, message, audience, symbolism, and honor.

Outstanding	Strong	Acceptable	Unacceptable

Effective Expression

The product expresses the creator's message effectively. The product clearly expresses both the subject's effect on the intended audience and on the product's creator.

Outstanding	Strong	Acceptable	Unacceptable

Quality of Research

The product contains appropriate and sufficient information about the subject and the subject's effect on the audience for whom the product is created.

Outstanding	Strong	Acceptable	Unacceptable

Habits of Mind

The product shows substantial creativity and effort in planning and execution. The product shows the creator's perseverance and exhibits a clear goal.

Outstanding	Strong	Acceptable	Unacceptable

SAMPLE 5.4—Jigsaw Discussion Questions

Patriotism and World War I Poems

Directions: In your expert groups, answer the questions for your group's assigned poem.

"The Soldier" by Rupert Brooke
1. Why will the "corner of a foreign field" be "forever England"?
2. How does the speaker feel toward England? How idealistic or realistic do you think his recollections are?
3. The speaker says his heart will become a "pulse in the eternal mind." In your own words, what does he mean?

"The Wirers" by Siegfried Sassoon
1. How do you think the wirers feel about what they have to do? How would they have to approach the job?
2. What is the speaker's attitude toward what has happened to young Hughes?
3. How is his attitude explained?
4. What irony is the poet pointing to in the last line?

"Dulce et Decorum Est" by Wilfred Owen
1. What is the poem's comment on the statement, "Dulce et decorum est pro patria mori"? (It is sweet and becoming to die for one's country.)
2. Which images in the poem help to show the reader the true horror of war?
3. What is the speaker's tone in the poem?

"This Is No Petty Case of Right or Wrong" by Edward Thomas
1. What does the poet mean when he says, in line 4, "to please newspapers"? What role do the media play in patriotic sentiment?
2. Explain the poet's sentiment in lines 20–22. Why would it be important to save a country that he views in this manner?
3. What is the poet's ultimate statement about patriotism and justification for war?

"Base Details" by Siegfried Sassoon
1. What are the officers' attitudes toward loss of life in war? How do these attitudes develop?
2. How does the poet's tone affect the reader's understanding of the officers' views? What words and images does Sassoon use to convey this tone?
3. How could perspective change these views? In Sassoon's view, what changes perspective?

SAMPLE 5.5—RAFT Activity Options and Rubric

RAFT Options: A Poet's View of Patriotism

Role	Audience	Format	Topic
Friend of a suicidal soldier (Sassoon)	Newspaper readers in 1918	Letter to the editor	"I am against this war, but I am still a patriot!"
Enlisted solider who has overheard the conversation of the majors in the bar (Sassoon)	Bartender	Monologue	"You know, buddy, those guys don't know what they're talking about."
President of the United States (Brooke)	Congress	Speech	"The war should continue because . . . "
Gassed soldier in a wagon (Owen)	Fellow soldiers	Multiple media collage	The cost of war
Eighteen-year-old about to enlist (Thomas)	Parents	Letter	"Let me tell you why I made this decision . . ."
Recruiter (Brooke)	Young men of 1918	Brochure	"You ARE England."
Grandfather (Owen)	Grandson interested in enlisting	Song	A soldier's life
Wirer (Sassoon)	Close friend or family member	Artwork or sculpture	My job
Parents of a new recruit (Thomas)	Each other (and viewing audience of 1918)	Dramatic scene	"He's leaving for war."
Widow or a mother who has lost a son (Sassoon)	The major at the base	Scrapbook/memory book	Loss

SAMPLE 5.5—RAFT Activity Options and Rubric—*(continued)*

RAFT Rubric: A Poet's View of Patriotism

Directions: As you plan your project, refer to the criteria presented below. After completing your RAFT activity, asses how well you have met the criteria. Submit this form when you turn in or present your activity.

ROLE: Student creates a specific role. Contextual cues within the product display a message from a defined point of view relevant to the content.

Evaluator	Very Strong	Strong	Acceptable	Unacceptable
Student				
Teacher				

AUDIENCE: Student addresses a specific audience. Contextual cues within the product display a content-relevant message to a defined audience.

Evaluator	Very Strong	Strong	Acceptable	Unacceptable
Student				
Teacher				

FORMAT: Student chooses a creative format—one that might showcase one of the student's strengths. The product's format not only enhances the message to the intended audience, but is also appropriate for the role and content.

Evaluator	Very Strong	Strong	Acceptable	Unacceptable
Student				
Teacher				

TOPIC: Student focuses upon a particular topic relevant to the field of study. The product's topic is relevant to the content. The student clearly displays his or her understanding of the major concepts within the content and of the role and audience for whom the product is intended.

Evaluator	Very Strong	Strong	Acceptable	Unacceptable
Student				
Teacher				

SAMPLE 5.5—RAFT Activity Options and Rubric—*(continued)*

Student Comments About the Project

Teacher Comments About the Project

SAMPLE 5.6—Target Notes Guidelines and Template

Name _____ Date _____

Directions: This note-taking template is designed to help you identify and analyze multiple perspectives on a common subject. Follow the prompts provided for your group, and see the teacher if you need assistance.

Group A

1. *Write the subject of this inquiry in the center circle.* For this assignment, your subject is yourself.
2. Think about the various individuals or groups with whom you interact. Examples might be your parents, a certain teacher (or your teachers in general), friends (or a specific friend), classmates, teammates, and so on. *Write the names of these individuals or groups in the inside ring of spaces.*
3. Think of the various ways in which these individuals or members of these groups might see you. What opinions do they have about you? What would they say your defining characteristics are? Your good and bad qualities? *Record this information in the outside ring of spaces.*

Group B

1. *Write the subject of this inquiry in the center circle.* For this assignment, your subject is yourself in the context of your role as a member of your generation—a young adult.
2. Think about the various individuals or groups in society who might interact with you in the context of this role—either directly or indirectly. Examples might be people in your parents' generation, your teachers, advertisers, politicians, and so on. *Write the names of these individuals or groups in the inside ring of blocks.*
3. Think of the various ways in which these individuals or members of these groups might view you in the context of your role as young adult. What opinions do they have about young adults? What would each identified individual or a typical member of the identified groups say are the defining characteristics of a young adult? Their good and bad qualities? *Record this information in the outside ring of boxes.*

Group C

1. *Write the subject of this inquiry in the center circle.* For this assignment, your subject is yourself in the context of your role as a part of American society and culture.
2. Think about the various individuals or groups who might interact with you or view you within context of this role—either directly or indirectly. Examples might be people in other countries, varying political or religious groups, the media, and other cultural groups. *Write the names of these individuals or groups in the inside ring of spaces.*
3. Think of the various ways in which these individuals or members of these groups might view you in the context of your role as a member of American culture and society. What opinions do they have about Americans? What would each identified individual or a typical member of the identified groups say about the American people? Their good and bad qualities? *Record this information in the outside ring of spaces.*

Target Notes

Name _____   **Date** _____

Subject _____   **Period** _____

SAMPLE 5.7—Spreadsheet Note-Taking Template

Taking Notes on Memorial Project Presentations

Directions: Record the presenter's name and project title in the first two columns. In the third column, record the subject of the memorial and several qualities about that individual that are evident in the project. In the fourth column, record elements of the project that you felt were effective in relaying those important qualities.

Presenter's Name	Project Title	Subject/Qualities	Effective Elements

6

Point the Way

A Mathematics Unit on Vectors

Unit Developer: Kim L. Pettig

Introduction

This two- to three-week mathematics unit focuses on the broad understanding of the interdependence of basic operations. To accomplish this, students investigate two-dimensional vectors in coordinate planes and come to understand how these represent magnitude and direction. The learning opportunities are highly interactive, providing students with experience working with vectors in a variety of kinesthetic and visual modes.

The unit begins with a challenge: Students attempt to direct a paper airplane toward a target through a cross wind. After brainstorming the factors that might influence a "successful trip," they go on to explore some of those factors, collecting different data by simulating magnitude and direction on an expanded floor or table-top grid.

Throughout the unit, lessons involve collaborative opportunities to experience, explain, and calculate results for different applications of vectors. Students learn about vectors through activities in like-readiness pairs, an exploration of interactive educational Web sites, a board game, and the development of creative designs. These activities promote proficiency in plotting vectors, translating vectors, and determining vector sums. They are differentiated to offer students a range of task options and various ways to demonstrate understanding, based on learning style. Targeted scaffolding helps students working at different readiness levels meet the requirements. Guidelines, rubrics, and contracts establish the parameters for responsible, independent work. Class presentations and explanations foster peer-to-peer discourse, and flexible grouping fosters cooperative work skills.

The unit also features a pretest to help clarify readiness levels. Embedded self-assessment activities help the teacher refine instruction to better suit students' readiness, learning profiles, and specific interests. On the final assessment, a menu of tasks allows the teacher to target both readiness and learning style differences.

Teacher Reflection on Designing the Unit

One of my favorite public television documentaries from years ago was *The Ascent of Man*, hosted and narrated by the brilliant mathematician, scientist, and poet, Jacob Bronowski. He had the gift of being able to peel back layers of history, invention, science, and archaeology to expose their dialectic relationships. This "interdependence of all things" has always fascinated me, and it ultimately guided the overall concept of this mathematics unit. Students today learn discrete skills but frequently miss how these skills connect. What better way to demonstrate the interdependence of mathematical concepts and calculations than by exploring vectors with hands-on learning?

I designed this unit for students who had mastered the three basic trigonometric ratios and had completed an Algebra I course that included constant and variable change, linear graphing, and beginning linear equations. It was relatively easy to select activities that would lead students to the key understandings about vectors. However, ordering the activities so that each concept adequately built toward the next step was more challenging. Small-group activities such as the ones I chose can be easily misconstrued as merely entertaining unless the expectations are explicit and the mathematics is essential for task completion. Piloting the lessons independent of one another was not as successful as implementing the unit as a seamless investigation. It became apparent early in the development of this unit that the "sum of the learning" was indeed greater than its parts.

Mathematics Standards Addressed

Numbers and Operations

SD1   Understand that vectors and matrices are systems that have some of the properties of the real-number system.

SD2   Develop an understanding of the properties of and representations for the addition and multiplication of vectors and matrices.

SD3   Develop fluency in operations with real numbers, vectors, and matrices.

Geometry

SD4   Explore relationships among classes of two- and three-dimensional geometric objects.

SD5   Use Cartesian coordinates and other coordinate systems to analyze geometric situations.

SD6   Understand and represent translations, reflections, rotations, and dilations of objects in a plane by using sketches, coordinates, vectors, function notations, and matrices.

SD7   Use trigonometric relationships to determine angle measurements.

Unit Concepts and Generalizations

Interdependence of Mathematical Operations, Properties of Mathematical Systems

GEN1   Interdependence of discrete elements is basic to the outcome of most all events.

GEN2   Prediction of events may require a synthesis of numerical and graphic data.

GEN3   Relationships among numbers and number systems are definable.

Unit Objectives

As a result of this unit, the students will *know*

- The definition and properties of vectors and how to represent them.
- The difference between magnitude (size, length) and direction.
- The procedure for plotting vectors and translating vectors using Cartesian coordinate geometry.
- The procedure for adding vectors.
- The definition and use of the term *resultant*.
- The definition and use of a *scalar* in relationship to vectors.
- That displacement, velocity, acceleration, and force involve magnitude plus direction, and are defined as *directed quantities*.
- That vectors and coordinates represent objects in a plane through translations, reflections, rotations, and dilations.
- Some practical applications for vector mathematics.

As a result of this unit, the students will *understand that*

- Interdependence of discrete elements is basic to the outcome of most events.
- Prediction of events may require a synthesis of numerical and graphic data.
- Relationships among numbers and number systems are definable.
- Systems, such as vectors, have specific properties of real-number systems.
- Mathematical modeling, as with vectors, simulates how interdependent properties behave.
- Real-world problems can be solved by modeling interdependent variations of an outcome.

As a result of this unit, the students will *be able to*

- Represent the elements of magnitude and direction with vectors.
- Explain some potential uses for vectors.
- Translate objects in a plane by using vectors.
- Calculate and solve problems using vectors.

Instructional Strategies Used in this Unit

- Activity guides
- Exit cards
- Scaffolding
- Tiered assessment
- Cooperative learning
- Flexible grouping
- Tiered activities

Sample Supporting Materials Provided

Sample #	Title	Page
6.1	Unit Pretest	238
6.2	Marble and Straws Activity Guide and Record Sheet	242
6.3	Ferry 'Cross the Mersey Tiered Activity Guide	243
6.4	Directions for "Vector"	244
6.5	From Here to Eternity Tiered Activity Guide	247
6.6	Pattern Challenge	248
6.7	Unit Post-test Menu	249

Unit Overview

LESSON	WHOLE-CLASS COMPONENTS	DIFFERENTIATED COMPONENTS
LESSON 1 **Unit Introduction and Exploration** *2–3 class periods*	Pre-assessment on vectors and the interdependence of magnitude and direction *30 minutes*	
	Pre-assessment follow-up *15 minutes*	
	Paper airplane demonstration to stimulate exploration *10 minutes*	
	Demonstration of the interdependence of magnitude and direction *10 minutes*	

LESSON	WHOLE-CLASS COMPONENTS	DIFFERENTIATED COMPONENTS
		Small-group work on reflection and translation differentiated by readiness and compatibility *20–30 minutes*
	Demonstration of adding vectors and introduction of the "How Far Away?" mini-project *10 minutes*	
		"How Far Away?" project work differentiated by readiness *30–35 minutes*
	Exit activity: "Tickets-to-Go" *5 minutes*	
LESSON 2 **Vector Applications** *2–3 class periods*	"How Far Away?" project follow-up and discussion *10 minutes*	
	Demonstration of measuring two unequal forces *5 minutes*	
	Hands-on "Marble and Straws" activity in self-selected small groups *20 minutes*	
	Exit activity: "Quickie-Stickies" *3 minutes*	
	"Marble and Straws" follow-up and connections discussion *10 minutes*	
	Video clip presentation and discussion *35–50 minutes*	
	Review of the three basic trigonometry functions for determining the specific angle of a vector *10–15 minutes*	
		"Ferry 'Cross the Mersey" practice activities differentiated by readiness *25 minutes*

LESSON	WHOLE-CLASS COMPONENTS	DIFFERENTIATED COMPONENTS
	Student presentations and whole-class follow-up discussion *20–30 minutes*	
LESSON 3 **Interactive Exploration** *2 class periods*	Demonstration of how to interact with the selected Web sites *10 minutes*	
		Web site exploration and response activities in readiness-based pairs *25–30 minutes*
	Exit activity: "iWeb Wonder" *5 minutes*	
	Web exploration follow-up and whole-class discussion *15–20 minutes*	
	Introduction to the board game "Vector" and review of the calculation skills for summing vectors *25 minutes*	
		"Vector" free play in readiness-based small groups *time varies*
LESSON 4 **Calculations and Translations** *2 class periods*	Introduction and whole-class investigation of geometric translation with vectors *20 minutes*	
	"From Here to Eternity" pattern translation activity in self-selected pairs *25–30 minutes*	"Stop-spot" whole-class mini-lessons based on readiness needs *Ongoing, time varies*
	"From Here to Eternity" pattern solution presentations *8–10 minutes*	
	Pattern quiz *5–8 minutes*	

LESSON	WHOLE-CLASS COMPONENTS	DIFFERENTIATED COMPONENTS
LESSONS 5 **Group Review and Assessment** *2 class periods*		Unit review in self-selected groups based on readiness needs *35–40 minutes*
	Exit activity: "Tickets-to-Go" *5 minutes*	
		Final assessment differentiated by learning profile *45 minutes*

Unit Description and Teacher Commentary

LESSON 1   **Unit Introduction and Exploration**   *(2–3 class periods)*
Concept: Interdependence of Mathematical Operations
GEN2; SD1, SD5–6

LESSON SEQUENCE AND DESCRIPTION	TEACHER COMMENTARY
Preparation note: Before this lesson, draw or use masking tape to create grids on pieces of poster board. There should be enough so that each group of three students will have its own grid.	
Pre-assessment on vectors and the interdependence of magnitude and direction. Distribute the **Unit Pretest** (see Sample 6.1, page 238) and give students 30 minutes to complete it. The item-by-item structure of the pre-assessment is designed to separately reveal the various key skills and understandings of this unit: • Items A, B, and G focus on attributes, definition, and essential vocabulary. • Items F and H focus on the concepts of interdependence for magnitude and direction. • Items C and E focus on the basics of coordinate geometry. • Item D focuses on the Pythagorean theorem.	The pretest was a way to give both the students and me a window into their current readiness levels. It examines skills, concepts, and an understanding of the basic principles. Additionally, it led students to assume more responsibility for their actions during this unit.

LESSON SEQUENCE AND DESCRIPTION	TEACHER COMMENTARY
Pre-assessment follow-up. Provide brief comments on the pretest. Reiterate and support successful performances that the students have revealed. Ask for and record a list of ideas that the students feel *least certain about* at this beginning point of the unit. Retain this list for later.	Here, I wanted to validate students' successes as well as their uncertainties.
Paper airplane demonstration to stimulate exploration. Give each student a half-sheet of plain, letter-size paper to fold into a paper airplane of any design. Challenge students to attempt to fly their planes into a centrally located receptacle. Then, use a variable-speed fan to attempt to alter the flight paths of the planes and cause them to miss the target. After everyone has had one try, discuss the combination of factors to know and the necessary calculations to make in order to fly the plane into the receptacle every time. Once again, record the students' ideas on a piece of chart paper, emphasizing the pairing of two or more pieces of information. Retain the list for later use.	
Demonstration of the interdependence of magnitude and direction. Using one of the prepared poster-board grids student volunteers, and two small objects (e.g., small-scale vehicles or figures), call out specific grid coordinates for two different "trips": 1. A "mime trip" (a geometric reflection, or mirror image shape that creates at least one line of symmetry). 2. A "copycat trip" (a geometric translation, or slide from one place to another while keeping the identical shape). For the mime trip (geometric reflection) 1. Ask Students A and B to place markers at the same coordinate point (0, –3). Record this location. 2. Call out coordinate point (3, –1) and ask Student A to move marker A to that point. Then, ask Student B to mirror that move by moving marker B to coordinate point (–3, –1). Record the new locations. 3. Next, ask Student A to move marker A to coordinate point (3, 2), which Student B mirrors by moving marker B to (–3, 2). Record these locations. 4. To finish the reflection, ask Student A to move marker A to (0, 4), at which time Student B moves marker B to the same point.	Students who self-assessed as being comfortable with this topic assisted with this demonstration. We marked and labeled each stage of movement to create maps, so that students could see the figures that emerged. After each demo trip, I displayed the list of coordinates alongside the map to underscore the mathematical relationships within or between the figure(s). This relationship is one basis for understanding symmetry and proportion.

LESSON SEQUENCE AND DESCRIPTION	TEACHER COMMENTARY

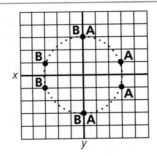

For the copycat trip (geometric translation)

1. Start Student A at coordinate point (1, 0) and Student B at (4, 3). Record these locations.
2. Call out coordinate point (4, 0) and ask Student A to move marker A to that point. Ask Student B to "copy" that move by moving marker B to point (7, 3). Record these locations.
3. Next, call out coordinate point (1, 3) for marker A, which Student B mirrors by moving marker B to (4, 6).
4. To complete the copy, ask Student A to move marker A back to (1, 0), at which time Student B returns marker B to (4, 3). Point out that each move was proportionally the same in the same direction, and the result is two copies of the same pattern.

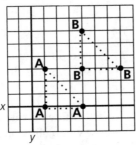

✳ **Small-group work on reflection and translation differentiated by readiness and compatibility.** Divide students into groups of three, based on readiness and interpersonal compatibility. Write specific coordinate instructions for the groups to take the reflection and translation "trips" and for them to record all of the coordinate data they used. So that the groups are not doing identical tasks, vary the instructions to suggest different patterns for the reflections (regular and irregular 2–D geometric shapes) and different positions of the translations (quadrant and rotation).

Stress that even though they are working in groups, each student is responsible for recording and submitting his or her own work.

With the airplane experience fresh in students' minds, transitioning to this activity focused them on finding the combination of necessary data that constitutes magnitude and direction. For the most part, they did not succeed with the paper airplane task and, therefore, were more motivated to make this task "work." I based readiness determinations on the pretest and compatibility judgments from classroom observation.

LESSON SEQUENCE AND DESCRIPTION	TEACHER COMMENTARY
There should be enough trials for each "trip" so that every student does each job (recording coordinate data, leading the trip for reflection, and leading the trip for translation) for both instances.	This structure allowed students to interact collaboratively and stay involved throughout the activity. In addition, requiring two students to complete the tasks successfully while the third one recorded the data for both of their movements underscored the concept of interdependence.
Close the session by telling students that during the next class session, they will be investigating a third type of trip called a "how far away" trip.	
Demonstration of adding vectors and introduction of the "How Far Away?" mini-project. Open the second class session in this lesson by introducing students to the scope and expectations of their first independent mini-project: They will learn to add vectors to determine solutions to a "how far away" type of situation (how far it is from a point of origin to a destination).	I provided a selection of actual maps (town, county, state, and region) and graphing tools from which the students could choose. Creating a new problem is an excellent embedded assessment.
Begin with a demonstration using the prepared grid and markers from the previous session's mime and copycat trips. Ask Students A and B to each move a marker from the origin (0, 0) to any coordinate in the NE quadrant (Student A) and any coordinate in the NW quadrant (Student B). Ask the students to call out both sets of coordinates and record them for the class to see.	
For example: Student A moves marker A to make vector a $\langle 4, 3 \rangle$. Student B moves marker B to make vector b $\langle -2, 2 \rangle$.	I used different students as demo assistants this time out.
Explain to the class that vector sums can show the result of actions that either take place one after another or result from two forces acting on an object at the same time.	The students saw this result in the video clips presented later, in Lesson 2.
Point out that the sum of these two vectors, called the resultant, is found by the following process: • Expressing $\vec{a}$ and $\vec{b}$ in ordered pair notations • Adding the x- and y-coordinates • Simplifying.	
Illustrate the process, using the coordinates chosen by Students A and B: $$a + b = \langle 4, 3 \rangle = (-2, 2 \rangle$$ $$= \langle 4 = (-2), 3 = 2 \rangle$$ $$= \langle 2, 5 \rangle$$	

LESSON SEQUENCE AND DESCRIPTION	TEACHER COMMENTARY
Point out that vectors can be added in any order and still produce the same resultant. Explain why, referencing the parallelogram rule and the diagonal that a resultant forms.	
"How Far Away?" project work differentiated by readiness. Assign like-readiness pairs and distribute readiness-based tasks and project guidelines with varying degrees of scaffolding.	The paperwork each pair-group received was quite similar. I wanted to minimize student awareness of different capabilities.
Task 1 (Advanced Students) A travel assistant at the auto club planned two routes for two different families to go from Rochester, New York, to New York City. One route went mostly south toward Corning and the other went mostly east toward Albany. The families stopped for the night in those cities. Assuming the roads were mostly straight, show and calculate which family had further to go the next day.	Task 1 requires applying the process of adding vectors twice and then determining the difference.
Task 2 (Grade-Level Students) A flight from Rochester, New York, to Charlottesville, Virginia, has a stopover in Philadelphia, Pennsylvania. Show how much farther the passengers traveling on that stopover route had to go than passengers who flew directly from Rochester to Charlottesville.	Task 2 requires the process of adding vectors to be calculated once; the "how much farther" question is derived from that first solution.
Task 3 (Entry-Level Students) A homing pigeon was released from Rochester, New York, to fly to its home. It landed 75 miles west and 23 miles south of the city. Pinpoint which town is nearest the pigeon's home. How far did the pigeon fly?	Task 3 requires the direct application of the process for adding vectors once.
As needed, adjust the directions for the tasks to fit students' readiness to work independently. For example: • *To provide little structure:* Leave the instructions very open, stating just the overall task and then suggesting resources if students "get stuck." • *To provide some structure:* State the overall task with reference to calculation processes; suggest possible first steps. • *To provide lots of structure:* State the overall task and provide a nearly complete example of the process included. Suggest several steps of the process and suggest possible materials to use.	Based on what I knew about the students, I mixed and matched the tasks and the degree of structure in the guidelines. For example, I gave some students very unstructured guidelines and assigned them to Task 2 (the grade-level task). This way of planning allowed for more flexibility to meet specific student needs.

LESSON SEQUENCE AND DESCRIPTION	TEACHER COMMENTARY
Exit activity: "Tickets-to-Go." During the last five minutes of the session, distribute "Tickets-to-Go"—slips of paper with this two-part prompt: 1. *What are some of the tools we use to measure magnitude?* 2. *Consider the following sentence: "The wind blows at 35 miles per hour." Does it contain enough information to describe a vector? Answer on the back of the ticket.* Collect tickets as students exit the classroom.	This provided me with some monitoring feedback about students' understanding of magnitude, measurement, and the interdependence of the components of what constitutes a vector. Based on what I saw in these tickets, I planned to discuss key ideas or prevalent misconceptions at the start of the next session.

LESSON 2

Vector Applications   *(2–3 class periods)*

Concept: Interdependence of Mathematical Operations
GEN1–2; SD3, SD7

LESSON SEQUENCE AND DESCRIPTION	TEACHER COMMENTARY
"How Far Away?" project follow-up and discussion. Begin by collecting student-generated problems from the previous session.	The problems students created were much more difficult than the ones in the original tasks. I checked them for appropriateness and accuracy and reserved them for extra credit "Peer Problems" (see page 249) on the final assessment.
Transition into the session by asking for two or three volunteer pair-groups to present their work on Tasks 1, 2, or 3. Discuss and clarify any misconceptions or errors.	✴ Students who were comfortable with class presentation and oral explanations volunteered to share their work.
Demonstration of measuring two unequal forces. Initiate the next learning activity by asking one student to help demonstrate the process of measuring two unequal forces. Reuse one of the large poster board grids, highlighting the central *x*- and *y*-axes.	
Hands-on "Marble and Straws" activity in self-selected small groups. Ask students to break into three-person groups. Give each group a large poster board grid, one marble, three straws, and a **Marble and Straws Activity Guide and Record Sheet** (see Sample 6.2, page 242).	✴ Students could choose to stay in their three-person groups from the previous lesson or switch partners. They readily recognized "compatible and working" relationships, and I found that they self-monitored on-task activity better after they formed their own groups.

LESSON SEQUENCE AND DESCRIPTION	TEACHER COMMENTARY
The directions for this task tell students to conduct a total of nine trials. Each trial proceeds as follows: 1. The students place the marble at a location on the grid (as directed). 2. The two students with straws align themselves with the axes at any point around the grid board. 3. The third student (the recorder) gives the start signal and the other two simultaneously blow through their straws to move the marble across the grid. 4. The recorder gives the stop signal at any time before the marble leaves the grid's edge and notes the starting and stopping location of the marble on his or her copy of the record sheet. Each student serves as the recorder for three trials, and as a "force of magnitude" for the other six. Then, they complete a set of drawing and calculation tasks based on the trials (see Sample 6.2).	The engaging nature of these tasks kept interest and on-task behavior at high levels, and the students were anxious to try all roles. What's more, rotating the roles gave everyone several opportunities to influence the outcome of a trial by controlling the "magnitude" factor—blowing through a straw. This helped to embed the key concept of interdependence. I noticed that students became more proficient with data collection and record keeping as they watched and experienced each successive trial.
Tell students that they should complete their calculations and determinations outside of class time and retain their work for the next session.	For the purpose of grading, I required students to complete the individual calculations, but the collaborative effect of this activity still led to peer mentoring and interaction.
Exit activity: "Quickie-Stickies." In the last three minutes of class, distribute sticky-note pads and announce that the students are to post a "Quickie-Sticky" response to the following prompt: *What is the variable that is influencing the magnitude for this activity?* Students post their responses as they exit the classroom.	My students like to use sticky notes, and they have a central poster board to use for these quick response activities. Here, it was a brief check to see if they understood the key aspect of the Marble and Straws activity. I addressed any misconceptions I found during the next session's opening discussion.
"Marble and Straws" follow-up and connections discussion. Facilitate an opening discussion about the previous activity and highlight interesting aspects of the students' results. Address misconceptions as necessary.	
Connect the application of wind velocity to air travel and to the initial experiment with the paper airplanes and fan, pointing out the need for both the Pythagorean theorem and basic trigonometry.	I very briefly modeled the paper airplane task during this discussion of the variability of the students' "wind" on their marble.

LESSON SEQUENCE AND DESCRIPTION	TEACHER COMMENTARY
Video clip presentation and discussion. Segue into another application for navigation requiring vector mathematics—travel on water with currents—by showing a short video clip from a movie that demonstrates unplanned or unmanageable vector paths. Good candidates include the following: • The scene from *The African Queen* when the boat is shooting the rapids. • The scene from *Homeward Bound: The Incredible Journey* when the animals cross the river. • A scene from *The River Wild* when the raft is going down the rapids. • Clips from classic Bugs Bunny or Road Runner cartoons that briefly depict the effects of water currents.	Additional visual input from a real-life type of situation is both engaging and instructive. Many students today are "video-oriented" and learn easily through this modality. I was careful to have the clips all queued so as not to distract from the purpose for showing them.
Review of the three basic trigonometry functions for determining the specific angle of a vector. Tell students that, as they observed in the video clips, in order for objects like airplanes and boats to travel directly from one point to another in the air or water, the navigator must calculate a vector path that considers both the object's speed and direction and the water (or air) current's speed and direction. Provide a brief review of the trigonometry functions: $$sine = \frac{opposite}{hypotenuse}$$ $$cosine = \frac{adjacent}{hypotenuse}$$ $$tangent = \frac{opposite}{adjacent}$$ Announce that in the next activity, students will figure out how to pilot a boat across a river, using trigonometry ratios.	Clearly, some students were relieved to have the trig functions and simple examples provided for them.
"Ferry 'Cross the Mersey" practice activities differentiated by readiness. Assign like-readiness pairs—different pairings than the ones used for the "How Far Away?" project in Lesson 1.	I based these pairings on students' responses to the pretest items related to trig functions (items C, D, and E) and on their general calculation-skills facility.

LESSON SEQUENCE AND DESCRIPTION	TEACHER COMMENTARY
Distribute the appropriate level of the **Ferry 'Cross the Mersey Tiered Activity Guide** (see Sample 6.3, page 243), which presents a task focused on determining the specific angle of a vector. Remind students that they should be ready to share their work with the rest of the class.	Students' versions of this activity guide contained only the task directions for their readiness level. The amount of scaffolding built into the task descriptions increases as the task readiness level decreases. However, all three task tiers indicate which trigonometry function is required: *tangent*. I provided a reminder for all students by posting the mnemonic *"SOH CAH TOA"*—the trig ratios.
Student presentations and whole-class follow-up discussion. As students share their work, prompt a discussion that helps to highlight two unit generalizations: event interdependence and the synthesis of numerical and graphed data to predict events.	

LESSON 3

Interactive Exploration
Concept: Properties of Mathematical Systems
GEN1–2; SD1, SD5

(2 class periods)

LESSON SEQUENCE AND DESCRIPTION	TEACHER COMMENTARY
Demonstration of how to interact with the selected Web sites. Explain the parameters of using specified Web sites to explore controlling one and two elements of a vector. Using a large-screen monitor (if available), go online and show students how to engage one of the interactive games on the Web site of the National Council of Teachers of Mathematics (NCTM): standards.nctm.org/document/eexamples/chap7/7.1/index.htm. Discuss the activity expectations: to explore the interdependent consequences of altering magnitude and direction.	Most students are comfortable with interactive computer games. I have found that using this pre-established modality is an effective way to refine conceptual understanding and reinforce skills.
Web site exploration and response activities in readiness-based pairs. Assign students to readiness pairs and give them their exploration assignment: one of two interactive games, both of which are available at the NCTM URL provided.	With two tiers here instead of three, the students were regrouped from the previous activity. It was important to establish "compatibility" of work styles for those students working as pairs.

LESSON SEQUENCE AND DESCRIPTION	TEACHER COMMENTARY
Grade-Level and Entry-Level Students Students play the *Components of a Vector* interactive game, which asks them to maneuver a "car" by adjusting direction and magnitude settings. Students follow the task directions on the Web site and answer the reflection questions, submitting their answers in writing. *Advanced Students* Students play the *Sums of Vectors and Their Properties* interactive game, which asks them to maneuver an "airplane" by adjusting magnitude and direction settings and factoring in "wind speed." Students follow the task directions on the Web site and complete the follow-up tasks, submitting their answers in writing. Other useful Web sites include the following: • *For student information:* mathforum.org/library/drmath/sets/select/dm_vectors.html and www.netcomuk.co.uk/~jenolive/homevec.html. • *For interactive practice:* mathforum.org/~klotz/Vectors/vectors.html. • *For interactive games:* naturalmath.com/matrix.html#1.	The game is designed to help students explore how characteristics of a vector affect the object's movement. This understanding creates the base for using and calculating vectors. This game takes the "car" activity a step further, and is designed to extend students' knowledge of number systems to the system of vectors. With this knowledge, application and calculation abilities become more durable.
Exit activity: "iWeb Wonder." Conclude this session by distributing slips of paper and asking students to respond in writing to this prompt: *Speculate about which other vector activities could be modeled interactively with a computer game/program. How did any of the Web activities you played demonstrate the main idea about using vectors?* Collect the iWeb Wonder slips as students exit the classroom.	Students' responses here were quite varied, ranging from very simple to ones with in-depth details. This was an opportunity for the students to reflect on their learning and a chance for me to get a look at their understanding of the applications for vectors. Some of the ideas formed the basis of the next session's discussion.
Web exploration follow-up and whole-class discussion. Facilitate a discussion of students' Web explorations based on their answers to the Web site questions. Incorporate various "iWeb Wonder" responses. Record students' general findings and conclusions about the interdependence of magnitude and direction as they experienced it in this task. Then, highlight the emergence of patterns and the subsequent predictable relationship between these factors. Refocus students on the overall unit principle concerning number system relationships.	Writing down students' ideas seemed to promote participation and stimulate more peer-to-peer discourse. I wanted the discussion about patterns to be extensive so that I could explicate the connections between the actions and the numerical aspect of the patterns.

LESSON SEQUENCE AND DESCRIPTION	TEACHER COMMENTARY
Introduction to the board game "Vector" and review of the calculation skills for summing vectors. Introduce "Vector," a board game designed to reinforce the calculation skills for summing vectors (see Sample 6.4, **Directions for "Vector,"** on page 244). To demonstrate how to play the game, create a transparency of the game board or use magnets on a vertical magnetic surface. Ask for a student volunteer to participate as your opponent. Use the rest of the class as "advisors" for you and your volunteer opponent. Play just enough moves to launch the basic game.	Students who struggled with some of the calculation aspects of this unit found the game approach illuminating, as it exemplified the interdependence aspect of vectors. I chose a board game format as a sequel to the online experience to maintain engagement while providing focused practice for calculation skills.
"Vector" free play in readiness-based small groups. Divide the class into groups of four based on readiness and distribute the game directions (see Sample 6.4), game pieces, and game boards. Permit students to sign out sets of game materials to play independently outside of class and ask them to report back about their games.	The students played this game at various levels of sophistication, and dividing them into readiness-groups encouraged them to be more competitive. I was careful to continually assess student progress so that the readiness groupings would match their evolving needs. Because of limited class time and the engaging nature of this game, almost everyone signed out the materials to play at home.

LESSON 4   **Calculations and Translations**   *(2 class periods)*
Concept: Properties of Mathematical Systems
GEN3; SD5–6

LESSON SEQUENCE AND DESCRIPTION	TEACHER COMMENTARY
Introduction and whole-class investigation of geometric translation with vectors. Introduce geometric translation with vectors through an investigation activity that incorporates geometric-design wallpaper samples. Distribute a wide variety of patterns and allow the students to select one they think might be interesting to translate on a coordinate grid. Discuss what kind of pattern might be easy to translate and what kind might be more challenging.	I carefully preselected the choices of samples so that there were mostly useable designs. I did include some nongeometric and difficult patterns to stimulate the discussion about the translation process.

LESSON SEQUENCE AND DESCRIPTION	TEACHER COMMENTARY
As a class, build a working definition of a translation. Use vectors (and a grid) to demonstrate the connection of translation. Show four situations: enlarging or reducing, overlapping, tessellating, and multidirectional translations. As part of this lesson, visually generate a wide variety of examples and nonexamples and then post them for ongoing reference.	
✸"From Here to Eternity" pattern translation activity in self-selected pairs. Ask students to form pairs and together choose any one pattern to translate. Discuss and then make available a wide range of appropriate materials, such as various-gauge grid papers and measurement tools.	The different-gauge grid papers inspired some students not only to translate their pattern, but to alter the proportions and scale. Those students who were demonstrating solid proficiency at the beginning of this activity completed the task and then created more complex versions. Students with a visual/graphic learning style tended to accomplish the task and then enlarge, colorize, or embellish the end product.
Distribute the **From Here to Eternity Tiered Activity Guide** (see Sample 6.5, page 247) and explain the tasks: Pairs must figure out how to use vectors to continue their selected pattern in all directions. Students explore the use of four-quadrant coordinate geometry, the expression of vector components, and the addition of vector values. The tasks highlight the importance of holding both direction and distance constant in order to accomplish a translation with vectors; they are interdependent for this function and this will be evident in the numerical notation.	✸Restating the basic information on this handout left me free to circulate and observe, providing key definitions and additional assistance as students worked. It had the secondary effect of encouraging students to take charge of resolving their own mini-problems. It also gave me insight as to larger issues we could use for our "stop-spot" lessons.
✸"Stop-spot" whole-class mini-lessons based on readiness needs. As students work on their pattern translations, do "stop-spot" whole-class mini-lessons on how to use vectors to represent translations graphically and numerically. Discuss the process and write down a specific example on chart paper, then post it for students' reference.	In this instance, it was important to review the addition of vectors as a whole class in order to translate a design twice in the same direction. We did this after students began work and then "discovered" they needed to know something else to complete the task. I've found that addressing this kind of immediate need-to-know usually leads to powerful and durable learning.

LESSON SEQUENCE AND DESCRIPTION	TEACHER COMMENTARY
	Here, students who grasped the concept enhanced their comfort level with it by explaining what they knew. Those who were less sure of the concept benefited from hearing a peer explain it in terms different from the original explanation.
"From Here to Eternity" pattern solution presentations. Pairs present their patterns and briefly explain their calculations to the whole class. Presentation order is determined through a sign-up sheet. After the presentations, collect students' work and assess it.	This sign-up strategy is a way of accommodating student differences in the ways in which they prefer to show their understanding. Here, it meant I didn't need to call on students who were either "always volunteering to speak" or "always first." This method also helps students control *when* they present. Some students' learning style is such that they truly prefer not to speak first or last.
Pattern quiz. Conclude this session with a quiz: the **Pattern Challenge** (see Sample 6.6, page 248). Students complete it on their own and hand in it for assessment.	This task was something moderately difficult but quick to accomplish and assess. The flexible grouping essential to successful differentiation includes opportunities for individual work and assessment.

LESSON 5   Group Review and Assessment   *(2 class periods)*

Concepts: Interdependence of Mathematical Operations,
Properties of Mathematical Systems
GEN1–3; SD1–7

LESSON SEQUENCE AND DESCRIPTION	TEACHER COMMENTARY
Unit review in self-selected groups based on readiness needs. Students self-select into one of three "focus groups," each of which reviews a different aspect of unit content: (1) vector plotting and calculation, (2) specific cases of magnitude, or (3) the interdependence of magnitude and directions.	Self-selection of the topic area allowed for differentiation based on both students' assessment of their own strengths as well as their particular interest in a type of activity experienced during the unit.

LESSON SEQUENCE AND DESCRIPTION	TEACHER COMMENTARY
Tell students that within their focus groups, they will discuss what they now understand about their chosen subtopic and use at least two visual examples. Everyone in the group must participate in the discussion. The rest of the class will observe the discussion and take notes. At the end of the discussion time limit (10 minutes per group), the observers may contribute up to three key points they feel were not covered.	The participation requirement resulted in high engagement. The not-so-subtle, secondary purpose for using this strategy was for the students to assume the major responsibility for shaping their own learning as well as assessing it.
Focus Group 1: Vector Plotting and Calculation Students' discussion should be built around the pattern challenge.	As we used it, the "focus group" format actually required a different physical set up in the classroom—a central circle of focus group participants inside a larger circle of observers.
Focus Group 2: Specific Cases of Magnitude Students' discussion should incorporate class suggestions from the iWeb Wonder activity (see page 232).	
Focus Group 3: The Interdependence of Magnitude and Direction Students' discussion should incorporate the comparative data collected from the initial table-top Marbles and Straws results (see page 228).	
Exit activity: "Tickets-to-Go." Conclude this session by asking students to respond to the following prompt: *Write a best <u>first</u> question on an exam about vectors. What do you think is the most important thing to know or understand?* Collect tickets as students exit the classroom.	Using this strategy almost always helps students at all readiness levels focus on their strengths and weaknesses, and thereby, study more effectively for a final assessment. Judging by the outcome of their final assessment, it worked well!
Final assessment differentiated by learning profile. Distribute prepared copies of the **Unit Post-test Menu** (see Sample 6.7, page 249), assigning each student to a combination of four tasks that considers his or her strongest working and learning modality. The item selection ensures assessment of a full range of skills and concepts for this unit. Each student must select a fifth task from the menu. Provide grid paper.	This menu gave some flexibility to adjust the post-test to meet both working and learning profiles (via Gardner's model).
Here are some possible task groupings: • For students who prefer verbal/language-based representations: Tasks A, B, C, and I. • For students who prefer calculation/numerical representations: Tasks C, E, G, and I. • For students who prefer visual/graphic modalities: Tasks B, F, H, and I.	I assigned Task I to all students because it represents a benchmark for the broad skills and conceptual basis for the unit. I did not assign Task D to any student; many students selected it as the "free-choice" item.

LESSON SEQUENCE AND DESCRIPTION	TEACHER COMMENTARY
• *For students who have mixed learning/working modalities:* Tasks A, E, F, and I. For extra credit, students may solve one of the Peer Problems generated back in their Lesson 1 "Tickets-to-Go." It may be necessary to custom-design an assessment to accommodate specific circumstances, such as fine motor skills coordination problems.	Interestingly, these problems reflected almost all of the essential points I covered on the assessment.

Teacher Reflection on the Unit

Teaching brings many rewards, but it's hard to beat students' exclamations as they "uncover" a new idea: "That's cool!" and "Awesome!" and an enthusiastic fist pump with a resounding "Yes!" When the hard work of unit planning, preparation, and implementation are repaid with these reactions, a teacher's reservoir of energy is instantly renewed. This was one of those units.

The various opportunities for choice, the regular regrouping, the variable work formats, and shifting responsibility for specific aspects of the learning to the students all combined to make this a unique mathematics experience. The openness of the give-and-take discussions ultimately led students to a better understanding of key concepts and provided an ongoing assessment of progress.

While the pretest and targeted post-test were a demonstration of one kind of mastery, the discussions spawned by the "Tickets-to-Go" and similar exit card–style assessments offered a richer basis for adjusting an upcoming task or focusing a mini-lesson. Teachers seldom repeat a whole unit or even a single lesson in the same way the next time they facilitate it; the response of each different group affects the path of instruction. This unit's design built that kind of necessary flexibility into most lessons. Furthermore, by sampling students' ideas about vectors through the exit activities, I acquired a treasure trove of new ideas to incorporate into both the discussions and future task options. Growing along with my students makes me say "Yes!" too.

Kim L. Pettig, EdD, is Project Challenge Coordinator for Allen Creek School in the Pittsford Central School District, Pittsford, New York. She provides instructional support for teachers as they implement new curricula and state standards. She can be reached at kim_pettig@pittsford. monroe.edu.

SAMPLE 6.1—Unit Pretest

Item A

Assign all of the phrases that apply to the diagrams by writing the phrase number under each diagram. Some diagrams may have none, one, or more than one matching phrase.

1 = All of these vectors are equal.
2 = None of these vectors is equal.
3 = These vectors are opposites.
4 = All of these vectors are parallel.
5 = Each of these vectors has the same initial point.
6 = None of these vectors is parallel.
7 = Each of these vectors has the same terminal point.

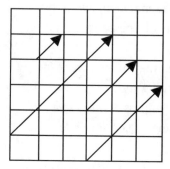

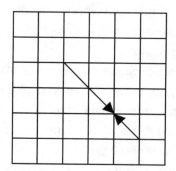

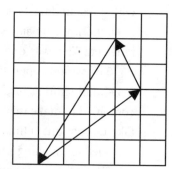

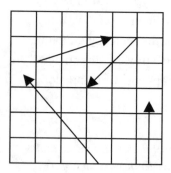

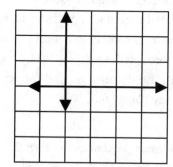

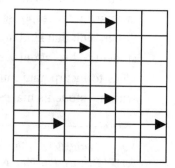

SAMPLE 6.1—Unit Pretest—*(continued)*

Item B
Read the following statements and check those that you think are true.

Vectors . . .
- [ ] are any quantity that has magnitude and direction.
- [ ] describe 2–D events.
- [ ] are directed line segments.
- [ ] can represent displacement.
- [ ] don't follow the rules of Associative Law for addition.
- [ ] describe a geometric translation.
- [ ] cannot represent force.
- [ ] describe 3–D events.
- [ ] can represent acceleration and velocity.
- [ ] describe honeybee movements for communication.
- [ ] graphically describe two numerical quantities at the same time.
- [ ] follow the rules for Commutative Property of Addition.
- [ ] are described as bearings with degrees for navigation.

Item C
1. Draw what you think a line segment would look like if it was described as having end points (–2, 5), and (7, –1). Label it.
2. Now, draw a new line segment parallel to the first one anywhere on the grid and describe its end points. Label it.

x

y

New Parallel Segment:
End point (_____)
End point (_____)

Item D

1. If you know the length of two legs in a right triangle, how can you figure out the length of the third side?

_____
_____
_____
_____
_____

2. If you know the length of two legs in a right triangle, how can you figure out the degrees of the acute angles of that triangle?

_____
_____
_____
_____
_____

Item E

1. Use each figure and vector to help you sketch a 3–D figure.

2. Explain how you could describe your 3–D figures by using coordinates.

_____
_____
_____
_____

SAMPLE 6.1—Unit Pretest—*(continued)*

Item F

A cheetah you want to photograph runs by at 68 miles per hour on his way to catch a young springbok. List <u>what else</u> you need to know in order to get your photo.

_____

_____

_____

_____

_____

Item G

What if you
— drew a simple shape like this one,
— asked a friend to wear a blindfold,
— and then tried to describe how to trace over it?

Explain what you would say.

_____

_____

_____

_____

Item H

Describe what you think going out in a rowboat on a river has to do with vectors.

_____

_____

_____

_____

SAMPLE 6.2—Marble and Straws Activity Guide and Record Sheet

Marbles and Straws

Name _____

Others in Your Group _____

Directions: Each member of your group must record the data from **three trials:**

Trial 1: Begin the marble at the *x*- and *y*-axes origin. Label the axes and intervals.
Trial 2: Begin the marble at any intersection of two grid lines in the SW quadrant.
Trial 3: Begin the marble at any one grid line along the *y*-axis.

You are the "start and stop" signaler for the three trials for which you record data. On the other six trials, you are one of the "forces of magnitude." (Use the straw to blow on the marble.)

For *each trial* you record, use the chart below to

1. Indicate the marble's starting and stopping points.
2. Draw the marble's paths as a vector and label each one.
3. Draw the vectors that represent the two forces on the marble.
4. Determine which force had the greater magnitude.

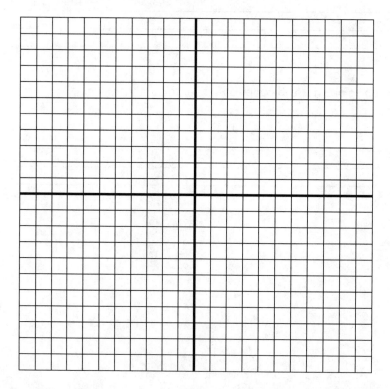

SAMPLE 6.3—Ferry 'Cross the Mersey Tiered Activity Guide

Ferry 'Cross the Mersey

Directions: Below is a map/location sketch of a river and two opposite ports on that river. Your task is to figure out how to take a ferry boat from one point (Bennett) to another point (Crawford) across that river. Assume the river's current forms a right angle to your boat's path. With your assigned partner, follow the prompts and guidelines to determine the direction the boat must travel to reach its destination. Use a calculator for both parts of the tasks. Show all your work and be prepared to explain your results.

Challenge Level
1. Choose the speed for your boat in still water and the current's speed. Determine the resulting speed of the boat on the river. (Pythagorean theorem)
2. Determine the angle of direction it would need to travel to reach its port. (tangent ratio)

Grade Level
1. The speed for your boat is 20 miles per hour. Choose the current's speed and write it here: _____. Now determine the speed of your boat on the river. (*Hint:* Use the Pythagorean theorem: $a^2 + b^2 = c^2$.)
2. Determine the angle of direction your boat would need to travel. (*Hint:* Use the tangent ratio: $\tan x° = \frac{opposite\ side}{adjacent\ side}$.)

Entry Level
1. The speed for your boat is 20 miles per hour in still water. The current's speed is 8 miles per hour. Determine the resulting speed of your boat on the river. (*Hint:* Use the Pythagorean theorem: $a^2 + b^2 = c^2$. For example, if the boat's speed was 22 miles per hour and the current's speed was 5 miles per hour, the calculation for the boat's resulting speed would be calculated by $22^2 + 5^2 = c^2$; use a calculator to take the square root.)
2. Determine the angle of direction your boat would need to travel to reach the port across the river. (*Hint:* Use the tangent ratio: $\tan x° = \frac{opposite\ side}{adjacent\ side}$. For example, using the same speeds as before, the boat's direction would be calculated by $\tan x° = \frac{5}{22}$; $x = \tan^{-1} \frac{5}{22}$); use a calculator.)

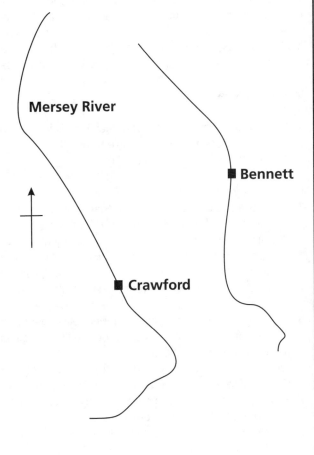

Mersey River

■ **Bennett**

■ **Crawford**

SAMPLE 6.4—Directions for "Vector"

Vector is a board game for two teams of two players, with the team of "North" and "South" facing off against the team of "East" and "West." The players maneuver a single playing piece toward team "goals"—areas on the board—by selecting various combinations of directions and distance (magnitude). Each player receives a set of eight direction cards (N, S, E, W, NW, NE, SE, SW) and a set of four numeral cards (0, 1, 3, 4).

The object of the game is for each team to accumulate as many points as possible. Players earn points when they move the playing piece to certain squares. The direction cards and numeral cards drawn during each round help determine the path of the playing piece on the grid. Using the coordinates drawn, players plan the piece's path toward their team's goal locations. *Note:* Even though this is a team game, each player is responsible for figuring out his or her next move. NO HINTS—verbal or nonverbal—are allowed between teammates.

What You Need
1. A game board.
2. One set of direction cards and numeral cards for each player.
3. A playing piece (a small object, like a coin, that will fit within one grid space).
4. A score sheet for 12 rounds of play.

How to Play
1. Sit on the side of the game board that depicts your direction. (For example, North and South side opposite one another on the north and south sides of the board.)
2. Put the playing piece in the board's center square.
3. Choose a direction card from your stack and place it *face up*. (In Round 1, "North" goes first, followed by East, South and West in a clockwise circle. In Round 2, East goes first; in Round 3, South draws first, and so on).
4. Choose a numeral card for your stack and place it *face down*, next to your direction card. (Follow the same clockwise choice-pattern until all players have placed a numeral card face down in front of them.)
5. The first player (North in Round 1) then turns over his or her numeral card and moves the playing piece that number of spaces in the direction specified by the direction card. Record any points or penalties and follow any directional instructions.
6. The next player (East in Round 1) turns over his or her numeral card and, starting from the square where the playing piece was left, moves it that number of spaces in the direction specified by his or her direction card.
7. Play continues until all players have had one turn; that ends the round. Players return their cards to their decks in preparation for the next drawings.
8. Calculate individual and team totals after each round.

Two Ways to Win
1. The game ends at the end of 12 rounds; the team with the most points wins.
2. The game ends when the playing piece enters any one of the four goal areas during any round. The points for the corresponding player (e.g., "North" if the piece enters the North goal) are doubled. The team with the most points wins.

SAMPLE 6.4—Directions for "Vector"—*(continued)*

About the Squares and Scores

25 Any player who lands on a square that designates just a number receives that number of points. If the next player has chosen a 0 numeral card, he or she also receives that many points.

S 75

E -60 If any player lands on a square that designates a single direction and a positive or negative number, only the designated player (South or East, for example) gains or loses that number of points.

NE 40

SW -50 If any player lands on a square designating two directions, he or she chooses which of these players will gain points (North or East?) or lose points (South or West?).

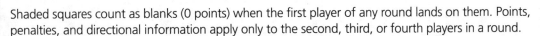 Shaded squares count as blanks (0 points) when the first player of any round lands on them. Points, penalties, and directional information apply only to the second, third, or fourth players in a round.

 If any player lands on a square containing an arrow and a number, he or she moves the playing piece that many spaces in the direction indicated and records any points or penalties from that location. (*Note:* These squares are shaded and count as blanks for the first player in a round.)

Squares with a direction and an *X* means that the corresponding player loses his or her turn in the next round. (*Note:* Again, these squares are all shaded.)

About the Border
If a player ends up on the border during play, he or she loses a turn in the next round. But first, he or she places the playing piece on the closest corner square and records any points or (additional) penalties from that location.

Strategy Suggestions
- Anticipate the moves of your partner and opponents.
- Remember that the first player in each round has many advantages. Use them!
- Watch the total score tallies. Ending the game early might be a good move.
- In certain situations, moving into the border area (and losing a turn) is a smart defensive play.
- Remember, verbal and nonverbal communication between teammates is prohibited.
- You need to carefully study all the possibilities presented by your teammate's directional move before you choose direction and number cards.

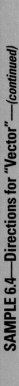

SAMPLE 6.4—Directions for "Vector"—*(continued)*

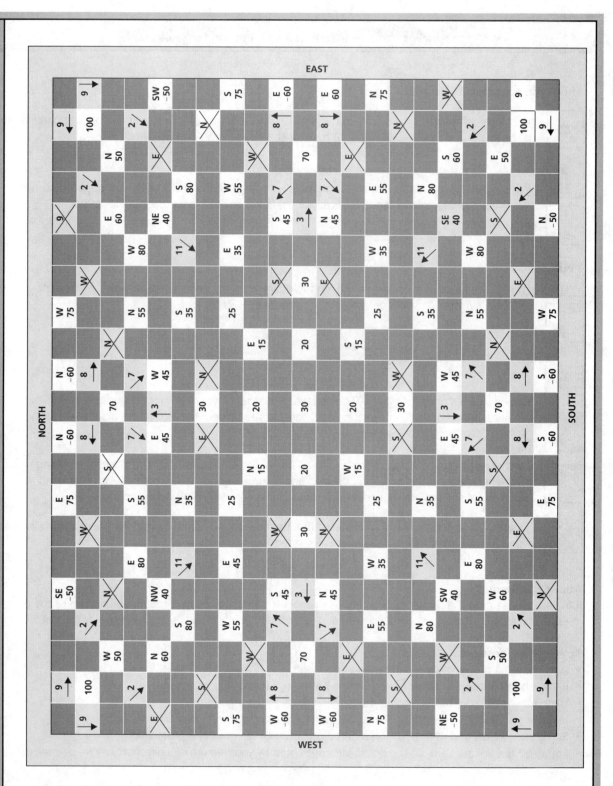

SAMPLE 6.5—From Here to Eternity Tiered Activity Guide

From Here to Eternity

Directions: Choose any one partner and together, choose any one pattern.
Show how your pattern can be continued in all directions using vectors.

We know that
- A **translation** of a shape to another spot means that you need to move the points, or vertices, of that shape in the **same direction** and the **same distance** (magnitude). This can be shown as a **vector.**
- A **translation** depends upon these two quantities being held constant for the duplication of the entire shape.

We also know that
- **Vectors** can be represented with **ordered pair notation** on a coordinate plane. In notation, *x* represents horizontal change from the initial point to the terminal point and *y* represents the vertical change, such that the notation from HERE to ETERNITY, or H to E, is (5, –3).

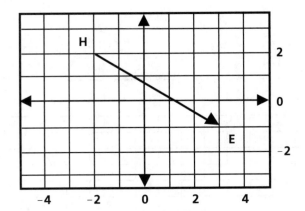

Guidelines
1. Copy your design (or a portion of your design) onto a four-quadrant grid; assign letter identifications to the vertices.
2. Translate that design (choose any two of these three tasks):
   a. In more than one direction
   b. In one direction twice
   c. As an enlargement or reduction
3. For **one** of the above translation tasks you chose
   a. Describe the design by using ordered pair notations for the vectors.
   b. Give the numerical grid change constant for this translation.
4. Formulate a question about any one of your translations to "challenge" another pair of students. Write it on a separate card. Example: *On our enlarged design, which vector has a notation of (–3, –6)?*

SAMPLE 6.6—Pattern Challenge

Directions: On the grid below . . .

1. Highlight and label the *x*- and *y*-axes.
2. Copy this pattern at any size entirely within one quadrant.
3. Translate it entirely within another quadrant.
4. Give the ordered pair notation of the vectors for any six (6) of the vertices.
5. In the space to the right of this shape, state the constants of direction and magnitude for the vectors to make your reproduction.

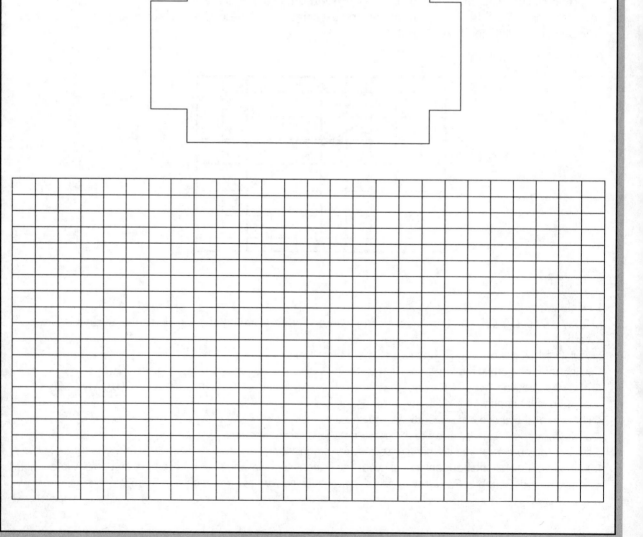

SAMPLE 6.7—Unit Post-test Menu

Directions: On a separate sheet of paper and the grid paper provided, complete the four items marked for you, and then choose **one** additional item to complete. Each task has an equal point value towards your final assessment. *Extra Credit: For 10 points, solve one "Peer Problem."*

☑	Tasks
	A. Write a clear definition of the term *vector* that includes at least four separate facts and attributes.
	B. Draw on grid paper an example of four vectors that are unequal, not parallel, and that have the same terminal point. Label your drawing.
	C. Find the sum of vectors a and c, where vector $\vec{a}$ = (35, –50) and vector $\vec{c}$ = (–35, 50). What does your answer tell you about vectors $\vec{a}$ and $\vec{c}$?
	D. A bear leaves home and ambles 12 km straight south. She turns and walks another 12 km straight west. Then she turns and wanders straight north another 12 km, ending up exactly where she started. What color is the bear? Why? Sketch the trip.
	E. A whale-watching boat leaves its home port and travels 110 miles directly east. It then changes course and travels 50 miles due north. In what direction should the boat head to return directly to its home port? How many miles is the whole trip? Sketch the trip.
	F. Sketch and find the sum of these three different vector pairs. Give your answers in ordered pair notation. a. $\langle -4, -4 \rangle + \langle 2, -5 \rangle$ = b. $\langle -3, 3 \rangle + \langle 4, -4 \rangle$ = c. $\langle -4, 4 \rangle + \langle -4, 2 \rangle$ = (Initial points are all 0) Sketch the answer to vector pair "b" if the initial point was –2,–1.
	G. Draw three vectors such that the sum of any two of them has a greater magnitude that the third one. Label the sketch and show all of your calculations.
	H. Sketch the vectors for the path of an outbound boat going due west at 24 km/h, if it had a north-to-south crosscurrent of 12 km/h. Where would it be after 90 minutes? How long would it take to get back to port?
	I. Translate any quadrilateral shape you choose *twice*. Show all calculations. The translations should not touch or overlap, nor be in the identical plane as the original shape; one translation should cross an *x*- or *y*-axis.

7

What Goes Up Must Come Down

A Mathematics Unit on Quadratics in the General Form

Unit Developer: Catherine Reed

Introduction

This three-week, second-year algebra unit studies quadratic equations from the larger perspective of systems. It addresses multiple mathematics curricular and process standards for algebra and geometry. Students explore real-life scenarios as they extend their understandings about a parabolic trace and consolidate their prior knowledge about this important class of quadratic functions. The goal is for students to create an enduring understanding of the nature of these functions, including the effect each parameter has on the trace of the function, and to grasp the links between this fundamental mathematical idea and its real-world applications. When students have completed the unit, they also will have reviewed the skills associated with solving quadratic equations.

The unit begins with a pre-assessment of the skills and understandings associated with quadratic equations as they are taught in Algebra I and Geometry, both standard prerequisites to Algebra II. Throughout, students work both independently and in flexible groups to create and test hypotheses about the parameters of quadratic functions and conduct research into the applications of quadratic functions.

The unit is designed to take from 14 to 17 class sessions of approximately 45 minutes each, although its actual length varies depending on student readiness, the length of investigative discussions, and the time needed to complete and present the research component.

Teacher Reflection on Designing the Unit

As I designed this unit, I thought about the many students who have entered my Algebra II classes with no conceptual understanding of quadratic functions. Although I knew they had spent weeks solving quadratic equations during their Algebra I and Geometry classes, many retained only fragmentary information and demonstrated truncated skills. They had been exposed to the mathematics, but they hadn't grasped the big ideas and supporting understandings.

I also thought about the wide range of mathematical skills and the limited interest in mathematics that many of these students brought. I wanted to create a unit that interested all these students and that was neither too high-end nor repetitive. And I wanted something that minimized direct instruction and emphasized exploration and discussion. It became clear that a differentiated unit would provide the structure and the freedom necessary to meet these various requirements.

Over the years, conversations with my students revealed that most came to Algebra II believing that mathematics was a disconnected compendium of skills. Many had not learned to value mathematics and were not confident about their ability to do mathematics, to reason mathematically, to problem solve, or to communicate their findings. In short, I found that my Algebra II students needed help developing mathematical dispositions.

To support their development as mathematical thinkers, I wanted to create the lessons in this unit (and all my units) to cement conceptual understandings and stress connections between mathematics and real-world experiences. To facilitate this with the study of quadratics, my lesson plans would need to allow all learners to hone their skills without limiting them to standard review drills. I would need to tier the unit activities and provide scaffolding to help students create personal understandings of what quadratic equations are and how different parameters change these equations.

Because parabolas are fundamental to technologies in widespread use, I wanted students to develop an appreciation for the form and the function of quadratics and to access the ideas behind quadratics. I wanted to craft a unit through which they would learn which parameters controlled the shape and direction of the parabola. I also believed that this unit was an ideal opportunity to allow the students to see a conceptual link to the concepts of dynamic change that are fundamental to calculus.

Mathematics Standards Addressed

Number and Operations

SD1 Understand numbers, ways of representing numbers, relationships among numbers, and number systems.

SD2 Compute fluently and make reasonable estimates.

Algebra

SD3   Understand patterns, relations, and function.

SD4   Use mathematical models to represent and understand quantitative relationships.

SD5   Analyze change in various contexts.

Geometry

SD6   Use visualization, spatial reasoning, and geometric modeling to solve problems.

Measurement

SD7   Apply appropriate techniques, tools, and formulas to determine measurements.

Problem Solving

SD8   Build new mathematical knowledge through problem solving.

SD9   Solve problems that arise in mathematics and in other contexts.

SD10   Apply and adapt a variety of appropriate strategies to solve problems.

SD11   Monitor and reflect on the process of mathematical problem solving.

Reasoning and Proof

SD12   Make and investigate mathematical conjectures.

SD13   Develop and evaluate mathematical arguments and proofs.

Communication

SD14   Organize and consolidate mathematical thinking through communication.

SD15   Communicate mathematical thinking coherently and clearly to peers, teachers, and others.

SD16   Analyze and evaluate the mathematical thinking and strategies of others.

SD17   Use the language of mathematics to express mathematical ideas precisely.

Connections

SD18   Recognize and use connections among mathematical ideas.

SD19   Understand how mathematical ideas interconnect and build on one another to produce a coherent whole.

SD20   Recognize and apply mathematics in contexts outside of mathematics.

Representation

SD21   Create and use representations to organize, record, and communicate mathematical ideas.

SD22   Use representations to model and interpret physical, social, and mathematical phenomena.

Unit Concepts and Generalizations

Quadratic Functions, Systems, Parabolic Shapes, Predictable Elements, Change

GEN1   Quadratic functions are systems.

GEN2   Quadratic functions must contain particular elements.

GEN3   The elements of quadratic functions are predictable.

GEN4   Modifying the elements of quadratic functions changes the outcome of the function: (a) different roots occur; (b) different min/max occurs.

GEN5   Quadratic functions model real events.

Unit Objectives

As a result of this unit, the students will *know*

- The form of the particular family of second-degree equations called "parabola."
- The function of the components of a quadratic equation.
- How to solve quadratic equations.
- The meaning of the number and of the kind of roots of any quadratic equation.

As a result of this unit, the students will *understand that*

- Quadratic functions model real-world events.
- Quadratic equations may contain a variety of variables.
- The methods for solving quadratic functions differ in their ease of application.
- Complex roots can be graphed.
- Second-degree equations need not be parabolic in shape.

As a result of this unit, the students will *be able to*

- Predict the shape of the graph of a quadratic equation.
- Solve any quadratic function.
- Discuss families of quadratic equations.
- Suggest connections between a quadratic equation and real-world events.
- Discuss changing rates of a parameter and relate these changes to a parabolic trace.

Instructional Strategies Used in this Unit

- Brainstorming
- Flexible grouping
- Paired/small-group assignments
- Pre-assessment
- Research
- Total Physical Response (TPR)

- Extension activities
- Jigsaw
- Peer coaching
- Presentations
- Tiered assignments
- Whole-class discussion

Sample Supporting Materials Provided

Unit Overview

LESSON	WHOLE-CLASS COMPONENTS	DIFFERENTIATED COMPONENTS
LESSON 1 **Introduction** *1 class period*	Beanbag toss activity in self-selected small groups *15 minutes*	
	Activity discussion and whole-class brainstorming *25 minutes*	
	Extension activities *time varies*	
LESSON 2 **Skills Pre-assessment** *1 class period*	Pre-assessment *20 minutes*	
	Pre-assessment review and discussion *20 minutes*	
	Preview of the Jigsaw activity *5 minutes*	

LESSON	WHOLE-CLASS COMPONENTS	DIFFERENTIATED COMPONENTS
LESSON 3 **Jigsaw Learning Circles** *1 class period*	Jigsaw preparation and procedure review *time varies*	
		Learning circle discussions differentiated by readiness *15 minutes*
	Peer-teaching in home groups *30 minutes*	
LESSON 4 **Quadratic Functions as Systems** *3–4 class periods*		Exploration activity I in pairs and quads based on readiness and learning profile *45 minutes*
	Whole-class discussion of outcomes from Exploration I *15–20 minutes*	
		Exploration activity II in pairs and quads based on readiness and learning profile *25–30 minutes*
		Extension discussion for advanced students *time varies*
	Whole-class discussion of outcomes and understandings of quadratic functions *45–60 minutes*	
LESSON 5 **Real-World Connections** *2–3 class periods*	Whole-class brainstorming *30 minutes*	
	NASA activity and follow-up discussion *45–60 minutes*	
		Interest-based team research into the applications of quadratic functions *ongoing, time varies*
	Research presentations and discussion *ongoing, time varies*	

LESSON	WHOLE-CLASS COMPONENTS	DIFFERENTIATED COMPONENTS
LESSON 6 **Applications of Quadratics** *2–3 class periods*	Whole-class investigation of the beanbag toss scenario *30 minutes*	
		Small-group exploration differentiated by readiness *45–90 minutes*
	Whole-class discussion of results *30 minutes*	
LESSON 7 **Summary of Unit Understandings** *1–2 class periods*	Unit assessment preview *15–30 minutes*	
		Understanding practice and discussion in flexible groups based on readiness and learning profile *20–40 minutes*
	Whole-class wrap-up discussion *15–20 minutes*	
LESSON 8 **Unit Assessment** *1 class period*	Final assessment in individual and/or small-group formats *45 minutes*	

Unit Description and Teacher Commentary

LESSON 1	**Introduction** *Concept:* Parabolic Shapes GEN5; SD 5–6, SD14–17, SD 20–22	*(1 class period)*

LESSON SEQUENCE AND DESCRIPTION	TEACHER COMMENTARY
Beanbag toss activity in self-selected small groups. Divide the students into groups of three and provide each group with a beanbag.	✳This activity uses Total Physical Response (TPR) (see Glossary, page 358). TPR actively supports kinesthetic, visual, and tactile learners.

LESSON SEQUENCE AND DESCRIPTION	TEACHER COMMENTARY
Before starting the activity, explain the steps and tasks involved: 1. Two students will toss a beanbag back and forth several times while the third student (the observer/recorder) watches. All three should pay attention to the path, height, and duration of their beanbag's flight and any apparent change the thrower makes that affects the height or time of the beanbag's flight. 2. At the teacher's signal, the groups will stop the toss and discuss the travel of the beanbag. The observer will enter the group's observations on the report form, using mathematically precise terminology whenever possible. 3. The groups will repeat this sequence three times, with students rotating responsibility so that each serves as the observer/recorder.	The data collection aspect supports aural and oral learners, who internalize and make connections with the material as they listen to fellow investigators and discuss possibilities. I postpone pre-assessing students' knowledge of quadratics until after this introductory activity because I want to "hook" my students by interesting them in some portion of the unit's material. At the same time, this introductory activity is a novel way to awaken the students' prior ideas about the subject. I also find that this "hook" provides a memory to which we can refer whenever students become lost or confused. It's a common experience that gives us talking points upon which to build understandings.
Activity discussion and whole-class brainstorming. After the third round of the beanbag toss, bring the class back together to discuss the activity. Create a chart on the board or on chart paper and initiate a comprehensive discussion of the students' observations, recording responses without attempting to arrange them into categories and without commenting on the observations' reasonableness or accuracy. If no one has used the term "parabola" to describe the path of the beanbag, pose a question that allows the students to make that connection. Ask: How could we describe the shape associated with the beanbag's path? When students have exhausted their relevant observations, ask for their ideas about the specific topics they will be investigating in these next weeks. Help them generate ideas about parabolic shapes and interesting features they know or suspect about quadratic functions. Ask: How does the beanbag toss help to connect the list of observations you made to the topics in this unit?	I encourage observations that discuss the speed of the beanbag and the height it reached and accept all input without judgment. I am seeking participation and trying to create an affectively supportive environment to minimize student embarrassment. I avoid questions that can be answered "yes" or "no" (e.g., I do *not* ask, "Is there a mathematical term that describes the path of the beanbag?") I'm careful to ask about ideas they will be "investigating" rather than the ideas they will be "studying." I am trying to link the mathematics of parabolas with real-world experiences, and "studying" can send a contrary message: that parabolas occur on the mathematics textbook page but not in the experienced world.

LESSON SEQUENCE AND DESCRIPTION	TEACHER COMMENTARY
Extension activities. If desired, proceed with one or both of the following extensions: *Extension 1* Group students for the purpose of organizing the class-generated list into categories that they determine. *Extension 2* Have students write a short explanation of which role in the beanbag activity they liked most and least and why.	Extension 1 allows the class to further their recognition of patterns and groups—a skill fundamental to the study of mathematics. Extension 2 allows students to investigate their own feelings, to inform me about their learning preferences in a sheltered format, and to practice communication, another of the "dispositions of a mathematician" supported by the National Council of Teachers of Mathematics (NCTM).

LESSON 2　　　　Skills Pre-assessment　　　*(1 class period)*

LESSON SEQUENCE AND DESCRIPTION	TEACHER COMMENTARY
Pre-assessment. Begin the class session by having students complete the **Skills Pre-assessment** (see Sample 7.1, page 270). The six items on the pre-assessment represent a cross-section of ideas from the study of quadratics and give a picture of students' mastery of a variety of fundamental tasks: • Recognizing common factors and squares. • Dealing with fractions. • Recalling and applying the quadratic equation. • Representing roots. Remind the students that they are NOT being graded on this material. The assessment is your way of gathering information that will help you tailor the lesson to their needs. (In other words, it is formative, not summative.)	Given the potential range of abilities and backgrounds that occur in Algebra II, I know that I need to differentiate many lessons. For differentiation to be meaningful, I need to establish which skill sets students remember and which they need to relearn. Although this pre-assessment is not designed to assess conceptual understandings, I can link this paper-and-pencil work with the observations and discussion in Lesson 1 to help me make decisions about how to structure appropriately challenging lessons. Students in upper-level mathematics courses are often concerned about earning top marks and building strong profiles for college admission. They can be reticent about engaging in any assessment activities until they are confident that they will be successful. I find that I need to teach my students *why* pre-assessment is necessary and valuable.

LESSON SEQUENCE AND DESCRIPTION	TEACHER COMMENTARY
Pre-assessment review and discussion. Provide the correct responses on an overhead transparency and ask students to mark their own work (placing a "C" next to correct responses and writing in the correct answers next to any problems answered incorrectly). Ask for additional answers to each problem and record those on the overhead as well. Do not discuss how to solve the problems. Collect the pre-assessment after the discussion and use the outcomes to help determine Lesson 3's groupings and the amount and kind of support to provide during the Lesson 3 activities.	I make green pens available for students to use when they correct any work. Color supports visually oriented students, and it allows all students to focus on specific items when the work is returned.
Preview of the Jigsaw activity. Preview the Jigsaw that will take place during the next class session. Explain to the students that the lesson will focus on employing the quadratic formula, factoring a trinomial that requires no modification, modifying a trinomial to permit factoring, and encountering complex roots. During the lesson, students will be working in two of the following groupings: • A "home" group, where each student will function as a peer teacher after he or she has reviewed and relearned a specific method. • A "learning circle" (or "specialty") group, where each student will review and relearn the specific method along with others assigned to that same method. • A "learning circle leaders" group, whose members function as peer teachers during the learning circle group meetings. After this group has facilitated the learning circle discussions, they will work together to investigate complex situations and conduct high-level research regarding complex roots.	Giving students a preview of the work they will do in the next lesson is a way of providing affective support. It allows them to mentally prepare for tasks that will be different from what they have experienced in previous mathematics classes. I am positioning them to become active learners. The learning circle groups are homogeneous, based on readiness.

LESSON 3   Jigsaw Learning Circles   *(1 class period)*
Concept: Predictable Elements
GEN2–4; SD1–2, SD10–11, SD14–18, SD21

LESSON SEQUENCE AND DESCRIPTION	TEACHER COMMENTARY
Jigsaw preparation and procedure review. Assign students to mixed-readiness home groups. Place the most advanced students—those who demonstrated understanding of all the solution techniques presented in the pre-assessment—in the "learning circle leader" group.	I determine group assignments based on the results from the pre-assessment, the whole-class discussion from Lesson 1, and my knowledge of group dynamics.

LESSON SEQUENCE AND DESCRIPTION	TEACHER COMMENTARY
Learning circle discussions differentiated by readiness. Once students are in their home groups, provide them with their readiness-based learning circle assignment: A, B, C, or D. Assign each student in the learning circle leaders group to facilitate a topic that they know well. Ask students to regroup so that they are sitting with classmates who have the same assignment that they do.	When I have more advanced students than I need to facilitate the four learning circle groups, I ask them to choose between that task or beginning independent or paired consideration of applications of quadratics that yield complex roots.
Distribute the **Learning Circle Specialty Assignments** (see Sample 7.2, pages 271–276) for each group. Each learning circle group should contain at least four students, plus a peer leader. *Learning Circle A: The Quadratic Formula* Students assigned to this learning circle demonstrated minimal to no understanding of how to find roots. They will become "specialists" in using the quadratic formula: the certain—although not necessarily the easiest—solution path for every quadratic equation. *Learning Circle B: Factoring Quadratic Equations* These are students who demonstrated that they could apply the quadratic formula, but were weak in other areas. They will learn more about factoring and about how to apply factoring. *Learning Circle C: Completing the Square* These students demonstrated they could apply the quadratic formula and accomplish some factoring. They will learn a complex factoring method that will serve them in future algebraic work. *Learning Circle D: Complex Roots* These students were accomplished in their use of the quadratic formula and in factoring. They should be able to approach complex roots without needing serious scaffolding in the basics of the quadratic formula or factoring, including completing the square.	The Jigsaw arrangement maximizes student time on task (no one has to wait for me to instruct the full class about how to use a particular skill). By giving students responsibility to peer-teach a small group after they have become more proficient in a particular solution technique, each has the chance to be "the expert," each is modeling leadership skills, and I am no longer the central focus of my students' learning—one of the NCTM paradigm shifts. While students participate in their learning circles, I monitor groups but do not teach. I want my students to accept that they are capable of learning without me. Because the skills targeted in these activities should have been taught in prior mathematics classes, I don't want to spend days repeating and drilling them. At the same time, I am supporting the reality that it's only when students can assess a problem and select potential solution methods that are they practicing mathematics.
Peer-teaching in home groups. When time is called, students return to their home groups to facilitate a review of their "specialties" and participate in reviews of the three other topics. Students in the learning circle leaders group begin research on complex roots (see Lesson 2).	While students are peer-teaching, I monitor those who are in Learning Circle A (the quadratic formula group) most carefully, as these students begin with the least understanding of how to solve quadratic equations.

LESSON SEQUENCE AND DESCRIPTION	TEACHER COMMENTARY
At this time, each home group completes the various worksheets. The student who "studied" a particular strategy during the learning circle becomes the peer teacher while the group focuses on that strategy's worksheet.	

LESSON 4　　**Quadratic Functions as Systems**　　*(3–4 class periods)*
Concepts: Quadratic Functions, Predictable Elements
GEN1–4; SD1–6, SD8, SD10–22

LESSON SEQUENCE AND DESCRIPTION	TEACHER COMMENTARY
✸ Exploration activity I in pairs and quads based on readiness and learning profile. With the baseline information established, in this lesson, students begin to work with the central concept of the material: that quadratic equations are systems.	
Distribute **Exploration Activity I** (see Sample 7.3, pages 277–278) and review the directions. Tell students that the explorations and questions will focus on developing their understandings about the number of roots, the nature of those roots, and the shape of the trace of the function. The activity will also help them determine which solution methods are easiest.	As Sample 7.4 shows, I sequence this activity carefully to prevent confusion from too much input. The format also encourages metacognition, as students are prompted to self-correct before they get too far off track.
Break students into pairs. Each pair will work together on the problems (developing and testing hypotheses regarding number and nature of roots and then answering the questions in the question sets) and then meet in a four-person team with a second like-readiness pair to discuss the results.	✸ I assign these pairs and quads based on the tangibles of the students' demonstrated skill with solving quadratic equations and the intangibles of learning style, pair-preference, and class dynamics.
Allow students who prefer to work alone to do so, but when they begin to address the questions, encourage them to consult with a classmate who is also working alone.	✸ Some students just aren't comfortable working in pairs. With gentle encouragement and monitoring by me, these singles often come to realize that cooperating with another student can ease their work and allow them to test ideas away from the perceived scrutiny of the whole class.
Although students should have graphing calculators at their disposal during this activity, encourage them not to use the calculators to create the initial sketches of their equations.	I prefer that the students develop their own understandings of the shape of the graphs and use the graphing calculators to check and correct their understandings.

LESSON SEQUENCE AND DESCRIPTION	TEACHER COMMENTARY
Whole-class discussion of outcomes from Exploration I. After all students have concluded the activity, lead a whole-class discussion of their findings. Key points to include in the discussion are • The sign of the coefficient on the quadratic term controls whether the graph opens up or down. • The real number roots coincide with the x-intercepts. • We can group these equations according to their similarities, and this enables us to "see" how each group behaves.	
Exploration activity II in pairs and quads based on readiness and learning profile. Distribute **Exploration Activity II** (see Sample 7.4, pages 279–280) and create new pairings, if desired. Exploration II provides additional practice with predictions, solution techniques, and sketching. It allows students to continue • Formulating personal ideas regarding which solution methods are the most manageable. • Creating and testing hypotheses regarding the number and nature of the quadratic roots. • Creating a link between the beanbag toss activity (see Lesson 1), the number of roots, and the "direction" of the parabola.	Students can be reluctant to trust newly developing skills of prediction. By providing the second set of equations to explore, I am scaffolding students' cognitive skills, affective sense, and metacognitive ability and also providing time for them to consolidate their understandings.
Extension discussion for advanced students. Expect high-end mathematics students to complete the second exploration activities rapidly. Ask them to extend their discussions by joining together prior to the whole-class discussion.	This discussion serves two purposes. First, I find that some of the high-end students may have excellent numeric sense, but may not necessarily comprehend the import of the changes to the quadratic that they have been investigating. Second, the cross-fertilization of ideas that sometimes occurs within a larger, high-end group can generate additional understandings and conjecture.
Whole-class discussion of outcomes and understandings of quadratic functions. Lead the whole class in a discussion that illuminates and considers the ideas the class has developed regarding quadratic functions.	Having an index card at hand that lists the unit concepts and generalizations helps me focus and refocus the conversation.

LESSON SEQUENCE AND DESCRIPTION	TEACHER COMMENTARY
Ask: Of the four ways to find roots, which was easiest and why? Prompt students who identify factoring as the easiest method to discuss why they find this easier than the quadratic formula, in view of the fact that not all quadratic equations can be factored. Point out that completing the square gets you around this objection. Discuss the pros and cons of completing the square. Ask: How do the problems that we solved in these investigations link to the beanbag toss on Day 1? If students don't see a link and need some scaffolding to make the connection, ask them about the trajectory (or "arc") the beanbag traveled when tossed. Use graphs or sketches as necessary. Ask: What constitutes a system? Bring the discussion back to the generalizations that frame the unit and prompt students to suggest why quadratic functions could (or could not) be considered a system. To help students assimilate what is, for most of them, the novel concept of functions as a system, ask them to think back to Algebra I and simultaneous linear systems (e.g., $y = 5x - 7$ and $y = -2x + 5$). From there, quickly review what these linear functions mean, how they are related, and why we call them a system. Guide the students to explicate the first three generalizations: 1. Quadratic functions must contain particular elements. 2. These elements are predictable. 3. Modification of these elements changes the outcome of the function in that different roots occur and different min/max occurs.	Before I am able to introduce the idea of a system that describes quadratic functions, students need to understand the multiple meanings of the word "system." Using this discussion as a parallel, I ask the students to use the reviewed ideas as they discuss quadratic functions. By now, my students are usually near the saturation point on the subject of new ways to consider quadratic functions. Occasionally, though, someone will suggest the idea of the fourth unit generalization: that quadratic functions model real events. When this occurs, I invite the class to consider if and when this could be true. I also tell them that they have just previewed our next lesson! They have worked very hard by the time they have reached this point. I find that praise for their accomplishments causes general euphoria—an affectively powerful cap to this lesson.

| LESSON 5 | Real-World Connections | (2–3 class periods) |

Concepts: Quadratic Functions, Parabolic Shapes
GEN5; SD4–7, SD9, SD12–17, SD22

LESSON SEQUENCE AND DESCRIPTION	TEACHER COMMENTARY
Whole-class brainstorming. Initiate the lesson by asking the students to brainstorm a list of the ways in which quadratic functions relate to real events. "Jump-start" the discussion by reminding them of the beanbag activity they did on the first day of the unit and provide additional guided questioning to lead them toward adding satellite dishes and trajectories to their list. When the students have exhausted their ideas, or when they have created an extensive list of possible connections, tell them that you are going to have them experience one such connection now.	Unless students connect quadratic functions to real-world situations, this unit becomes another series of classes in which the students find themselves using discrete skills for no reason other than the teacher requiring them to. Lesson 5 has the students discovering and experiencing some of the ways in which quadratic functions model real events.
NASA activity and follow-up discussion. Move outside to participate in the NASA activity "Capturing a Whisper from Space," available at solarsystem.nasa.gov. Students experience an application of the focusing effects of a parabolic receiver. The distance over which they are able to hear the "signal" seems impossible, making for a lively discussion upon returning to the classroom. Back in the classroom, discuss the experience and relate it to quadratic functions. Allow the students to add additional ideas to their previous list of connections between quadratic functions and real events.	NASA has prepared numerous activities that allow active engagement in mathematics and science. I selected this one because it is easy to execute and yields interesting results that intrigue students. Discussion and reflection are powerful tools with which to create new ideas, form new connections among ideas, and cement new learning.
Interest-based team research into the applications of quadratic functions. Have students self-select into research teams to explore an area of interest—a specific model/example of quadratic equations—and prepare a short, informal presentation on their findings. (Visual aids are not required.) They may pursue extension activities from NASA or research one of the topics from this lesson's introductory brainstorming session.	These teams are not the same as the quads in Lesson 3. I want the fertilization of ideas and effort that new groupings can yield. I also want to provide a different working structure; when students get too comfortable within a group, they can start to coast. Allowing students to form their own groups here acknowledges their growth in mathematical ability, in interest in the topic, and in the ability to participate, due to enhanced interpersonal skills.

LESSON SEQUENCE AND DESCRIPTION	TEACHER COMMENTARY
Keep a list of students' selections and hold conferences about these topics to provide oversight, scaffolding, and guidance. If any high-end learners express no preference for a topic, suggest that they research the real application of complex roots, which link to very high-level applications (in descriptions of alternating electric current and in the calculations that characterize harmonic motion and wave motion).	If an advanced student decides to research an "easy" topic, I hold a mini-conference to find out why. If the student admits to seeking an easy topic, we investigate other ideas, and I encourage the student to embrace something more challenging. Similarly, if students express preferences for topics that I feel may be too difficult, I discuss this choice and provide appropriate guidance. Still, if a student articulates a compelling interest in a topic, I allow him or her to proceed.
The time allotted for this activity depends on the students, their abilities, and the resources available. Students conduct the bulk of their research during class. Provide access to the Internet, advanced mathematics books, encyclopedias, and books on the history and application of mathematics. Access to professionals (a physicist or an electronics teacher/professor) is desirable, but not a necessity.	
Research presentations and discussion. Each research team presents its findings regarding the links between quadratic functions and real models. These are informal "mini-presentations." No visual aids are required.	I believe that all students should have the opportunity to hear about the interesting connections their peers are making.
Space presentations over the remaining days of the unit, scheduling them to take advantage of the historic chronology of developments or to group similar topics.	Ideally, I want the historical pieces to precede the models that are similar to the structures the students are presenting.

LESSON 6   **Applications of Quadratics**   *(2–3 class periods)*

Concepts: Quadratic Functions, Systems, Change

GEN1–5; SD1–22

LESSON SEQUENCE AND DESCRIPTION	TEACHER COMMENTARY
Whole-class investigation of the beanbag toss scenario. Begin by presenting the equation that models a beanbag toss: *When a ball is thrown directly upward, its height at time* t *is determined by the following formula:* $h = -\frac{1}{2}gt^2 + v_0t + h_0$ *. . . where* g *is the gravitational constant,* v_0 *is the initial velocity of the ball, and* h_0 *is the ball's initial height. Near the surface of the Earth,* g *is close to 32 feet/second², or 9.8 meters/second². Assume the initial velocity is 80 feet/second² and the height at which the ball is released from your hand is 4 feet above the ground.*	Usually, the students are a little overwhelmed by the information this equation contains. Some do not recognize that it is quadratic.

LESSON SEQUENCE AND DESCRIPTION	TEACHER COMMENTARY
Discuss this equation, prompting students to reflect on what they understand the problem to be asking. To facilitate the discussion, have the students jot some notes to themselves. Then deconstruct the equation, providing guidance as necessary. Ask: What shape would the trace of this function take? Next, consider pieces of the function as separate functions. 1. Students need to understand that h_0 may be treated as a constant, here equal to the height of the ball-throwing arm. To support this realization, center the discussion on the equation $h = h_0$. 2. Move next to a consideration of $h = v_0 t$. Through careful questioning, bring the students to the realization that $h = v_0 t$ generates a distance equivalent to the $d = rt$ formula, where h is the distance of the ball above the ground and v_0 is the speed of the ball. This leaves $-\frac{1}{2}gx^2$ as "new" material. The original equation, which might have seemed strange and unapproachable, can now be understood to consist of two familiar equations joined with only one new expression. This expression is similar to the $y = x^2$ parabola. We need only consider the coefficient as being $-\frac{1}{2}g$ rather than a particular number. The remaining issue is how to make sense of the presented variables. Turn the discussion to the norms surrounding independent and dependent variables, which should allow students to make the link between the apparently four different variables presented and the "normal" x- and y-variables associated with the usual algebraic work and graphing calculators. Of the four symbols presented in the equation, three (g, v_0, and h_0) are constants.	I find that few students have considered the discrete terms of an equation in a systematic manner. By guiding this discussion about the parts of the equation, I am modeling a powerful mathematical tool: the power of deconstructing an equation into its components. I am seeking to scaffold the development of the mathematical disposition that not only "sees" how families of equations have common elements, but that also understands that within each type of system, unique features may occur.
Small-group exploration differentiated by readiness. Provide students with the **Tiered Quadratic Exploration** (see Sample 7.5, page 281) and ask them to begin work at their assigned level: *Level 1 (Struggling Students and Concrete Learners)* The material in this level investigates skills and connections all students should have when they investigate and use quadratic equations or use graphing calculators, but which may still elude struggling learners.	I allow all students to see all three levels of material. Doing this reinforces the notion that no group is being asked to do more than the others. Students also see that some questions are the same for all groups. In class discussion, I underscore the importance of developing a body of understandings and abilities.

LESSON SEQUENCE AND DESCRIPTION	TEACHER COMMENTARY
Level 2 (Grade-Level Students) The material in this level supports the consolidation of basic understandings of quadratic equations and graphing calculators. It furthers abstract thought and speculation about mathematical possibilities. *Level 3 (Advanced Students)* The material in this level provides a quick check for understanding of quadratic equations and calculator use, followed by challenging, high-level questions that call for abstract understanding of the parameters for the given equation. These explorations will extend through one or two class periods.	Students' readiness can change over the course of any unit's study. Often, students who start the unit slowly have "a-ha" moments and are no longer struggling by this point. Conversely, some of the initially quick students have not progressed toward high-level skills or understandings. In addition, if I believe a student is teetering on the brink of higher-level capability, I want to nudge that student with a slightly higher-level challenge. For these reasons, I reformat the groups to provide the best learning opportunity for all.
Whole-class discussion of results. Shortly after the start of the final day in this lesson, bring the class back together and facilitate a discussion about the students' findings during the Tiered Quadratics Exploration activity. Allow time for questions and answers among the students in a whole-class discussion.	

LESSON 7

Summary of Unit Understandings

(1–2 class periods)

Concepts: Quadratic Functions, Systems
GEN1–5; SD1–22

LESSON SEQUENCE AND DESCRIPTION	TEACHER COMMENTARY
Unit assessment preview. Explain the nature of the next day's two-part unit assessment: Students will work alone and without calculators on Part I; they may use their calculators and either work alone or in pairs on Part II. Point out that the option of working with a partner reflects both the philosophy of the class as a community of learners and the reality of the workplace.	I encourage students who worked together on the pre-assessment to work together on the unit assessment too. I also ask all pairs to "register" as such before they leave class to help to avoid confusion during the assessment.
Understanding practice and discussion in flexible groups based on readiness and learning profile. Distribute copies of the **Unit Summary of Understandings** (see Sample 7.6, page 282), a type of study sheet. Students will work on it in assigned like-readiness pairs or alone, as they prefer.	Note that these are assigned pairs, not the self-selected pairs students may opt for during the unit assessment.

LESSON SEQUENCE AND DESCRIPTION	TEACHER COMMENTARY
Monitor students' progress; when individuals and groups have completed the activities, facilitate the sharing of understandings in small groups so that students do not need to wait for the full class to finish before commencing discussion.	
Whole-class wrap-up discussion. Invite students to ask any remaining questions they have about any aspect of the unit content.	I work to provide an engaging and affectively supportive environment so that students will feel welcome to pose questions about any areas of lingering confusion.

LESSON 8 — Unit Assessment *(1 class period)*

Concepts: Quadratic Functions, Systems, Parabolic Shapes, Predictable Elements, Change
GEN1–2; SD1, SD4

LESSON SEQUENCE AND DESCRIPTION	TEACHER COMMENTARY
Final assessment in individual and/or small-group formats. Present the students with the first part of the two-part **Unit Assessment** (see Sample 7.7, pages 283–284).	This assessment asks students to verbalize, sketch, or even create generalized equations that describe their new understandings and that are transferable to a new or unique situation.
Part I Students work on Part I independently and turn it in when it is complete. The tasks are open-ended and ask students to describe certain features. Calculators are not permitted.	The two-part design allows me to assess both individual and small-group understandings. It also models another aspect of the link between the mathematics we are using and the real world. Just as mathematics does not occur in a vacuum, what people create with mathematics is rarely created alone. Shared responsibility is a fact in the workplace too.
Part II Students work in previously determined self-selected pairs or alone if that is preferable to them. (To minimize downtime and distractions, partners begin work independently if one finishes Part I before the other.) The tasks in Part II ask students to confirm some information on similar but not identical equations. Calculators are permitted.	

Teacher Reflection on the Unit

This unit reflects my belief that the study of quadratic equations can be more than acquiring a compendium of skills. It takes the larger view of quadratics as a system. With the understanding that certain conditions pertain to a system, my students learn to look for patterns and predictable events. Throughout, they are engaged in building their own learning, moving forward with guidance in small discovery groups. All students have rich opportunities to investigate ideas and receive the support they need to develop the dispositions of a mathematician: to conjecture, to model, to predict, to test, and to refine. Regardless of students' future learning path, this experience opens the possibilities of linking mathematics to a world that they value.

Catherine (Kate) Reed, PhD, teaches in the Department of Teacher Education for California State University, Hayward, where she is responsible for the elementary mathematics methods courses for the Multiple Subjects credential program. In addition, she teaches graduate mathematics curriculum, assessment and evaluation, and gifted and talented education courses, and supervises credential candidates. She can be reached at creed@csuhayward.edu.

SAMPLE 7.1—Skills Pre-assessment

Directions: Factor the following equations any way you choose, and then state your method (or briefly describe it).

#	Equation	Solution Method
1.	$9x^2 + 3x + \frac{1}{4}$	
2.	$0 = \frac{x^2}{4} + 2$	
3.	$-16t^2 + 16t + 5$	
4.	$0 = -.005x^2 + 2x - 4.5$	
5.	$\frac{1}{2}x^2 + \frac{1}{2}x$	
6.	$0 = x^2 - 4x + 3$	

SAMPLE 7.2—Learning Circle Specialty Assignments

Focus on the Quadratic Formula

Mathematicians know all quadratic equations can be rearranged into this form

$$ax^2 + bx + c = 0$$

where a is the coefficient of the quadratic—or x^2—term; b is the coefficient of the linear—or x—term, and c is the constant term.

Either or both the linear and constant terms may be missing. If the linear term is missing, $b = 0$. If the constant term is missing, $c = 0$.

Do NOT overlook that the quadratic coefficient = 1 when we see only x^2 with no number in front of it.

Practice identifying the values of a, b, and c in these equations.

1. $3x^2 + 11x - 4 = 0$

2. $5x^2 + 8x = 0$

3. $x^2 - 2x - 3 = 0$

The quadratic formula is $x = \dfrac{-b \pm \sqrt{b^2 - 4ac}}{2a}$

Use this formula to solve each of the three equations above.

SAMPLE 7.2—Learning Circle Specialty Assignments—*(continued)*

Focus on Factoring Quadratic Equations

Recall that we are factoring a trinomial (a polynomial with three expressions). We know that this usually results from the multiplication of two binomials, such as $(a + b)(c + d)$. When we multiplied the two factors, the common acronym to remind us of the parts of the multiplication problem was FOIL. This stands for "first times first," "outside times outside," "inside times inside," and "last times last."

For example, for $(a + b)(c + d)$ we get $ac + ad + bc + bd$. Any terms that have the same pair of variables raised to the same power can be gathered (summed). The full multiplication using one variable and numbers or two variables yields a trinomial rather than the four-part polynomial we just generated.

The above information suggests that the quadratic equations with which we are working could have been generated by binomial multiplication. **Factoring** attempts to return the quadratic equation to its "premultiplied" form. We are trying to find the factors of the multiplication problem.

Several patterns and general rules can be tested. Rather than memorizing a list of rules, we can find the factors by focusing on the factors of the first term and the last term. Test these for the middle term by looking at the sum of the "outside" and "inside" terms.

1. Factor: $x^2 - 2x - 3 = 0$

2. Find the factors of the first term (of the x^2) and write them into a pair of binomial factors.

3. Find the factors of -3 and write them into that pair of binomials.

Because there is a choice of where to place the negative, you will need to test both possibilities. Start with the 3 being positive and the 1 being negative:

$$(x + 3)(x - 1)$$

If you test the outside and inside products, you'll see that this is the wrong placement for the signs:

$$+3x - x = +2x$$

Because the $2x$ has the correct absolute value but the wrong sign, you can switch the signs on the factors (the other possibility referred to above) and find the correct sum of the products:

$$(x - 3)(x + 1)$$

Never trust your results without testing them! Also, sometimes you will find that it is impossible to factor a trinomial. This does NOT mean that there is no way to solve the quadratic equation; it just means that *this kind of factoring is not the method that will work*.

SAMPLE 7.2—Learning Circle Specialty Assignments—*(continued)*

Factor the following examples. One of them is not factorable using the FOIL analogy.

1. $x^2 + 4x + 3 = 0$

2. $x^2 + 5x - 24 = 0$

3. $x^2 + x - 1 = 0$

4. $3x^2 + 11x - 4 = 0$

SAMPLE 7.2—Learning Circle Specialty Assignments—*(continued)*

Focus on Completing the Square

Sometimes trinomials do not factor and using the quadratic formula yields very large or small numbers that are difficult to use. Such occasions are good opportunities to use the technique called **Completing the Square**. This method takes advantage of patterns developed from binomial expansions in which the multiplication uses the same factor two times.

From practice with such binomial expansions, mathematicians have discovered that the expansion of a binomial square will yield a constant term that is equal to the square of one-half the coefficient of the linear term *when the coefficient of the quadratic term is +1*. To use this technique to solve a quadratic function, pay attention to the rules that govern equation solving and use the information about adding the square of one-half the coefficient of the linear term.

To factor the following equation, move the constant term to the right side:

$$x^2 + 4x + 3 = 0$$
$$\underline{\ -3\ -3}$$
$$x^2 + 4x = -3$$

If the coefficient of the quadratic term is not +1, divide through by the non-+1 coefficient. When this has been done, or if it is not necessary, find the coefficient of the linear term. In this example, the coefficient is +4. To complete the square, take one-half of this coefficient (+2), square it (+4), and add this amount to the equation (on both sides, of course!):

$$x^2 + 4x = -3$$
$$\underline{+4+4}$$
$$x^2 + 4x + 4\ =\ 1$$

Factor the trinomial portion of the equation:

$$x^2 + 4x + 4\ = 1$$
$$(x + 2)(x + 2) = 1$$

Write this as a binomial squared:

$$(x + 2)^2 = 1$$

Take the square root of both sides, considering both roots:

$$\sqrt{(x + 2)^2} = \sqrt{1}$$

Evaluate the results:

$$
\begin{array}{ccc}
(x + 2) = 1 & & (x + 2) = -1 \\
\underline{-2\ -2} & \text{or} & \underline{-2\ \ -2} \\
x = -1 & & x = -3
\end{array}
$$

SAMPLE 7.2—Learning Circle Specialty Assignments—*(continued)*

Solve the following examples by completing the square:

1. $x^2 + 18x + 6 = 0$

2. $x^2 - 4x + 3 = 0$

3. $3x^2 - 6x - 9 = 0$

4. $x^2 + 2x + 3 = 0$

SAMPLE 7.2—Learning Circle Specialty Assignments—*(continued)*

Focus on Complex Roots

The real number system is composed of many different kinds of numbers. Usually we limit our consideration of values to those numbers that exist within the real number system. There are occasions when we need to expand the numbers needed to include the so-called "complex" numbers. The complex system includes the square roots of all negative numbers. The basic unit of this complex system is the square root of -1, written $\sqrt{-1}$. Because writing the square root symbol with a negative under the radical sign can become tedious, $\sqrt{-1}$ is replaced with a lower case "i."

For example: $\sqrt{-4} = 2i$ and $\sqrt{-8} = 2i\sqrt{2}$ although the i is usually written at the end, $2\sqrt{2}i$

Solve each of these problems by any method and express the answer using the complex numeration system:

1. $x^2 + 2x + 3 = 0$

2. $x^2 + 4x + 24 = 0$

3. $5x^2 + 8x + 10 = 0$

SAMPLE 7.3—Exploration Activity I

Directions: Conduct this exploration with a partner. Solve each pair of equations on a separate page. For each equation set, you will need to

- Predict the shape of the graph, the number of roots, and which method of solving will be easiest.
- Solve each equation *three times*—once by each of the three methods we have practiced.
- Sketch both equations on the SAME graph, using care to locate the *x*- and *y*- intercepts accurately. Label the intercepts.

Answer the questions in the corresponding **Question Set,** and then discuss your answers with the pair or your team. When you are satisfied that you have good "ideas" to test, work with your partner to predict the shape, the actual roots, and the easiest solution method for the next two equations.

Equation Set I
1. $y = x^2 - 9$
2. $y = x^2 - 16$

Question Set I
A. What is the shape of each of these two functions?
B. Look ahead to the other equations. What will the shape of all the graphs be? What leads you to believe this?
C. Look ahead to the other equations. Do they all follow the same pattern? If your answer is yes, identify that pattern. If your answer is no, what differences do you notice? Try to group the equations into sets that share the same characteristics.
D. Think about the equations 1 and 2 again. What do you notice about the roots?
E. Use your answer to the preceding question to predict the roots to the equations in Set II. Write your predictions down before you start working on these equations.

Equation Set II
3. $y = -x^2 + 6x - 9$
4. $y = -x^2 + 8x - 16$

Question Set II
A. Did you correctly predict the shape of each of these two functions? If yes, what allowed you to make this correct prediction? If no, what do you believe caused you to make a different prediction?
B. Make a generalized prediction about what controls the direction in which the parabola opens. Then predict which of the remaining equations will open "up" and which will open "down."
C. Did you correctly predict the value of the roots for equations 3 and 4? If yes, what allowed you to make this correct prediction? If no, what do you believe caused you to make a different prediction?
D. Predict the roots to the equations in Set III. Write your predictions down before you start working on these equations.

SAMPLE 7.3—Exploration Activity I—*(continued)*

Equation Set III
5. $y = x^2$
6. $y = -x^2$

Question Set III
A. Compare your predicted roots to the roots you calculated. What are the differences?
B. Compare your predictions about the shape of the graphs to your actual sketches. What are the differences?
C. Which solution method seems easier than the other two for the purposes of making predictions and solving the equations? Why do you believe this?
D. Predict the roots to the equations in Set IV. Write your predictions down before you start working on these equations.

Equation Set IV
7. $y = x^2 - 4x - 5$
8. $y = -x^2 - 6x - 5$

Question Set IV
A. Did you correctly predict the value of the roots for equations 7 and 8? If yes, what allowed you to make this correct prediction? If no, what do you believe caused you to make a different prediction?
B. Discuss your prediction of the shape of these two graphs and how they agreed/disagreed with the actual graphs.
C. Why is it possible/impossible to predict the roots of quadratic functions?
D. What elements must an equation have in order to be classified as a parabola? How can you test your answer? Go ahead and test it! Explain what you did to confirm/disprove your prediction. Give details.

SAMPLE 7.4—Exploration Activity II

Directions: Conduct this exploration with a partner. Solve each pair of equations on a separate page. For each equation set, you will need to . . .

- Predict the shape of the graph, the number of roots, and which method of solving will be easiest.
- Solve each equation *three times*—once by each of the three methods we have practiced.
- Sketch both equations on the SAME graph, using care to locate the x and y intercepts accurately. Label the intercepts.

Answer the questions in the corresponding **Question Set**, and then discuss your answers with the pair on your team. When you are satisfied that you have good "ideas" to test, work with your partner to predict the shape, the actual roots, and the easiest solution method for the next two equations.

Equation Set V
9. $y = x^2 + 9$
10. $y = x^2 + 16$

Question Set V
A. What are the roots to these two equations?
B. Discuss why your predictions about the roots were correct or incorrect.
C. Given the roots, what can you say about your prediction of the shape of the graph? Be specific.
D. Look ahead to the other equations. Do they all follow the same pattern? If your answer is "yes," identify that pattern. If your answer is "no," what differences do you notice? Try to group the equations into sets that share the same characteristics.

Equation Set VI
11. $y = x^2 + 6x - 9$
12. $y = x^2 + 8x - 16$

Question Set VI
A. Did you correctly predict the value of the roots for equations 11 and 12? If yes, what allowed you to make this correct prediction? If no, what do you believe caused you to make a different prediction?

SAMPLE 7.4—Exploration Activity II—*(continued)*

Equation Set VII
13. $y = -x^2 - 9$
14. $y = -x^2 - 16$

Question Set VII
A. Compare your predictions about the roots to equations 13 and 14 to the roots you calculated. What are the differences?
B. Which solution method seems easier than the other two for the purposes of making predictions, solving the equations, and answering the questions? Why do you believe this?
C. Predict the roots to the equations in Set VIII.

_____

Equation Set VIII
15. $y = x^2 - 4x + 5$
16. $y = -x^2 - 6x + 5$

Question Set VIII
A. Did you correctly predict the value of the roots for equations 15 and 16? If yes, what allowed you to make this correct prediction? If no, what do you believe caused you to make a different prediction?
B. Why is it possible/impossible to predict the roots of quadratic functions?
C. Develop a way of graphing two or more of the equations in this Exploration activity. Describe this method (in words) and then give two examples of your method using your selected equations.

SAMPLE 7.5—Tiered Quadratic Exploration

Directions: Work in your groups to complete this exploration at the assigned level. Each group member is responsible for generating his or her own written responses to the exploration prompts.

Level 1
1. To work on this problem, you will need to find an appropriate window for your graphing calculator. What should it be? Why?
2. Can you predict from the equation what the graph will look like? Draw a rough sketch of what you expect your calculator to show. Why do you expect to see this?
3. Use your calculator to confirm or correct your prediction.
4. What does each axis represent?
5. What is the height of the ball one second after it is thrown? Describe at least two ways to answer this question.
6. When is the ball 80 feet high? When is the ball 20 feet high? Explain your answers.
7. Write two questions about the behavior of the ball in this situation that you would like to investigate.
8. Investigate these two questions, writing your results in full sentences.

Level 2
1. To work on this problem, you will need to find an appropriate window for your graphing calculator. What should it be? Why?
2. Can you predict from the equation what the graph will look like? Draw a rough sketch of what you expect your calculator to show. Why do you expect to see this?
3. Use your calculator to confirm or correct your prediction.
4. What does each axis represent?
5. When is the ball 80 feet high? Explain your answer and how you found it. Describe at least one other way to find this answer. Is one method preferable to the other? Why?
6. For how many seconds is the ball in the air?
7. What is the maximum height of the ball? When does the ball attain this height?
8. Consider when the ball is at its maximum height, when it is 80 feet high, and how long it is in the air. If you are told that the ball reaches a height of 30 feet after .4 seconds, can you predict when it will again be at that height? What feature of this graph allows you to make such a conjecture?

Level 3
1. To work on this problem, you will need to find an appropriate window for your graphing calculator. What should it be? Why?
2. Can you predict from the equation what the graph will look like? Draw a rough sketch of what you expect your calculator to show. Why do you expect to see this?
3. Use your calculator to confirm or correct your prediction.
4. For how many seconds is the ball in the air?
5. What is the maximum height of the ball?
6. What value do you get for the height at $x = 7$? Explain this value in terms of the equation and then in terms of this particular situation. Do you need to put some restrictions on the value of x in this situation? If so, what are they?
7. Suppose someone else throws the same ball and it reaches a height that is one-fourth the height that your ball reached. What was the initial velocity of this throw?
8. What happens if someone else throws the ball at an initial velocity of 20 ft/sec^2?

SAMPLE 7.6—Unit Summary of Understandings

Directions: Although you may work alone on this summary, you may recall and learn more by working with another member of the class. When this summary is complete, check in with me. I will pair you with another person/team to share your results and discuss your findings.

1. Give an example of a quadratic function.

2. Describe the shape and roots of your example function.

3. What does the shape mean?

4. What do the roots mean?

5. How is your example similar to all quadratic functions?

6. How is your example different from other quadratic functions?

7. Describe at least three examples of real-world events that quadratic functions model, and explain how these events are linked to quadratics.

8. We have discussed quadratic equations as systems. Explain what this means. Give at least one specific example.

9. On the back of this page, write one question related to quadratic systems that you would like to investigate. Explain why you would like to investigate this question.

SAMPLE 7.7—Unit Assessment

Directions: This is a two-part assessment. In Part I, you will work alone to share your ideas about quadratic functions. When you have finished Part I, return it to me and pick up Part II. In Part II, you may work with a partner to confirm some information on similar but not identical equations. (Your partner will join you when he/she has returned Part I to me.) You have the remainder of the period in which to complete these tasks.

Part I: Individual Assessment

Name _____

1. Sketch a parabola that opens up. Then sketch a second parabola that also opens up but does NOT intersect the first one you sketched. Describe the similarities and differences of your two sketches.

2. Propose equations that would be similar to (but not necessarily identical to) the ones you just sketched.

3. Explain why you believe these proposed equations are similar to your sketches.

SAMPLE 7.7—Unit Assessment—*(continued)*

Part II: Individual or Paired Assessment

Name(s) _____

1. Select two of the three equations listed below and *write about these equations as a system*, including any ideas you think are interesting or important. You may use your graphing calculator and talk about your ideas with your partner.

$$y = x^2 \qquad\qquad y = x^2 + 3 \qquad\qquad y = x^2 - 3$$

2. Consider the following equations as a system. In what ways are they different from the pair of equations you discussed in the previous question?

$$y = x^2 + 3 \qquad\qquad\qquad y = -x^2 + 8x - 16$$

8

The Little Prince and Me

A World Languages Unit on Reading Target-Language Literature

Unit Developers: Cindy A. Strickland and Molly Wieland

Introduction

This four- to eight-week unit is designed for a high school French class at level 3 or higher—the point at which students are taking their first steps into in-depth literary study in the French language. Through close reading and discussion of Antoine de Saint-Exupéry's *Le Petit Prince* in the literature circle format, students work toward standards focused on communication, cultural understanding, and seeing connections between disciplines. Both the differentiation strategies and the activities are easily adaptable to other world language classes.

A good deal of time-flexibility is built into the unit. The main scheduling considerations are the amount of reading that students conduct outside of class and the amount of time they will need to devote to grammar review and product preparation. The schedule presented is set up for classes that meet on a modified block schedule: once per week for 45 minutes and twice per week for 90-minute blocks.

Teacher Reflections on Designing the Unit

This unit's present form is the result of two teachers working in tandem. When one of us (Molly) first designed and taught it, her goal was to spark advanced discussion of literary themes and life lessons, thus linking what students were learning in English class to what they were learning in French class. Although creating a differentiated unit was not her express intent, the original design did provide opportunities for individualized work responding in part to student interest and readiness.

Then Cindy, who had experience teaching *Le Petit Prince* at the high school and college level, set out to transform the already strong unit into a more fully differentiated one. The first change was the addition of pre-assessments for vocabulary, grammar, and learning profile to capitalize on existing student strengths and encourage growth in areas of relative weakness. A contract component was added to promote individual growth in vocabulary and grammar. The incorporation of literature circles, a strategy familiar to English and reading teachers, provided students with multiple opportunities to practice and improve their skills in listening and speaking, as well as the chance to wrestle with the "big ideas" found in this rather little book. The revised unit also accommodates learning preferences with the roles students play in the literature circles, the extension/anchor activity products they complete, and the final project they choose. The emphasis on higher-level thinking and personalized learning, present in the original unit design, remains.

World Languages Standards Addressed

Communicate in Languages Other Than English

SD1   Students engage in conversations, provide and obtain information, express feelings and emotions, and exchange opinions.

SD2   Students understand and interpret written and spoken language on a variety of topics.

SD3   Students present information, concepts, and ideas to an audience of listeners or readers.

Gain Knowledge and Understanding of Other Cultures

SD4   Students demonstrate an understanding of the relationship between the products and perspectives of the culture studied.

Connect with Other Disciplines and Acquire Information

SD5   Students reinforce and further their knowledge of other disciplines through the target language.

SD6   Students acquire information and recognize the distinctive viewpoints that are only available through the target language and its cultures.

Develop Insight into the Nature of Language and Culture

SD7   Students demonstrate understanding of the concept of culture through comparisons of the cultures studied and their own.

Participate in Multilingual Communities at Home and Around the World

SD8   Students show evidence of becoming lifelong learners by using the language for personal enjoyment and enrichment.

Unit Concepts and Generalizations

Perspective, Exploration, Growth, Relationships

GEN1 Who you are and what you value affects your view of the world.

GEN2 People hunger for exploration and growth of both the external and the internal world.

GEN3 Relationships confer responsibility.

Unit Objectives

As a result of this unit, the students will *know*

- The background of Antoine de Saint-Exupéry, author of *Le Petit Prince*.
- The characters, setting, plot, and themes of *Le Petit Prince*.
- Key French vocabulary necessary to understand the story.
- The verb tenses used in the text.

As a result of this unit, the students will *understand that*

- Reading literature in the target language is one way to improve vocabulary and increase fluency.
- It is possible to read for pleasure in more than one language.
- As in native language literature, it is possible to see reflections of ourselves in target-language literature.

As a result of this unit, the students will *be able to*

- Read more fluently in French.
- Demonstrate improved grammatical accuracy in writing and speaking.
- Incorporate new vocabulary into discussion and writing.
- Discuss literary elements in the French language.
- Analyze a theme found in *Le Petit Prince*.
- Examine personal beliefs and values through a textual lens.

Instructional Strategies Used

- Entry points
- Learning contracts
- Pre-assessment
- Rubrics
- Tiered questions
- Extension menus
- Literature circles
- Product choice
- Tiered assignments

Sample Supporting Materials Provided

Unit Overview

LESSON	WHOLE-CLASS COMPONENTS	DIFFERENTIATED COMPONENTS
PRE-ASSESSMENT *1 class period*	Pre-assessment *45 minutes*	
LESSON 1	Unit introduction *10 minutes*	
		Entry point activities differentiated by interest and learning profile *30 minutes*
Introduction to *Le Petit Prince*	Regrouping and sharing of entry points *20 minutes*	
	Text distribution and introduction *10 minutes*	
	Read-aloud and discussion *20 minutes*	
1 block		Tiered homework differentiated by readiness

LESSON	WHOLE-CLASS COMPONENTS	DIFFERENTIATED COMPONENTS
LESSON 2 **Introduction to the Unit Requirements and Literature Circles** *1 block*	Discussion of unit requirements *30 minutes*	
	Introduction, discussion, and demonstration of literature circles *40 minutes*	
		Literature circle planning in self-selected groups *10 minutes*
		Homework and contract work differentiated by readiness, interest, and learning profile *10 minutes*
LESSON 3 **Contract Work and Literature Circles** *4 class periods and 8 blocks*		Individual vocabulary and grammar contract work based on readiness *ongoing, time varies*
		Extension/anchor activities differentiated by interest and learning profile *ongoing, time varies*
		Reading comprehension assessments differentiated by interest *ongoing, time varies*
	Literature circle preparation and discussion *ongoing, time varies*	
		Mini-lessons based on readiness needs and interest *ongoing, time varies*
		Final project work differentiated by interest and learning profile *ongoing, time varies*
		Individual conferences *ongoing, time varies*
	Film clip/music presentations and whole-class discussion *ongoing, time varies*	

LESSON	WHOLE-CLASS COMPONENTS	DIFFERENTIATED COMPONENTS
LESSON 4 **Final Project Presentations** *1 class period and 2 blocks*	Final project presentations and whole-class discussions *ongoing, time varies* Unit evaluation *15 minutes*	

Unit Description and Teacher Commentary

PRE-ASSESSMENT   *(1 class period)*

LESSON SEQUENCE AND DESCRIPTION	TEACHER COMMENTARY
Pre-assessment. One to two weeks prior to the unit start, students complete a pre-assessment focused on the grammar tenses and constructions that feature most prominently in *Le Petit Prince*. If necessary, include a survey- or checklist-style assessment of student learning profiles in the pre-assessment exercise. There are several good online sources to explore: • For learning preference questionnaires in multiple languages, including French, Spanish, German, and Arabic, try www.vark-learn.com. • For several resources (en français) on Gardner's multiple intelligences, including questionnaires and observation checklists, try www.cslaurentides.qc.ca/Public/CarrefourPedagogique/webIntelMulti/section%20enseignant%20outils.htm. To introduce a learning profile pre-assessment, tell students that the upcoming unit will offer several opportunities to work on products that respond to a variety of learning preferences. Completing the learning profile survey will help them identify how they learn best.	Administering the pre-assessment in advance gave us the lead time we needed to develop the personalized learning contracts (see Lesson 2). Our source for pre-assessment questions was the workbook *Découverte du Petit Prince: An Enrichment Workbook for Exploring Languages and Themes* by Ann Brown and Anne Gassaway Brown. Our students used this workbook throughout the unit as source for vocabulary lists and reading comprehension questions. There are other similar resources available, in print and on the Web. For more information about learning styles and language learning, see Johnston and Orwig (1999).

LESSON 1	**Introduction to *Le Petit Prince***	*(1 block)*

Concepts: Perspective, Exploration, Growth, Relationships
GEN1–3; SD1–3, SD5, SD8

LESSON SEQUENCE AND DESCRIPTION	TEACHER COMMENTARY
Unit introduction. Tell students that for the next few weeks they will be studying a very well known French novel. Although the book is popular among children the world over, it was really written for adults. The book contains many important lessons about life and raises philosophical questions about a person's perspective on the world, exploration, growth, and the building and maintaining of relationships. These are likely topics with which the students themselves have wrestled. Ask students if they are aware of any books in English (or their native language) that provoke these kinds of questions and thoughts. What do they enjoy about such books? What can be difficult with such books? Distribute individual copies of the **Unit Overview** (see Sample 8.1, page 301).	
Entry point activities differentiated by interest and learning profile. As an introduction to their study, assign or have students choose one of the following activities set up in stations around the room. (It is not necessary for the groups to be equal in size.) Announce that the activities are designed to provide a glimpse into the world of *Le Petit Prince* and its author, Antoine de Saint-Exupéry, and to get everyone excited about studying the text and its themes. *Narrational Entry Point* Provide excerpts from *Le Petit Prince* in written and audio formats (such as Universal Music's CD version, read by Gerard Philipe) and, if desired, excerpts of other Saint-Exupéry works (see www.saint-exupery.org). Ask students to go through the excerpts quickly to get a feel for the author's style. Remind them that they are not trying to get all the details, just an overall sense of the meaning and the style of the language. Ask them to make a list or use a graphic organizer to help them remember their impressions.	Howard Gardner's work on multiple intelligences includes a discussion of the importance of offering students a variety of ways to "enter into" a subject. The activities here address Gardner's five categories of entry points (see Glossary, page 351). They respond primarily to learning profile and interest, but can also be differentiated by readiness. For more information, see Carreiro (1998).

LESSON SEQUENCE AND DESCRIPTION	TEACHER COMMENTARY
Logical/Quantitative Entry Point Provide biographies of Saint-Exupéry or access to a number of Web sites featuring biological information about him. Ask students to profile the author by collecting, compiling, and displaying important facts about his life.	
Foundational Entry Point Provide students with philosophical or profound quotes from *Le Petit Prince.* Ask students to choose three of the quotes and journal their thoughts about each quotation. They may want to speculate about the specific meaning of the quote in the context of the story or take a larger view and discuss how the quote relates to their own philosophy of living. If there is time after the journaling, they may share their impressions as a small group.	Our choice of quotes was influenced by *A Guide for Grownups: Essential Wisdom from the Collected Works of Antoine de Saint-Exupéry.*
Aesthetic Entry Point Provide a listening station so students can play selections from the CD of the musical version of the story (*Le Petit Prince: L'Intégral du Spectacle Musical,* music by Richard Cocciante and words by Elisabeth Anais) and look at the liner notes. Stress to students that the point of this exercise is not to understand every word of every song, but to get a sense of the music's tone and style in order to get an idea of the tone and style of the book. After listening, students should draw a picture or write a paragraph illustrating their impressions.	Another idea here would be to offer audio excerpts of the book and reconfigure this station to be more like the narrational entry point. Students could focus on the aesthetic qualities of the reader's voice—especially if there is more than one audio version. They could talk about which rendition they like best and why. Or, the aesthetic focus could be on the costumes used in the musical. Video clips on the topic are available at www.lepetitprince.com/fr/xDivers/Castelbajac.php.
Experiential Entry Point Provide a series of drawings that represent key symbols in the book: a rose, stars, a desert landscape, trains, water, a fox, a snake, and so on. Ask students to look at the drawings and reflect on the meaning each symbol has for them and why. Ask students to arrange the symbols into sequence and compose an original story or poem to accompany them.	Note that this entry point illustrates and reinforces a unit generalization: "Who you are and what you value affects your view of the world" (GEN1).
Regrouping and sharing of entry points. After students have spent about 30 to 40 minutes at their chosen station, regroup them so that there is a representative from each entry point activity in each of the new groups. Ask students to share their work and their impressions with the other group members.	It is important to expose students to the entry points they did not choose. This provides them with multiple perspectives about the text and can spark an interest in trying a new entry point the next time this type of activity is offered.

LESSON SEQUENCE AND DESCRIPTION	TEACHER COMMENTARY
Text distribution and introduction. Pass out copies of *Le Petit Prince* and ask students to read the back cover synopsis and the dedication and skim the illustrations. Provide important cultural information and background on the text and the author to set the stage for reading the novel. Possible topics might include • The eventual disappearance of the author. • Parallels between the author and the character of the aviator. • The novel's adaptation into a musical in France. • Movie versions of the text. If necessary, provide a brief introduction to the literary past tense.	
Read-aloud and discussion. Ask students to spread out around the classroom and make themselves comfortable for listening. Read Chapter 1 aloud two times. The first time through, students should just listen. The second time, allow them to read along silently if they wish. Discuss the chapter, making sure that all students have the opportunity to relate the reading to their own lives and experiences. Post and review a set of general guidelines for reading a French novel. Tell students that for best understanding, they should follow a standard process for each chapter: 1. Look at the vocabulary and questions for the chapter. 2. Read the chapter rapidly to get a general idea of what happens. Try to avoid using your vocabulary lists, and do not use a dictionary. 3. Read the chapter a second time more slowly, and consult the vocabulary list as needed. 4. Try to answer as many of the assigned comprehension questions as you can. 5. Read the chapter a third time to find the answers to the rest of the questions. 6. If desired, read the chapter a fourth time, rapidly, to get an overall feel for the text.	We addressed different levels of questions to students based on their skills in reading and speaking. We provided students with a hard copy of these directions so that they could refer to them throughout the unit. Because this was our students' first experience reading a French novel, we wanted to provide a scaffold to help them be more productive in their reading.

LESSON SEQUENCE AND DESCRIPTION	TEACHER COMMENTARY
Tiered homework differentiated by readiness. Ask students to reread Chapter 1 and answer an assigned set of questions. Distribute the appropriate version of the **Tiered Chapter 1 Comprehension Questions** (see Sample 8.2, pages 302–303) based on readiness.	The questions in this handout are differentiated according to skill in reading comprehension and abstract thought. Please note that unlike the version of the handout in Sample 8.2, the questions students received were written entirely in French.
All three levels of questions (novice, intermediate, and advanced) include questions about the text's literal meaning and symbolic meaning and prompts for reflection. However, as the levels increase, the questions focus more on abstract thought. Each level also asks student to analyze the use of grammatical constructions in the text, but there is more scaffolding at the novice and intermediate levels than at the advanced level.	All questions, regardless of tier, draw on higher-level thinking skills and connect the text to students' lives. No student should be "stuck" with questions that draw only on concrete knowledge and comprehension of the text.

LESSON 2

Introduction to the Unit Requirements and Literature Circles

(1 block)

Concepts: Perspective, Growth
GEN1–2; SD1, SD8

LESSON SEQUENCE AND DESCRIPTION	TEACHER COMMENTARY
Discussion of unit requirements. Distribute individual copies of a packet that includes three key documents:	Many students appreciate an overview of what to expect in a unit of study. It's necessary to support students with auditory processing difficulties, but it also provides an organizational structure that can help all students manage their time and stay on task.
1. The **Unit Requirements** (see Sample 8.3, page 304). This document explains the major components of the unit (reading; literature circle discussions; individualized grammar, vocabulary, and comprehension work; the final project; and extension/anchor activities).	
2. The **Unit Contract** (see the **Unit Contract Template,** Sample 8.4, pages 305–306). Explain to students that you have used information from their unit pre-assessment to determine the grammar points and the vocabulary they need to review. Provide individual students with a card that lists the grammar (by topic) and vocabulary (by chapter) that they need to review and the number of extensions they are required to complete.	Due to the great variability in student readiness, interest, and learning profile, we decided to put students on a grammar and vocabulary building contract to accompany the study of the text. It was an effective way to help them concentrate on the areas in which they needed additional practice.

LESSON SEQUENCE AND DESCRIPTION	TEACHER COMMENTARY
Have students fill out their contracts accordingly—checking which vocabulary quizzes they need to complete and highlighting which grammar topics they need to work on (or do this for them in advance). Tell them you will be offering mini-lessons on the grammar topics throughout the unit. Answer any questions they have on the unit assignments.	
3. The **Extension/Anchor Activities and Product Rubric** (see Sample 8.5, pages 307–309). When students reach the "Number of Extensions Required " portion of the contract, explain that there will be times when they finish their work earlier than others or when they do not have a grammar or vocabulary requirement for a particular chapter. At those times, they may choose to work on an extension/anchor activity. Point out that they are required to complete a certain number of these activities (the number is included in their contract) and that any others they choose to complete will count as extra credit points.	The number of extensions each student had to complete was based on the individual's vocabulary and grammar readiness. We asked the most advanced students to complete between four and five extension activities and struggling students to complete only one or two.
Review the list of extension activities and the product rubric, providing clarification and answering questions as needed.	
The activities provide multiple options for students to explore up to four key elements of literary analysis (character, setting, plot, and theme) through various modalities. Some of the activities are highly analytical (1B), while others are more introspective (4B). Some have a more practical (4C) or creative (2A) bent. Gardner's multiple intelligences are also evident, particularly musical/rhythmic intelligence (2C), visual/spatial intelligence (3B), and bodily/kinesthetic intelligence (3D).	With extension activities like these, it can be easy for students to avoid doing their very best work. The addition of the product rubric (see page 309) was our way of trying to prevent this. Although the rubric could be fleshed out with other criteria for specific products, we kept the focus on elements applicable for all: content, accuracy, and mechanics/aesthetics.
Introduction, discussion, and demonstration of literature circles. Explain to the class that they will be discussing *Le Petit Prince* in a literature circle environment. Talk about the purpose and advantage of literature circles. Explain what a good literature circle discussion looks like, the various roles available, and the importance of strong group-interaction skills. Share with students the **Rubric for Literature Circle Discussions** (see Sample 8.6, page 310), which will be used to evaluate their literature circle performance.	We found out from colleagues in the English department if the students had ever been exposed to literature circles. There are many books and Web sources devoted to the literature circle instructional strategy. For more information, try these: • home.att.net/~teaching/ litcircles.htm. • teachers.net/gazette/MAR02/ zeiger.html.
Ask: How can the roles in a literature circle help us to gain a variety of perspectives on what we read? How can they help us with our own growth in reading, writing, speaking, and listening in French?	

LESSON SEQUENCE AND DESCRIPTION	TEACHER COMMENTARY
Refer students to unit generalizations 1 and 2: "Who you are and what you value affects your view of the world," and "People hunger for exploration and growth of both the external and the internal world." If possible, ask other teachers or students with particularly strong verbal skills to help you demonstrate a successful literature circle discussing Chapter 1 of the text. Ask students to use the rubric to evaluate the discussion. If a demonstration is not possible, ask students to help you fill out sample role sheets for Chapter 1 as if they were preparing for a literature circle meeting.	• www.allamericareads.org/ lessonplan/strategies/ during/litcirc2. htm. • fac-staff.seattleu.edu/kschlnoe/ LitCircles/Discussion/focus. html.
Literature circle planning in self-selected groups. Ask students to break into literature circle groups so that there is one student for each of the roles. Provide each student with a **Unit Calendar Template** (see Sample 8.7, pages 311–312), and explain that they need to make a schedule to follow for the rest of the unit—something to clarify which person will take on which role for each portion of the reading. Remind students to refer to their learning profile surveys to help them assign roles for the first literature circle meeting. They should begin with a role that is quite comfortable for them. Over the course of the unit, they should also try out other roles with which they are less comfortable in order to stimulate their own growth in text interpretation.	Setting reasonable goals is a skill that can be difficult for many students to master, so it's always a good idea to check in on their work. And, of course, some groups of students need more monitoring than others. Literature circle groups can be formed in many ways, depending on the teacher's specific learning goals and the student population. Here, we planned for students who would be using literature circles in a world language class for the first time, and decided to let them work with others with whom they felt comfortable. In general, though, we often place advanced readers in one group and group at-grade-level and below-grade-level students heterogeneously. We also consider learning profile as well as readiness, striving for groups of students who have a variety of interests and learning profiles.
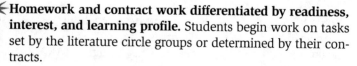**Homework and contract work differentiated by readiness, interest, and learning profile.** Students begin work on tasks set by the literature circle groups or determined by their contracts.	

LESSON 3	Contract Work and Literature Circles	*(4 class periods*
	Concepts: Perspective, Exploration, Growth, Relationships	*and 8 blocks)*
	GEN1–3; SD1–8	

LESSON SEQUENCE AND DESCRIPTION	TEACHER COMMENTARY
Note: This lesson extends over four weeks, with students working independently and in flexible groups to complete the unit requirements.	This unit required a *lot* of upfront work, but things slowed down a bit for us once students began their independent and small-group work.
Here are some guidelines for facilitating a productive working environment during this lesson: • Provide places in the classroom where students can work and meet, making sure that necessary supplies are available, including computers with PowerPoint and video and audio equipment. • Post a daily schedule with times of mini-lessons, video clip screenings, or other teacher-led activities. • Designate a central place (a file box or basket) for students to turn in work as it is completed.	Small tables and groups of desks facilitated both individual and small-group extension work. Study carrels worked well for quizzes and for those students who had difficulty concentrating in a multitasking classroom.
Individual vocabulary and grammar contract work based on readiness. As indicated in their individual contracts, students complete grammar exercises in *Découverte du Petit Prince* and complete chapter-specific vocabulary quizzes.	We used this workbook because it was readily available to us. Other appropriate review exercises might come from a grammar-review text.
Extension/anchor activities differentiated by interest and learning profile. Students work independently or in groups to complete their assigned number of extensions, or complete them as anchor activities when time permits (see Sample 8.5).	
Reading comprehension assessments differentiated by interest. Students complete two **Reading Comprehension Quizzes** (see Sample 8.8, pages 313–314) focused on the big ideas of the text and the unit generalizations. To differentiate the quiz for learning profile, allow students to answer the questions orally via a tape recording if they choose.	Each section offers students a choice of which questions they wish to answer. Some of the questions are harder than others, so readiness differentiation is built in too. In each section, the first question is the simplest or most concrete, and the last is the most complex or most abstract. However, to answer any of the questions, students needed to have a good comprehension of the story and had to move beyond recall and summarization to analysis, synthesis, and evaluation.

LESSON SEQUENCE AND DESCRIPTION	TEACHER COMMENTARY
Literature circle preparation and discussions. Students prepare for and meet in their literature circles, following their group schedule. Provide them with chapter-specific comprehension questions to help stimulate discussion.	As noted, our students used the *Découverte du Petit Prince* reading comprehension questions.
Meet with each literature circle at least twice formally and as often as possible informally. Use the literature circle discussion rubric (see Sample 8.6) to evaluate student participation.	Sometimes we just observed the literature circle meetings, while at other times, we participated in the discussion in order to push student thinking to the next level.
✳ Mini-lessons based on readiness needs and interest. Observe sticking points that come up as students read and discuss, and provide mini-lessons as needed. Topics might include troublesome grammar points or particularly complicated passages in the novel. These lessons should be limited to 30 minutes or less.	We posted mini-lesson topics on the board each day and invited students we knew needed the help, but we also encouraged anyone who wished to attend to do so.
✳ Final project work differentiated by interest and learning profile. At the beginning of this lesson (or earlier, if desired) distribute the **Final Project Guidelines and Evaluation Rubric** (see Sample 8.9, pages 315–317). *Choice 1: Multimedia Project* This targets students who enjoy working with technology, students who are fairly verbal, and students who are highly visual. The project is completed independently or with a partner. *Choice 2: "Book Talk" Video Presentation* This targets students with strong interpersonal intelligence and students who are highly verbal. The project is completed in pairs. *Choice 3: Written Analysis of a Theme* This targets students who are both analytical and creative and students who have strong intrapersonal intelligence. The project is completed independently.	The "ideas for themes" provided in the project handout were just a jumping-off point. We included both concrete themes (column one) and themes that are more abstract (column two). We designed the three product choices to be at about the same level of difficulty and focused all of them firmly on the themes in the text and the first unit generalization (GEN1). Each choice has a "twist" to make it appealing to students with varied interests and learning profiles. We also allowed students to come up with their own ideas for a project as long as it maintained the focus of the other choices and stretched student skills in technology or mechanics.
✳ Individual conferences. Meet one-on-one with students on a biweekly basis or more frequently, if necessary. Students should bring their contracts and supporting documents with them to every meeting and be prepared to talk about their progress on the various components of the unit.	We differentiated the amount of structure—such as check-in dates and progress reports—we provided individuals. However, all students, including the most advanced, benefited from individual attention and support.

LESSON SEQUENCE AND DESCRIPTION	TEACHER COMMENTARY
Film clip/music presentations and whole-class discussion. Throughout this lesson, show and discuss clips from a film adaptation of the novel (such as the 1974 American musical version, directed by Stanley Donen) or play and discuss particular songs from the soundtrack.	Students vary in their skill with the various components of communication in a language they are learning. Some are better at reading; others, at listening. Because a lot of this unit focuses on understanding and analyzing themes, we were comfortable offering alternative ways to access its "big ideas."

LESSON 4

Final Project Presentations

Concepts: Perspective, Exploration, Growth, Relationships
GEN1–3; SD1–8

(1 class period and 2 blocks)

LESSON SEQUENCE AND DESCRIPTION	TEACHER COMMENTARY
Final project presentations and whole-class discussion. Students present their final projects over three class sessions. Before the first presentation, post the following guidelines: *As you listen to each presentation, respond in writing to the following prompts:* *1. Which of the unit generalizations does this presentation best support and why?* *GEN1: Who you are and what you value affects your view of the world.* *GEN2: People hunger for exploration and growth of both the external and the internal world.* *GEN3: Relationships confer responsibility.* *2. What does this presentation (or the theme it analyzes) help you discover or rediscover about the novel? About yourself?* Discuss responses to the presentations as time allows.	As noted, we used the rubric in Sample 8.9 to evaluate presentations and also had presenters submit their own filled-in rubrics as self-assessment. We collected these responses to get insight into students' thought processes. We also allowed the presenters to see the written feedback and announced this intention in advance, knowing that some students would rather not share personal thoughts and feelings with their classmates.
Unit evaluation. During the final class session, after the last presentation, have all students fill out the **Unit Evaluation** (see Sample 8.10, page 318).	Note the clear link between the unit objectives and the questions posed on this evaluation. Getting this kind of information helps teachers determine those parts of a unit that were successful as well as the parts that need a bit of tweaking.

Teacher Reflection on Designing the Unit

When first working to differentiate, it is unreasonable (we think) to start from scratch on every unit. Often, it makes better sense to select an existing unit that you feel is already strong and look for opportunities to make the unit even stronger by reworking it to be more responsive to student differences in readiness, interest, and learning profile. We feel we accomplished both objectives in redesigning this unit.

One benefit of using contracts, even though they require a lot of preparatory work on the part of the teacher, is the opportunity they offer high school juniors and seniors to practice the skill of time management—something that will be critically important once they arrive at an institute of higher learning. An especially exciting aspect of the unit is the use of literature discussion (via literature circles) and literary analysis (via the final project) in the target language. These skills should certainly help students feel more comfortable in advanced French discussion and literature courses at the college level.

Cindy A. Strickland has taught French to students from kindergarten to college in Minnesota, Indiana, and Virginia. She is currently a doctoral student at the University of Virginia. She can be reached at cas2k@virginia.edu.

Molly Wieland, PhD, is a French teacher at Hopkins High School in Minnetonka, Minnesota, and the world language curriculum coordinator for the Hopkins School District. She can be reached at molly_wieland@hopkins.k12.mn.us.

SAMPLE 8.1—Unit Overview

The Little Prince and Me

In reading and analyzing *Le Petit Prince,* you will need to develop and exercise a variety of skills. At times you will need to act like a philosopher; at others times, a literary critic. You will need to exercise your imagination and examine your own philosophies of life. You will need an analytical spirit as well as openness to fantasy, imagination, and symbolism. You will also need to spend time reflecting on what you read, as there are important lessons throughout the text. But you must read between the lines to get a full understanding of the meaning of the story.

As a result of this unit

You will *know*
- The background of Antoine de Saint-Exupéry, author of *Le Petit Prince.*
- The characters, setting, plot, and themes of *Le Petit Prince.*
- New vocabulary words.
- The verb tenses used in the text.

You will *understand that*
- Reading literature in the target language is one way to improve vocabulary and increase fluency.
- It is possible to read for pleasure in more than one language.
- As in native language literature, it is possible to see reflections of ourselves in target-language literature.

You will *be able to*
- Read more fluently in French.
- Demonstrate improved grammatical accuracy in writing and speaking French.
- Incorporate new vocabulary into discussion and writing.
- Discuss literary elements in the French language.
- Analyze a theme found in *Le Petit Prince.*
- Examine your own beliefs and values through a textual lens.

Note: You cannot achieve these objectives by reading the book in English. For this reason, you are **forbidden** to read the English version of the text.

SAMPLE 8.2—Tiered Chapter 1 Comprehension Questions

Novice Level

Literal Comprehension *(what happened in the chapter)*
1. How old was the narrator when he first saw a boa?
2. Draw the narrator's first drawing and describe what is inside.
3. How is the narrator's second drawing different from his first drawing?
4. What advice do adults like to give?

Symbolic Comprehension *(abstract action, symbolism, big ideas)*
5. What do the following symbolize: open boas, closed boas, virgin forests, and stars?

Reflective Comprehension *(the meaning of the text)*
6. Has an adult ever misunderstood you? Explain.
7. According to the narrator, what qualities do adults seek in other adults? What qualities does the narrator seek? What qualities do *you* seek?

Text Analysis
8. Give an example from the book that reflects the following:
   — A formative or defining moment from the narrator's or the Little Prince's life.
   — Something the narrator or the Little Prince did routinely.
   — Circumstances or description.

   What verb tense is used in each situation?

Intermediate Level

Literal Comprehension *(what happened in the chapter)*
1. Draw the narrator's first drawing and describe what is inside.
2. How is the narrator's second drawing different from his first drawing?
3. Over the course of his life, what experiment did the aviator conduct to see if an adult "truly understood"?

Symbolic Comprehension *(abstract action, symbolism, big ideas)*
4. What is meant by the following question, posed by adults: "Why should a hat inspire fear?"
5. What do the following symbolize: open boas, closed boas, virgin forests, and stars?

Reflective Comprehension *(the meaning of the text)*
6. Describe a defining moment from your life.
7. In your opinion, what is the fundamental meaning of this chapter?

Text Analysis
8. In what situations does the author use the imperfect tense? Give specific examples and tell why the author used that tense.

Note: These questions were adapted from www.richmond.edu/~jpaulsen/petitprince/chapitre1.html with permission of the author, Janice Paulsen.

SAMPLE 8.2—Tiered Chapter 1 Comprehension Questions—*(continued)*

Advanced Level

Literal Comprehension *(what happened in the chapter)*
1. Draw the narrator's first and second drawings and describe what is inside.
2. Over the course of his life, what experiment did the aviator conduct to see if an adult "truly understood?"

Symbolic Comprehension *(abstract action, symbolism, big ideas)*
3. What is meant by the following question, posed by adults: "Why should a hat inspire fear?"
4. What do the following symbolize: bridge, golf and ties, open boas, closed boas, virgin forests, stars?

Reflective Comprehension *(the meaning of the text)*
5. Describe a defining moment from your life.
6. In your opinion, what is the fundamental meaning of this chapter?
7. Is adults' lack of comprehension a universal problem? Explain.

Text Analysis
8. In what situations does the author use the past perfect tense? The imperfect tense? Give specific examples and explain why the author used that tense.

SAMPLE 8.3—Unit Requirements

The Little Prince and Me

Here are the major expectations for this unit:

1. Nightly *reading assignments.*
2. Full participation in whole-class and small-group (literature circle) *discussions about the readings.*
3. *Quizzes on vocabulary, grammar, and comprehension* as indicated in your Unit Contract.
4. *A final project on the analysis of a theme.*
5. *Extension activities* as assigned or negotiated.

Vocabulary Requirements

You are responsible for improving your vocabulary as you read. Because reading fluency is related to your recognition and understanding of sight vocabulary, you will spend some time during this unit adding to your current repertoire.

Look carefully at the results of your vocabulary pre-assessment. If you scored lower than 80 percent on the words associated with a particular chapter, you will need to take a quiz on that chapter's vocabulary. Decide how you will go about learning the meaning of the words. Many students find flashcards helpful, for example. See me if you need more suggestions. When you are ready, you may take the appropriate vocabulary quiz. In each quiz, you will need to provide the English equivalent of the underlined vocabulary words. Here is an example item:

Le dessin représentait un serpent boa qui avalait <u>un fauve</u>.
Your response would be to write, <u>a wild beast</u>.

A quiz for each chapter is available in the file box on my desk. Take the quiz and correct it. Place your corrected quizzes into the proper folder in the file box and mark the date you did so in Column 3 on your contract.

Grammar Requirements

You will receive a list of grammar topics you need to review during this unit. (You will need to highlight them in Column 5 of your contract.) For each required grammar topic, complete the corresponding sections in your workbook, *Découverte du Petit Prince*. *If the topic is not on your requirement list, you do not need to do those workbook sections.* Turn in the completed sections to the appropriate file and mark the date you did so in the last column of your contract.

Reading Comprehension Requirements

Your comprehension of the text will be evident in your large- and small-group discussions. In addition, you need to schedule a time to take a general comprehension quiz after reading Chapters 1–15 and again after reading Chapters 16–27. For each quiz, choose two questions to answer (you will have access to the various question options beforehand) and respond in essay form or orally. You may practice or write out sample answers, but you may not bring any notes with you when you take the quiz.

Final Project Requirements

You will choose a theme in the novel that you find particularly intriguing and prepare and present an analysis of it by completing one of three project options. As you read the novel, be sure to note themes that come up and mark these passages so you can find them later. At the end of the unit, you will present your final project to your classmates. For more information on the final project, see the **Final Project Guidelines and Evaluation Rubric.**

SAMPLE 8.4—Unit Contract Template

This contract belongs to _____

Key

PC = Past perfect tense

IMP = Imperfect tense

PS = Literary past tense

Subj = Subjunctive

Futur = Future tense

PP = Present participle

PQP = Pluperfect tense

Impér = Imperative

PQPS = Pluperfect subjunctive

Cond = Conditional tense

Accord = Past participle agreement

FA = Anterior future tense

CP = Past conditional tense

Phrases = Conditional Phrases

Temps = Future after expressions of time

Chapter	Vocabulary Quiz (Check if required)	Date Completed	Grammar Topics (Complete workbook pages only for those topics that are highlighted)	Date Completed
1			PC, IMP	
2			PS	
3			Subj	
4			Futur	
5			PS, Subj	
6			IMP	
7			PP, PQP	
8			Impér	
9			Futur	
10			Impér	
11			PS, PQP	
12			IMP, Subj, PQPS	
13			Cond	
14			Cond, IMP, Subj	
15			Accord, PQPS	

SAMPLE 8.4—Unit Contract Template—*(continued)*				
Chapter	**Vocabulary Quiz** (Check if required)	**Date Completed**	**Grammar Topics** (Complete workbook pages only for those topics that are highlighted)	**Date Completed**
Comprehension Quiz on Chapters 1–15				
16			FA, CP, PQP, Phrases	
17			PP, Phrases	
18			PQP, PP, Phrases, Subj	
19			PQP	
20			Temps, Subj	
21			FA, IMP, PC	
22			PP, Phrases	
23			PQP, PP, Phrases, Subj	
24			PQP	
25			Temps, Subj	
26			FA, IMP, PC	
27			None	
Comprehension Quiz on Chapters 16–27				

* Number of Extensions Required _____

SAMPLE 8.5—Extension/Anchor Activities and Product Rubric

Individual Extension Activities

Choose no more than one option under each numbered topic category. Use the attached **Product Rubric** to guide your work.

1. Character

A. Draw a concept map showing the major hurdles the Little Prince had to overcome in the novel and the major hurdles *you* (or adolescents in general) have to overcome during this time of your life. Be sure your map represents your ideas clearly. Include a brief explanation on the back of the map.

B. Complete an analysis matrix that specifies the fox's feelings about responsibility toward those we tame and why he believes as he does. Consider your own feelings about this topic. Develop notes on both views of responsibility with reasons and illustrations from the text and from your life.

C. Imagine that it's 20 years after the events in the novel took place. Write a feature piece for a magazine on one of the characters in the book. Where has life taken him? Why? Now imagine it's 20 years from now. Write a feature on yourself that addresses the same questions.

D. Create a fortune-lines visual (with narration) that shows the emotional state of the Little Prince at what you believe are the 8 or 10 most important points in the book. Explain why you selected these events and the personal meaning these scenes have for you.

2. Setting/Mood

A. Make up your own planet with a corresponding inhabitant and write a short chapter about the Little Prince's visit to the planet. Include an illustration. Be ready to defend why the stereotype represented by your planet is a good addition to the book.

B. Draw or paint three greeting cards that invite viewers into the scenery and mood of the book at three different points in the story. Be sure the verse in each card helps us understand what is important in the scene and why.

C. Listen to excerpts from Gustave Holst's *The Planets*. Create and record brief soundscapes of what at least three of the planets that the Little Prince visited might sound like. Write a CD liner-note explanation of your soundscapes to make the link between the music and the stereotype represented by the planets' inhabitant(s).

D. Design a map that illustrates the Little Prince's journey (physical, emotional, or spiritual) throughout the book. Annotate the map so we can see the importance of the "places" you chose to include.

3. Plot

A. Prepare and videotape a music video in which you dance and lip-sync the words to one of the songs from the soundtrack to the musical. You may use cue cards if necessary. You will need props and costumes that clearly fit the mood of the song.

B. Choose five to seven significant scenes from the book and make a series of illustrated bookmarks that reveals the sequence of the storyline. Include some written descriptions (perhaps on the back?) to clarify what's happening in each scene and why it is important.

Note: These activities were adapted from http://fac-staff.seattleu.edu/kschlnoe/LitCircles/Extension/extension.html with permission of the creator, Katherine L. Schlick Noe, and from "Novel Think-Tac-Toe" (Tomlinson, 2003, pp. 131–132).

SAMPLE 8.5—Extension/Anchor Activities and Product Rubric—*(continued)*

    C. Fold a piece of paper into three sections. On side 1/section 1, write the name of your book, the author, and your name. On side 1/section 2, draw the problem of the story. On side 2/section 3, draw how the problem was solved. On side 2/section 1, draw something that happened at the beginning of the book. On side 2/section 2, draw something that happened in the middle of the book. In the last section, draw something that happened at the end of the book.

    D. Present a dramatic interpretation of one section of text. You may work alone or with a partner to perform a key scene from the book. You do not need to memorize the text of the chapter. You may use certain words or expressions, but this is not intended to be a verbatim performance of the chapter. Use your own words and make it sound spontaneous.

4. Theme

    A. Compose lyrics to an original song related to one of the book's themes. Design the front and the back cover for a CD of your "hit single" that captures its spirit. Include your original lyrics to the hit single inside.

    B. Find and illustrate a set of quotes by the Little Prince. Annotate the quotations, explaining their significance to the themes of the novel.

    C. Make a treasure box that contains artifacts representing ideas, events, characters, and themes in the book. Label each artifact and briefly write about its importance to the book.

    D. Using magazine photos, original drawings, or both, create a mobile symbolizing key themes in the book. On the back of each section, explain what the image symbolizes and how it draws on key material from the text.

Group Extension Activities

Choose one of the following to complete in your literature circle group. Use the attached **Product Rubric** to guide your work.

    A. Using strips of adding machine tape, work with your group to create a visual representation of significant ideas or themes in the book. Use symbols, ideas, colors, and words to capture these ideas or themes on strips of paper (one symbol, idea, or theme per strip). Weave the strips together and attach them to a border that literally and figuratively binds them together.

    B. Work with your group members to create a paper "quilt" illustrating the wisdom of the book. Select important quotes from the book and incorporate them into individual quilt squares or their border. "Sew" the quilt squares together.

    C. Create an alphabet book that focuses on key characters, settings, symbols, and themes from the text. Include an illustration on each page as well as one or two sentences explaining each illustration's significance to the story.

    D. Videotape a literature circle discussion of one or more chapters. Edit the tape and provide narration demonstrating the various literature circle roles and their contribution to a deep understanding of the novel.

SAMPLE 8.5—Extension/Anchor Activities and Product Rubric—*(continued)*

Product Rubric

Criteria	Novice	Emerging	Competent	Expert
Content	Product does not show evidence that the instructions leading up to the product or the product requirements were seriously considered.	Project shows attention to task instructions leading up to the product and to the product requirements, although some parts seem to have received less attention than others.	Project demonstrates clear and consistent attention to task instructions leading up to the product and all the product requirements have been met.	Project demonstrates clear and consistent attention to the task and the execution (research, discussion, contemplation) exceeds requirements.
Accuracy	Product contains inaccurate or misleading information.	Product information is accurate with the exception of minor details or omissions that do not detract from its overall impact.	Product contains accurate information.	Product content is accurate and insightful, fresh, and surprising to the viewer.
Mechanics and Aesthetics	Errors in mechanics (spelling, grammar) or aesthetics (balance, contrast, emphasis) distract the viewer.	Errors in mechanics (spelling, grammar) or aesthetics (balance, contrast, emphasis) are noticeable, but do not distract from the product's overall impact.	There are no mechanical errors and the product is aesthetically pleasing.	There are no mechanical errors and the overall product is not only aesthetically pleasing, but is on par with what you would expect from a professional in the field.

SAMPLE 8.6—Rubric for Literature Circle Discussions

Criteria	Student of Literature	Professor of Literature	Nobel Laureate
Preparation	Student completed assigned reading and role sheet.	Student completed reading and fully prepared for his/her role.	Student completed reading and brought extensive notes that correspond to and expand upon his/her role.
Participation	Student answers and asks appropriate questions; student does not interfere with the functioning of group.	Student listens to others, asks questions, and responds appropriately; student is part of the solution when it comes to addressing and clarifying group misunderstandings.	Student actively listens to others, asks thoughtful questions, and helps keep the group on task; student anticipates and works to resolve potential conflicts before they arise.
Reflection	Student has thought about and refers to the text, although on a surface level.	Student contributes thoughtful, clearly supported ideas demonstrating careful and reflection on the text.	Student thinks both deeply and broadly about text, building on others' questions and comments and elaborating on his/her own thoughts; student effectively and consistently uses the text to share passages and support ideas and opinions.

SAMPLE 8.7—Unit Calendar Template

The Little Prince and Me

For the next four weeks, you will be working in your literature circles to read and discuss *Le Petit Prince*. Fill in the Unit Calendar template (attached) to schedule your reading assignments and literature circle activities, including required discussions with me.

1. Make a tentative plan for reading the text. Remember, you must finish reading and discussing the entire novel by the end of Day 14. Everyone in your group must agree on the schedule, because everyone's preparation and participation is vital for the success of your literature circle. Be sure you write down the role you are assigned and the pages you need to read for each class period in your Unit Calendar. You may need to adjust the schedule after the first week, so write in pencil! You do not have to meet every class period, but I suggest you meet at least twice a week.

2. You need to schedule a discussion time with me at least twice during Weeks 2–6. I will probably drop in unannounced as well.

3. You also need to schedule two general comprehension quizzes (one for Chapters 1–15 and one for Chapters 16–27), during which you will choose from a series of questions to answer in written or oral form.

4. Remember to keep your contract record sheet up to date. Staple this calendar and your contract together and keep them in a safe place!

SAMPLE 8.7—Unit Calendar Template—*(continued)*

Unit Calendar

Week	45-minute period	90-minute block	90-minute block
Week 1		Day 1 Entry point activities; read Chapter 1	Day 2 Unit overview; introduction to literature circles; meet with literature circles and set tentative calendar
Week 2	Day 3 Assignment: Role: ☐ Discussion with teacher Time:	Day 4 Assignment: Role: ☐ Discussion with teacher Time:	Day 5 Assignment: Role: ☐ Discussion with teacher Time:
Week 3	Day 6 Assignment: Role: ☐ Discussion with teacher Time:	Day 7 Assignment: Role: ☐ Discussion with teacher Time:	Day 8 Assignment: Role: ☐ Discussion with teacher Time:
Week 4	Day 9 Assignment: Role: ☐ Discussion with teacher Time:	Day 10 Assignment: Role: ☐ Discussion with teacher Time:	Day 11 Assignment: Role: ☐ Discussion with teacher Time:
Week 5	Day 12 Assignment: Role: ☐ Discussion with teacher Time:	Day 13 Assignment: Role: ☐ Discussion with teacher Time:	Day 14 Assignment: Role: ☐ Discussion with teacher Time:
Week 6	Day 15 Final project presentations	Day 16 Final project presentations	Day 17 Final project presentations and unit evaluation

SAMPLE 8.8—Reading Comprehension Quizzes

Comprehension Quiz, Chapters 1–15

1. Choose one of the following options and respond.

   A. Le Pilote
      Who was this man? Why did he seem less absurd than others the Little Prince had met? What traits and virtues did he have that made the Little Prince want to be his friend?

   B. Le Petit Prince
      Describe the melancholy life of the Little Prince up until he travels to other planets. Talk about both physiological and psychological traits. According to the Little Prince, how should we judge others?

   C. La Rose
      Describe the rose and her rather contradictory nature. Explain how and why the rose tormented the Little Prince. Why did the Little Prince decide to leave his planet and his rose?

2. Choose one of the following options and respond.

   A. What did the Little Prince learn at the businessman's planet? Compare their thoughts about the value of material possessions. What do you think about the value of material possessions?
   B. What did the Little Prince learn at the geographer's planet? Compare the Little Prince's and the geographer's thoughts and ideas about "the ephemeral." What is your opinion about "serious things" in life? Do you agree more with the Little Prince or the geographer? Explain.
   C. Summarize and explain your thoughts about what the Little Prince learned on his voyage to the six planets. What did you learn?

3. Choose one of the following unit generalizations and explain how what you have read so far supports or refutes that generalization.

   A. Who you are and what you value affects your view of the world.
   B. People hunger for exploration and growth of both the external and the internal world.
   C. Relationships confer responsibility.

SAMPLE 8.8—Reading Comprehension Quizzes—(continued)

Comprehension Quiz, Chapters 16–27

1. Choose one of the following options and respond.

   A. Talk about the scene between the Prince and the fox. What is the significance of "taming"? Give the fox's definition and description of the process. Also provide your own interpretation of the process. The fox says that he will cry when the Little Prince leaves, yet he will also have won. What does he mean by this? Do you agree? What is the symbolic meaning of the entire conversation between the fox and the Little Prince?
   B. What was your first impression when you saw the final drawing in the book? Why was the narrator worried? How did he explain why he drew this final drawing? What is the symbolic meaning of this last drawing? What is your understanding of the ending of the book? Has your understanding of "existence" changed or been reinforced by reading this text? Explain. Why, in your opinion, did Saint-Exupéry write this book?

2. Choose one of the following quotes or expressions of wisdom. Explain how the quote fits into the story. Talk about what this quote means to you. Give a specific example from your own life or the life of someone close to you.

   A. It is not enough to read and write about a lot of things . . . you must experience them! You can read lots of books about mountains, but you don't really know them if you don't see them and experience them.
   B. And now here is my secret, a very simple secret: It is only with the heart that one can see rightly; what is essential is invisible to the eye.
   C. "Men have forgotten this truth," said the fox. "But you must not forget it. You become responsible, forever, for what you have tamed."
   D. One runs the risk of weeping a little, if one lets oneself be tamed.
   E. What makes the desert beautiful is that somewhere it hides a well.
   F. You become forever responsible for that which you have tamed.

3. Choose one of the following unit generalizations and explain how your own thinking about that generalization has changed over the course of the book.

   A. Who you are and what you value affects your view of the world.
   B. People hunger for exploration and growth of both the external and the internal world.
   C. Relationships confer responsibility.

SAMPLE 8.9—Final Project Guidelines and Evaluation Rubric

Directions: For this assignment, you will choose a theme in the novel that you find particularly intriguing and prepare and present an analysis of this theme by completing one of three product options and presenting to the rest of the class. As you read, be sure to note themes that come up, and mark these passages so you can find them later. Here are some ideas for themes:

friendship/love	life and death	equilibrium
exploration/discovery	quality vs. quantity	social critiques/societal problems
good and evil	superficiality	Saint-Exupéry's philosophy of life
the visible vs. the invisible	what it means to be rich	fragility and the protection of
children's vs. adults'	stereotypes	fragile things
outlook on life	justice	materialism
happiness	beauty	possession
duty and responsibility	imagination	hunger and thirst
loyalty	light vs. shadow	
solitude	circles/circularity	

Choice 1: Multimedia Project

1. You may work alone on this project or with one other person. If you work in a pair, be sure to divide the work into equivalent parts or work together to write the text. What I *don't want* is one person to do the writing of text and the other to do the drawings.
2. Choose a theme from the text that you wish to explore. Analyze and present the theme in a manner that exploits the technology available to you. This analysis should include your own thoughts and feelings about the theme and how you explored and clarified these thoughts and feelings through reading the story. Be careful! I expect you to analyze a theme from the book, not simply point out or summarize parts of the story where the theme is evident.
3. Create a presentation of 7 to 10 slides. The number of slides is not as important as the quality and thoroughness with which you address the analysis. WATCH OUT! Always back up your files, and generate a hard copy of your text in case of technical difficulties.
4. Type in all of your text before you spend considerable time on illustrations or fancy effects. Remember that illustrations and effects must enhance the message you are conveying rather than detract from it.
5. Be sure to include the following elements:
   — An introduction that includes an appropriate title as well as the name of each creator.
   — A concluding slide that summarizes the message of your presentation.
   — Appropriate visuals and effects. Remember: Your analysis counts more than your drawings or effects. Don't spend all of your time making it look pretty!
   — Five to eight citations from the text that support your analysis. Keep your citations less than four lines long. This is not the spot to reproduce whole sections of the novel!
   — Vocabulary from your contract and/or your partner's contract.
   — Enough words to discuss your theme, your analysis, your reflections, and so on. (This will probably be at least 250 words, spread over several slides.)
6. You will need to do some work outside of class. Be sure to plan wisely so you will have the time you need in the computer lab and with your partner.

SAMPLE 8.9—Final Project Guidelines and Evaluation Rubric—*(continued)*

7. I also expect you to use this opportunity to enhance your skill with PowerPoint. Make a plan for your work that includes an opportunity for you to try something new. For example, if you have never imported a graphic or a video clip, challenge yourself to do so. Share your previous PowerPoint presentations with your partner or a peer and get feedback on ways to improve the impact of your work. Your PowerPoint growth goals will be evaluated in the "technique" section of the assessment rubric.

Choice 2: Book Talk Video Presentation

1. You will need to work on this project with a partner.
2. Choose a theme from the text that you wish to explore.
3. Prepare a 10-minute video segment for a new cable show called "Book Talk." In this segment, you and your partner will need to introduce the book you will discuss (*Le Petit Prince,* of course!) and the theme you will focus on during your discussion. You will probably want to include a brief summary of the story as part of your introduction, but remember that the focus of your work should be the theme and its analysis, *not the plot.* Be careful! I expect you to analyze a theme from the book, not simply point out or summarize parts of the story where the theme is evident. Your segment should then proceed as a discussion (conversational or a more formal point–counterpoint format) in which you analyze the theme you chose. Your analysis should include the thoughts and feelings of you and your partner about the theme and how you explored and clarified these thoughts and feelings through reading the story. You should each support your viewpoint with examples and brief citations from the text and your interpretation of the examples and citations. Be sure to conclude the segment in such a way that the viewer experiences a sense of closure and wholeness to the presentation.
4. Incorporate vocabulary words from your contract and your partner's contract wherever appropriate.
5. I also expect you to use this opportunity to improve your visual presentation skills and your skill with the camera. Meet with me early in the process to set specific goals. Your technical and presentation growth goals will be evaluated in the "technique" section of the assessment rubric.

Choice 3: Written Analysis of a Theme

1. This project must be completed on your own.
2. Choose a theme from the text that you wish to explore. Be careful! I expect you to analyze a theme from the book, not simply point out or summarize parts of the story where the theme is evident.
3. Write a paper of at least five paragraphs. Each paragraph should contain five to eight sentences. In the first paragraph, introduce your subject and the ideas you will present. You may wish to include a brief summary of the story, but you should quickly transition to the theme you will discuss in the rest of the paper. The next three paragraphs should develop the theme you have chosen. Your analysis should include your own thoughts and feelings about the theme and how you explored and clarified these thoughts and feelings through reading the story. Support your viewpoint with examples and brief citations from the text and your interpretation of the examples and citations. The final paragraph should present your personal conclusions about the theme and its treatment in the text.
4. Incorporate vocabulary words from your contract wherever appropriate.
5. I also expect you to use this opportunity to improve your writing skills. Early in the process, meet with me to go over previous examples of your writing and set specific goals for improvement. Your writing growth goals will be evaluated in the "technique" section of the assessment rubric.
6. Remember, your paper must be word processed and double-spaced. Have a trusted peer review your paper for mechanical errors before you print out your final copy. Prepare a written and oral outline of your major points to share with the whole class.

See the **Final Project Assessment Rubric**, attached.

SAMPLE 8.9—Final Project Guidelines and Evaluation Rubric—*(continued)*

Final Project Assessment Rubric

Names: _____

Chosen Theme: _____

EVALUATION: 50 points

If your project is missing one or more required elements, it will be returned to you. After you have completed the missing sections, you will need to resubmit the project for grading.

I. Content (quality, depth, and originality of analysis)

_____ / 25 points:

25   *Wow! An original and rather profound analysis.* I learned something new by listening/reading your project. You really made me think. Bravo!

23–24   *Very fine analysis.* You went well beyond class discussions, and your ideas were original and thoughtful. You made several interesting links between the book and the outside world or the book and your own life.

20–22   *Good analysis.* You expanded on what was discussed in class. However, I would have liked to have seen
    _____ Less description and more analysis of ideas.
    _____ A more complex or profound analysis.
    _____ Better links between the book and the outside world or the book and your own experiences.
    _____ More original ideas (ideas beyond what we discussed in class).

17–19   *You chose a theme, but didn't analyze it.* Instead
    _____ You provided a simple series of examples instead of illustrating/analyzing the link between the author's ideas and the outside world.
    _____ Your ideas were correct, but you mostly reiterated what was discussed in class.

14–16   *You chose a theme, but*
    _____ You did not provide enough examples of this theme in the text.
    _____ Your examples did not appropriately illustrate your chosen theme.
    _____ You did not analyze the theme.
    _____ Your interpretation of class discussion was incomplete or incorrect.

II. Form (overall comprehensibility of your French, including use of vocabulary, grammar, and sentence structure)

_____ / 20 points

III. Technique (appropriate use of and skill with technology involved and/or mechanics of writing and presenting)

_____ / 5 points

TOTAL: _____ / 50 POINTS

SAMPLE 8.10—Unit Evaluation

Directions: Please answer YES, NO, or UNSURE to the numbered questions and then respond to the two prompts that follow.

During this unit, did you

1. Learn something new about Saint-Exupéry?

2. Learn key features of the plot, characters, and setting of the novel?

3. Improve your sight vocabulary?

4. Improve your fluency in speech?

5. Improve your facility with grammar?

6. Read for pleasure?

7. Increase your personal understanding of unit concepts (perspective, exploration, growth, relationships)?

8. See a reflection of yourself or your life in the text?

9. Gain perspective on your learning preferences and skills?

Which aspects of this unit did you especially enjoy?

How could this unit be redesigned to help you learn better?

9

Water, Water, Everywhere

An Earth Science Unit on Water and Watersheds

Unit Developer: Andrea Trank

Introduction

This three-week earth science unit is built on state and national standards and benchmarks and addresses water, weather, environmental quality, and natural resources. It begins with some basic lessons on understanding water and expands into a look at watersheds, a consideration of water as a natural and managed resource, and an investigation of how water affects humans though weather events.

The opening activities are inspired by Project Wet, a national environmental education curriculum and activity guide developed by Montana State University and the Council for Environmental Education. I served as a teacher tester on this curriculum and have been certified as a Project Wet instructor by the Virginia Department of Environmental Quality and Virginia Department of Education. This part of the unit focuses on engaging student interest and correcting some of the misconceptions they might have about water and the water cycle through demonstration and exploration of water properties and the water cycle. In addition to covering key science concepts, the early lessons involve hands-on activities, movement, mathematics, reading, and possibly drawing. The follow-up activities are differentiated according to interest and readiness.

Students next focus on their own watershed, using both online resources and local maps. Depending on students' readiness levels, they either investigate a watershed their neighborhood and draw it on a map or investigate a watershed in the schoolyard. The unit then transitions to an exploration of water-related weather and its consequences. Students break into heterogeneous groups to investigate particular aspects of an actual weather-related event, such as a drought or a flood. A concluding problem-based community outreach project pulls the unit together, allowing the students to synthesize their understanding of water and apply it to a real-world issue.

319

Teacher Reflection on Designing the Unit

Earth science is a very comprehensive curriculum with, in my opinion, far too many areas of concentration. Within a one-year period, teachers must cover four very large topics: geology, oceanography, meteorology, and astronomy. Many teachers have seen this as a deterrent to developing interesting differentiated units. However, some concepts within earth science are broad enough to allow the flexibility to develop such a unit. Water comes up within the curriculum in many different places—as a resource to be managed, as a driving force behind weather, and as an agent of great geological force. Students enjoy explorations of water because it is relevant to and prevalent in their lives. My goal was to differentiate the instruction through readiness and interest to engage more students in these lessons and allow more students to master this crucial content.

Science Standards Addressed

SD1   The student will investigate and understand how to read and interpret maps, globes, models, charts, and imagery.

SD2   The student will investigate and understand the differences between renewable and nonrenewable resources. Key concepts include water and vegetation; resources found in an area; use of resources and their effects on standards of living; and environment costs and benefits.

SD3   The student will investigate and understand how freshwater resources are influenced by geologic processes and the activities of humans. Key concepts include identification of other sources of freshwater (including aquifers, with reference to the hydrologic cycle and dependence on freshwater resources) and the effects of human usage on water quality.

SD4   The student will investigate and understand the origin and evolution of the atmosphere and the interrelationship of geologic processes, biologic processes, and human activities on its composition and dynamics. Key concepts include atmospheric regulation mechanisms and potential atmospheric compositional changes due to human, biologic, and geologic activity.

SD5   The student will investigate and understand that energy transfer between the sun, Earth, and Earth's atmosphere drives weather and climate on Earth. Key concepts include observation and collection of weather data, prediction of weather patterns, and weather phenomena and the factors that affect climate.

SD6   The student will implement a proposed solution; evaluate the solution by testing it against the needs and criteria it was designed to meet; and communicate the problem, process, and solution orally, in writing, and in other forms, including models, diagrams, and demonstrations.

Unit Concepts and Generalizations

Patterns of Change, Scale and Structure, Stability

GEN1   Earth does not have infinite resources; increasing human consumption places severe stress on the natural processes that renew some resources and depletes those resources that cannot be renewed.

GEN2   Natural ecosystems provide an array of basic processes that affect humans.

GEN3   Humans are part of Earth's ecosystems and human activities can, deliberately or inadvertently, alter the equilibrium in an ecosystem.

GEN4   Freshwater is essential for life and most industrial processes, yet it is limited in supply and vulnerable to pollution and depletion.

GEN5   Cleaning up the pollution of national resources can be difficult and costly.

Unit Objectives

As a result of this unit, the students will *know*

- Earth is a water-based planet.
- Water is essential for life.
- The water cycle is a closed system.
- Water is a natural resource that is managed for human use.
- Humans affect water quality and the quantity of water available.

As a result of this unit, the students will *understand that*

- They can and do affect decisions related to water pollution and consumption.
- Water is a local issue, not just an issue for scientists and politicians.
- Although water seems to be unlimited, the amount available for human use is dwindling due to pollution and poor management.
- The water they use today is the same water used by their ancestors and the same water that will be used by their children's children.
- Science is about discovery, and technology is often the application of science to real-world problems.

As a result of this unit, the students will *be able to*

- Give an accurate and detailed description of the water cycle.
- Explain the relationship between weather and water.
- Develop and communicate solutions to a community problem involving water.

Instructional Strategies Used

- Brainstorming
- Cooperative learning
- Extension/anchor activities
- Independent study
- Problem-based learning

- Coaching
- Demonstration/modeling
- Flexible grouping
- Learning stations
- Tiered assignments

Sample Supporting Materials Provided

Sample #	Title	Page
9.1	Independent Study Contract	339
9.2	Water Cycle Activity Handout	340
9.3	Water Cycle Activity Options	343
9.4	Weather Information Note-Taking Guide	344
9.5	Research Presentation Rubric	345
9.6	Article Review Template	346
9.7	Community Outreach Project Group Rubric	347
9.8	Community Outreach Project Individual Evaluation Form	348

Unit Overview

LESSON	WHOLE-CLASS COMPONENTS	DIFFERENTIATED COMPONENTS
PRE-ASSESSMENT *15–20 minutes*	Unit pre-assessment *15–20 minutes*	Independent study option *ongoing*
LESSON 1 **Understanding the Water Cycle** *1 block*	Whole-class kinesthetic activity on the water cycle *30 minutes* Follow-up discussion in random small groups *15 minutes* Whole-class discussion of the water cycle *45 minutes*	

LESSON	WHOLE-CLASS COMPONENTS	DIFFERENTIATED COMPONENTS
		Independent water cycle activities differentiated by interest and learning profile *30 minutes*
LESSON 2 **All the Water in the World** *1 block*	Sharing of water cycle products and whole-class discussion of water cycle patterns *15 minutes*	
	Demonstration: "Where's the Water?" *25 minutes*	
		Small-group guided discussions differentiated by readiness *20 minutes*
	Whole-class follow-up discussion of water as a resource *30 minutes*	
LESSON 3 **Water and the Land** *2–3 blocks*	Introduction to watersheds *10 minutes*	
	Small-group work to identify the local watershed and study land use *45 minutes*	
	Optional activities: "Watershed walk"/stream testing *1 block*	
		Small-group watershed project work differentiated by learning profile *1–2 blocks*
	Watershed presentations and whole-class follow-up discussion of environmental quality, interdependence, and conservation *45 minutes*	
LESSON 4 **Water and Weather** *2 blocks*	Brainstorming on the connection between weather and water *20 minutes*	

LESSON	WHOLE-CLASS COMPONENTS	DIFFERENTIATED COMPONENTS
	Review of recent weather in self-selected small groups *15–20 minutes*	
		Small-group weather event research and presentation preparation differentiated by interest *90 minutes*
	Weather event presentations *30–40 minutes*	
	Exit card activity *5 minutes*	
LESSON 5 **Getting Involved in Your Community** *4–5 blocks*	Opening problem and whole-class discussion *30 minutes*	
	Community outreach project launch *25 minutes*	
		Small-group project research, planning, and product development differentiated by interest *2–3 blocks*
		Extension/anchor activities differentiated by interest *ongoing, time varies*
	Small-group project presentations and product sharing *1 block*	
LESSON 6 **Sharing Your Research** *1 block*	Community outreach project presentation *90 minutes*	
		Homework: Final essay differentiated by interest

Unit Description and Teacher Commentary

PRE-ASSESSMENT	*(15–20 minutes)*
LESSON SEQUENCE AND DESCRIPTION	TEACHER COMMENTARY
Unit pre-assessment. The day before beginning Lesson 1, have students do the following: 1. Draw or describe in writing what the water cycle looks like. 2. Explain how weather affects the water cycle. 3. Describe the distribution and availability of water on Earth. 4. Describe the relationship between water and humans.	I reviewed the pre-assessments to determine students' prior knowledge and used this information as the foundation for readiness-group determinations.
✴**Independent study option.** If there are students who show an unusually advanced knowledge of the unit concepts and generalizations, work with them to design independent study projects. In the project, the student should act as an environmentalist to identify and work on an issue of current concern to environmentalists. For example, the student might investigate sources of pollution and how they affect the water cycle or choose a particular location and investigate the water cycle of that region, focusing on unique problems such as the damming of a river, the diversion of water, or the pollution of groundwater from buried wastes.	Monitoring independent study projects can be challenging. I often work with the gifted resource teacher to develop a contract. See the **Independent Study Contract** (Sample 9.1, page 339) for an example.

LESSON 1	**Understanding the Water Cycle** *Concepts:* Patterns of Change, Scale and Structure, Stability GEN1–4; SD2–5	*(1 block)*

LESSON SEQUENCE AND DESCRIPTION	TEACHER COMMENTARY
Whole-class kinesthetic activity on the water cycle. Prepare for this lesson by setting up nine stations throughout the classroom, each reflecting a location where water can be found in the water cycle: glaciers, oceans, clouds, rivers, lakes, groundwater, soil, animals, and plants. Each station should have a sign indicating its name, a box or pillowcase to hold a set of "game cards" so that students can conduct a blind drawing, and a cup containing colored paper clips that students will use to track their path from station to station. They'll use a different color per station (e.g., a green paper clip for the Plant station, a brown one for the Soil station, a blue one for the Ocean station).	This activity involves students in a movement game to simulate the diverse nature of the water cycle. A common misconception students have is that all water travels in a circuit from clouds to the ground to an ocean and then back to clouds.

LESSON SEQUENCE AND DESCRIPTION	TEACHER COMMENTARY
Begin by telling students they will play a game in which they take on the role of a water droplet and document that droplet's trip through the hydrologic cycle, also known as the water cycle.	This activity clarifies that individual water droplets can follow very different paths.
The first step in this activity is to enlist the students' help in creating the game cards for each station. Each card will indicate a possible "next step" that a droplet of water might take at a particular stage in the water cycle. Distribute blank index cards; the **Water Cycle Stations Handout** (see Sample 9.2, pages 340–342), which provides directions for this part of the activity; and any necessary art supplies. Randomly assign each student a certain number of cards to create.	One of the strengths of this activity is that it incorporates Gardner's multiple intelligences. For example: kinesthetic learners enjoyed the hands-on aspect and movement, mathematical learners enjoyed the probability aspect, and artistic and verbal students enjoyed creating the cards and documenting their journey in the form of a cartoon or an imaginary story as part of the associated activity options.
Once all the cards have been created and deposited in the blind drawing box at each station, the game can begin.	

1. Students select a starting station. If necessary, assign some students to certain stations so that there are a few people at each station.

2. At the stations, each student draws a card, copies the process description in the appropriate space on the handout, and returns the card to the box or pillowcase. The "Next Location" on Side 2 of the drawn card also indicates which station to visit next. Before leaving the station, each student takes the station's color-coded paper clip. If Side 2 shows the name of the current station (e.g., a student draws Soil Card #6 while at the Soil Station), that student must remain at the station and draw again, along with the next incoming group, and collect a second paper clip from that station. In this way, students record all steps of their journey and create a paper clip chain as a form of secondary documentation.

3. Have each student make 15 stops on their journey and collect 15 paper clips.

4. Conclude the game by asking students to write out a description or draw a diagram of their own trip through the water cycle, using their paper clip chain and filled-in handout as a guide.

LESSON SEQUENCE AND DESCRIPTION	TEACHER COMMENTARY
Follow-up discussion in random small groups. Form small groups to have students discuss the various journeys they took as a water droplet. There should be great variety. Guide this activity by walking around and looking for paper clip chains that show unusual combinations. Select some of the more interesting journeys to discuss as a whole class. Questioning the students about how they moved from place to place can help generate discussion.	When questioning students, I checked not only their understanding of the process by which water moves through the cycle, but also their reactions to their journeys. Students who were "stuck" going from cloud to ocean again and again tended to be frustrated, while those who traveled through the entire cycle felt more fulfilled. It was interesting to note their use of personification in this activity.
Whole-class discussion of the water cycle. After prompting students to share their journeys, post a list of the unit concepts and generalizations. Ask students which of these were illustrated in the kinesthetic water cycle activity. Did the activity help them view the water cycle in new ways?	I kept unit concepts and generalizations posted on a bulletin board throughout the unit so that we could refer to them often.
Independent water cycle activities differentiated by interest and learning profile. Distribute the **Water Cycle Activity Options** (see Sample 9.3, page 343). Students choose one of six possible activities to complete in class (time permitting) or as homework. The options are designed to appeal to different types of learners: • Choices A (drawing a cartoon), C (writing a fictional story), and D (designing another game similar to the one just completed) all appeal to students with high levels of creative intelligence. • Choice B (creating an accurate drawing of the water cycle, including all steps) appeals to students with high levels of visual/spatial intelligence. • Choice D (designing a game) also appeals to students with high levels of practical intelligence. • Choice E (graphing) appeals to students with high levels of mathematical intelligence or analytical intelligence. • Choice F (investigating a local water cycle) appeals to students with high levels of naturalistic intelligence.	These are designed to appeal to a variety of interests and learning styles as defined by both Gardner (1993) and Sternberg (1988). My goal was to encourage students to solidify their understanding of water and cycles in nature. Observing the activity choices students made here gave me further insight into their learning preferences. Note that some of the activities are more difficult than others. I also watched to see which students took on the extra challenge.

LESSON 2	All the Water in the World	(1 block)

Concepts: Patterns of Change, Scale and Structure, Stability
GEN1–4; SD2–3, SD5

LESSON SEQUENCE AND DESCRIPTION	TEACHER COMMENTARY
Sharing of water cycle products and whole-class discussion of water cycle patterns. Ask for volunteers to share their products from the water cycle activity. Ask: What kinds of changes take place in the water cycle? What patterns do you notice? What about the water cycle remains constant or stable?	
Demonstration: "Where's the Water?" Begin by asking students to estimate how much of our planet is covered with water. How much of that water is freshwater? Where is most of the freshwater located? How much of that freshwater is available for human use? Prompt students to share and discuss their ideas. To demonstrate the amount of water on Earth, use a model where 1 liter (1,000 ml) represents all the water on the planet (billions and billions of liters). Pour all but 30 ml of the water into a second beaker, and add salt to represent that 97 percent of the water on Earth is salt water in oceans. Next, take 24 ml of the 30 ml and pour it into an ice cube tray to represent the 80 percent of the planet's freshwater that is locked up in glaciers. Hold up the beaker to show the 6 ml remaining. Explain that of the rest of the freshwater on the planet, only the equivalent of one drop of it is available for human consumption. The rest is too far underground, trapped in the soil, or polluted. Use an eyedropper to remove a single drop (.003 ml) and drop it onto a glass slide. Walk around the class and allow each student to take a look. Stress that the ever-increasing human population means there are growing demands on the drinkable water we have available, and that practices that contribute to pollution are threatening to reduce the "size of the drop" even further. Consider allowing students to recreate the demonstration, as the hands-on aspect may help them gain a better understanding of the concept.	Students often have difficulty understanding very large-scale concepts such as the amount of water on Earth, and they tend to think that the water they use is "magically" made and will always be available when they need it. Models can help them visualize concepts and make abstraction concrete. Models can also be misinterpreted. One of the dangers with this one was that students would come away thinking that we have very little water. I was careful to explain that that 6 ml. (which doesn't look like much) represents 1.68 billion liters.

LESSON SEQUENCE AND DESCRIPTION	TEACHER COMMENTARY
Small-group guided discussions differentiated by readiness. Place students in homogenous small groups of three according to their degree of scientific understanding and ability to handle abstractions. Ask each small group to choose a discussion leader, a discussion scribe, and a discussion reporter, who will share the high points of the group's conversation with the rest of the class. Provide each group with the appropriate question card:	The use of tiering helps adjust the discussion to the readiness levels of all students. Each tier provides a greater level of abstraction.
Card 1 (Below Grade-Level Groups) 1. What does this demonstration help you understand about the amount of water on Earth? What new questions does it raise in your mind? 2. Make a list of ways in which humans need or use water. Who or what else depends on Earth's water for survival? 3. How could we increase the amount of Earth's water that is available for human consumption?	The first-tier question set asks students to summarize what they just learned. Listing is a concrete way to get them to think beyond the activity.
Card 2 (Grade-Level Groups) 1. What were your initial reactions to this demonstration? What was new or surprising to you? 2. In what ways do humans affect the amount of water available on the planet? What can we change about this? What should we change? 3. What other analogy can you come up with to help people understand both the abundance and the scarcity of water on this planet?	The second-tier question set asks students to explore their reactions to this activity and draw upon prior understandings of environmental issues involving water.
Card 3 (Above Grade-Level Groups) 1. What were your initial reactions to this demonstration? What was new or surprising to you? 2. Who does Earth's water belong to? Explain your thinking. What changes in the availability of water could nature have in store for us? What about other humans? 3. What if humans figured out a cheap way to desalinate large quantities of water? Should we do it? Why or why not?	The third-tier question set prompts students to explore the relationship between environmental quality and technology.
Have students report on their discussions. When groups talk about the questions unique to their tier, solicit reactions and additional answers from all students, including those in the other tiers.	The practice of "blending" the discussions helps ensure that readiness designations don't inadvertently limit the thinking of any students. It also helps me to gauge student readiness for later activities.

LESSON SEQUENCE AND DESCRIPTION	TEACHER COMMENTARY
Whole-class follow-up discussion of water as a resource. Relate the day's activity and discussions to unit generalizations 4 and 5. Ask: How does the amount of water available on the planet relate to what we learned about the water cycle in the previous class period? At what points in the water cycle could humans interfere? What effects might this interference have? What if the amount of useable water suddenly decreased dramatically? How would we adapt? *Could we adapt?*	This discussion also related this lesson's work to the previous lesson.

LESSON 3   **Water and the Land**   *(2–3 blocks)*

Concepts: Patterns of Change, Scale and Structure, Stability
GEN2–5; SD1, SD3

LESSON SEQUENCE AND DESCRIPTION	TEACHER COMMENTARY
Introduction to watersheds. Introduce the concept of a watershed by showing the following pictures: a bathtub with a drain, a shed, and an umbrella. Ask students to brainstorm a definition of the word "watershed" based on these pictures. Record their ideas, and then write the following definition on the board: *A watershed is the land area from which surface runoff drains into a stream, channel, lake, reservoir, or other body of water; it is also called a drainage basin.* Ask students to pair up and talk briefly about how the definition relates to the three pictures. Back in the whole-class group, display a large topographic map of the local community. Invite all students to write their names on individual sticky notes and affix the notes on the map to indicate where they live. Explain that a watershed is usually named according to the river or stream that drains the land area. For instance, the Meadow Creek watershed is all the land that surrounds Meadow Creek; rain that falls within this watershed's boundaries drains through Meadow Creek.	As documented in the science education literature, using everyday objects to represent an unfamiliar scientific concept is a particularly effective approach. I obtained maps from the United States Geological Service (USGS): www.usgs.gov. These kinds of maps are also available through local water and conservation district offices.

LESSON SEQUENCE AND DESCRIPTION	TEACHER COMMENTARY
Small-group work to identify the local watershed and study land use. Divide students into groups based on where they live, and provide a variety of maps and aerial views of the local area. Ask them to locate the stream, river, or lake that is closest to their home and to determine their watershed drainage area. Where does the body of water drain? What are the various ways that land is used within their watershed? Next, ask students to look up information about their watershed by visiting the Web site of the Environmental Protection Agency: epa.gov. Have them compare the information on this site to the information they gleaned from the other maps. As an alternative, use the school grounds as the basis for this activity. Finally, ask groups to explore the land uses in their watersheds by completing the following tasks: • Come up with a list of all the ways land is used in our watershed (e.g., farming, business, parking lots). • Think of the ways in which humans have already affected the water supply and the watershed in our area. What effects do you predict for the future?	My maps already had the watersheds marked. Otherwise, I would have asked students to delineate the watershed themselves by locating all the rivers on the map, finding the highest points of the land surrounding each river, and drawing in the watershed boundaries to completely encircle those rivers. Students are used to identifying their home according to street addresses; learning their watershed address gave them a new way of defining where they lived and connected them with many different people. I wanted them to realize that the rain that falls on their yard can affect the quality of water in a stream that is a mile away. Connecting science with the students' own lives makes it seem more relevant to them and is critical to developing greater understanding of scientific concepts.
Optional activities: "Watershed walk"/stream testing. Time permitting, take a "Watershed Walk" on school grounds identifying the land use. Alternatively, use the Izaak Walton League's method to survey a nearby stream. See www.iwla.org and www.sosva.com for detailed instructions and downloadable forms to use for stream surveys. Consider archiving the stream study and using it in following years to track a stream's health depending on the changes in land use.	Even though I teach earth science, I like to take my students to a stream to do biological testing. The students who seem to appreciate outdoor lab experiences the most tend to be the ones who are least successful with traditional school work. It is a way of engaging hard-to-reach students and helping other students connect school work with the world around them.
Small-group watershed project work differentiated by learning profile. Students break into small groups based on Gardner's multiple intelligences. The groups will take different approaches to demonstrate the concept of a watershed.	Multiple intelligence theory encourages teachers to reach students through strategies that take advantage of their unique forms of intelligence.

LESSON SEQUENCE AND DESCRIPTION	TEACHER COMMENTARY
Option 1 (Students with Verbal/Linguistic, Visual/Spatial, and Interpersonal Strengths) Write, design, and perform a play intended to show elementary school students what a watershed is and why it is important to know about watersheds. The play must include appropriate costumes and props.	
Option 2 (Students with Bodily/Kinesthetic, Logical/ Mathematical, and Naturalist Strengths) Build a scale working model of a local watershed. Be sure to accurately depict the environment of the watershed area.	
Alternative (Students Who Prefer to Work Alone) Working independently or with a partner, research a current issue concerning watersheds. Prepare a flowchart or other visual that depicts the problem, some possible solutions, and the probable outcomes of those solutions.	Some students just do not enjoy working in groups. When possible, I try to honor this learning preference either by allowing them to do the assignment alone or by providing an alternative assignment they can tackle independently or with a partner.
Watershed presentations and whole-class follow-up discussion of environmental quality, interdependence, and conservation. Students present their plays, demonstrate their models, and share their visuals. Afterward, discuss the ways in which humans impact the watershed and brainstorm ways to approach the various problems that result.	Having to present in front of their classmates makes some students so uncomfortable that they just read their notes or act very silly. I try to counter this by offering concrete suggestions: "Make note cards," "look at your audience," and "summarize." I also let students know that I will be evaluating and grading their presentation's style, not just its content, because presenting work to others is a key skill of practicing scientists.

LESSON 4	**Water and the Weather** *(2 blocks)*
	Concepts: Patterns of Change, Scale and Structure, Stability
	GEN2; SD1, SD4–5

LESSON SEQUENCE AND DESCRIPTION	TEACHER COMMENTARY
Brainstorming on the connection between weather and water. Open the lesson by asking each student to make a two-column chart. In the left-hand column, ask them to write down everything they know about weather and water's role in it; in the right-hand column, ask them to list things they want to know about how water affects weather.	Units on water are often taught separately from those on weather and atmosphere, which can leave students with the misunderstanding that these topics aren't connected. By including part of my weather unit within my water unit, I can make the connections clear.

LESSON SEQUENCE AND DESCRIPTION	TEACHER COMMENTARY
Ask student volunteers to share one item from each column. Record the ideas on an overhead transparency.	In my experience, asking students what they want to know about a topic usually leads to a lively discussion.
Review of recent weather in self-selected small groups. Ask students to form small groups, and then distribute copies of the local newspaper extending back a week or so (as many days are there are small groups). An alternative option is for students to access this information via The Weather Channel's Web site: www.weatherclassroom.com. Distribute the **Weather Information Note-Taking Guide** (see Sample 9.4, page 344) and explain that each group will review a different day's weather forecast and the accompanying weather map.	I use current events a great deal in my earth science classes because a lot of the news concerns weather and weather-related hazards or events. It is important for students to see the application of scientific understanding to events that could affect their own lives. The bonus questions on high and low pressure systems and fronts focus on clarifying common points of confusion.
If the local weather has been uneventful in recent weeks, choose an earlier time period when the area experienced a drought, flood, or record snowfall (contact the local paper for archived articles) or choose another area of the country that is currently experiencing these conditions.	I keep a scrapbook of articles on weather-related events in my area.
Have each group report on the relevant weather for the day, going in order: the "Sunday" group first, then "Monday," "Tuesday," and so on. Stress that the purpose of sharing these reports is to identify patterns in the weather. For instance, Sunday was a sunny day with no rain; Monday was partly cloudy (i.e., there was water in the clouds); and on Tuesday, a cold front came through, bringing thunderstorms and rain showers.	These reports provided multiple opportunities to explore patterns of change and stability. Students became the meteorologists and very quickly learned to identify the reoccurring patterns in the weather.
Ask students to reflect on the past few months and see if they can come up with significant weather patterns that were related to water or the lack of water.	
Small-group weather event research and presentation preparation differentiated by interest. In advance of this lesson, solicit student input about a water-related weather event—a specific drought, flood, or blizzard—that they would be interested in studying. Set up a research library of articles related to that kind of weather and specific event, being sure to provide articles at a variety of reading levels.	This activity allowed students to specialize in aspects of weather that they had some prior knowledge of and found interesting.

LESSON SEQUENCE AND DESCRIPTION	TEACHER COMMENTARY
Classify the articles into five topic categories and set up five learning stations in the classroom: 1. Socioeconomic effects 2. Environmental effects 3. Scientific data 4. Tips for consumers 5. Governmental response Introduce the research activity and ask students to indicate which of the learning station topics interests them most. Announce group assignments based on these preferences.	For example, I classified an article providing an historical look at the rainfall in the area as topic 3, "scientific data," and classified an article that focused on the best water-saving devices on the market as topic 4, "tips for consumers." With this kind of activity, the goal is always to give everyone his or her first choice while also ensuring that all topics are investigated and all groups are fairly equal in size so that no group is burdened with excessive reading. Sometimes this requires asking students for a second or third choice.
Once at their assigned station, students divide the articles among themselves. Stress that they need to read their articles closely so that they will be able to clearly and succinctly summarize each article and present the information to rest of the members of their group. Working together, each group synthesizes the information gleaned from all of the articles and prepares a 3- to 5-minute presentation that includes an appropriate visual aid. The goals for the presentation are to help the rest of the class understand the topic and to show how their research supports or refutes one or more of the unit generalizations. Distribute the **Research Presentation Rubric** (see Sample 9.5, page 345) and indicate that students should attend to all of the elements listed.	During this kind of heterogeneous group research, I steer my most advanced students to the articles that require the strongest reading and comprehension skills or concern the most sophisticated concepts. Struggling readers receive various kinds of scaffolding, which may including pairing them with a reading buddy, highlighting the important points of the articles in advance, and providing a graphic organizer or template (see Sample 9.6, **Article Review Template,** page 346).
Weather event presentations. Conduct presentations and use the rubric to evaluate each group's performance.	
Exit card activity. To assess and reinforce what students learned during the research presentations, ask them to take out a sheet of paper and respond in writing to the following prompts: 1. *What are three things you learned today that you did not know about the relationship between water and weather?*	Exit activities help students sift through information and identify the most important concepts. They also help the teacher to decide on the next step for each student: Did he "get" the concept? Is she ready to move ahead? Do some students need reinforcement of concepts already taught?

LESSON SEQUENCE AND DESCRIPTION	TEACHER COMMENTARY
2. What are two things you still want or need to find out about this water-related weather event? *3. What is one idea you have that would help educate a community about this water-related weather event?*	

LESSON 5	**Getting Involved in Your Community**	*(4–5 blocks)*
	Concepts: Patterns of Change, Scale and Structure, Stability	
	GEN5; SD6	

LESSON SEQUENCE AND DESCRIPTION	TEACHER COMMENTARY
Opening problem and whole-class discussion. Discuss local weather- and water-related issues that have come up throughout the unit. Ask: What have you found particularly interesting or intriguing? What don't you know yet that you would like to know?	This lesson, loosely based on the problem-based learning model, pulls together all preceding elements. For more information on problem-based learning, see www.samford.edu/pbl/.
Community outreach project launch. As a whole class, decide on a community outreach project that will showcase the knowledge and understanding students have developed during the unit.	Our region had recently experienced a severe drought, and that influenced my students' decision on a topic. The objective we decided on was this: "To educate the community about water-related resources and human and natural factors that affect these resources."
Discuss the components of a successful community outreach project/education campaign and brainstorm the components of the project that students will pursue.	To guide my students during this activity, I needed to understand the community's water resources. Our school is in a residential rural area, and many households get water from wells. Using the U.S. Geological Service Web site as a resource, I developed a working knowledge of groundwater and its fluctuating levels. I also contacted the Soil and Water Conservation Districts for maps and other local information and got information from my county planning department.

LESSON SEQUENCE AND DESCRIPTION	TEACHER COMMENTARY
Small-group project research, planning, and product development differentiated by interest. Ask students to place themselves in work groups based on their interests and their talents to research one of the components of the project and develop a product that will help to achieve the project objective. For example: *Group 1* Create a drought meter for the class or school. Use the meter to monitor daily consumption of water and to evaluate reservoir levels. Research other areas that have experienced a drought and compare those conditions to the conditions in our region. *Group 2* Create a water conservation plan for the school. Investigate school usage of water as well as policies that could control usage. *Group 3* Design a list of water conservation tips for homeowners and businesses that could be broadcast on television or put in an educational brochure. *Group 4* Create posters and signs for the school and help produce an educational video that explains the link between water use and water resources. *Group 5* Create a drought histogram that will show the history of the drought and help others to see patterns of water consumption and rainfall. Use the histogram to make predictions about future trends. Each group must create a plan for their project component that includes 1. A list of the group's objectives. 2. A set of procedures for accomplishing their objectives. 3. A list of materials they will need to accomplish their objectives. 4. A time line for accomplishing their objectives. 5. A description of their final product and how it fits into the overall campaign.	I allowed students who did not want to work in a group to propose independent research that would still contribute to the overall effort. I met with students in their small groups at the beginning to develop group plans and have them sign a work contract.

LESSON SEQUENCE AND DESCRIPTION	TEACHER COMMENTARY
Distribute and discuss the **Community Outreach Project Group Rubric** (see Sample 9.7, page 347) and the **Community Outreach Project Individual Evaluation Form** (see Sample 9.8, page 348). While each group's role in the class project will be unique, some of the features of the project should be uniform. Students should use the expectations outlined in the rubrics to guide their work.	One of the challenges in a class project such as this is uneven work distribution. The fairness issue inevitably comes up when attempting to differentiate lessons, and it can be addressed first by knowing each student's capabilities, strengths, and weaknesses, and second, by using carefully constructed rubrics. I adapted the rubric in Sample 9.7 from models available at the Rubistar Web site (rubistar.4teachers.org).
To monitor student progress toward completion of their activities, set up regular meetings with the groups. Offer coaching as needed.	The work students do during problem-based learning is as important as their final products.
✳ **Extension/anchor activities differentiated by interest.** Because each group will be working on its own schedule, there will be times when one group finishes early while another needs more time to accomplish its task. To address this, provide the following anchor activity options.	These anchor activities are designed to help students understand the difference between *weather* (conditions of the atmosphere at a particular time and place) and *climate* (weather conditions in an area over a long period of time). This is a common area of confusion.
Option 1 Research a major water-related climatic event (a hurricane, a flood, a drought, a blizzard) and prepare a brief report about how it changed people's lives. Your report should be short and to the point, not an in-depth project.	✳Here, I provided struggling students with a list of events to choose from or an outline of what I wanted them to find out.
Option 2 Research climate classification systems and transfer your findings onto a map, establishing a color coding system or some other key. Remember: Climate zones are largely determined by two factors: how hot or cold and how wet or dry. Next, choose a region and write about how the climate controls other factors, such as plant and animal or local weather conditions.	✳I coached students during this activity by guiding them toward helpful print and online resources.
Small-group project presentations and product sharing. All groups present their individual contributions to the project in class for discussion and group evaluation. Each student fills out an individual rubric and submits it after his or her group presentation.	

<table>
<tr><td colspan="2">LESSON 6   Sharing Your Research   (1 block)
Concepts: Patterns of Change, Scale and Structure, Stability
GEN1–5; SD1–6</td></tr>
<tr><td>LESSON SEQUENCE AND DESCRIPTION</td><td>TEACHER COMMENTARY</td></tr>
<tr><td>Community outreach project presentation. There are many options for sharing the work students have done on this project, including

• Publication in the school newspaper or on the school Web site, or broadcast over the school television network.
• Presentation through local media. Newspapers and television stations are often covering these kinds of stories and might appreciate a new angle.
• Presentation to the school board.
• An educational forum (an assembly).
• Production of an educational video.</td><td>My students opted to produce a video. It was distributed to schools throughout our region and state during Virginia's drought in 2002. It was also made available through a teacher's Web site via video streaming.</td></tr>
<tr><td>Homework: Final essay differentiated by interest. Have students choose one of the unit generalizations and write a brief essay or create a visual in which they clarify how their thinking about this idea has evolved over the course of the unit.</td><td>We concluded the unit by returning to the unit generalizations.</td></tr>
</table>

Teacher Reflection on the Unit

Students feel empowered when the work they do in school can connect them to the community and help educate others. I have always found that I know far more about a subject after I have taught others about the topic. A unit like this allows students to become the teachers and take with them an earth science experience that they are unlikely to forget.

_____

Andrea Trank, EdS, teaches earth science and journalism at Monticello High School in Albemarle County, Virginia. She can be reached at atrank@albemarle.org.

SAMPLE 9.1—Independent Study Contract

Directions: During this unit, you will be working independently on a project while other students work in large or small groups on the set unit content. Please read this work contract carefully. Write your initials next to each point to indicate that you understand and agree to the conditions stated. Sign and date the contract and submit it for teacher review. I will initial the contract, make a copy of it, and return the original to you.

Learning Conditions

_____ I will demonstrate an understanding of the work that other students are learning in class even though I will not be participating in their whole-group/small-group learning.

_____ If my teacher feels I need to join the class for key areas of discussion or pertinent lessons, I will do so.

_____ I will keep a daily log of my progress and maintain a weekly meeting log with my teacher or independent study mentor.

_____ I will share a progress report or a project with the rest of the class at regular intervals during my independent study and will contribute my work to the final group project.

_____ At the conclusion of my independent study, I will complete a self-evaluation.

Working Conditions

_____ I will check in with my teacher at the beginning of every class period.

_____ I will keep this contract with me as I work in other parts of the school.

_____ I will not disturb my classmates' work or attempt to get my teacher's attention during class if the teacher is otherwise occupied.

_____ I will not call attention to the fact that I have different work to do and different guidelines to follow.

_____ I will work on my independent study during the allotted class time and not waste that time.

Student signature _____ Date _____

_____ Teacher initials

SAMPLE 9.2—Water Cycle Activity Handout

Directions: You will need your textbook during this activity. You will be assigned to create a certain number of game cards for our next activity on the water cycle. For each card you are assigned to create, consult the Information Chart below and write the *Current Location in the Water Cycle* on Side 1 of an index card. On Side 2 of the card, write the *Next Location in the Water Cycle* and a short *Process Description:* an explanation of how a droplet of water moves from the current location to the next location. If the current location and next location are the same, explain why. Here are some examples:

Soil Card #1

Soil		Plant
		Process: Plant roots absorb water.
1		

Soil Card #6

Soil		Soil
		Process: Water remains on the soil surface as a puddle or adheres to soil particles.
6		

SAMPLE 9.2—Water Cycle Activity Handout—*(continued)*

Information Chart

☑	Card #	Side 1: Water's Current Location in the Water Cycle	Side 2: Water's Next Location in the Water Cycle	Process Description
X	Soil Card #1	Soil	Plant	
	Soil Card #2	Soil	River	
	Soil Card #3	Soil	Groundwater	
	Soil Card #4	Soil	Cloud	
	Soil Card #5	Soil	Cloud	
X	Soil Card #6	Soil	Soil	
	Plant Card #1	Plant	Clouds	
	Plant Card #2	Plant	Clouds	
	Plant Card #3	Plant	Clouds	
	Plant Card #4	Plant	Clouds	
	Plant Card #5	Plant	Plant	
	Plant Card #6	Plant	Plant	
	River Card #1	River	Lake	
	River Card #2	River	Groundwater	
	River Card #3	River	Ocean	
	River Card #4	River	Animal	
	River Card #5	River	Clouds	
	River Card #6	River	River	
	Clouds Card #1	Clouds	Soil	
	Clouds Card #2	Clouds	Glacier	
	Clouds Card #3	Clouds	Lake	
	Clouds Card #4	Clouds	Ocean	
	Clouds Card #5	Clouds	Ocean	
	Clouds Card #6	Clouds	Clouds	
	Ocean Card #1	Ocean	Clouds	
	Ocean Card #2	Ocean	Clouds	
	Ocean Card #3	Ocean	Ocean	

	SAMPLE 9.2—Water Cycle Activity Handout—*(continued)*			

☑	Card #	Side 1: Water's Current Location in the Water Cycle	Side 2: Water's Next Location in the Water Cycle	Process Description
	Ocean Card #4	Ocean	Ocean	
	Ocean Card #5	Ocean	Ocean	
	Ocean Card #6	Ocean	Ocean	
	Lake Card #1	Lake	Groundwater	
	Lake Card #2	Lake	Animal	
	Lake Card #3	Lake	River	
	Lake Card #4	Lake	Clouds	
	Lake Card #5	Lake	Lake	
	Lake Card #6	Lake	Lake	
	Animal Card #1	Animal	Soil	
	Animal Card #2	Animal	Soil	
	Animal Card #3	Animal	Clouds	
	Animal Card #4	Animal	Clouds	
	Animal Card #5	Animal	Clouds	
	Animal Card #6	Animal	Animal	
	Groundwater Card #1	Groundwater	River	
	Groundwater Card #2	Groundwater	Lake	
	Groundwater Card #3	Groundwater	Lake	
	Groundwater Card #4	Groundwater	Groundwater	
	Groundwater Card #5	Groundwater	Groundwater	
	Groundwater Card #6	Groundwater	Groundwater	
	Glacier Card #1	Glacier	Groundwater	
	Glacier Card #2	Glacier	Clouds	
	Glacier Card #3	Glacier	River	
	Glacier Card #4	Glacier	Glacier	
	Glacier Card #5	Glacier	Glacier	
	Glacier Card #6	Glacier	Glacier	

SAMPLE 9.3—Water Cycle Activity Options

Directions: Choose and complete one of the following activities.

A. Design a cartoon that illustrates your journey as a water droplet. Include an appropriate caption.	B. Draw an accurate version of the water cycle that includes all steps. Be sure to show the processes that get a water droplet from one step to another.
C. Create a fictional story about the journey of a water droplet. Base it on your water droplet's journey.	D. Design a similar game using another cycle we have studied (for example, the carbon cycle or the nitrogen cycle). Write out or sketch one possible journey. How does this journey differ from your journey as a water droplet?
E. Create a bar graph of your journey and the journey of two other droplets, based on the amount of time spent at each station. For data, refer to your paper clip chain and the chains of two classmates.	F. Create a local version of the water cycle. Be sure to include the names of local rivers, bays, oceans, mountains, and so on.

SAMPLE 9.4—Weather Information Note-Taking Guide

Directions: Record the following information for your assigned day and be prepared to present your findings to the rest of the class.

1. What was the weather forecast?

2. What were the high and low temperatures for the day?

3. Describe the weather conditions: Cloud cover? Wind speed and direction?

4. What kind of front was passing through the region? Warm, cold, or stationary?

5. Was there a high pressure system or a low pressure system in control of the weather?

6. Look to the west of our region and speculate about the kind of weather that we will have in the next few days.

Bonus Items:

A. What kind of weather is associated with high and low pressure systems?

B. Describe the weather associated with warm, cold, and stationary fronts.

SAMPLE 9.5—Research Presentation Rubric

Group Members _____

Presentation Title _____

Presentation Date _____

Element	4	3	2	1	Total Points
Organization	Group presents information in a logical and engaging sequence that allows the audience to follow it easily.	Group presents information in a logical sequence that the audience can follow.	Audience occasionally has difficulty following the presentation due to some illogical sequencing of information.	Audience cannot understand the presentation.	
Content Knowledge	Group demonstrates a thorough understanding of the content and can answer all questions in depth and with elaboration.	Group is at ease with the content and can answer the questions raised.	Group seems uncomfortable with the content and is able to answer only rudimentary questions.	Group does not have a solid grasp of the content and cannot answer questions.	
Unit Concepts and Generalizations	Presentation increases our understanding of unit concepts and generalizations by making illuminating connections between the basic content and these ideas.	Presentation references one or more unit concepts and generalizations and clearly connects them to the basic content.	Presentation references one or more unit concepts and generalizations, but the connection to the basic content is unclear or inaccurate.	Presentation ignores unit concepts and generalizations.	
Visual	Group visuals reinforce and clarify the information.	Group visuals are related to the text and the presentation.	Group visuals do not support the presentation.	Group does not create a visual.	
Delivery	Group members speak clearly and easily; the delivery is polished.	Group members speak clearly and at an appropriate pace.	Group members are sometimes difficult to hear; delivery is not smooth, but is understandable overall.	Group members speak too quietly to be heard; delivery is slow or halting.	

SAMPLE 9.6—Article Review Template

Article Title _____

Information Source _____

Article Date _____

Summarize the article in one paragraph. Be sure to use complete sentences.

Five major points in the article:

1.

2.

3.

4.

5.

Two reasons why this article is of interest:

1.

2.

Two personal reflections on the article:

1.

2.

SAMPLE 9.7—Community Outreach Project Group Rubric

Group Members _____

Project Title _____   Project Presentation Date _____

Element	4	3	2	1	Total Points
Ideas	Group independently identifies the key issues in the project.	Group identifies most of the key issues in the project and requires little teacher help.	Group identifies some key issues in project but needs significant teacher help.	Group cannot identify key issues in the project with teacher help.	
Group Time Line	Group independently develops a reasonable, complete time line describing when different parts of the work (e.g., planning, research, draft, and visuals) will be complete; each group member can describe the high points of the time line.	Group independently develops a time line describing when different parts of the work will be complete; each group member can describe the high points of the time line.	Group independently develops a time line describing when most parts of the work will be complete; most group members can describe the high points of the time line.	Group needs teacher help to develop a time line and/or several group members cannot describe the high points of the time line.	
Delegation of Responsibility	Each group member can clearly explain what information the group needs, what information he or she is responsible for locating, and when the information is needed.	Each group member can clearly explain what information he or she is responsible for locating.	Each group member can, with minimal prompting from peers, clearly explain what information he or she is responsible for locating.	One or more group members cannot clearly explain what information they are responsible for locating.	
Project	Group completes the project within the set time frame; it contains all the components that they planned for and is thorough and imaginative.	Group completes the project within the set time frame; it contains most of the components they planned for and has some creative elements.	Group completes the project within the set time frame; however, the project lacks creativity and thoroughness.	Group does not complete the project within the set time frame and the project is lacking many components.	

SAMPLE 9.8—Community Outreach Project Individual Evaluation Form

Student Name _____

Group Project Title _____

Project Presentation Date _____

Directions: Rate your contribution to the Community Outreach Project (use +, ✓, or –) and elaborate as needed in the "Student Comments" space.

Student Rating	Teacher Rating	Responsibilities
		Actively participated with other group members.
		Showed respect and support for fellow group members.
		Listened to group members' ideas.
		Provided ideas that contributed to the success of the project.
		Did a fair share of the project work.
		Held self accountable for high-quality work.
		Held others in the group accountable for high-quality work.
		Made a difference in quality of the group's work.

Student Comments:

Teacher Comments:

Glossary

Activity guides—These are packets of written material containing different sets of instructions for students who are working on the same task but with qualitatively different levels of complexity. Activity guides may contain some or all of the following: specific instructions, suggested steps for solutions, partial models of solutions, performance rubrics, presentation options, and various tools or resources.

Anchor activities—These are tasks students automatically move to when they complete assigned work. Teachers may provide a list of possible anchor options and should encourage students to suggest other ideas. Anchor activities must be important to essential student learning and never just time-fillers. In classes with flexible pacing, all students will need anchor options. Still, if a student is consistently finishing work early, it's likely that either the student is finding the work too easy or the student is working at a lesser level of craftsmanship.

Big idea—This term is sometimes used as a synonym for a **generalization**. It refers to the key understandings a student should derive from a lesson or unit.

Brainstorming—Brainstorming is a thinking and problem-solving process. The goal of the initial phase of brainstorming is to get participants to generate a list (the longer, the better) of examples of a topic or solutions to a problem. The rules of brainstorming require that all contributions be accepted without judgment.

Compacting—Compacting is a process in which students who have demonstrated mastery of a topic or set of skills are allowed to opt out of unit material that would be redundant for them or that they could learn more quickly and efficiently on their own. Ways in which teachers can gauge students' eligibility for compacting include pretesting, observation, looking at work samples, and one-on-one discussions. Students who compact use the time they gain to pursue independent projects or extensions to the unit. For more information, see Reis, Burns, and Renzulli (1992).

Complex instruction—This instructional strategy, developed by Elizabeth Cohen (1994), enables students to work in heterogeneous groups in ways that benefit each member of the group and call on each member to make a critical contribution to the success of the group as a whole. Complex Instruction tasks call on students to work in small, heterogeneous groups on tasks that are high level, open ended, and personally interesting, and that require many different talents for successful completion. Reading and writing are integrated into the tasks. Students' group assignments are based on the teacher's increasing knowledge of the intellectual strengths of each learner, and teachers design the tasks to call on the varied intellectual strengths of all learners. Multilingual groups should always have a bilingual student who can serve as a bridge between languages. Materials required for group success are often available in the primary language of English language learners. The teacher continually moves among groups, probing student thinking, helping students plan for success and quality, and making sure students are aware of the strengths various learners bring to the task at hand. Used appropriately, Complex Instruction can address student readiness, interest, and learning profile needs.

Concept—A concept is a name assigned to a category of objects or ideas with common attributes. Concepts are abstract, broad, and universal. They help learners make sense of ideas and information because they help organize and distinguish entities. They help learners look at likenesses and categorize objects or ideas. Concepts are generally stated in one word (for example, *pattern, probability, habitat, poem, perspective, energy, fraction, number, justice*). Sometimes concepts require two or three words to communicate an idea (for example, *rights and responsibilities, balance of power, checks and balances, relative size, supply and demand, central tendency, point of view*).

Concept attainment—This instructional strategy, developed by Hilda Taba (1971), guides students in discovering the key components or elements of a particular concept.

1. The teacher selects a concept that will be central to a topic or unit and determines the components or elements that define the concept. (For example, *symmetry* is a concept and is defined as correspondence in size or arrangement of parts along a plane.)
2. The teacher selects positive and negative examples of the concept. A positive example has all the components or attributes of the concept. (For example, a jacket, a cone, a square, a valentine heart, the name *ANNA*, and an Oreo cookie are all positive examples of symmetry.) A negative

example does not have all the key attributes. (For example, some paintings, most puzzle pieces, a tree, and the numeral *4* are negative examples of symmetry.)
3. The teacher explains the process of figuring out a concept and shows students a succession of positive and negative examples through objects, pictures, and words. However, the teacher usually does not yet use the name of the concept.
4. As students look at an example, they decide whether an example might be positive or negative by speculating on its attributes. The teacher (or a student) lists the examples in a "positive" or "negative" column as directed by the students. (For example, a student might say, "I think all these things are made of wood, so I'd put 'tree' in the positive column.") If a hypothesized attribute fails to pan out in later examples, students tell the teacher to strike out the attribute in the "positive" column and add it to the "negative" column.
5. Through the process of testing attributes over successive examples, students arrive at the key components of a concept and, ultimately, write their own concept definitions.
6. The teacher gives additional examples so students can test their definitions.
7. The teacher brings closure to the activity by ensuring that all students have a common understanding of the concept and its key components.

Concept-based teaching—Concept-based teaching uses the essential concepts and key principles of a discipline as a primary way of organizing curriculum content. For example, a history teacher might tell her students that history is the study of "CREEPS." The acronym stands for *C*ulture, *R*eligion, *E*conomics, *E*sthetics, *P*olitics, and *S*ocial issues. Students define each of the concepts in their own words, and these concept definitions give students a yearlong (and, in fact, lifelong) lens for viewing history. It also helps them make connections between their own lives, current events, and historical events. Principles that relate to each concept help students think more specifically about patterns in history. One key principle they might examine is, "People shape culture and culture shapes people." Students can see how this principle plays out in history and in their own lives.

Creative problem solving—The Osborne-Parnes Creative Problem Process provides a specific set of steps to be used in solving a problem. These steps include Mess Finding (Objective Finding), Fact Finding, Problem Finding, Idea Finding, Solution Finding (Idea Evaluation), and Acceptance Finding (Idea Implementation). For more information, see Davis (1998).

Culture-based differentiation—Culture affects many facets of our lives. Because our own culture is integral to and pervasive in our lives, we may be unconscious of how it shapes us. More to the point, we are unlikely to be aware of how our culture shapes us in ways that differ from how other people's cultures shape them. It is easy to assume "our way" is everyone's way. In education settings, this habit of thinking is particularly problematic for students from minority cultures who attend schools shaped largely by the majority culture. Culture-based differentiation emphasizes the need to (1) understand the cultures and cultural expectations of all students in the classroom; (2) develop classrooms that are sensitive and responsive to a variety of cultures; (3) ensure that all students' cultures are represented in materials and perspectives on issues; (4) ensure equity of attention, participation, and high expectations for students from all cultures; and (5) ensure learning approaches and options that span the full range of culture-influenced possibilities. Culture can affect how we relate to authority, whether we prefer contextualized or decontextualized learning, whether we are more reserved or expressive, whether we prefer working alone or with peers, whether we feel constrained by time, whether we stress the individual or the group, and so on. There is great variance of learning preference within each culture. The goal of culture-based differentiation is not to label or pigeonhole students, but to understand and actively address the fact that a classroom that runs counter to a student's cultural norms and needs will impede that student's learning.

Double-entry journals—Double-entry journals ask students to react to classroom content in a two-column format. Students record information about content in the left-hand column (e.g., key ideas from the reading, brief summaries, list of symbols, important vocabulary) and react to that information in the right-hand column (e.g., give a personal reaction to the reading, drawing on memories and emotions; ask questions; agree or disagree with a character's choices; compare and/or contrast the passage with another passage or another work of literature; make a prediction based on reading already accomplished; identify the theme; and/or explain and interpret figurative language and motif as a representation of theme).

Entry points—In *The Unschooled Mind* (1991), Howard Gardner includes a discussion of the importance of offering students a variety of ways to "enter into" a subject. Gardner identifies five types of entry points: narrational, logical, experiential, aesthetic, and foundational. Entry points respond primarily to learning profile and interest, but can also be differentiated by readiness.

Equalizer—The Equalizer is a visual guide to help teachers think about tiering tasks and products (*see* **Tiering**). As the figure here illustrates, it suggests several continuums along which teachers can adjust task or product difficulty. By matching task difficulty with learner readiness, a teacher can provide appropriate challenge for a given learner at a given time. For example, if students in a math class are working with measurement, their teacher might ask them to measure the surface area of a desk. If the teacher asks students having difficulty with measurement to measure the surface area of their bedroom floors as a homework assignment, that task, on the Equalizer, would be relatively "foundational"—that is, similar to the familiar, in-class task. If, on the other hand, the teacher finds that some students have a solid grasp of the in-class task, the teacher might assign homework asking them to

The Equalizer: A Tool for Planning Differentiated Lessons

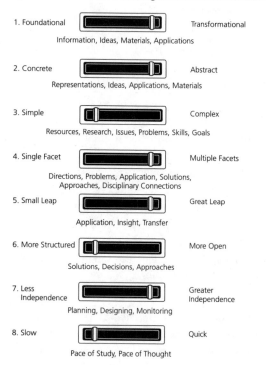

1. Foundational — Transformational
Information, Ideas, Materials, Applications

2. Concrete — Abstract
Representations, Ideas, Applications, Materials

3. Simple — Complex
Resources, Research, Issues, Problems, Skills, Goals

4. Single Facet — Multiple Facets
Directions, Problems, Application, Solutions,
Approaches, Disciplinary Connections

5. Small Leap — Great Leap
Application, Insight, Transfer

6. More Structured — More Open
Solutions, Decisions, Approaches

7. Less Independence — Greater Independence
Planning, Designing, Monitoring

8. Slow — Quick
Pace of Study, Pace of Thought

develop a plan for measuring the surface area of a tree. That task is much more "transformational," or unfamiliar. In this way, both groups of students can continue to advance their ability to measure surface area, but at appropriately different degrees of difficulty.

Exit card—An exit card is a quick and easy method of assessing student understanding on a particular idea, skill, or topic. The teacher teaches the skill or concept that is central to the lesson and gives students a chance to work with it and discuss it. Just a few minutes before the class ends, the teacher distributes index cards to all students. Then, the teacher poses a question that probes student understanding of the topic (rather than information recall) and asks students to write their name and a response to the question on their index card. Students turn in the card as they leave the room (or someone may collect the cards). The teacher does not grade the exit cards, but rather sorts them in categories representative of student understanding. A teacher might elect to use only two

categories (students who seem to grasp the idea and those who don't) or might elect to use as many as four or five categories (students who understand little, understand some, have a basic understanding, have only a few gaps, and have a solid grasp). In this way, the exit cards become a vehicle for planning subsequent lessons aimed at helping each student continue to grow in knowledge and skill from a current point of understanding. As an alternative, teachers sometimes use a "3–2–1 format" on exit cards. In this instance, students might be asked to write the three most important ideas in the lesson, two questions they still have about the lesson, and one way they can use what they learned. Either approach can be modified to match lesson goals and learner needs.

Extensions—Extensions refer to unit or lesson activities that go beyond the scope of the basic curriculum. Extensions are typically offered to students who complete unit work at a faster pace, pretest out of some of the unit work, or are particularly interested in the topic.

Flexible grouping—Flexible grouping is the purposeful reordering of students into working groups to ensure that all students work with a wide variety of classmates and in a wide range of contexts during a relatively short span of classroom time. Flexible grouping enables students to work with peers of both similar and dissimilar readiness levels, interests, and learning preference and allows the teacher to "audition" each student in a variety of arrangements. At various points in a lesson, most students have a need to work with peers at similar levels of readiness on a given topic or skill. But they also benefit from heterogeneous groupings in which the teacher takes care to ensure that each student has a significant contribution to make to the work of the group. Likewise, although most students enjoy the chance to work with peers whose interests (or learning profiles) match their own, they may be challenged and enriched by blending their interests (or learning profiles) with students of differing talents and interests (or learning profiles) to accomplish a task that draws on multiple interests (or approaches to learning). Additionally, it's important for students to work as a whole class, individually, and in small groups—and when doing so, to learn to make good choices related to working relationships. A teacher who uses flexible grouping systematically groups and regroups students as a regular feature of instructional planning.

Gender-based differentiation—It is likely that there are predominantly male learning preferences and predominantly female learning preferences. On the other hand, it is clearly the case that not *all* members of the same gender learn in the same ways. The goal of gender-based differentiation, then, is to understand the range of learning preferences that may be influenced by gender and to develop learning options that span that range, allowing students of either gender to work in ways that are most effective for them. Among the continuums of learning preferences that may be gender-influenced are abstract vs. concrete, still vs. moving, collaboration vs. competition, inductive vs. deductive, and silent vs. talking. Although there is great variance within each gender, *in general*, females prefer the first approach in each pair, and males the second. However, it is important to remember that there is great variance within each gender. Gender-based differentiation is one facet of learning profile differentiation.

Generalization—A generalization is an essential understanding central to a topic or discipline. It's a statement of truth about a concept. Generalizations transfer across events, time, and culture. Like the concepts they help explain, generalizations are broad and abstract. Unlike concepts, generalizations are written in complete sentences. An example of a generalization is, "Parts of a system are interdependent."

Intelligence preference—According to psychologists such as Howard Gardner and Robert Sternberg, human brains are "wired" differently in different individuals. Although all normally functioning people use all parts of their brains, each of us is "wired" to be better in some areas than we are in others. Gardner suggests eight possible intelligences, which he calls *verbal/linguistic, logical/mathematical, bodily/kinesthetic, visual/spatial, musical/rhythmic, interpersonal,*

intrapersonal, and *naturalist* (Gardner, 1993, 1995). Sternberg suggests three intelligence preferences: *analytic* (schoolhouse intelligence), *creative* (imaginative intelligence), and *practical* (contextual, street-smart intelligence) (Sternberg, 1988, 1997). Differentiation based on a student's intelligence preference generally suggests allowing the student to work in a preferred mode and helping the student to develop that capacity further. Sometimes, teachers also ask students to extend their preferred modes of working, or they opt to use a student's preferred areas to support growth in less comfortable areas. Differentiation based on intelligence preference is one kind of learning profile differentiation.

Interest-based differentiation—As learners, we are motivated by things that interest us, and we tend to be more confident in our ability to succeed when we work with those things. Interest-based differentiation attempts to tap into the interests of a particular learner as a means of facilitating learning. Interest-based differentiation can build upon existing interests or extend interests. Further, interest-based differentiation can link student interests with required learning outcomes or can provide students the opportunity to extend their own talents and interests beyond the scope of required learning goals.

Jigsaw—This cooperative strategy, developed by Elliot Aronson (see Aronson, Blaney, Stephin, Sikes, & Snapp, 1978), allows students to become experts in a facet of a topic they're particularly interested in. Students first meet in small groups, sometimes called *home-base groups.* Here, they review the task they must complete and clarify goals for individuals and the group. They then divide into specialty groups, or *work groups.* Each specialty group is responsible for one facet of the overall task. Every member of the specialty group works to develop a full understanding of the assigned subtopic or subtask. After an appropriate amount of time, students reassemble in their home-base groups. Each member of the group shares the information about his or her specialty. All group members are responsible for asking questions and learning about all facets of the topic. In effective jigsaw arrangements, all students are both teachers and learners. Teachers may assign students to specialty groups based on assessed needs or interests, or students may select their own. Appropriately used, Jigsaw can address readiness, interest, and learning profile needs.

Learning contracts—A learning contract is an agreement between a student and a teacher (and sometimes parents, too). Contracts establish the parameters for responsible, independent work. Contracts may respond to interest, learning profile, and readiness differentiation. One benefit of using contracts is the opportunity they offer students to practice the skills of time management, taking responsibility for their own learning, and self-assessment.

Learning stations—Learning stations are designated areas in a classroom to which students move on a specified timetable to complete particular tasks. For example, there may be a discussion station to which students go to engage with peers in guided discussions about key topics. There may be a station where students check their work using an answer key. There may be another station designated for Internet research on a targeted topic. Students may rotate through several stations in a day or over several days. It is not necessary that every student go to every station.

Learning style—Learning style refers to a student's best way of working in terms of personal and environmental factors. For example, some students need quiet when they work, while others prefer interaction or some noise. Some students work best while sitting up straight at a table or desk; others learn best in a more relaxed position. Differentiation based on a student's learning style is one facet of learning profile differentiation.

Literature circles—This is an instructional technique in which students take on specific roles (such as discussion director, artist, connector, etc.) as they read a text and prepare to discuss it. Literature circle groups typically make their own decisions about how many pages they will read each day and when, within limits, they want to schedule their literature circle meetings.

Metacognition—This term refers to students' thinking about their own thinking. For example, a teacher might ask students to explain how they solved a problem or to monitor their understanding of a particular concept so that they might ask for clarification. It is likely that students are more effective learners when they are aware of both the kind of thinking a particular instance calls for and the thinking processes they use to make this decision. It is important for teachers to help students develop a "vocabulary of thinking" and to monitor their own thinking processes.

Mini-workshops/mini-lessons—This is another name for small-group instruction. When a teacher senses that some learners need additional help with a topic, understanding, or skill, the teacher might conduct a small-group teaching session on that topic to help learners make necessary progress. The teacher may open the workshop to all students interested in attending, invite specific students to attend, or do both. A student who is particularly strong with a topic or skill might conduct a mini-workshop for peers, as long as the student is also effective in working with agemates and teaching what he or she knows. Mini-workshops can be particularly helpful in guiding students through complex product assignments in which some requirements are not familiar to all learners. They are also useful for helping groups of students at all skill levels know how to move to the next level of proficiency.

Negotiated criteria—This term refers to the process of developing criteria for student success based on more than one perspective. Some criteria for success may be required of most or even all learners due to the nature of a task or previously established benchmarks. However, it is helpful for a student to establish personal goals important to his or her growth. In addition, the teacher can generally set one or more criteria for success that are uniquely important for an individual learner. The "collection" of criteria for quality becomes a student's guideposts for work that meets both group and personal standards. This negotiated approach to establishing benchmarks for success is important to ensure that work is appropriately challenging for and interesting to individual students, while still supporting shared goals.

Peer critiques—This is a means of helping students provide useful feedback on peer work in progress. Typically, partners read one another's work and then provide both positive and constructive feedback by following a critique guide developed by the teacher (often with student input). The peer critique guide should adhere to criteria for success made available to students at the outset of the work in a rubric or some other format. Goals of peer critiques include helping students succeed with work, helping students work at increasingly high levels of quality, developing collegial relationships among peers, and helping students develop their ability to evaluate the quality of work.

Process log—A process log is a mechanism for helping students keep track of their thinking as they work on a product or other complex task. The goal of a process log is not so much to record concrete details such as the names of books read or the length of time spent working on a task; its main purpose is to help students think reflectively about their work (see Metacognition). What are their goals for a work session? Why have they selected those goals? How do they know whether they are on the right track with their work? What are they doing to achieve at the highest possible level? When they get stuck, what do they do? These sorts of prompts may guide students as they write in their process logs. Typically, teachers collect and review process logs at assigned checkpoints while work is in progress and again when students turn in a finished product. The process log allows insight into the process of working *and* the product of the work.

RAFT activities—RAFTs take their name from the first letters of four words—*R*ole, *A*udience, *F*ormat, and *T*opic—and are based on the work of Doug Buehl (2001). In a RAFT, students play a specified role, for a particular audience, in a named format, regarding a topic that gets at the core of meaning for that topic. For example, during a study of punctuation, a student may take on the role of a semicolon, for an audience of 5th graders, in the format of a personal letter, and on the topic, "I wish you really understood where I belong." Or in a history class, students might be assigned (or choose) the role of President of the United States, speaking to Congress, in the format of a speech, on the topic, "Why should we continue in this war?" RAFTs allow differentiation by readiness, interest, and learning profile.

Readiness-based differentiation—Our best understanding of how people learn is that they begin with past knowledge, understanding, and skill and extend these to new levels of complexity or sophistication. Further, we learn best when the work we do is a little too hard for us. What that means is that we have a sense of both what the task calls for and the gaps in our capacity to do what it asks of us. When these gaps are not present (in other words, when we can do a task effortlessly), we do not learn because we do not stretch what we already know. Similarly, when the gaps are too great, we cannot span them and do not learn. Learning takes place when we have to stretch a manageable amount and do so. Readiness-based differentiation attempts to design student work at varied levels of challenge so that each student has to stretch a manageable amount and is supported in doing so.

Reading workshops—Reading workshops are extended periods of time set aside for students to read, discuss, and respond in a variety of ways to texts that they themselves have chosen.

Rubrics—Rubrics are tools that guide the evaluation of student work and clarify student understanding of expectations for quality work. Generally, rubrics specify several categories of significance in achieving quality (for example, quality of research, quality of expression, and quality of work habits). In addition, a rubric describes how various levels of quality in each of the designated categories would look. The most effective rubrics help students explore *qualitative* differences in their work, rather than quantitative differences. For example, it is not necessarily an indication that a student has done better work if he or she used five resources rather than four. A more appropriate indication of quality is that the student synthesized understandings from several reliable resources.

Scaffolding—Scaffolding refers to any support system that enables students to succeed with tasks they find genuinely challenging. The goals of scaffolding include helping students be clear about the task's purpose and directions and helping students stay focused, meet the expectations for quality of work, find and use appropriate sources of information, and work effectively and efficiently. The many types of scaffolding include study guides, step-by-step directions, comprehension strategies, use of a tape recording or video to support reading or understanding, modeling, icons that help interpret print, guided lectures, and multimode teaching. When tasks are appropriately challenging (a little too difficult for the student attempting the task), all students need scaffolding in order to grow and succeed.

SCAMPER—SCAMPER is an acronym for *Substitute, Combine, Adapt, Modify* (or *Magnify* or *Minimize*), *Put to other uses, Eliminate* (or *Exaggerate*), *Reverse* (or *Rearrange*). It serves as a tool to help develop creative thinking skills by facilitating fluency and flexibility in thinking as students alter an original idea or design to be more complex or interesting.

Skills—Skills are the actions students should be able to perform or demonstrate as the result of a lesson, a series of lessons, or a unit of study. There are many categories of skills important to student learning. Some of those categories (with examples of skills in each) are *basic skills* (reading, writing, computing), *thinking skills* (synthesizing, summarizing, creating, defending a point of view, examining evidence), *production skills* (planning, goal setting, evaluating progress, asking important questions), *skills of a discipline* (map reading in geography, recognizing tones in music, interpreting metaphorical language in language arts), and *social skills* (listening, empathizing, considering multiple

perspectives on an issue, taking turns). When identifying the skills students should master in any unit, lesson, or lessons, teachers should be aware of both the categories of skills and the specific skills. Teaching those skills explicitly is at least as important as teaching information explicitly.

Socratic seminar—A Socratic seminar is a structured discussion that opens with a question that has no right answer, but is designed to lead the group into a deeper consideration of the text or topic. As the inquiry unfolds, responses lead to new questions, new responses, new questions, and so on. The teacher keeps questions "fuzzy," speculative, clarifying, and focused on the text or topic. The teacher's role as guide and participant should encourage explicit thinking out loud and model the sharing of thoughtful exchanges as students explore ideas. Students should read the text in advance to search for issues, questions, and evidence and be active, respectful listeners throughout the seminar. Students take turns, react, talk with each other as well as with the teacher, focus on ideas, and agree to disagree with issues rather than each other. Students and teacher share the responsibility for developing a deeper understanding of the text or topic throughout the seminar.

Synectics—The synectics process is an analogy-based way of problem solving, consisting of six steps:
1. *Description.* Begin with a description of the present condition, or problem to be solved (for example, how tone affects a piece of writing).
2. *Direct analogy.* Suggest direct analogies to the present condition and describe it further, looking to other realms like nature, technology, history, economy, society, and so on. For example, "The way that tone affects a piece of writing is analogous to the way a thunderstorm affects a summer day. The clouds can be dark and ominous, inspire fear, or cause anticipation or excitement. The approaching storm can build tension. The downpour can be refreshing, awe-inspiring, or intriguing. Lighting strikes can punctuate wind, rain, and thunder in a variety of ways."

3. *Personal analogy.* This step asks students to imagine that they are the thing—the suggested direct analogy—as a way to distill the emotion combined with the problem. For example, "As a thunderstorm, I would have the power to create the mood of the day. People would react to me personally, in a unique way, depending what they were doing when I arrived, whether they were outdoors or inside, whether they love thunderstorms or fear them, and so on. Therefore, my effect can't be limited to a single interpretation. Also, along with sunny weather, I am part of the balance of the landscape, and the rain I bring is cleansing and nurturing."

4. *Second direct analogy.* Suggest a second direct analogy to the present condition, choosing a different realm. For example, "Consider a new analogy for tone in writing: the terrorist attacks on September 11, 2001. How are the characteristics of tone and the attacks similar and different?" "Like tone, the attacks affected the emotions of people differently, relative to individuals' personal lives and experiences. The attacks shaped how people thought about daily life as well as the past and the future. The attacks created new frameworks for thinking, new schema for understanding, new perspectives and perceptions of people and events. Unlike tone in writing, the attacks had a primarily negative effect. Unlike tone, which influences every reader directly, most people experienced the attacks through the filter of media reporting."

5. *Analyze the analogies.* List the characteristics and features of the two selected analogies and decide on a core commonality. For example, "Both a thunderstorm and 9/11 are explosive, dramatic, powerful, and agents of change. They shape and reshape perception. Their core commonality is that a thunderstorm and the 9/11 terrorist attacks frame an individual's understanding in dramatic and unique ways, depending on the individual's prior experience.

6. *Force fit.* Reconsider the present condition—the original task or problem to be solved—and use the second direct analogy or the entire

experience to proceed with a new mindset. For example, "Authors use tone to shape the reader's experience much like a summer thunderstorm and the terrorist attacks of 9/11 shape those who experienced them. This shaping will be unique for each reader: possibly pleasing for one, maddening for another, dramatically altering for some, reinforcing for others. Tone allows the reader to connect with a text in some unique, highly personal way."

A thorough explanation of the synectics process is presented in *Synectics: The Development of Creative Capacity* (1968) by W. J. J. Gordon, a book now unfortunately out of print. Other information can be found on the Web. Try innovation.im-boot.org.

Target notes—This is a teaching strategy that combines the benefits of categorizing and note-taking with the visual mapping of a graphic organizer (one that's shaped like a target). After "targeting" a key idea, person, term, or process by writing it in the organizer's "bull's-eye," the student uses the first concentric circle to define, describe, or explain it. The next concentric circle invites deeper or broader definitions, descriptions of relationships or interactions between elements, or expanded analysis of characteristics or conditions. This strategy is very open-ended and offers almost limitless possibility for application. For a thorough explanation of target notes, along with student work samples, see Burke (2002).

Think-alouds—A "think-aloud" is a comprehension building strategy in which a competent reader verbalizes the connections, inferences, reactions and questions that go through his or her mind while reading. Think-alouds give struggling readers the opportunity to hear what more sophisticated readers do to make sense of text. Teachers should model thinking aloud multiple times before asking students to do so.

Think–Pair–Share (T–P–S)—This instructional strategy, developed by Frank Lyman (1992), is used to engage all learners in thinking and talking about a question or issue important to a current area of study. Typically, the teacher begins a T–P–S by posing an important thought question. Students are asked to write their ideas or think about the question, working silently until the teacher calls time (usually two to three minutes). This is the "thinking" phase of the process. In the second phase, pairing, students turn to a peer and exchange their thoughts about the question. In the final phase, sharing, the teacher restates the question for the class as a whole and leads the class in a discussion of the question. The Think–Pair–Share strategy increases the likelihood that all students will engage with the question, will have something to contribute to the final discussion, and will be more invested in the outcome of the discussion than they would have been if the question had simply been posed once to the entire class and answered by the first student to raise a hand.

Tiering—Tiering is a process of adjusting the "degree of difficulty" of a question, task, or product to match a student's current readiness level. To tier an assignment, a teacher 1) determines what students should know, understand, and be able to do as a result of the task; 2) considers the readiness range of students relative to these goals; 3) develops or selects an activity that is interesting, requires high-level thought, and causes students to work with the specified knowledge, understanding, and skill; 4) determines the complexity level of that starting-point task compared with the range of student readiness; 5) develops multiple versions of the task at different levels of difficulty, ensuring that all versions focus on the essential knowledge, understanding, and skill; and 6) assigns students to the various versions of the task at levels likely to provide attainable challenge. To guide development of multiple versions of the task, a teacher may refer to the continuums of the Equalizer (*see* **Equalizer**), use supporting materials that range from basic to advanced, provide forms of expression that range from very familiar to very unfamiliar, and relate the task to experiences that range from very familiar to very unfamiliar.

Total Physical Response (TPR)—Developed by James Asher (2000), TPR is a language-learning method involving the coordination of speech and action. It is based on the theory that the memory is enhanced through association with physical movement. In a TPR lesson, teachers typically model a series of actions as they pronounce associated commands in the target language, then ask students to join in the actions as the teacher speaks the command. Once students are able to perform the action and repeat the commands, they may be asked to assume the teacher role and prompt others to do the actions. For more information see Asher (2000) or www.tpr-world.com.

Transparency talk—In a transparency talk, students use an overhead projector, transparencies, and markers to anchor a presentation that summarizes or synthesizes their research or thinking.

Resources on Differentiation and Related Topics

Adler, M. J. (1982). *The Paideia proposal.* New York: Touchstone.

Armstrong, T. (1994). *Multiple intelligences in the classroom.* Alexandria, VA: Association for Supervision and Curriculum Development.

Aronson, E., Blaney, N., Stephin, C., Sikes, J., & Snapp, M. (1978). *The jigsaw classroom.* Beverly Hills, CA: Sage Publications.

Asher, J. (2000). *Learning another language through actions* (6th ed.). Los Gatos, CA: Sky Oaks Productions.

Ball, W., & Brewer, P. (2000). *Socratic seminars in the block.* Larchmont, NY: Eye on Education.

Billmeyer, R., & Barton, M. L. (1998). *Teaching reading in the content areas.* Aurora, CO: Mid-continent Regional Educational Laboratory.

Black, H., & Black, S. (1990). *Organizing thinking: Book one.* Pacific Grove, CA: Critical Thinking Press & Software.

Buehl, D. (2001). *Classroom strategies for interactive learning* (2nd ed.). Newark, DE: International Reading Association.

Burke, J. (2002). *Tools for thought: Graphic organizers for your classroom.* Portsmouth, NH: Heinemann.

Campbell, L., Campbell, C., & Dickinson, D. (1996). *Teaching and learning through multiple intelligences.* Needham Heights, MA: Allyn & Bacon.

Carreiro, P. (1998). *Tales of thinking: Multiple intelligences in the classroom.* York, ME: Stenhouse Publishers.

Cohen, E. (1994). *Designing groupwork: Strategies for the heterogeneous classroom* (2nd ed.). New York: Teachers College Press.

Cohen, E., & Benton, J. (1988). Making groupwork work. *American Educator, 12*(3), 10–17, 45–46.

Cole, R. (Ed.). (2001). *More strategies for educating everybody's children.* Alexandria, VA: Association for Supervision and Curriculum Development.

Cone, J. (1992, May). Untracking advanced placement English: Creating opportunities is not enough. *Phi Delta Kappan, 73*(9), 712–717.

Darling-Hammond, L., Ancess, J., & Ort, S. (2002, Fall). Reinventing high school: Outcomes from the Coalition Campus Schools Project. *American Educational Research Journal, 39*(3), 639–673.

Davis, G. A. (1998). *Creativity is forever* (4th ed.). Dubuque, IA: Kendall/Hunt Publishing.

Erickson, H. (2002). *Concept-based curriculum and*

instruction: Teaching beyond the facts (2nd ed.). Thousand Oaks, CA: Corwin Press.

Gamoran, A. (2003). Tracking and the literacy achievement gap. Retrieved 08/05/03 from cela.albany.edu/newslet/spring03/tracking.htm.

Gardner, H. (1991). *The unschooled mind.* New York: Basic Books.

Gardner, H. (1993). *Multiple intelligences: The theory in practice.* New York: Basic Books.

Gardner, H. (1995, November). Reflections on multiple intelligences: Myths and messages. *Phi Delta Kappan, 77*(3), 200–203, 206–208.

Gartin, B., Murdick, N., Imbeau, M., & Perner, D. (2003). *Differentiating instruction for students with developmental disabilities in inclusive classrooms.* Arlington, VA: Council for Exceptional Children.

Good, E. P. (1987). *In pursuit of happiness: Knowing what you want, getting what you need.* Chapel Hill, NC: New View Publications.

Hyerle, D. (2000). *A field guide to using visual tools.* Alexandria, VA: Association for Supervision and Curriculum Development.

Johnston, C., & Orwig, C. J. (1999). *Your learning style and language learning* [electronic publication]. Available: www.sil.org/LinguaLinks/Language Learning/OtherResources/YorLrnngStylAndLngg Lrnng/contents.htm.

Kiernan, L. (Producer). (1997*). Differentiating instruction* [Videotape]. Alexandria, VA: Association for Supervision and Curriculum Development.

Kiernan, L. (Producer). (2001). *At work in the differentiated classroom* [Videotape]. Alexandria, VA: Association for Supervision and Curriculum Development.

Kiernan, L. (Producer). (2001). *A visit to a differentiated classroom* [Videotape]. Alexandria, VA: Association for Supervision and Curriculum Development.

Kiernan, L. (Producer). (2003). *Instructional strategies for the differentiated classroom, part 1* [Videotape]. Alexandria, VA: Association for Supervision and Curriculum Development.

Kiernan, L. (Producer). (2004). *Instructional strategies for the differentiated classroom, part 2* [Videotape]. Alexandria, VA: Association for Supervision and Curriculum Development.

Lyman, F. (1981). The responsive classroom discussion: The inclusion of all students. In A. Anderson (Ed.), *Mainstreaming Digest* (pp. 109–113). College Park, MD: University of Maryland Press.

Lyman, F. (1992). Think–Pair–Share, Thinktrix, Thinklinks, and Weird Facts: An interactive system for cooperative thinking. In N. Davidson & T. Worsham (Eds.), *Enhancing thinking through cooperative learning* (pp. 169–181). New York: Teachers College Press.

Marx, G. (2000). *Ten trends: Educating children for a profoundly different future.* Arlington, VA: Educational Research Service.

Millis, B. J., & Cotell, P. G., Jr. (1998). Cooperative learning for higher education faculty. Phoenix, AZ: Oryx Press.

Moeller, V., & Moeller, M. (2002). *Socratic seminars and literature circles for middle and high school English.* Larchmont, NY: Eye on Education.

National Association of Secondary School Principals. (2004). *Breaking ranks II: Strategies for leading high school reform.* Reston, VA: Author.

National Board for Professional Teaching Standards. Five core propositions. Retrieved 02/21/04 from www.nbpts.org/coreprops.cfm.

Nottage, C., & Morse, V. (2000). *Independent investigation method: A 7-step method of student success in the research process.* Kingston, NH: Active Learning Systems.

Parks, S., & Black, H. (1992). *Organizing thinking: Book two.* Pacific Grove, CA: Critical Thinking Press & Software.

Perry, T., Steele, C., & Hilliard, A. G. (2003). *Young, gifted, and black: Promoting high achievement among African-American students.* Boston: Beacon Press.

Reis, S. M., Burns, D. E., & Renzulli, J. S. (1992). *Curriculum compacting: The complete guide to modifying the regular curriculum for high ability students.* Mansfield Center, CT: Creative Learning Press.

Roberts, T. (1996). *The Paideia seminar: Guide and workbook.* Chapel Hill, NC: New View.

Sarason, S. (1990). *The predictable failure of educational reform: Can we change course before it's too late?* San Francisco: Jossey-Bass.

Schlick Noe, K. L. (2005). Literature circles resource center [Web site]. Available: fac-staff.seattleu.edu/

kschlnoe/LitCircles/Extension/extension.html.

Sharan, S. (Ed.). (1999). *Handbook of cooperative learning methods* (2nd ed.). Westport, CT: Greenwood Press.

Sizer, T. (1992). *Horace's compromise: The dilemma of the American high school.* Boston: Houghton Mifflin.

Sternberg, R. (1988). *The triarchic mind: A new theory of human intelligence.* New York: Viking Press.

Sternberg, R. (1997, March). What does it mean to be smart? *Educational Leadership, 54*(6), 20–24.

Strachota, B. (1996). *On their side: Helping children take charge of their learning.* Greenfield, MA: Northeast Society for Children.

Strong, M. (1996). *The habit of thought: From Socratic seminars to Socratic practice.* Chapel Hill, NC: New View Publications.

Taba, H. (1971). *A teacher's handbook to elementary social studies; an inductive approach* (2nd ed.). Reading, MA: Addison Wesley.

Tomlinson, C. (1995, Spring). Deciding to differentiate instruction in middle school: One school's journey. *Gifted Child Quarterly, 39*(2), 77–87.

Tomlinson, C. (1996). *Differentiating instruction for mixed-ability classrooms: An ASCD professional inquiry kit.* Alexandria, VA: Association for Supervision and Curriculum Development.

Tomlinson, C. (1998, November). For integration and differentiation choose concepts over topics. *Middle School Journal, 30*(2), 3–8.

Tomlinson, C. (1999a). Leadership for differentiated classrooms. *The School Administrator, 9*(56) 6–11.

Tomlinson, C. (1999b). *The differentiated classroom: Responding to the needs of all learners.* Alexandria, VA: Association for Supervision and Curriculum Development.

Tomlinson, C. (1999c, September). Mapping a route toward differentiated instruction. *Educational Leadership, 57*(1), 12–16.

Tomlinson, C. (2000, September). Reconcilable differences: Standards-based teaching and differentiation. *Educational Leadership, 58*(1), 6–11.

Tomlinson, C. (2001). *How to differentiate instruction in mixed-ability classrooms* (2nd ed.). Alexandria, VA: Association for Supervision and Curriculum Development.

Tomlinson, C. (2003). *Fulfilling the promise of the differentiated classroom: Strategies and tools for responsive teaching.* Alexandria, VA: Association for Supervision and Curriculum Development.

Tomlinson, C., & Allan, S. (2000). *Leadership for differentiating schools and classrooms.* Alexandria, VA: Association for Supervision and Curriculum Development.

Tomlinson, C., & Eidson, C. C. (2003a). *Differentiation in practice: A resource guide for differentiating curriculum, grades K–5.* Alexandria, VA: Association for Supervision and Curriculum Development.

Tomlinson, C., & Eidson, C. C. (2003b). *Differentiation in practice: A resource guide for differentiating curriculum, grades 5–9.* Alexandria, VA: Association for Supervision and Curriculum Development.

Tomlinson, C., & Kalbfleisch, L. (1998, November). Teach me, teach my brain: A call for differentiated classrooms. *Educational Leadership, 56*(3), 52–55.

Tomlinson, C., Kaplan, S., Renzulli, J., Purcell, J., Leppien, J., & Burns, D. (2001). *The parallel curriculum: A design to develop high potential and challenge high-ability learners.* Thousand Oaks, CA: Corwin Press.

Tomlinson, C., & McTighe, J. (in press). *Integrating Differentiated Instruction and Understanding by Design.* Alexandria, VA: Association for Supervision and Curriculum Development.

Tomlinson, C., Moon, T., & Callahan, C. (1998, January). How well are we addressing academic diversity in the middle school? *Middle School Journal, 29*(3), 3–11.

Tompkins, G. (1998). *50 literacy strategies step by step.* Upper Saddle River, NJ: Prentice Hall.

Wiggins, G. (1993). *Assessing student performance: Exploring the purpose and limits of testing.* San Francisco: Jossey-Bass.

Wiggins, G., & McTighe, J. (2005). *Understanding by design* (2nd ed.). Alexandria, VA: Association for Supervision and Curriculum Development.

Winebrenner, S. (1992). *Teaching gifted kids in the regular classroom: Strategies and techniques every teacher can use to meet the academic needs of the gifted and talented.* Minneapolis, MN: Free Spirit Publications.

Winebrenner, S. (1996). *Teaching kids with learning*

difficulties in the regular classroom: Strategies and techniques every teacher can use to challenge and motivate struggling students. Minneapolis, MN: Free Spirit Publications.

Also helpful:

Exemplars K–12 (www.exemplars.com) is a source for standards-based, tiered lessons with rubrics and student examples in mathematics, science, reading, writing, and research skills. Contact Exemplars, 271 Poker Hill Road, Underhill, VT, 05489.

HOTT LINX (www.hottlinx.org) is an online source for differentiated units, lessons, and instructional strategies, K–12.

Index

Note: References to figures are followed by the letter *f*. References to are followed by the letter *s*.

363

About the Authors

Carol Ann Tomlinson, EdD, is Professor of Educational Leadership, Foundations, and Policy at the University of Virginia and was a public school teacher for 21 years. In 1974, she was Virginia's Teacher of the Year. During Carol's time in public school, she taught in many differentiated classrooms and directed district-level programs for struggling and advanced learners. Today, as co-director of the University of Virginia Summer Institute on Academic Diversity, she works with an international community of educators committed to academically responsive classrooms.

In addition to the other books in the Differentiation in Practice series, Carol has authored the ASCD books *How to Differentiate Instruction in Mixed-Ability Classrooms, Leadership for Differentiating Schools and Classrooms* (with Susan Allan), and *Fulfilling the Promise of the Differentiated Classroom.* She consulted on and authored facilitator's guides for ASCD video staff development sets and developed ASCD's Professional Inquiry Kit on Differentiated Instruction.

Carol can be reached at Curry School of Education, The University of Virginia, P.O. Box 400277, Charlottesville, VA, 22904, or via e-mail at cat3y@ virginia.edu.

Cindy A. Strickland is pursuing her doctorate in educational psychology with an emphasis in gifted education at the University of Virginia and serves as teaching assistant to Carol Ann Tomlinson. She is an international consultant in the areas of differentiation of instruction, the Parallel Curriculum Model, and gifted education.

Cindy has been a teacher for more than 20 years. She has taught music, French, humanities, and gifted education to elementary through college-age students.

Her ASCD publications include the online course *Success with Differentiation* and a unit in the book *Differentiation in Practice: A Resource Guide for Differentiating Curriculum, Grades 5–9.* Cindy's other publications include *In Search of the Dream: Designing Schools and Classrooms that Work for High Potential Students from Diverse Cultural Backgrounds* and *The Parallel Curriculum Model in the Classroom: Applications Across the Content Areas.*

Cindy can be reached via e-mail at cas2k@ virginia.edu.

Related ASCD Resources: Differentiated Instruction

Audio

Affective Differentiation by Ellen Hench and Cindy A. Strickland (tape: #204230; CD: #504364)

Differentiated Instruction: The Complex Issue of Academically Diverse Classrooms Instruction by Carol Ann Tomlinson (tape: #203173; CD: #503266

Differentiated Instruction: Meeting the Needs of All Learners by Carol Ann Tomlinson (tape: #203064; CD: #503060

Help for Your Struggling Learners: Strategies and Materials that Support Differentiated Instruction by Char Forsten, Betty Hollas, and Jim Grant (#202214)

Teaching Students with High Academic Ability in Mixed-Ability Classrooms by Susan Winebrenner (#299060)

Understanding by Design and Differentiated Instruction: Partners in Classroom Success by Grant Wiggins, Jay McTighe, and Carol Ann Tomlinson (tape: #203188; CD: #503281)

Mixed Media

ASCD Professional Development Planner: *Differentiated Instruction and Resource Package* (#701225)

ASCD Professional Inquiry Kit: *Differentiating Instruction for Mixed-Ability Classrooms* by Carol Ann Tomlinson (#196213)

Networks

Visit the ASCD Web site (www.ascd.org) and search for "networks" for information about professional educators who have formed groups around topics like "Differentiated Instruction" and "Multiple Intelligences." Look in the Network Directory for current facilitators' addresses and phone numbers.

Online Resources

Visit ASCD's Web site (www.ascd.org) for the following professional development opportunities:

Online Tutorial: *Differentiating Instruction* (free)

PD Online Course: *Differentiating Instruction* (for a small fee; password protected)

Print Products

The Differentiated Classroom: Responding to the Needs of All Learners by Carol Ann Tomlinson (#199040)

Differentiation in Practice: A Resource Guide for Differentiating Curriculum, Grades K–5 by Carol Ann Tomlinson and Caroline Cunningham Eidson (#102294)

Differentiation in Practice: A Resource Guide for Differentiating Curriculum, Grades 5–9 by Carol Ann Tomlinson and Caroline Cunningham Eidson (#102293)

Fulfilling the Promise of the Differentiated Classroom: Strategies and Tools for Responsive Teaching by Carol Ann Tomlinson (#103107)

How to Differentiate Instruction in Mixed-Ability Classrooms (2nd ed.) by Carol Ann Tomlinson (#101043)

Leadership for Differentiating Schools and Classrooms by Carol Ann Tomlinson and Susan Demirsky Allan (#100216)

Videos

At Work in the Differentiated Classroom (3-tape series, plus Facilitator's Guide) (#401071)

Differentiating Instruction (2-tape series, plus Facilitator's Guide) (#497023)

A Visit to a Differentiated Classroom (videotape, plus Online Viewer's Guide) (#401309)

For additional information, visit us on the World Wide Web (http://www.ascd.org), send an e-mail message to member@ascd.org, call the ASCD Service Center (1-800-933-ASCD or 703-578-9600, then press 2), send a fax to 703-575-5400, or write to Information Services, ASCD, 1703 N. Beauregard St., Alexandria, VA 22311-1714 USA.